The French Radical Party
in the 1930's

The French Radical Party
in the 1930's

PETER J. LARMOUR

1964
Stanford University Press
Stanford, California

Stanford University Press
Stanford, California
© 1964 by the Board of Trustees of the
Leland Stanford Junior University
Library of Congress Catalog Card Number: 64-14554
Printed in the United States of America

Acknowledgments

The idea for this book was formed in the graduate seminars of Shepherd B. Clough and John Wuorinen at Columbia University. My interest in French politics was first aroused by Philip Williams. Many Radical deputies and politicians aided me in my research for this work. I am particularly indebted to the very kind help of the late Jacques Kayser, and to the hospitality of Michel Geistdoerfer and his family, of Robert Fong, and of Maurice Rolland; I should also like to thank those who let me have the use of unpublished material—Lucien Bauzin, Lucien Lamoureux, André Lorgeré, Jacques Mitterand, Hippolyte Ducos, Julien Durand, and Roland Manescau.

I was enabled to carry out the research by the award of a J. W. Dafoe Foundation Travelling Fellowship and a MacKenzie King Fellowship. The manuscript has greatly benefited from the criticisms of Gordon Wright, John Cairns, John Sherwood, and Rudolph Binion. Many others have contributed to my understanding of French politics, among whom Donald Baker should especially be mentioned. Finally, I should like to thank Muriel Davison of the Stanford University Press for her energetic editing.

Without the tireless editing, unsparing criticism, and timely encouragement of my wife Ronda, this book could never have been completed.

Contents

The French Radical Party
in the 1930's

Introduction

During the dismal decade of the 1930's, France was governed principally by the Radical party.* From 1932 to 1934 and again from 1938 to 1940, the Radical predominance was unquestioned; from 1934 to 1938, Radicals shared power first with the right and then with the Socialists. These eight years transformed the French Republic. France's army, which in 1932 was the world's strongest, crumbled in 1940. Her system of alliances, which guaranteed the Versailles settlement, collapsed following 1936. Her parliament, which had survived for over sixty difficult years, was paralyzed by 1938 and dismissed in 1940. The French economy stagnated and regressed. For France, the 1930's opened a period of political and social instability that has not yet closed.

The subject of this study is the response of the Radical politicians to the enormous challenges of these years. The story is less a history of the Radical party in the 1930's than a history of France in the 1930's through the Radical party. Radicals were not, of course, the only politicians in power; Gaston Doumergue, Pierre-Etienne Flandin, and Pierre Laval on their right and Léon Blum on their left dominated the crucial years from 1934 to 1937. To maintain that Radicals alone were responsible for the decisions taken during the 1930's would

---

* The official name of the Radical party from its foundation in 1901 was the Republican Radical and Radical-Socialist Party. The name, obviously, was too cumbersome for normal use, and two terms were commonly substituted—Radical-Socialist and Radical. The former was employed when precision seemed necessary—for example, on electoral returns, Radical-Socialist designated a party member; Radical, an unattached centrist candidate of Radical orientation. For ordinary political purposes, however, Radical was the name applied to the party and to party members, and this form will be used henceforth.

be a distortion. Yet, because of their location in the political spectrum, the Radicals played a decisive role denied the other parties and politicians. All governments required Radical support; ultimately, the Radical party or the majority of Radical deputies determined the nature of every government.

Although the Radicals were only one party out of many, they were always recognized as something special. Today when Frenchmen reminisce about Third Republic politics, they naturally speak first of the Radical party, then perhaps of the Socialists and Communists or of outstanding personalities; the other parties and groups have been consigned to limbo. The inter-war Republic was the Radical Republic: although even during the party's greatest prosperity only one-quarter of the deputies were Radicals, the party not only strategically dominated parliament,[1] but set the political style as well. For this reason the Radicals were always considered the principal enemy by the right, who would attack them in preference to the theoretically much more dangerous Socialists and Communists.[2]

What was the Radical party? Institutions are deceptive, since corporate permanence generally conceals shifting social realities. Radicalism still existed following World War II, and even played an important role. Edouard Herriot and Edouard Daladier continued to wage their classic "war of the two Edouards," and it is easy to forget that this quaint quarrel between two slightly comic relics was only a vestige of what had once been a vital struggle for power between two outstanding politicians. Distortion may also result from transferring the doctrinaire anti-clericalism of the Radicals of the 1900's to their less dogmatic successors. By the 1930's the militancy of the turn of the century had changed to the complacency of established power; but it was not yet the unabashed opportunism of the 1950's.

The Radical party was the oldest of France's formal political parties. Founded in 1901, it concealed behind its impressive façade a loose confederation of pre-existent and still autonomous committees. The heroic age of the party lasted only the four years of the crisis over the separation of church and state; in those days the Radicalism of the Radicals was a potent, lived faith. The transition from militancy to satisfied participation in the benefits of what Stanley Hoffmann has labeled "the stalemate society" was easily made; and in a period when parties "were primarily parliamentary collections of 'fief-holders' [whose] function was to occupy power rather than govern,"[3] the Radicals quickly became the archetypal party. They occupied or shared power complacently until World War I destroyed their position. Their outstanding leaders, Joseph Caillaux and Georges Clemenceau, who were excused from political fence-mending by their personal authority and consequently no longer interested themselves in party affairs, became the proponents of two basically opposed war policies. With Clemenceau's victory, the hard line triumphed, and Caillaux was hounded into prison. Clemenceau himself by the end of the war could no longer be considered a Radical, but rather a man of the right. The Radicals emerged from the war a tired, leaderless, conservative group; their parliamentary representation was halved by the general elections of 1919, from 172 to 86. Throughout the country, party organization had disintegrated. This was the first of their many apparent deaths. Resurrection, however, followed quickly. Herriot now came forward, and with his leadership the party rebuilt its organization and returned doctrinally to the left. In alliance with the Socialists, the Radicals swept into power in 1924, with wide-eyed visions of democratic reform.

This reforming bubble burst in the first great democratic crisis of the inter-war period, the overthrow of the alliance by the "Mur d'Argent." The strains of the war had unbalanced the budget, undermined the currency, unsettled the traditional social order, and transformed politics from the prewar game into something more serious. The Radicals were not prepared to act seriously, and so, in 1926, when a speculative panic threatened the country with chaos, the Radicals broke the alliance with the left and fled to the reassuring shelter of Raymond Poincaré, Union Nationale, and sound finances. In this new right-wing government the Radicals played a secondary, though honored, role until 1928. They fought and lost the elections of 1928 in a typically disintegrated fashion, some allying with the Socialists locally, some allying with the right.

After these two unheroic years, an unprecedented grass-roots revolt shook the party structure, forced the Radical contingent from the government, and replaced the now chastened Herriot by a young, militantly left-wing Daladier as president of the party. For three and a half years this classic "party of government" voluntarily withdrew into opposition, organizing in the country and capitalizing on the deepening depression and the hesitancies of the right-wing governments of Laval and André Tardieu. It was a reinvigorated party that fought the elections of 1932.

The Radicals of the 1930's appealed to a new kind of supporter.

In 1939, one of the contributors to an admirable political study in
the periodical *Esprit* made the following observation about the evolution of Radicalism:

The emotional significance of a given group may change with time, or even
from one region of a country to another during a given period. The Radicalism of the first years of the Republic was something entirely different
from the average Radicalism of today. When the outstanding men age,
when the program has been achieved, when reforms no longer have to be
put across, but need only be preserved, then such a party becomes less attractive to a person with a combative temperament and more acceptable to
one who enjoys tranquillity.[4]

The Radical's image during the 1930's was being refashioned, in
part by a spate of political analyses which appeared during the late
twenties and early thirties, notably Albert Thibaudet's *La République
des professeurs* and *Les Idées politiques de la France,* André Siegfried's *Tableau des partis en France,* Jacques Fourcade's *La République de la province,* Daniel Halévy's *La République des comités,* and
Emmanuel Berl's *La Politique et les partis.* These analyses were typically French—literary, qualitative, delighting in paradox. Their authors were indifferent to geographical and sociological variation. Even
Siegfried, otherwise a pioneer in electoral sociology, pursued an elu-
sive essence of Radicalism. These books helped create the stereotype
of the Radical politician as timid, provincial, bizarre, and yet quint-
essentially French.

"I begin with [the Radicals]," wrote Siegfried, "because they are the
salt of the left—in the biblical sense of the word salt—and perhaps the
most typically French of all the parties."[5] "The Radical party," wrote
Berl, "in many ways, is France itself."[6] And only France could have
produced the Radical party:

It cannot be meaningfully compared to any foreign party. It is a specifically
French product. It is not defined by a doctrine or a program; it is a certain
mode of existence, the balance slowly achieved in our villages between a
former age and the present, between the humanism, the individualism of
France, and the increasingly harsh discipline that the collectivists demand
of men.

Conservative like France, reasonable like France, contradictory like
France, niggardly like France but also generous like her, Radicalism was
not imported from abroad, nor has it ever enjoyed any vogue. Even when
Alain was a young man, he was smiled at for being a Radical.[7]

There can be no question that this uniqueness existed. Yet a sort of national uniqueness is characteristic of center parties, and many of the Radicals' attitudes and aims coincided fairly closely with those of similar parties abroad. A general description of the ideology of "liberal" parties runs: "[The] liberal position means, by and large, minimal regulation by the government, opposition to strong trade unions and apprehension concerning the giant companies, belief in equal opportunities for achievement and hence an opposition to entrenched, traditional groups such as the clergy and the aristocracy."[8] This cluster of attitudes characterizes the Radicals nicely. It encompasses their anti-clericalism and their single-minded devotion to education, their opposition to the chain stores and their antipathy to exchange control, their fear of the strikes of 1936 and their verbal violence against the "money powers" and the "trusts."

From its beginnings, intellectuals treated the party with condescension, which grew through the years into immoderate contempt: "The estheticians of politics have already said all there is to say [about Radical style], the French people have experienced it all; this party, which covets the functions of state, which lives in electoral slime, which raises fraud into a system of government, which is morally lax and fawns before its electors."[9] And Halévy declared: "The only ideal known to the Radical party is a mediocre egalitarianism which carries no risk."[10] Not everyone disliked the Radical party so thoroughly, but only its members ever really admired it. About the most charitable outside judgment was the grudging recognition that it fulfilled a useful moderating function. "If the Radical party disappeared," wrote L.-O. Frossard, "it would soon be seen that something essential was missing in our public life."[11] The party's role was to damp the violent swings of opinion and power to the extremes of right and left.

This role gradually came to be accepted by the Radicals themselves. "I hold that the Radical party is necessary in a democratic regime," said the Radical Premier Camille Chautemps. "It is a steadying element without which two great, violently antagonistic movements, like two armies on the march, would clash and dispute ceaselessly in an atmosphere of social hatred and civil war."[12] This thought was voiced over and over during the days of the Popular Front.[13] Such an appreciation was new. It is one thing for a party to fulfill a useful function; it is quite another for it to proclaim that function as its *raison d'être.* In the heroic first decade of the century, such a thought would never have occurred to anyone; the Radicals then were one of the "two violently antagonistic movements." After World War I and even into the early thirties, Radicals saw themselves as many things— the only real democrats, the true defenders of the rights of man, the party of the little man—but not as a moderating influence.

This change in role made many observers uneasy; a political party was supposed to represent an ideal. When, during the late 1930's, men came to look for that ideal among the Radicals, they found none, and concluded that the party was moribund. A right-wing journalist wrote, "We see in the Radicals a party that has lost its purpose [with the abandonment of anti-clericalism], like the monarchists when the restoration of the monarchy had become impossible."[14] This kind of critique of the party has continued. The outstanding analyst of the politics of the Fourth Republic, Philip Williams, has written:

The Radicals are old-fashioned. . . . [They] no longer possess a mystique to inspire their followers to a wider and more vigorous outlook, and their leadership is not of a kind to supply the deficiency. . . . Essentially a defensive party, protecting the citizen against the government, they are inhibited from vigorous action when in office by their own traditions and outlook. They prefer weak and conformist leaders, and avoid or repress dangerously strong personalities.

Williams reproduced Siegfried's statement, "From the American point of view, [the Radicals] express what is most outmoded in France."[15]

Yet are these criticisms to the point? Lack of doctrine seems to be becoming a political asset, not a liability. The most successful modern parties have been abandoning their doctrinal baggage, and their platforms have become little more than a clever balancing of the interests of their electors.[16] If in form the Radical party may have been pleasantly and provincially anachronistic, in fact its politicians were disturbingly modern. Here is Nathan Leites' description of a contemporary politician: "In the Fourth Republic—and this corresponds no doubt to a general trend in the West—a politician had to be, above all, smooth if he wanted to maximize his chances." Leites continued, "The politician convinces himself that everything can always be arranged, settled, smoothed out. It is all a matter of skill. With sufficient ingenuity, one will be able to conciliate conflicting positions that seem at first sight utterly incompatible."[17] Compare this with a description of an old-fashioned Radical, the most characteristic politician of the 1930's: "Chautemps told me that he would certainly find a formula for agreement. His quick and supple intelligence gave him an extraordinary mastery of the art of conciliation. He adored the word and the thing. He said laughingly of himself, 'Though I may have to split hairs four ways or even twenty ways in order to conciliate, I am ready to do it!' "[18] Another observer portrayed Chautemps as "a wily, adroit parliamentarian who is not embarrassed by principles, an alert navigator ready to veer and to avoid shoals."[19]

The Radicals may have had something quaint in their appearance, something ineffably French; but they were the closest French approximation to the amorphous, shifting, chameleon party that is becoming the standard in the Western world. They were a politician's party; and as politicians who had risen by the easy, glad-handing path to power, they were faced with the deepest crisis in France's history. This study, therefore, is in part a case study of the reactions of such a party to an extreme situation.

Radicals occupied, sociologically, a strategic position in the France of the 1930's. Radicalism was the political expression of what Marx called "the dangerous class," the petty bourgeoisie, which the French prefer to call the *classes moyennes*—a category approximating our lower middle classes, but embracing the liberal professions and the peasant proprietors as well. Then as now these classes had an affinity for fascism; in the frightening world of the 1930's, men both on the right and on the left anticipated that France, like its neighbors, would be faced with an indigenous fascist movement. Whether the Radicals would be able to withstand a fascist bid for their clientele became a question of immediate importance. Leon Trotsky, during his brief stay in France, wrote, "Fascism can become a mass force only by conquering the petty bourgeoisie. In other words, fascism, in France, can increase above all at the expense of the Radicals."[20] Daladier made the same point.[21] Although the Radicals in the 1930's were not dynamic enough to deflect a fascist thrust had there been one, the fact that Radicalism had brought the *classes moyennes* to political consciousness more than a generation earlier, and infused them with a democratic mystique, was probably sufficient to prevent a rapid spread of fascism. In the 1930's, however, it was by no means apparent how weak French fascism was, and the fear of fascism prodded the left into feverish activity.[22]

Often in this study the Radical party has been judged and found wanting. Since the very nature of the party was diversity, it may be asked whether meaningful judgments can be made on the party rather than on its individual members: the parliamentarians, after all, were ultimately sovereign, and in most matters of importance they were divided into three groups—those for a policy, those opposed, and those who abstained. Yet the Radical party is more than a convenient fiction for several reasons. In the first place, the party was regarded by Radicals and by others as a corporate entity capable of action. When the Radicals joined the Popular Front, for instance, not only the Popular Front Radicals were included, but the anti-Popular Front Radicals as well; thus the anti-Communist, anti-Socialist Georges Bonnet could legitimately be Minister of Finance in a Popular Front government. Again, the purest Radicals were smeared by the Stavisky scandal because the public treated the corruption as a corporate, not an individual, fault. In the second place, although the Bureau, the Congress, and the Group had no coercive powers over their members, decisions made in these bodies were usually followed by the majority of deputies. At critical moments, such as the beginning of the 1932 legislature or the crisis of February 6, 1934, the party opted for one of two possible courses of action, thereby swinging the passive, indecisive majority of deputies in the chosen direction. On almost all the big issues the decision of the party as a whole was crucial.

It may seem unfair to judge the actions of a party one of whose essential functions was to reconcile and represent the interests of its voters: surely the voters, not the blotter-like party, ought to be blamed. Yet in practice the Radical deputies represented the interests of their voters rather poorly, and on issues of national importance the deputies were usually free to act as they saw fit. If they followed the common prejudices, it was not because they could not oppose them, but because they shared them. In studying the history of the 1930's, one cannot but be struck by the degree to which the political class failed in its role of directing and instructing the public. The leaders quite simply refused to lead.

The 1930's saw the reversal of the long-range drift of French opinion to the left. Until 1936, the right had been electorally on the defensive; following 1936, with the first real appearance of anti-Communism as a mystique, the right was able to drive the left from many of its former electoral strongholds. Anti-Communism, the fear of war, and the successes of the fascist countries affected all of French politics, and not least the Radical party. The ideological animosities of the larger body politic were reproduced on a smaller scale in the Radical party—it had its proto-fascists as well as its proto-Communists. The economic crisis produced the same futile reactions among the Radicals as in the population at large.

Before we begin the analysis of the party, a word must be said about the principal source for this study, the press. Any political study of the 1930's must be based primarily on newspaper accounts; there are very few useful alternatives—a few memoirs and the reports of a few investigating committees.[23] (The archives of the Ministry of the Interior either have been destroyed or remain inaccessible.) A mistaken assessment of the press's role has led many historians to use the press only as illustration for what is taken to be public opinion and to reject much political information as biased and inaccurate. Yet as a source for public opinion, the venal Paris press is extremely suspect; but as a source for political events, it is highly valuable not only because it was a key political force in itself, but also because its information is more accurate than is generally supposed.

The press was an important channel of communication among politicians and an essential source of information. Most important politicians had a press-clipping service,[24] and much of what was called the "confidential press" was distributed free to deputies. Every important political article, whether accurate or not, became a political fact in its own right, and often as important a fact as the event it purportedly described. A press account may have had political effects even though it was a distortion of the facts. On November 8, 1933, for instance, *Le Temps* reported that Daladier made a speech in the Radical Group hostile to the Socialists. The key passage of the article read as follows:

Be careful, he said in substance, about collaborating with the Socialists. I was one of those who made the most extensive sacrifices to the Union des Gauches, sometimes going so far as to back Socialist solutions and to give them preference. . . . And yet it was to me that M. Léon Blum said no!

Never forget that it was the Socialists who broke the Union des Gauches with their own hands.

This quotation was copied verbatim by most of the press, including the Socialist *Le Populaire*.[25] Yet, according to Jean Zay, a leader of the pro-Socialist Radicals, who was very closely connected with the incident, Daladier said no such thing. Some of the press later stated that the report had been in error.[26] Whether Daladier did or did not make this statement is not very important. The distortion—or the truth—was plausible and had the effect of publicly promoting Daladier as the Radical most liable to break with the Socialists. He accepted the image and actually tried to create a non-Socialist majority in January 1934. In this instance, the report—whether true or false—is the important fact, and what lies behind it is secondary. Only the reports in generally reliable papers like *Le Temps* were elevated into political facts in their own right.

Also, whereas in any given situation the facts of a report may or may not have been correct, the nature of the explanation was probably accurate. If in reporting a political incident the press emphasized electoral considerations and ignored foreign policy, then although the details of any given newspaper account may be questionable, the general nature of the incident cannot reasonably be doubted. A report widely accepted by politicians must have been intellectually plausible to that class, and must therefore have reflected the sort of behavior they were familiar with. However distorted such reports may have been in individual instances, the style of political behavior they relate is almost certainly the dominant style, and therefore it seems reasonable to assume that the aggregate image of politics gained through the political press is substantially correct.

In the early 1930's at least, political society was very much an open society. Few secrets were kept; major political decisions almost immediately became public knowledge. The "revelations" in Herriot's memoirs—not published until the 1950's—about the overthrow of the Doumergue government were in the 1930's in such papers as *La Lumière, Candide,* and *Aux écoutes*. Daladier's secret negotiations for the formation of a centrist majority in the late summer of 1933, which were confirmed in the findings of the commission formed to investigate the riots of February Sixth and in the more recently published memoirs of Lucien Lamoureux, were known at the time. Herriot's opposition to Laval's Ethiopian policy was public knowledge by September 1935, and his tortuous four-month indecision over whether or not to overthrow the government was chronicled in print.

Very often the journalistic account was written by one of the actors. The pseudonymous Pierre du Clain of *La Lumière* was François Albert, president of the Radical Group and leader of the left-wing Radicals before January 1933. Accounts in *La Dépêche de Toulouse* of events in which Yvon Delbos or the Sarraut brothers, Albert and Maurice, were very closely involved obviously have a particular sort of authenticity: they give, at the very least, these men's version of their actions. Jean Piot, the editor of *L'Oeuvre,* was a member of the Radical Group from 1932 to 1936 and of the Bureau in 1937 and 1938. The editor of *L'Ere nouvelle,* Léo-Abel Gaboriaud, was a member of the Bureau in 1932 and 1933. The secretary-general of the party from 1932 to 1934, Albert Milhaud, wrote daily in *L'Ere nouvelle.* The secretary-general from 1934 to 1936, Raoul Aubaud, was closely connected with *La République de l'Oise.* There was a similar overlapping of parliamentary and journalistic roles in the weekly provincial press.

It seems unlikely that any source for the meetings of the Radical Group other than the press reports of the proceedings will ever be discovered; any records the party might have had were destroyed in 1940. An incident in 1937 concerning the Group and the press is reassuring about the accuracy of press reporting. On their return to parliament after a trip to Republican Spain, some members of a Radical delegation made derogatory remarks about the Republican government that were picked up by the press. Supporters of the Popular Front were outraged, and to calm the storm the Group claimed that the press had misreported the incident. The press union was indignant and directed its president to protest, which he did so successfully that the Radicals were forced to retract: "The delegation gladly recognizes first of all that the information was published in good faith, according to the usual methods of information of the parliamentary press." Published statements by Lucien Galimand, the principal Radical involved, subsequently showed that the press report had been substantially accurate.[27]

One cannot, of course, take the press at face value, for the press reports contained many of the intentional and unintentional errors customarily associated with journalism. But the most interesting political events are documented only in press reports; therefore the press must and can be used.

The Basis of Radical Politics

CHAPTER I

Party Structure and Organization

I

The subject of this book is the Radical-Socialist party, defined simply as its senators, deputies, and *militants* (party workers).* It may be asked whether a party of such feeble organization and contradictory tendencies is a suitable subject for study. Georges Dupeux and Jean-Jacques Chevallier lump the Radicals with the neighboring splinter parties—the Republican Socialists, French Socialists, and the Indépendants de Gauche.[1] All these groups represented substantially similar areas and classes; and their joint treatment is justified in a primarily electoral study. But this study is not electoral: the parliamentarians are the subject, not the voters, and Radical and dissident Socialist parliamentarians were formed by different intellectual heritages. Moreover, there was a very strong group unity among Radicals which excluded outsiders, particularly the renegades who filled the ranks of the splinter groups. When Bergery and Cudenet seceded to the left, or Pfeiffer, Creyssel, Montigny, and Franklin-Bouillon to the right, the party cut them off. During the crisis of December 1932, for instance, the president of the Radical Group let it be known that the

---

* There is no English equivalent for the French term *militant,* but for the sake of convenience, "party worker" will henceforth be used. It should be remembered, however, that whereas the "party worker" of American politics connotes work in anticipation of tangible benefits, *militant* connotes participation in an ideological enterprise. Gabriel Almond (p. 397) points out that *militants* exist only in continental political systems. All real parties in France tend to reflect what Almond calls a "political culture" and try to encompass their members' whole social existence. The most striking instance is the Communist party, with its trade unions, athletic clubs, and cultural organizations. To a lesser extent, this was true also of the Radicals, who considered working for the party a commitment to a philosophy that competed with the philosophies of Marxists and Christians.

party would not tolerate in the new cabinet any renegade Radicals.[2] Only very occasionally was an outsider like Paul Painlevé accepted; great republicans of the past were assimilated into the Radical galaxy only after they were dead. There was an institutional unity as well: the Radical party worker lived for the annual Congress, and the deputy's life centered around the Group meeting. The members of the party shared a self-conscious, exclusive Radicalism.

This group feeling was never endangered by the chronic disunity of the party's parliamentary behavior. For the Radical, freedom to vote as he pleased was a basic right which the party generally respected. All types of Radicals were remarkably tolerant toward dissent within the party. For example, in the partial election of Lapalisse in the Allier in 1936, Lucien Lamoureux, the Radical candidate, though ostracized by his party because of Daladier's antipathy to him and his outspoken opposition to the Popular Front, was helped by four personal friends—Léon Archimbaud, Robert Lassalle, Albert Le Bail, and César Campinchi. All four men were strong partisans of the Popular Front; yet, as Campinchi said, they felt that all Radicals should support all Radicals, no matter what their leanings.[3]

The Radical party's formal organization is of little concern to us, but before examining the party's history in the 1930's we must examine at some length the main classes of people who comprised it: its electoral clientele, its party workers, its deputies and senators, its leaders, and the Radical press.

II

What did the Radicals represent in parliament? The answer is fairly simple on one plane. It can be arrived at simply by drawing a map, or rather two, and shading in the areas represented by deputies on one and the percentage of votes on the other. Several blocs emerge: the Southwest and Languedoc, parts of the West, of the East, of the Paris area, and so on. The most striking observation is the blankness in the urban, industrial centers: Paris, Nord, Lorraine, Marseilles, Bordeaux. Only in the towns of Lyons, Rouen, Le Havre, and St.-Etienne were Radicals to be found. The Radicals represented rural, provincial France.

When one moves from such simple observations to the more complex questions—who voted for them? whose interests did they defend?—the clarity disappears. Since public opinion polls were unknown, conclusions about the composition of the Radicals' electorate are problematical.

By the 1930's, the Radicals had ceased appealing to the working classes. They were generally acknowledged to represent the independent peasants and the lower middle classes—the *classes moyennes.*[4] For Pierre Cot, the Radical party "is, and always has been, the party of the small independent proprietors, farmers, shopkeepers, artisans, *fonctionnaires* [minor civil servants], men of the liberal professions— that is to say, all those who live from their work, but work that they pursue as individuals; from their craft, but a craft that is distinctly theirs."[5] This is a good description of the *classes moyennes.* Albert Chichery told the party members to win new adherents among the shopkeepers, peasants, and members of the *classes moyennes.* The Communists saw the Radical party as the authentic representative of the petty bourgeoisie, and this belief had far-reaching political consequences at the time of the Popular Front.[6] Nobody bothered to verify the commonly held opinions scientifically, and it is no longer possible to do so. Probably what the Radicals themselves and the world believed they represented was fairly accurate: they were the representatives of the petty bourgeoisie and the peasantry.

This conglomerate is politically intriguing, for it contains within it the new and the old France. The peasantry and petty bourgeoisie, who traditionally supplied the Radical party's votes, were threatened by the process of modernization and industrialization. These classes were declining in numbers, and the Radical party fought a delaying action for them with legislation hindering the expansion of large industrial and commercial establishments.[7] Yet other segments of the population which were traditionally Radical—professional men and "cadres" of all sorts except the highest—were being created by those very forces of modernization. These "new men," whose increase in numbers has been extraordinary during the past generation, were potentially Radical, and the party therefore had a chance to bring about a gradual shift in its electoral support by consciously catering to them. It ultimately failed to do so, and though these new men were momentarily attracted to Mendès-France, the majority have probably ended with de Gaulle.

In the Fourth Republic, the Radicals were strongest among the peasant proprietors and the pensioners, and strong also among the shopkeepers, middle bourgeoisie, liberal professions, and fonctionnaires; they were very weak among industrial, agricultural, and white-collar workers. The moderates had as high a proportion of peasant voters as the Radicals, who also shared the rest of the *classes moyennes* with the Socialists, the MRP, and the moderates.[8] Presumably there was a comparable division in the 1930's. To call the Radicals the representatives of the *classes moyennes* was an oversimplification.

Although their voters were peasants and petty bourgeois, can it be said that the Radicals represented them? Can it be assumed, for instance, that those who represented rural districts really championed peasant interests? Louis Chevalier has shown that in this period the rural constituency, made up of distinctly urban and peasant sectors, was dominated by the urban sector, which provided the political personnel for constituency politics and which supported urban interests against those of the countryside. Most of the Radical "peasant" spokesmen in the Chamber in reality were defending the rural "urban" interests—the grain dealers, for example, against the grain growers at the time of the Popular Front's Wheat Board.[9]

Yet if the Radicals did not really represent the peasant interests, neither did anyone else, and the belief that they were the spokesmen for these groups affected their parliamentary behavior—from 1933 to 1935 on the wheat question, in 1936 and 1937 on inflation and the social laws.

III

The party worker presents a different problem. Our knowledge of him is at once more and less certain. Whereas the number of Radical voters can be known with precision and their social composition inferred in a general way, the number and social composition of active party workers can only be guessed at.[10] In a list of officers of the local committees of the Federation of the Seine, occupations are given for about half the men named; these are shown in Table 1. This list is not wholly representative, the officers being higher in the social scale than the average party worker.[11] Presumably the total body of party workers contained a higher proportion of skilled workers, artisans, and shopkeepers. The list is atypical, since in provincial France the role of the peasant proprietor as party worker was extremely important. The absence of workers is striking. The socio-economic status of these party workers is much lower than that of the deputies. Petty bourgeois—particularly fonctionnaires and artisans—clearly domi-

TABLE I
Occupations of Local Radical Party Officers in the
Federation of the Seine, 1939[a]

Occupations	Number of Officers
Wage Earners and Salaried Workers	
Unskilled workers	0
Skilled workers	4
White-collar workers	8
Fonctionnaires	21
Salesmen	7
Professional Classes	
Teachers	2
Journalists	1
Professors	2
Doctors, veterinarians, pharmacists	2
Lawyers, magistrates, etc.	12
Higher fonctionnaires	3
Engineers and architects	8
Businessmen	
Executives	5
Shopkeepers and artisans	25
Small businessmen	8
Small industrialists	4
Other	
Retired army officers	3
Retired policemen	2
Retired	2
Students	1
Farmers	0

[a] The list was kindly furnished me from the papers of Lucien Bauzin, past president of the federation. The categories in this table were adapted from the socio-professional divisions used by Dogan in *L'Origine sociale*, p. 295; I have omitted his Category II (farmers) and Category V (officers and clergy).

nate, and the intellectual professions are not so strikingly over-represented as among the deputies. Lawyers are naturally strongest, followed rather surprisingly by engineers and architects (the desire for public contracts may play a part here); teachers, journalists, and professors are strikingly under-represented. Business representation is also weak.

How many Radical party workers there were can never be known. Radicals never exhibited the statistical propensities of the Socialists, who recorded not only the membership of every Socialist federation, but also the strength of each ideological group within it. Most Radical federations compiled no membership figures, and the twenty-five or so that made some efforts in this direction were evidently concerned only with a very general indication of size, too unreliable to be used here. The number of party cards held varied during our period from perhaps 70,000 to 120,000.[12] The number of cards reflected only faintly the number of members. On the one hand, cards were very cheap and could be purchased indiscriminately by persons seeking influence within the party. The commune of Mus-des-Cours in the Aude in 1936, for example, had only 11 electors, all Radicals, yet 28 party cards were held; in Félinus-Termeues in the same department, the number of cards jumped from six to 42 between 1932 and 1933, but only 15 Radical votes were cast in 1936. On the other hand, many of the strongest Radical constituencies held no cards whatsoever. Indeed, federations tended to be organized only in periods of declining strength. In Barbezieux in the Charente, for example, after the seat "fell by surprise into reactionary hands" a committee was formed to restore the situation.[13] After the shock of the 1936 elections, official Radical committees were established for the first time in such strongholds as Saintes and Louis-Jean Malvy's fief in Lot. Since the unregistered party workers probably compensated for the excessive purchase of cards, the official figures are not necessarily too high.

A membership of 120,000 is ludicrously small compared with the 2,800,000 members of the Conservative party in Great Britain,[14] or indeed with the membership of most foreign parties. But French parties have notoriously small memberships. In 1932, the Socialists, who were the one "mass party," had a membership of 137,701.[15] The Communists had between 15,000 and 30,000.[16] The comparison with the British Conservative party, moreover, is misleading. Most of the Conservative membership consisted of inactive sympathizers. According to Robert McKenzie, "Even at an election the average association cannot rely on the active support of more than three or four hundred of its members and the turnout of such numbers at an annual general meeting would be considered very large indeed."[17] If the press accounts are even roughly accurate, such turnouts among Radicals at meetings of an arrondissement federation (comparable to an English constituency association) were relatively common,[18] and a banquet could usually count on more.[19] Radical party membership was probably made up principally of party workers, with the supporters, to use Maurice Duverger's distinction, remaining outside.

The Radicals were the prototype for Duverger's model of the "cadre party," "restricted to a few, dependent upon rigid and exclusive selection"; such a party had no need to recruit members, and therefore "the problem [of numbers] is meaningless."[20] To the committees, however, it was a matter of concern. There were lively recruiting drives in the Charente-Inférieure, Allier, Aude, Nord, Indre, and elsewhere. There was a simple pride when, for instance, the Federation of St.-Claude in the Jura could vote a motion "in the name of its 795 members," or when the Federation of Finistère announced that its membership had risen from 1,000 to 2,500.[21]

The presence of party workers in a commune seems to have had little effect on election results. Comparison of the list of actual party workers with Radical votes, commune by commune, in the first arrondissement of Dinan shows no correlation between the percentage of Radical votes in a commune and the number of party workers there.[22] One suspects that the party workers' role was not so much to mobilize the vote as to allocate claims and favors.

The local committees differed enormously in their organization and nature. Duverger has called the party "an incoherent agglomeration of associations linked by vague and variable bonds."[23] But apart from the effects the differences had on the Executive Committee and the Congresses, discussed below, the variations had little apparent bearing on national politics.

Commentators have denounced the Radicals as parochial, but Daniel Bardonnet has shown that whereas the Committee of Montluçon was concerned only with local matters, the Committee of the Sorbonne in Paris spent much of its time discussing national issues.[24] The impressions of deputies are contradictory.* An analysis of the content of the constituency press, however, unequivocally supports the broad-interest hypothesis. In all but one or two papers (for example, *Dinan-républicain,* examined in Chapter 3), national and international questions dominated, local politics were treated with reluctance, and polemics with neighboring local parties were rare. In the newspaper

---

* André Liautey told me that in the 1930's his electors were little interested in national problems (interview, October 29, 1960); Julien Durand said the contrary (interview, November 5, 1960). Henri Clerc quoted a peasant: "We want to hear you speak on national questions, because then we will learn something we don't already know" (*La République,* July 3, 1932). Pierre Cot said that when he talked with the peasants of his constituency, he was always astonished to find them "informed about the smallest details of politics" ("Le Rajeunissement des partis," p. 158).

Royan there were 54 major articles from May 1932 to April 1933; 20 concerned foreign affairs, 32 national domestic policy, two miscellaneous questions, and none local affairs.

La République de Chinon in 1934 had nine articles on foreign affairs, three on economic conditions, and 26 on national domestic politics, principally the Stavisky affair, but none on local politics or problems. This emphasis was wholly characteristic. Undoubtedly local politics were discussed at party meetings and banquets, but such discussions were not reported in the papers; newspaper reports dealt almost exclusively with the formal addresses that invariably concerned public policy.

In spite of his interest, the party worker's influence on policy was slight. The meetings of his committee were rare. His essential function was to act as an intermediary through whom the constituents' wishes were transmitted to the Radical deputy and the Radical ministers in Paris. For the party worker, the main purpose of political power was to mitigate the impact of the bureaucratic state (whose general legitimacy was not questioned) in individual instances. The party worker's letters to his deputy, if one is to believe Hippolyte Ducos, concerned private affairs exclusively.[25] For this reason, the Radicals regarded the Ministry of the Interior—the source of such dispensations from government regulations—as their private preserve.[26] If the deputy filled this role adequately, his obligations to his local supporters were fulfilled, and he was free to follow his own inclinations in matters of general policy. Typically, in the Radical party the local committee seems to have had very little control over, or even interest in, the deputy's actions. Occasionally a deputy would have to explain his stand on a particular issue, but widespread explanations seem to have occurred only twice—at the time of Herriot's policy of paying the American war debts, and after the highly unpopular Wheat Bill was passed by Flandin in the winter of 1934–35. There was also considerable pressure from below to force deputies to join the Popular Front in 1935. But face to face with the deputy, the committee was generally impotent.

In two of the party's institutions the party worker could act independently of his local deputy: the Congress and the Executive Committee. But the parliamentarians and the professionals usually managed to neutralize the party workers' influence even here by such devices as fixing the order of business and setting the proportion of ex officio members to elected delegates at roughly two to one.[27]

The Executive Committee and the Congress were huge, unwieldy bodies; they were more or less independent of each other, although the Congress had the ultimate authority to change the statutes. In 1935, the Executive Committee had 2,388 members, of whom 1,406 were ex officio members—men who held or had held the position of deputy, senator, departmental councillor, or mayor, and former candidates for these positions. The potential ex officio membership was almost limitless—there were perhaps 1,600 Radical departmental councillors alone. The representation to both bodies was shockingly unequal from one department to the next. The figures brought forward by one exasperated party worker are eloquent: one department had 2,536 cards and 11 delegates to the Executive Committee; another, 1,500 cards and 49 delegates; a third, 350 cards and 42 delegates; a fourth, 19 cards and ten delegates.[28] The Congress had a somewhat more equitable representation, but it was a fairly easy thing to fix a Congress by buying cards—the Congress of Biarritz in 1936 was the most notoriously rigged during our period. Usually about 1,200 delegates attended. Voting was not by mandate or even by ballot, but simply by raised hands, which facilitated steam-roller tactics. The order of business was worked out ahead of time by the Bureau of the Executive Committee, which was, as we shall see, dominated by the president of the party. The meetings were chaired by parliamentarians. All these characteristics have led Duverger to claim that these bodies were simply rubber stamps for the parliamentarians.[29]

Yet the question is not so easily settled. Both bodies on occasion made difficulties for the directors of the party. The annual fall meeting of the Congress was an outstanding political event. The federations took the Congress seriously, conscientiously electing delegates and sometimes defraying their traveling expenses. Moreover, the largest federations were located in areas from which few deputies were elected—notably the Seine, Seine-et-Oise, Nord, Ariège, Haute-Garonne, and Bouches-du-Rhône. With no deputies to overawe them, these large federations could become strongly organized. The Federation of the Seine was more like a Socialist organization than a rural Radical federation; some of the committees of the Seine went so far as to call themselves by the Socialist term *section* (branch). The Seine, which had scarcely any Radical deputies, sent as many as 250 delegates to the Executive Committee, whereas the Charente-Inférieure, where Radical deputies dominated, sent between 17 and 25.

The preponderance of ex officio members, moreover, was not a very effective means of diluting the influence of the party worker. For most federations, those who went to the Congress ex officio would have been delegated if they had not qualified for ex officio status. Many ex officio members were of local eminence only; a vast spiritual distance separated them from the parliamentarians, who often felt ill at ease in Congresses. The domination of the parliamentarians was resented and the latent antagonism occasionally was expressed in interruptions like: "Let the party workers speak first!"[30] At the Congress of Nantes in 1934 there was a notable run-in between party workers and the party structure. On this occasion Gaston Martin made the interesting statement: "[The parliamentarians] feel very much as if they were on trial before the party workers."[31]

The Congress was a war machine of considerable power when properly handled. Although the party workers by themselves could do nothing, they could be very effective in the hands of a discontented leader. The Congress in fact had far more real power than the annual conference of the Conservative party in Great Britain, in spite of the Conservatives' superior organization.[32]

The power of the Congress had been demonstrated by the so-called Coup d'Angers of 1928, when Caillaux and Bergery maneuvered the Congress into condemning continued Radical participation in the Poincaré government unexpectedly, and thus forced Herriot to resign. This was the only time a Radical Congress directly overthrew a government; yet the precedent haunted all subsequent governments, and they approached the Congress very delicately. In 1933, the Congress was called early and the budget published late so that there would be no chance for its unpopular provisions to spark a revolt. Before the extraordinary Congress of May 1934, there was endless speculation about a new "Coup d'Angers," all of it in vain, since no leader dared to muster the party workers. The Congress of Nantes in October 1934, which is often cited as overthrowing the Doumergue government, simply endorsed Herriot's clear intention to do so. But Herriot approached the Congress of 1935 with trepidation and ran into considerable opposition led by Daladier. The greatest dangers came during the Congresses of Biarritz in 1936 and Lille in 1937, when the party workers, led the first year by Albert Milhaud and Emile Roche and the following year by Roche and Georges Bonnet, threatened to destroy the Popular Front.

Because the Radical Congresses were so large—attracting as many as 6,000 people—they had to be held in large cities or resorts, where the Radicals were generally an insignificant minority. Of the cities chosen, Vichy, Toulouse, Clermont-Ferrand, Nantes, Biarritz, Lille, and Marseilles had conservative or reactionary local memberships, and conservative support was thus inevitably over-represented at provincial Congresses. But the Congress that preceded the legislative elections was traditionally held in Paris, which was very left-wing. The federations of the Seine and surrounding departments also had few deputies but were numerically and organizationally strong, and pushed the Congress further to the left than the party as a whole. Thus accidents of location accentuated the existing tendency toward radicalism before elections and moderation afterward. The most striking shift was from the Popular Front Congress of Paris in 1935 to the almost reactionary Congress of Biarritz in 1936.

The Executive Committee was not so formidable as the Congress. It met more often, and the attendance at its meetings was smaller. But it always met in Paris and was therefore dominated by the left-wing federations of the Paris area. On occasion, it could cause the party leaders difficulty. After February Sixth, the conservative secretary-general Milhaud simply refused to let it meet. When it finally met in July 1934, after Milhaud's replacement by a left-wing secretary-general, there was a real effort by the party workers to wrest control of the party from the parliamentarians.[33] In January 1936, after Herriot's resignation as president of the party, the Federation of the Seine packed an Executive Committee meeting to ensure the election of Daladier as president and to give the party a decisive push toward the Popular Front. In January 1939, Daladier capped his triumph over the left-wing elements of the party when he had Ernest Perney replaced as president of the Federation of the Seine by the more conservative and malleable Lucien Bauzin, in what may have been a fixed election. With this done, the Executive Committee was fairly well brought under control.

Above the Congress and the Executive Committee stood the Bureau of the Executive Committee and the president of the party.[34] According to the original intention expressed by Herriot in 1906, "The Bureau's members should be replaced frequently so that we do not appear subjected to a dictatorship, so that we do not seem always to be led by the same men."[35] Although the terms of election to the Bureau were ostensibly democratic—16 party workers and 16 parliamentarians, half of whom were replaced every year—in fact the Bureau was cliquish and dominated by the parliamentarians. The representatives of the party workers were not typical. Many were professional politicians, and journalists.[36] Others were simply parliamentarians out of a seat. Throughout the period, eight of the 72 positions reserved for party workers were filled with former parliamentarians.[37] Although consecutive terms were not permitted, from 1932 to 1940 no fewer than 23 people served more than once.[38]

The Bureau met every week and handled the routine affairs of the party. It made the important day-to-day decisions and did the stage managing for the Congress and the Executive Committee. It arranged each year for the elections for its own replacements. It handled delicate political affairs. During the summer of 1933, Herriot reportedly used the Bureau to contact the Socialists to try to avert a government crisis.[39] It was clearly an institution of weight, yet it led a tranquil, unworried existence. When the Bureau decided to join the Popular Front, for instance, the decision was not opposed, according to Kayser, even by such an anti-Popular Front member as Paul Marchandeau.[40] The conflicts that throve in other parts of the party by-passed the Bureau. Although Daladier and Herriot each had their supporters and each was entitled to attend the meetings of the Bureau ex officio, neither interfered with the other's presidency.[41] The leaders found the Bureau much more manageable than the Group, to which all Radical deputies belonged. Herriot wrote concerning one incident: "The Radical Group was very hostile to the government. The Bureau of the party, which met afterward, was much more conciliatory."[42]

The party's central organization was a logical, complex, highly structured sham. The Bureau stood at the top of an elaborate pyramid of committees for general policy, propaganda, commerce, agriculture, and so on. These committees were so ineffectual that often the Radicals in the government were unaware of their existence. Indeed, the whole party bureaucracy, such as it was, existed in a never-never land between the party workers in the country and the deputies in parliament. The party would occasionally print a brochure.[43] Now and then it attempted to organize teams of speakers to be sent out across the country. It even established an Ecole Supérieure du Radicalisme, which was quickly laughed out of existence. There was just enough organization to make everyone acutely aware of its monumental deficiencies. Since the form was there, the feeling persisted that there should be some substance. Emile Kahn, at the Congress of Biarritz, complained that the departmental federations systematically neglected to answer the questionnaires sent out to them.[44] When a "vast rural enquiry" was made in the summer of 1937, the party received responses from sixteen federations.[45] When I asked Bauzin about the existence of Radical party archives, he replied that the party was so disorganized that he doubted that there ever were any—which was not strictly true. Urgent pleas were ritually made for the production of propaganda, and were ritually ignored.

Occasionally the Bureau was called upon to intervene in local affairs. In the Isère in the fall of 1932 it had to settle a dispute between the left-wingers and the right-wingers concerning alliances with the Socialists in the senatorial elections. During the election of Saintes in May 1938, the Bureau ineffectually tried to get the local federation to withdraw its candidate in favor of the Socialist on the second ballot, and received the sharp rebuke: "The Executive Committee has no right to give orders. The federations are autonomous. Such a gesture must not be repeated."[46] One or two other instances complete the list of the party's local interventions.

The party, therefore, exercised only limited control over events. It was a convenient instrument for producing policy statements when they were needed, and it exercised a general tutelary role. But its ultimate power was limited.

IV

The real authority within the party, as in all liberal bourgeois parties, lay with the parliamentarians.[47] In France this position approached absolute sovereignty. The Radicals' "ingrained" indifference to discipline limited the leader's authority; then, too, the structure of party finances forced the deputy to raise his own campaign funds. Nationally, the deputy dominated the Bureau; locally, he had only to keep his electoral fences mended.

A basic difference of type existed between the Radical senators and the Radical deputies. The two played different political roles. The senatorial electors were rural notables who enforced their conservatism on their senators.[48] In the Seine-et-Marne, for example, three incumbent Radical senators were rashly persuaded by their left-wing federation to run on a Popular Front platform in the senatorial elections of 1935; all three were resoundingly defeated.[49] Such disasters were rare, since the senators usually shared their electors' attitudes. In Loiret, the deputies were all very left-wing and the senators all very conservative; yet they managed to coexist peaceably. In Eure-et-Loir, the left-wing deputy Jules Mitton and the conservative senator Jean Valadier both regularly wrote in *Le Patriote de Châteaudun* although the doctrines they presented were usually diametrically opposed.

The senators were less involved with the party than the deputies. There was not even a Radical Group in the Senate; the Gauche Démocratique, of whose 160 members roughly 90 were Radicals, was the closest approximation. Very occasionally the Radical senators would meet separately. In January 1936, for example, they tried to stem the leftward drift of the Group in the Chamber. But such gestures were without effect.

The Radicals of the Senate were a breed apart. With rare exceptions, they represented an older generation than the deputies; the Senate was a haven for the declining years. With the notable exceptions of Léon Perrier and Emile Lisbonne, who were left-wing, Radical senators were generally conservatives. The average Radical senator was a local notable who had been rewarded for faithful service, and who did not make the slightest impression on national politics; often years would go by without his attending a session. There were a number of senators who politically dominated their departments, but played a minor role in Paris—Valadier in Eure-et-Loir, Plaisant in Cher, de Kerguézec in Côtes-du-Nord, Sireyjol in the northern part of Dordogne, Germain in Indre-et-Loire, Delthil in Tarn-et-Garonne, and Perreau in Charente-Inférieure. In Isère, Perrier was far more important than the nationally better known Paganon. The smallest group of senators were those few active conservatives who personified the Senate and whose importance was derived from this role. In his last years, Caillaux dominated the Senate and made it almost equal to the Chamber in political importance. The rest of the group consisted of Régnier, Gardey, Roy, and Bienvenu-Martin.[50] The principal concern of the Radical senators was to assure the financial orthodoxy of the government.[51] They opposed all dangerous experiments from 1932 to 1934, and, within the limits of the possible, from 1936 to 1938. Other Radical senators were politicians of importance, but not because they were senators. During the 1930's, there was a gradual drift of the important Radical deputies into the Senate: Palmade, Bertrand, Jac-

TABLE 2

*Occupations of Radical Deputies in the 1932 and 1936 Legislatures
Classed by Importance in the Party*

Occupations	Minis-trables	Lesser Minis-trables	Active Non-minis-trables	Others	Total
Workers	0	0	0	0	0
White-collar workers	0	0	0	0	0
Fonctionnaires	0	0	3	3	6
Farmers	0	1	1	9	11
Teachers	0	1	1	4	6
Professors	7	5	4	4	20
Journalists	4	5	4	5	18
Doctors, veterinarians, pharmacists	2	4	2	16	24
Lawyers, etc.	11	15	9	25	60
Higher fonctionnaires	2	2	1	1	6
Engineers and architects	1	2	0	3	6
Shopkeepers and artisans	0	0	0	3	3
Small businessmen	0	0	0	15	15
Industrialists and executives	1	1	2	10	14
Miscellaneous	3	0	1	6	10
Total	31	36	28	104	199

quier, Queuille, Paganon, Berthod, and Chautemps himself. These men, like Albert Sarraut and René Renoult, regarded the Senate more as a suitable resting place than a source of power. Powerful personalities like Albert Sarraut and Camille Chautemps had far less influence over their fellow senators than Caillaux or even Gardey and Régnier.

In the end, Radical politics centered on the Chamber of Deputies. What was the Radical deputy? Table 2 shows the deputies' occupations as given in the parliamentary handbook.[52] It is clear that the Group, especially the *ministrable** class, was totally dominated by the liberal and intellectual professions at the expense of the social categories that the party was supposed to represent.[53]

The farmers, businessmen, shopkeepers, and fonctionnaires all belonged to the submerged class of deputies. Workers, of course, were

---

* A *ministrable* was a person who had been, was, or was likely to be a minister. Not all *ministrables* actually became ministers, because of the chances of the game; but their status was generally recognized.

completely absent. The important ministers were exclusively professors, lawyers, journalists, doctors, and higher fonctionnaires.

On the surface, the Radical deputies were an amorphous amalgam
of individuals whose only predictable behavior was that on every legislative vote they would divide into three sections. "The parliamentary
Group," writes Duverger, "has no will of its own, no common action,
no discipline in its voting. When it comes to an important ballot it is
unusual to see all Radical deputies adopt the same attitude: generally the Group divides into three, some voting 'for,' others voting
'against,' and the rest abstaining."[54] It is true that discipline was lacking, but certain clear patterns of legislative behavior indicate that the
voting was not purely capricious. Radical deputies can be categorized, albeit somewhat arbitrarily, into four distinct voting groups:
left, moderate left, moderate, and conservative. These categories are
the basis of much of the analysis in this study. Except for the left after
1934, and the conservatives after 1936, the deputies did not self-con-
sciously identify with a voting group. Between the left and the conservatives were one hundred deputies, a morass of indistinct contours
and loosely held convictions, who have branded the entire party with
the stereotype of hesitancy and inertia universally associated with
French Radicalism in its declining years. But even within this group,
clear divisions can be easily discerned. In the 1932 Chamber there were
roughly 28 left-wingers, 54 moderate left, 38 moderates, and 37 conservatives. In the 1936 Chamber there were roughly 24 left-wingers,
35 moderate left, 21 moderates, and 25 conservatives. The edges of
these categories are, of course, blurred. The left-wing deputies are generally those who opposed Doumergue in 1934 and who were unhappy
with Daladier in 1938 and 1939. The Conservatives, generally, are
those who supported Laval in 1935 and 1936 and opposed Blum in 1936
and 1937. The moderate left and moderates are the crucial groups,
since they drifted, and it is their drifts which are ultimately the pivotal
facts in French parliamentary history during the 1930's. The moderate left permitted the creation of the Popular Front by drifting into
opposition to Laval, and supported Daladier after the fall of the Popular Front. The moderates drifted into opposition to Laval toward
the end, and into opposition under Blum, thus permitting both governments to be destroyed. Voting records on particular issues are not
absolute criteria, however; some unequivocal left-wingers, like Michel Geistdoerfer, did not vote against Doumergue.

The character of the deputies changes with the category. The men of the moderate left emerged from the depths of the provinces—Brittany, Landes, Aube, Haute-Marne. They constituted the biggest bloc within the party. They tended to be demagogically left-wing in the provinces and rather prudent in Paris—the sort that was characterized as a radish, red on the outside, white within. With rare exceptions—such as Jean Piot, editor of *L'Oeuvre,* and Henri Guernut, former secretary-general of the Ligue des Droits de l'Homme—they were modest provincials with limited ambitions.

The moderates were more imposing. Most ministers came from this group: Chautemps, Bastid, Dalimier, Hesse, Bertrand, Delbos, Palmade, Durand, Ducos, Paganon, Marcombes, Miellet, Maupoil, Jacquier, Meyer, Bernier. They were conservative but not intransigent, tempered always by political expediency. They correspond fairly accurately to the postwar group that has been called "les radicaux de gestion."[55] They were politicians of the purest sort. A description of one of them in action at a meeting of his local General Council runs: "As for M. le ministre André Hesse, deputy of La Rochelle, vice-president of the Chamber of Deputies, he passes through the room . . . smiling, witty, telling one of his inimitable anecdotes, shaking hands, shaking hands, shaking hands."[56]

The conservatives were a disparate bunch, a curious collection of fossils, ministrables, and bright young men. The fossils with their winged collars and handle-bar mustaches or mutton-chop side whiskers were few and declining in number—Jacques de Chammard, for example, with his plaintive incomprehension when defeated in the elections of 1936: "How could the electors have repudiated de Chammard? He was perfectly honest!"[57] Among the conservatives there were astute and seasoned politicians of ministerial rank who refused to submit to the Popular Front—Queuille, Bonnet, Lamoureux, Malvy, Marchandeau. There were finally a surprisingly large number of bright young men, although fewer than on the left—Potut, Martinaud-Déplat, Riou, Mistler.

On the left, as on the right, there was a mixture of the old and the new. There were modern young reformists—Zay, Mendès-France, Bergery, Cot. But with them there were intransigents from the provinces, representing "significant survivals, 'outcroppings' of older cultures, . . . remnants of the older middle classes who are still primarily concerned with the secularization of the political system itself."[58]

They were a strange breed—Geistdoerfer, Crutel, Longuet, Gout—the "pure" Radicals who were living symbols of what the party had once been: unbendingly anti-clerical, anti-authoritarian, intransigent, and provincial. Then there were others, also of the old school but intellectually sophisticated—Bayet, François Albert, Jammy Schmidt, Aubaud, Archimbaud.

In the 1930's the existence of left-wing and right-wing Radicals was commonly explained by the electoral system of two ballots: if on the second ballot a Radical required Socialist support to get elected, he was left-wing; if he had to run against a Socialist, he was right-wing. Such an intelligent commentator and wily politician as L.-O. Frossard wrote: "According to whether a deputy is obliged to campaign with or against [the Socialists and Communists], he is for or against the Popular Front."[59] Another commentator wrote that there were two equally important types of Radicals, those elected with the help of the Socialists and those elected without it.[60] This argument was occasionally used by those who supported a left-wing policy. It must be understood, said Jean Zay,

that the 160 Radical deputies—this is a political fact—have the duty, not the right, but the duty, to remember at certain times that they were not elected by specifically Radical votes alone. [Protests.] What kind of democracy would there be if elected representatives paid no attention to representing those who elected them!

Party Worker: No! No! We cannot accept that![61]

Undoubtedly, there was a relationship between a deputy's electoral support and his behavior in parliament, and some deputies may have inclined toward the left from fear of reprisals by their electoral allies. But, particularly in the 1932 Chamber (see Table 3), such relationships were far from universal. In general, the table shows the expected tendency; yet 30.5 per cent of the deputies who required Socialist votes for election were moderate or conservative, and 36 per cent of the deputies who ran against Socialists and Communists were left-wing or moderately left-wing in parliament. Only in the case of an outright second-ballot contest between a Radical and a Socialist does there seem to be a necessary connection between a deputy's attitude and his electoral support. To be sure, opinions had not yet crystallized in 1932, and there was little pressure on the deputies to follow consistent poli-

TABLE 3

*Classification of Radical Deputies in the 1932 Legislature
by Parliamentary Voting Group and Electoral Opposition*

Electoral Opposition	Left No.	Left % of Group	Moderate Left No.	Moderate Left % of Group	Moderate No.	Moderate % of Group	Conservative No.	Conservative % of Group
Elected on 1st ballot:								
Principal opponent on the right...	12	43	12	22	11	30	7	18
Principal opponent Socialist or Communist	2	7	5	9	4	11	8	21
Elected on 2d ballot:								
Elected because Socialist or Communist withdrew	12	43	25	46	13	35	8	21
Elected after, but not because, Socialist or Communist withdrew .	2	7	11	20	9	24	9	24
Defeated Socialist or Communist .	0	0	1	2	0	0	6	16
Total	28	100	54	99	37	100	38	100

cies. The elections of 1936, following two years of agitation, were fought in a much more politically conscious atmosphere. Table 4, for the 1936 Chamber, shows a much clearer, although still not absolute, correlation between parliamentary faction and electoral support.

We have seen that the party worker had little control over the action of the deputy, especially when national issues, rather than local interests, were involved; if a deputy took care of his constituents in matters of patronage, he seems to have been free to follow whatever political course he pleased. Daladier represented one of the most conservative federations; yet through much of his career he posed as leader of the left for tactical reasons. The electors of Cot, Geistdoerfer, and Pierre Dezarnaulds were considerably more moderate than their deputies. Léon Perrier remained true to his left-wing upbringing even after his supporters in the Isère had become moderates. Albert Chichery was always conservative, yet he was elected by a Popular Front majority.

The chief reason for these discrepancies was simply personality. A good example is the 1939 election of a successor to William Bertrand, a moderate deputy who had decided to move up into the Senate. His constituency, Marennes in the Charente-Inférieure, had recently moved rapidly toward the right. Only a year earlier the federation

TABLE 4

*Classification of Radical Deputies in the 1936 Legislature
by Parliamentary Voting Group and Electoral Opposition*

	Left		Moderate Left		Moderate		Conservative	
Electoral Opposition	No.	% of Group	No.	% of Group	No.	% of Group	No.	% of Group
Elected on 1st ballot:								
Principal opponent on the right ..	4	15	5	15	0	0	1	4
Principal opponent Socialist or Communist	1	4	1	3	2	11	9	39
Elected on 2d ballot:								
Elected because Socialist withdrew	3	11	12	36	5	28	2	9
Elected because Socialist and Communist withdrew	14	54	7	21	5	28	1	4
(Total of the two preceding)	(17)	(65)	(19)	(57)	(10)	(56)	(3)	(13)
Elected after, but not because, Socialist and Communist withdrew	4	15	6	18	5	28	2	9
Defeated Socialist or Communist .	0	0	2	6	1	5	8	35
Total	26	99	33	99	18	100	23	100

had disavowed the Popular Front by a vote of 150 to 7. The by-election took place at the height of the anti-Communist, anti-Popular Front reaction within the party. There were two candidates for the Radical nomination: a moderate named Gautier and a die-hard supporter of the Popular Front, Jean Hay. Both men addressed the committee, Gautier pallidly (one gathers), Hay with conviction. In asking for the nomination, Hay made some minor concessions to the conservatives, but no constricting promises about his future political behavior. Hay won by 236 votes to 21, simply because he was the dominant personality in his constituency.[62] Before the rise of intra-party tensions in the Popular Front era, this preponderance of personality was presumably even greater. For this reason, electoral sociology is of only limited usefulness in explaining legislative behavior.

Accidents of personality did not, however, completely eliminate the effect of regionalism on deputies' attitudes. There was undoubtedly a general tendency of the deputy to conform to the inclinations of the local party, for the dominant personality was more likely to come, after all, from the majority segment. Thus in certain regions Radicalism tended to be conservative, and in others, left-wing. In three major votes of confidence a total of 58 Radicals voted against the Doumergue government. These votes generally indicated a leftward orientation. Grouping these by region gives the following results:

North and Paris.............14 out of 28, or 50%
West....................... 7 out of 16, or 44%
East ....10 out of 24, or 42%
Southwest ....11 out of 26, or 42%
Southeast ....12 out of 29, or 41%
Center .... 3 out of 23, or 13%
Languedoc .... 1 out of 12, or 8%

This distribution clearly shows regional variations; but any division between a northern-radical and a southern-conservative Radicalism is inaccurate; the Southwest and Southeast are far more left-wing than the much more northerly Center. The Radicalism in Languedoc, the relatively small area around Toulouse, with its powerful, conservatively oriented newspaper, *La Dépéche,* is quite conservative, which has given rise to the erroneous impression that the whole Midi was conservative. Paris and the north are somewhat left-wing. The rest of the country is about equally divided between left and right. The regional pattern is not strong, however, and the variations in political attitude are striking even within the boundaries of a single department. Local Radicalism can meaningfully be studied only on the level of the arrondissement, which means studying individual deputies.

Overlapping the four basic political groupings were the phenomena of Freemasonry, the conflict of generations, and cliques, all of which created strong allegiances and significantly affected legislative behavior.

We can only speculate about the real influence of Freemasonry. The Masons were, of course, a secret society, and most of the literature devoted to them is the hostile product of the lunatic fringe. In the early years of the century, Masonry dominated the Radical party and gave it its strength.[63] This influence was definitely weaker in the 1930's than in the great days, but it remained profound in the Radical committees of many provincial towns.[64] The most prominent Radical Masons were Chautemps, Bertrand, and Jammy Schmidt. There were Masons in all four voting groups of deputies. The role Masonry played in parliament must remain conjectural—the normal twilight enveloping government crises is deepened by Masonic secrecy. Masonry may have helped Chautemps survive in December 1933. It certainly had something to do with the unrolling of the Stavisky scandal. It was involved in the formation of the Popular Front. Possibly its most important single function was to create a bond between the Radical and Socialist deputies. Given the natural animosity of these two parties, this was no small accomplishment.

The age of Radical deputies significantly affected their political behavior. The average age of the Radical deputy in 1933 was 51, which was also about the average of the Chamber as a whole.[65] The great majority of the Radical deputies studied—175 out of 191—reached maturity before the First World War. Rudolf Heberle writes about the general effect of a party's age distribution:

A generation enters active political life as the *ruling* generation only when it has already *passed through* the formative period of life. The politically dominating generation is composed of adults roughly between forty and sixty-five years of age. Consequently, the actual political situations and issues which confront the ruling generation are not the same as those from which it received its decisive experiences. But the issues of the day are seen, so to speak, in the light of those decisive experiences.[66]

The Radicals of the 1930's were particularly ill-prepared by their political training for the problems they had to face, since social and economic questions had been so completely submerged by the purely political agitations of the turn of the century.

The age distribution of the deputies helps explain why they became Radicals. The older ones simply grew into it. They tended to be second-generation republicans. Many had fathers or relatives who had been important in the republican camp—the Sarrauts, Chautemps, Bastid, Lamoureux, Zay. I asked Pierre Le Brun, now a high official in the Confédération Générale du Travail (CGT) and therefore a most improbable Radical of the 1930's, why he had joined the party; he said that his father was a professor and a Freemason, and so there seemed to be no alternative.[67] Pierre Cot invoked his republican ancestors to explain his affiliation, and only secondarily the ideology of the party.[68]

The conflict of generations was never very severe in France. As can be seen from Table 5, there is little correlation between political atti-

TABLE 5

*Radical Deputies in the 1932 and 1936 Legislatures
by Decade of Birth and Parliamentary Voting Group*

Born	Left		Moderate Left		Moderate		Conservative		Total	
	No.	% of Group	No.	% of Group	No.	% of Group	No.	% of Group	No.	% of Group
Before 1865 ...	—	—	1	1.5	—	—	2	4	3	1.5
1865–1875	3	10	19	27.5	10	24	2	4	34	18
1875–1885	11	33	21	30	13	31	24	50	69	36
1885–1895	10	30	22	32	12	29	15	31	59	31
1895–1905	5	15	5	7	6	15	5	10	21	11
1905 & after ...	4	12	1	1.5	—	—	—	—	5	2.5
Total	33	100	69	99.5	41	99	48	99	191	100

tude and age. Conservatives are over-represented in the group that came of age during the Dreyfus Affair, and almost absent from the generation whose first political crisis was Boulangism. It is rather surprising to note the relative youth of the conservatives and the relative age of the moderate left. Otherwise, there is nothing very significant in the age distributions.

Only the Young Turk movement of the early 1930's showed any conscious conflict between old and young within the party.[69] The Young Turks were essentially a generational phenomenon rather than a specifically left-wing movement. Some of the Young Turks were very conservative—Martinaud-Déplat, Potut, Raoul Girard, Mistler, Tony Révillon, Creyssel. A Young Turk was either very conservative or very left-wing; there were no moderates.[70] There was a clear distinction between the Young Turks and the "Radicals of the left," which was pointed out by one of the latter, Raoul Aubaud.[71] Jammy Schmidt, François Albert, Bayet, Perrier, and Perney were left-wing by tradition, a different phenomenon entirely; Jammy Schmidt was as much a "vieille barbe" as Herriot or the rest.[72] Some politicians simply became fixed on the left in their childhood and remained that way through life, whereas others evolved to the left; but neither group shared the desire for modernization of the Young Turks. In the department of the Isère, which was dominated by Léon Perrier, who was on the extreme left, the younger generation that wished to supplant him became extremely conservative for personal rather than doctrinal reasons.[73] In the end, however, the conflict between old and young came to very little. One Young Turk, Jean Mistler, explained why:

In the literary and artistic worlds, the vigorous war cry "Make room for the young!" has succeeded, if not in eliminating the prewar establishment, at least in clearing the way for the young. In politics, this slogan has been proclaimed only feebly and has not caught on. Political personnel are replaced slowly; the subtlest rules of the game have to be learned before you can play a match. Men in their seventies are kept young by their rivalries and their determination to bury their contemporaries; and the political skill and staying power of such men makes newcomers look like school children.[74]

The younger men were not only outmaneuvered, but also decisively outnumbered by their elders. Even more important was the great skill with which the party quieted the impatience of the young by early giving jobs to the most outspoken. Martinaud-Déplat was secretary-general of the party in 1928 at the age of 29; Kayser entered the Bureau of the party in 1923 at the age of 23, and remained as a permanent fixture; Cot was Minister of Air at 37, Zay Minister of Education at 32, Mistler Undersecretary at 35; Mendès-France at 25 gave the principal economic report at the Congress of Toulouse, and at 31 was Undersecretary of the Treasury. The energies of the young left-wingers were so completely absorbed in government after 1936 that the left lacked parliamentary leadership to combat the conservative reaction within the party. One way or another, the Radical party proved itself fully able to guarantee the smooth and steady transition between generations that Sigmund Neumann sees as an essential factor in political stability.[75]

The final set of relationships modifying the ideological tendencies was the clique or the clan. Not all deputies belonged to cliques, and indeed it is difficult to say exactly what belonging to a clique meant. A man might be entirely the creature of a leader: Herriot's deputies from the Rhône, for example, owed their political existence entirely to him. On the other hand, such an important figure as Chautemps himself was often said to be in the Herriot sphere of influence. A man might have an independent local position and attach himself more or less closely to one of the leaders for parliamentary convenience or in hopes of a ministerial position.

There were four principal cliques in the party, clustering about Herriot, Daladier, Chautemps, and the Sarraut brothers. The lines between them were never very clear, and the Herriot, Chautemps, and Sarraut spheres of influence occasionally overlapped. Thus one deputy, André Cornu, started out as a protégé of the Sarrauts and later came into the sphere of Chautemps.

Each clique had certain characteristics. The Sarraut domain was principally geographical, consisting chiefly of the deputies of some twenty departments of the Southwest under the very potent control of *La Dépêche de Toulouse*;* it extended beyond *Dépêche* territory, however, to include such disparate characters as Pierre Dezarnaulds from Loiret and André Cornu from Brittany. Chautemps promoted a certain number of deputies assiduously, among them Cornu, Marchandeau, Laurens, and Bertrand, men in the mold of Chautemps himself—smooth, skillful politicians, without very strong principles, and generally moderate. Herriot's group had to put up with his oversensitivity; men with ability like Kayser and Bergery were first attracted to him, then broke away. His local deputies from the Rhône and his other steady followers tended to be flunkies. Curiously, cliques were not necessarily determined by ideological considerations. Michel Geistdoerfer, for instance, an intransigent left-wing Radical from Brittany, supported Herriot and opposed Daladier even when Herriot was entirely conservative and Daladier supposedly the left-wing leader. Dezarnaulds, another left-winger, was closest to the Sarrauts. The Daladier clique had certain peculiarities that will be dealt with later.

The central institution of parliamentary Radicalism was the Group. Membership in it was desirable and fairly expensive; it cost a thousand francs a year to belong. During government crises, the Group was expanded into what was called the Cadillac Committee, which consisted of the deputies, the senators, and the members of the Bureau of the party. It met off and on for the duration of the crisis.

The Group held frequent debates, in an effort to determine what a

---

* The political power of *La Dépêche* derived from its control of local political communication. The regional editions of *La Dépêche,* which could print, withhold, or distort important information concerning the local deputy, were well done and left little room for the independent political weeklies that flourished elsewhere in France. Radical politicians, therefore, had to be on reasonably good terms with the paper's manager, Maurice Sarraut, since otherwise their position could be made uncomfortable. The great skill and restraint with which Sarraut used the resources of his paper account for the quite exceptional role it played among provincial dailies.

better disciplined party would regard as the party line. Most Radicals thought that there should be more discipline. At the Executive Committee meeting following the elections of 1936, Armand Dupuis said, to the approval of his audience: "We have paid too dearly for the spectacle of a divided group of parliamentarians . . . who, when they meet, argue for hours, only to decide at the end of the meeting that everyone will be free to vote as he pleases. . . . Once a vote has been taken, once the decision has been made, I maintain that no one, party worker or parliamentarian, has the right to oppose the carrying out of this decision."[76]

The party consequently decided to invoke discipline in support of the Blum government. They had enforced discipline for the Chautemps government in December 1933, for the Daladier government in February 1934,* and for the vote on the second Sarraut government, to the considerable annoyance of the conservative Radicals. The ability to enforce discipline was regarded seriously enough for *Le Temps* to predict that the Group would vote for the Sarraut deflationary measures only if discipline were invoked.[77] From 1932 to February 6, 1934, the Radicals voted as a bloc on questions of confidence except on four occasions.[78]

When the issue was serious, however, discipline was unenforceable. In January 1936, for example, after the Laval government had come through repeated tests in parliament because of the unfailing support of some 30 to 40 Radicals,[79] anti-Lavalist Radicals made an effort to defeat the government by enforcing discipline. They had tried to get the Bureau of the Executive Committee to impose unity on the deputies, but the Bureau felt that the Group should manage its own discipline.[80] A crucial meeting of the Group was held on January 16; the majority was strongly, evenly passionately, opposed to Laval, and voted a motion condemning his policy by 61 to 28. Immediately afterward it was demanded that discipline be invoked for this condemnation; the motion was defeated 41 to 40, thanks to deputies reluctant to enforce their views on their colleagues. Similarly, Daladier was unable to enforce sanctions against those who opposed him in 1938.

The habit of undisciplined voting, therefore, limited the importance of the Group as a decision-making body. Its importance lay elsewhere.

* At this time, Malvy, Colomb, and Grisoni asked to be excused because of their friendship for Chiappe; this was granted to Malvy, but refused to the two others; they voted in favor of Daladier, but immediately thereafter Grisoni resigned from the party.

In the first place, the Group distributed the Radicals' allotment of committee seats among its members. In 1937 and 1938 the Popular Front majority of the Group obstinately kept Malvy and Lamoureux out of the powerful Finance Committee; conversely, after the fall of the second Blum government, the left-wing deputies were kept out. Second, a deputy had much greater authority in debate if he spoke in the name of the Radical Group than if he spoke simply in his own name. In the Popular Front Chamber Lamoureux was consistently refused the right to speak in the name of the Group; the majority proposed that he speak in his own name, which he refused to do, since in the past he had always spoken for the party. He was effectively silenced for over a year in this way. Third, the Radical nominees for the presidency, vice-presidencies, and other offices of the Chamber were chosen by the Group. Finally, the Group constantly sent delegations to petition ministers, with considerable success until the time of Daladier's third government.

The Group—actually, the Cadillac Committee—was theoretically supposed to have sovereign authority in government crises, but was in fact ineffectual on such occasions. Usually the Committee was first told not to compromise the designated premier's chances, and then presented with a fait accompli. After the fall of the Laval government, Henri Guernut made the following protest:

What are we doing here? When we were first called to the Cadillac Committee, the crisis had scarcely begun. . . . The head of State has not yet given anyone the task of forming a cabinet, and we are now therefore asked to adjourn out of deference for the President of the Republic, whose choice we must not dictate. Then, when a candidate has been chosen, we shall again be asked to do nothing, because a decision on our part might inconvenience him, or interfere with his plans. Finally, after the ministry has been formed, it will be considered useless for us to comment on it. And so we go on doing nothing. If it is going to be this way again, I'd rather go work in the library.[81]

Only during Bonnet's attempt to form a government in January 1938 did the Cadillac Committee exert decisive influence during a government crisis.

The presidency of the Group was a prize and an object of competition. The president spoke for the party in major debates, and during the party's eclipse in 1936 and 1937 was almost the only Radical who spoke at all. In June 1932, François Albert defeated Bonnet for the position; in 1934, Delbos won over Daladier, although this was not an open struggle;[82] in June 1936, Campinchi defeated Bonnet in the most dramatic contest;[83] in June 1937, Paul Elbel edged out Chichery. All these contests were to some extent struggles between the left and right wings of the party. The presidents during the early period were imposing figures—François Albert, Herriot, Chautemps, Delbos, Daladier. Later the quality of the men declined along with the importance of the office; at the end the president, Chichery, was little more than Daladier's "parliamentary attaché" for manipulating legislative behavior.[84]

Attendance at Group meetings was not large. The highest figure I have found is 130 of the 160 deputies,[85] and that was exceptional. At the crucial debate of January 16, 1936, there were only 89 present, and usually no more than 30 or 40 attended. The debates were dominated by a relatively small number of deputies. The only remaining records of Group meetings are the newspaper accounts, which usually mention the names of the main speakers. At 84 important meetings of the Group, the Cadillac Committee, and the Delegation of the Left during the 1932–36 legislature, only 32 deputies were reported as speaking more than four times; 62 spoke from one to four times, and 77 not at all. This distribution was not simply a matter of leaders speaking and followers listening. There is no exact correlation between a deputy's importance in the party and his activity in the Group. Of the 32 deputies who spoke most, only 18 were ministers during the period and three others were ministrables. Of the 139 less talkative deputies, no fewer than 33 were former ministers, and six more were ministrables. Of the 77 who did not speak at all, nine were ministers. The most talkative of all was Henri Guernut (27 times), who was not in the first rank. Daladier was reported as speaking only 12 times, and Chautemps a scarcely respectable three. Reassuringly, however, the lowest-ranking deputies tended to be silent; and on the whole the highest-ranking were heard from most.[86] Some deputies assumed a special role as spokesmen for different groups within the party—Lamoureux and Marchandeau on the right; Zay, Archimbaud, and Mendès-France on the left.

The meetings of the Group were frequent and long—three hours was not uncommon—and they provided the only formal association for Radical deputies. At these meetings, all subjects of importance to the party were discussed frankly and exhaustively. Although the decisions taken by the Group were not binding, they were important in the formation of opinion.

Clearly there were other roads to success within the party besides the Group. Indeed, many of the most effective Radicals had only limited relations with any part of the formal party structure. Caillaux came to an occasional Congress, but in general held himself aloof; his power stemmed from his position in the Finance Committee of the Senate and from entirely personal factors. Albert Sarraut had nothing to do with the Bureau, the Group, the Senate, the Congress, or the Executive Committee; his force was based on his brother's prestige, and on ownership of *La Dépêche de Toulouse*. Chautemps was somewhat closer to the party, but preferred to operate informally in the lobbies of the Chamber and by an intricate network of personal relations. Queuille did very little within the party; his power stemmed from his presidency of the Société Nationale d'Encouragement à l'Agriculture.

Not all held aloof, however. Lamoureux and Marchandeau and, to a lesser extent, Bonnet on the right, Zay and Archimbaud on the left, worked through the Group and the party organization and made their name there. Significantly, only Daladier and Herriot had close ties both among the parliamentarians and in the formal party structure. Only these two pre-eminent leaders could consistently succeed in uniting its two antagonistic elements—the party workers and the parliamentarians.

One more question must be asked, though it cannot really be answered. Who financed the Radical party?[87] No figures were published, but the legitimate income of the Radical party can be fairly easily computed. Assuming that all members paid their dues, the party's resources in 1936 can be estimated as follows:*

* According to the party statutes passed in 1936 (Parti Républicain Radical et Radical-Socialiste, *Statuts et règlements,* sec. 14, pp. 15–18), party cards were sold for four francs; each deputy and senator paid a fee of 1,000 francs, each member of the Executive Committee 50 francs, each newspaper that was a party member 25 francs, each base committee ten francs. My estimate is based on a membership of about 100,000, roughly 200 deputies and senators, 1,600 non-parliamentary members of the Executive Committee, 400 newspapers, and 500 committees. Jammy Schmidt (*Les Grandes Thèses radicales,* p. 250) quotes Daladier at the Congress of Angers as claiming 400 weeklies.

Party membership cards............400,000 francs
Deputies and senators..............200,000
Executive Committee 80,000
Newspapers 10,000
Committees..................... 5,000
    Total ....695,000 francs

In 1928, an individual election was calculated to cost 50,000 francs; perhaps the cost was less during the 1930's.[88] If the total funds of the party had been devoted to electoral ends, the expenses for barely 14 deputies would have been covered.[89] In fact, dues were probably insufficient to pay the rent for the party's spacious quarters on the Place de Valois.*

The Radical method of financing had direct consequences on the party structure and on the position of the deputy. Since the party provided the deputy little money, it had little control over him. Even within the feeble party structure that existed, the power relations were distorted by party financing. First, finances enhanced the deputies' preponderant position. Before 1936, when the Radical parliamentarians numbered over 250 and party cards cost only two francs, parliamentary dues were the party's major legitimate source of income. The loss of a deputy financially equaled the loss of 500 party members. Second, finances interfered with what little party democracy existed. In 1935, when it was decided to make a minor reform of the Executive Committee in favor of greater democracy, the loss of income from the displaced ex officio members was serious enough for the party to ask that the measure be rescinded.[90] Finally, the minimal price of party cards permitted the cheap purchase of influence and votes within the party. The Radical budget need only be compared with the Socialist budget to understand the totally different financial commitment of the Socialist party worker and the relatively lesser role of the Socialist deputy. According to official figures, the Socialists in 1938 received 2,949,798.60 francs from party cards and only 477,320 francs from the parliamentarians.[91]

---

* In the early 1930's, the party moved its headquarters from the Rue de Valois to the Place de Valois. However, since French practice is to name institutions after their address, and the Radicals had been referred to as "le parti de la rue de Valois," it was apparently too inconvenient to acknowledge the change of address in the appellation. Thirty years after the move, the party is still referred to as "la rue de Valois."

The more serious aspect of Radical finances was, of course, the extent to which the party's financial weakness invited corruption. Denouncing the reluctance of the parliamentarians to follow Radical policy, the president of the Federation of Paris observed: "In the shadow of local political figures there are always a number of mysterious interests that run the city and see to it that a man cannot always do what he would like to see done."[92] Elections were expensive. One contemporary commentator wrote: "Judging by their occupations, the great majority of candidates were unquestionably unable to raise the necessary funds for the electoral campaign by themselves and therefore had to get financial support from their friends."[93] According to one study, the electoral campaigns themselves were cheap in relation to those in other countries, but there was the additional peculiarly French expense of having to buy second-ballot withdrawals.[94] "Politicians know that a candidate who withdraws expects to be reimbursed by an amount at least equal to what he has spent for the first ballot. I have been present at meetings where charges were made of gifts of money to secure *désistement*."[95] Such practices were probably more extensive on the right than between the Radicals and Socialists.

Where the money came from is far from clear. Overt connections with big business and industry were relatively rare in the party. Augustin Hamon's monumental muckraking work, *Les Maîtres de la France*, lists only a few Radicals, most of whom were included simply because of their friends or their châteaux.[96]

Party corruption is an awkward question about which little can be established. Jean Meynaud has written: "As for the importance of [business] support and the list of beneficiaries, only hypotheses based on the most dubious evidence can be put forward. This is another factor in political life whose effects and extent must be recognized as almost totally unknown. It is therefore impossible to attempt to make the slightest evaluation of the influence, not in winning—some would say 'buying'—seats but in affecting general political orientation."[97] Yet party finances can be ignored only at the risk of falsifying history. The only study of the subject based on reliable documentation was done on Sweden and showed that the Liberal party—which is the approximate equivalent of the Radicals—got only 6 per cent of its funds from dues and the rest from outside sources, mostly industry, in the election year of 1948.[98] This evidence, the obvious inadequacy of legitimate funds, and the party's postwar connections with business, suggest that, as the principal governing party in France, the Radicals probably received a substantial part of their income from interested parties.

Who these interested parties were is a still more difficult question. In a period when journalism throve on scandal and inside information, there is surprisingly little concern with political finance. The results of the investigation of the Union des Intérêts Economiques were almost suppressed; a certain light flickered through when it was discovered that Alexandre Stavisky had given a lot of money to the Comité Mascuraud, but this was soon forgotten. The outright purchase of a deputy for criminal purposes—as happened with Gaston Bonnaure and Joseph Garat in the Stavisky affair—was sensationally publicized, but not the more subtle and serious issue of how the average deputy paid his expenses. In 1924, the secretary-general of the Radical party testified before an investigating committee that the party had collected 136,879 francs for propaganda purposes, but this is a very small figure.[99] The party was reported to have received no less than 1,500,000 francs from Raymond Patenôtre alone.[100]

Two institutions existed for collecting money from industry and disbursing it to deputies: the Union des Intérêts Economiques of Senator Billiet and the Comité Républicain du Commerce et de l'Industrie, or Comité Mascuraud, which was closely tied to the Radical party —its president, Louis Proust, was expelled from the party for his role in the Stavisky affair. The UIE probably helped finance at least half the Radical deputies in 1919.[101] The fonctionnaires' union accused it of influencing Herriot in the elections of 1932, and indeed a meeting of 700 UIE members did give him a vote of confidence in November 1932.[102] But by the 1930's both the UIE and the Comité Mascuraud were declining in influence. François Goguel wrote in 1938 of "the continuous twenty-year decline" of the Comité Mascuraud,[103] and he claimed that the Radicals were not to his knowledge receiving money from any of the industrial syndicates.

All this is very indefinite. In contemporary political squibs, however, one source of funds crops up again and again—the insurance companies.* This money had important political implications, since

---

* Goguel wrote, "I am also aware that the party of the Rue de Valois has ties with bodies like the Comité des Assurances" ("Le Comportement," p. 658). Danos claims that the 1936 elections were paid for by the insurance companies ("Le Front populaire," p. 1815). See also Goguel, *La Politique des partis,* p. 519; and Bardonnet, *Evolution,* p. 261.

the nationalization of the insurance companies was part of the Radical program and a live political issue. It had come up on three occasions: in January 1933, nationalization would have been passed by an ad hoc coalition of Radicals and Socialists in the Finance Committee if the attitude of some Radical deputies had not suddenly shifted; it was envisaged for the program of the Popular Front; and, during the 1932 elections, it was one of the points Léon Blum presented to the Radicals as a possible joint program. In all these instances, particularly the last, the Socialists may have specified insurance simply to make the proposal unacceptable.[104] In any event, the refusal to consider nationalizing insurance fed the discord between Radicals and Socialists, and thus helped hamstring the 1932 legislature.

The few Radicals who were openly linked with business interests were strategically placed: Malvy was retained by the Compagnie Internationale des Wagon-Lits while president of the Finance Committee; Lamoureux was connected with Etablissements Pernod and the Compagnie Fermière de Vichy while rapporteur-général of the Finance Committee.[105] We do not know how these men used their business contacts to promote their private ventures, but we do know that in the Chamber they followed the ultra-conservative financial and economic policies that such ties encouraged. Where influence ends and conviction begins in such instances is hard to determine; but that acknowledged representatives of business should have power within a supposedly left-wing, anti-capitalist party was a falsification of party roles. A conservative party, or a liberal party of the Swedish or Belgian type, may legitimately be financed by business interests because there is no ideological conflict. The Socialist and Communist parties in France solved the problem by heavily taxing their supporters. The Radicals, however, were in the falsest of positions; they claimed to be a popular party but were incapable of financing themselves as such. Furthermore, their deputies rarely had the large private incomes that made the more right-wing candidates financially independent. The party was therefore dependent on the very interests that its rather demagogic anti-capitalism attacked. Consequently, electoral duplicity was inevitable.

V

At the top of the complex hierarchy of party workers and parliamentarians were the party leaders, condottieri with their retinues, engaged in obscure vendettas. Herriot, in a moment of lyricism, proclaimed that he, Daladier, and Chautemps were "a trinity, a Radical entity in three persons";[106] but the more common description of the relations of the first two persons was "the war of the two Edouards." When Herriot moved left, Daladier moved right. When Herriot became pro-Russian, Daladier became pro-German. When Herriot opposed full emergency powers, Daladier supported them. All the while, the two men engaged in a vicious form of infighting, which greatly distressed the ordinary party workers and which the two leaders publicly denied, with effusive protestations of eternal brotherly devotion. When Herriot was dangerously ill during the fall of 1933, Daladier rushed to his bedside on the eve of the Congress. "This step," wrote a harassed party worker, "should finally end the carefully cultivated legend of hostility, particularly if it were known how moving and touching Daladier's visit was."[107] When Herriot resigned as president of the party in December 1935, Daladier "threw himself on him," begging him to stay, although he was perfectly delighted by this opportunity to become president himself.[108]

Herriot was unquestionably the outstanding Radical of his generation. He defies sociological explanation. "M. Herriot not only represents a dominant influence in French politics today as the leader of the greatest party of the left, but is also the prime mover of all the spiritual and intellectual forces of this country."[109] A more sophisticated observer, the French ambassador Robert Coulondre, wrote:

I have never come across a man who knows so much, and I doubt if one exists. A remarkable phenomenon that defies the laws of physics—on one side of the scale the incredible weight of his intellectual equipment; on the other, balancing it, his unpretentiousness. Edouard Herriot is clever enough not to show off. He knows that his worth is great enough to make this unnecessary.

Coulondre adds, with a certain lowering of tone, "If you insist [on a qualification], there is this: I think President Herriot eats too much."[110]

After the death of Briand, Herriot was the foremost political orator in France. The impact of such a character on the simple party worker in the provinces was profound, and the normal reaction was unthinking adulation. During a controversy, the party workers "applaud Herriot almost without wanting to know which of the conflicting positions he has chosen. Trust in him is absolute."[111] The real purpose of a Radical Congress was to give Herriot an ovation; when he was sick in 1933, the whole Congress was downcast. He was the chosen object of the Radicals' latent authoritarian urge to submit to an overwhelming personality. Although this study is generally critical of Herriot, the unique position he held and the impact he had on others must be regarded as a great personal accomplishment. To temper his awesome erudition, Herriot never let it be forgotten that his roots were among the people. "Je suis peuple," he announced, and rode with the engineer on the Lyons train. His vast girth, his enormous gourmandise, his pipe, and his rumpled clothing endeared him to the man in the street.

Herriot's relations with his colleagues were less happy. He was on constantly bad terms with the two men who could rival him in the party, Daladier and Caillaux, and his proverbial sensitivity made him extremely difficult to deal with. His entourage was made up of ciphers. He invariably entered a meeting a few minutes late, preferably in the middle of a speech by Daladier, in order to receive the maximum applause. He would periodically resign as president in order to eliminate opposition.

Running into strong opposition from several deputies, Herriot left the conference room, announcing that he was going to resign as president of the Group and of the party. Several of his friends caught up with him just as he reached the corridor, and insisted that he return to the Group. The alarm that had seized the Group soon subsided, and Herriot again began exhorting his colleagues to support the cabinet.[112]

He generally recommended sensible policies—support of Ethiopia, support of Czechoslovakia, resistance to Hitler, resistance to Pétain— but he did so after so much hesitation and soul-searching that his advocacy had little effect.

Herriot's great rival was Edouard Daladier. He, too, was a professor, but did not have Herriot's dogmatism. Daladier was a curious figure, as abrupt as Herriot was urbane. He created an impression of vigor and determination; he spoke little, but when he did, it was in short, explosive phrases, which he punctuated by pounding his fist on the table. His habitual expression was a frown. He is portrayed as "solidly planted on his short body, his large head sunk between two broad shoulders, remaining generally silent like a sullen peasant, absorbed by some obscure and interminable meditation."[113] He possessed at this time, and strangely managed to maintain until the end of the Republic, the reputation of a strong man. The adjectives invariably used to describe him are: "abrupt," "brutal," "sulky," "rude," and "thickset." He was generally regarded as preferring action to talk. Although, or perhaps because, he was so different from Herriot, he was also immensely popular with the party workers; his brooding gaucheness, his ineradicable air of remaining a provincial baker's son, and his unpretentiousness made him seem like the party worker writ large. And although he was not a polished speaker, he was a very successful demagogue. After Herriot, he was the most successful manipulator of the mass of Radical party workers. When he was president of the party—in complete contrast to Herriot, who took no interest in party organization—Daladier was an efficient organizer and administrator.

Despite the popular image, Daladier was weak and indecisive. His manner was deceptive. "Experience has shown . . . that when he bangs on the table with his fist, it is a sign that he is preparing to give in."[114] The carefully constructed image was disastrously shattered by his sorry capitulation on February 7.[115] His indecision was a byword in the party; sometimes he would literally take months to make up his mind.[116]

For all his weakness, Daladier was probably the most likable of the Radical leaders. He had none of the pretension of Herriot, none of the slickness of Chautemps, none of the haughtiness of Caillaux. Cot calls him the most straightforward of all Third Republic leaders.[117] He was scrupulously honest. He was loyal to his friends and mistrustful of the flattery that Herriot demanded. Though he was on bad terms (in varying degrees) with all the Radical leaders, he had an enthusiastic and devoted clientele among the lesser deputies of the left; and the leaders of the left, even after they thought he had betrayed them in 1938, retained an affection for him that they felt for no other leader.

Daladier usually posed as a man of the left, but that was because Herriot was usually on the right. He was amazingly versatile, shifting without qualm in whatever doctrinal direction seemed advantageous —to the right in 1933, 1934, and 1938, and to the left in 1935.

Daladier was at the focal point of the critical events of the period between the wars. His first government marked the failure of the legislature; his second government was defeated by the riots of February Sixth; his personal disgrace in 1934 came at the same time as the eclipse of the party. It was Daladier who brought the Radicals into the Popular Front, and later took them out; it was Daladier who went to Munich, and later as Minister of War, faced the military defeat of France.

Three other leaders shared high responsibility with Herriot and Daladier, but their personalities were so different that the same conflicts did not arise. They were Chautemps, Caillaux, and Maurice Sarraut.

Chautemps was an extraordinarily unassuming, soft-spoken, and even-tempered man. He was on friendly terms with everyone—Bonnet, the Sarrauts, Herriot (a great achievement), Caillaux, Lamoureux, Paul-Boncour (who came from the same department), Léon Blum, and Marshal Pétain. It was he who used to run out of meetings to persuade Herriot not to resign. Like Caillaux and Sarraut, he was born into a well-known political family. A lawyer by training, he was an excellent speaker in the Chamber, but nervous at Radical Congresses. His political skill made him indispensable. According to de Monzie, no one could equal his ability to arrange compromises; this gift, combined with his extreme kindness, enabled him "to exercise a decisive influence over his colleagues."[118] He developed a habit of smoothing over differences of principle, a practice that he carried over into the tragic days of June 1940, when it suddenly seemed inappropriate. Since then he has lived in retirement, covered with obloquy.

Joseph Caillaux was entirely different. He was out of place in the Radical party. Aristocratic, autocratic, brilliant, and bizarre, he frightened the party workers and lacked the compensating hominess that made Herriot attractive to them. Emile Buré remarked on his "classicism" in contrast with the "disorganized romanticism" of Herriot.[119] "You never knew with this man," wrote Jean Zay, "if he were cultivating his legend, contriving to appear fantastic, disconcerting, and formidable by a sort of studied aristocratic bad temper, or spontaneously giving in to a volcanic temperament. Within two hours, on the same issue, he would be accommodating and impossible, flexible about principle, unbending on detail."[120] When Zay, as Minister of Education, proposed a minor cut in the budget, Caillaux jumped up: " 'The Committee is against it!' [Caillaux] sat down. Then I [Zay] got up and, trusting neophyte, dared to express my surprise at not finding support in the Finance Committee for a budget cut. Joseph Caillaux jumped up again and said in his most acid voice: 'A minister who suggests a cut in the budget is suspect!' And the Senate, without further debate, rejected my suggestion by voice vote."[121]

Caillaux's role in the party was limited to controlling the Gauche Démocratique in the Senate; but his virtual dictatorship of the Senate Finance Committee probably made him the most consistently influential politician of the 1930's.

Almost as bizarre as Caillaux was Maurice Sarraut. No democratic politician in the Third Republic came closer to being an *éminence grise*. He was timid and self-effacing, but hot-tempered. Though never Premier, he was senator for a while until he resigned to devote himself fully to his job as editor of *La Dépêche de Toulouse*. From the paper's offices he controlled the deputies of some twenty departments; he worked hard, answering all letters in his own hand. He had a part in the making and unmaking of most cabinets—the first Daladier government and the Doumergue government in particular. He was briefly president of the Radical party in 1926, and undertook a great reorganization, which apparently soured him on formal party activities.[122]

Below these five came the lesser men, ranging from Georges Bonnet and Albert Sarraut at the top to the obscurest deputy at the bottom. Bonnet was brilliant, consumed by ambition, and never entirely trusted by anybody; his Munich foreign policy, however, aroused lasting devotion among the defeatists. Albert Sarraut was a real political war-horse, blunt and unpretentious, the object of delicious anecdotes, the right man for the caretaker government of 1936, but not for the crisis provoked by the German occupation of the Rhineland. Léon Meyer was so inveterately anti-ministerial that he once helped overthrow a government in which he was a minister. There was Pierre Cot, American in style, very modern and jaunty, extremely competent, forceful, and partisan. There were Bertrand Nogaro and Paul Bastid, who felt that a permanent plot frustrated their ministerial ambitions. There were Alfred Margaine, "très original," who voted against every government, and André Liautey, who considered himself a pure Proudhonian. Two hundred and fifty personalities, old men and young, each the focus of conflicting claims of friendship and animosity, of party ideology and small-town Masonic voodooism. The very origin of political action is often traceable to bruised egos and forgotten favors; this is the heart of the Radical Republic.

As a group they were curiously admirable. Most were honest, many very earnest; some even had that frighteningly complete culture and competence of the polished Frenchman. They easily surpass their successors in the Fourth and Fifth Republics as human beings and as leaders. They were part of that republican aristocracy which, in spite of its surface futility, gave a tough and durable tone to the Republic. No political party could reasonably have had better personnel, and that makes the tragedy of their failure the more profound.

VI

In the haphazard organization of the Radical party, the one institution that assured the continuity of political life was the press. It provided the party worker with his one steady contact with the party. Although every Radical politician did not come to the party as a professional journalist, it was the exception who did not become one. This was the road to power. According to one observer, in the 1936 elections for the French Chamber, "35 per cent of the Radical-Socialist deputies moved directly from the editorial rooms to the Palais Bourbon, while around 85 per cent were continually in contact with the press, as editors or as regular or occasional contributors."[123] Professional journalists such as the Sarraut brothers, Delbos, and François Albert attained the highest political positions.[124] Daladier helped to found *La République*; Herriot was a regular contributor to *L'Ere nouvelle*, *Le Progrès de Lyon*, and other papers. Bayet was as much a journalist as a professor, such was the fluidity between professions.

The Radical press in Paris consisted of five daily papers: *La République*, *L'Ere nouvelle*, *L'Oeuvre*, *Le Quotidien*, and *La Volonté*. None of these was officially affiliated with the Radical party, or as representative of the party as *Le Populaire* was of the Socialists. By the early 1930's, *Le Quotidien* and *La Volonté* were declining in importance, having moved to the right. *L'Oeuvre* inclined to the left, *L'Ere nouvelle* to the right. Before 1934 *La République* was the most varied; its owner, Emile Roche, and its editor, Pierre Dominique, were conservative, but young and open to new ideas; the Young Turks did most of their publishing in this paper. After 1934, Roche moved further to the right, and so did the paper.

Besides the Paris dailies, there were a number of provincial Radical dailies, the principal one being *La Dépêche de Toulouse*, which served as the bastion of the Sarraut brothers within the party. Other impor-

tant Radical or pro-Radical provincial dailies were *Le Petit Provençal,
La France de Bordeaux,* and *Le Progrès de Lyon.* Among less important dailies were *Le Petit Comtois, Le Petit Haut-Marnais, L'Eclaireur
de l'Est, Le Petit Troyen, La Dépêche dauphinoise,* and *La Dépêche
de Rouen.* The Radical press had an overall circulation of 2,000,000,
representing 17 per cent of the French press, according to a 1939 estimate.[125] Toward the end of the decade, many ostensibly Radical papers
were owned by non-Radicals like Patenôtre or even by anti-Radicals
like Laval.

A large part in the life of the Radical deputy was played by the
"confidential press" and the financial press. The confidential press
consisted of papers like *La Concorde* or *Le Courrier du Parlement,*
dailies with extremely limited circulation, financed heaven knows
how, which printed articles by lower-ranking deputies. Geistdoerfer,
for instance, frequently contributed to *La Concorde.* The financial
press, so far as the Radicals were concerned, consisted principally of
Le Capital, inspired by Caillaux and Régnier, and *L'Agence économique et financière.* According to Hamon, *Le Capital* paid as much as
several thousand francs for a single article, a figure that is probably
exaggerated but demonstrates the function of this press.[126] One deputy told me that *Le Journal de commerce* had asked him for articles,
which he contributed occasionally and was well paid for. Then one
day the editor asked him "to be understanding" about a forthcoming
bill—significantly for compulsory insurance—for which the deputy
was *rapporteur.* When he refused, the demand for articles ceased.[127]

Most Paris papers were, of course, notoriously corrupt, and the
Radical papers were no exception. Bernard Sérampuy (François Goguel), writing in 1939 about the Radical papers, said that every one of
them was sold out to someone.[128] Since four of the five Radical papers
were very conservative, the opinion they expressed was scarcely representative. This unrepresentative character of the Radical press should
be stressed, because it is common practice to cite *La République,* for
example, as "Radical opinion."[129]

The Paris press is generally an unsatisfactory means of discovering
the origins of Radical action. The reverse is true of the weekly provincial press; it is manifestly clear what the local weekly represents
when the name of the local deputy is on the masthead as political director. The study of the local press is not a vague study of "Radical
opinion," but a study of the opinion of specific Radical deputies, who

were, in fact, the arbiters of governments. In many instances, the local paper was the keystone of the local organization. The federation, if it existed, was a seasonal affair, coming to life only for elections; the paper provided continuity. The deputy used it for communicating with his electors. Since the deputy and the senator were, for all practical purposes, the Radical party, when they expressed themselves in the paper, it was not simply a snippet of public opinion, but the direct expression of the party itself.

The actual number of Radical weeklies is uncertain.* The party claimed 400 in unconvincing round figures.[130] For major events, a number of accounts can usually be found by deputies of different orientations. When these opinions are correlated with parliamentary votes on political issues, we have a solid quantitative basis for analysis. When several deputies of one voting group give similar explanations of votes, they are probably representing the position of that group fairly accurately. Furthermore, argument a fortiori is possible when the bias of the deputy is known. When, for example, Jean Zay, on the extreme left wing of the party, rejected the Socialist plan to overthrow the Laval government, it is likely that the less radical members of the party shared this point of view, unless demonstrable personal factors intervened. If, on the other hand, it had been Lamoureux who opposed the Socialist scheme, we could not assume that this reflected the position of any but his conservative friends.

The importance of the local paper varied considerably, from the imperious *Dépêche de Toulouse* with its 19 regional editions and circulation of 300,000 to the paper that produced two or three issues before each election and then lapsed into silence. Occasionally, the legally required statement indicating the number of copies printed can be found in a library's collection of the local paper. This figure—usually 3,000 or 4,000—is small when compared with the circulation of the dailies, but significant when compared with the number of voters in the district.[131]

By means of this local press, the Parisian Radical papers acquired their political importance. *La République* maintained a free press service that distributed its articles to 256 weeklies, of which an average of

* The files of the Bibliothèque Nationale are deficient, as are the local archives. A list of the papers that have been identified is given in the Bibliography. Over 60 parliamentarians expressed their ideas fairly frequently in local papers. Another 40 had their speeches printed and wrote an occasional article for their local papers.

100 printed them. If we assume an average circulation of 3,000–4,000 copies, the audience for a political article was comparable in size to that of all but the largest Paris dailies. An important article, therefore, did not reach only the 15,000–25,000 subscribers of *La République,* but perhaps twenty times that number.[132] It seems likely that *L'Ere nouvelle* and *L'Oeuvre* maintained similar services, if we can judge by the frequent appearance of their articles in local papers.

Where the local deputy did not provide the editorial, the Paris press services did. The political complexion of a paper can generally be determined by looking at its list of contributors. The writers who appeared most frequently were, on the left, Bayet and Kayser; on the right, Milhaud, Roche, and Pierre Dominique.[133] These opinion-molders were either conservative or left-wing; the center, which dominated parliament, produced little widely read political propaganda.[134] Between 1932 and 1934, however, ideologies had not yet jelled, and Bayet and Milhaud, Roche and Kayser frequently appeared in the same paper. After 1934 there was much less tolerance.[135] The earlier attitude was the traditional one, and illustrates the Radicals' close spiritual unity. Although a person like Albert Bayet was as far removed politically from someone like Albert Milhaud as a Socialist is from a conservative, before 1934 they coexisted easily.

The provincial paper was at once the focal point of local Radicalism and its symbol. As a symbol, the most important aspect was its title, and great care went into choosing this. When a new Radical paper was established in Verdun, it was first called *L'Avenir de la Meuse,* later *Meuse-républicaine,* and finally *La Tribune républicaine.* In Lot-et-Garonne, the paper was called *Le Radical de Lot-et-Garonne* during the elections of 1932, but immediately afterward its title was changed to *Le Démocrate de Lot-et-Garonne,* to demonstrate to those non-Radicals who had supported the successful candidate, Gaston Martin, that they would be welcomed as readers. The choice of titles reveals a partially conscious order of ideological priorities; a title could not reasonably contain more than two political symbols (*La République démocratique,* for example), and so it was rigorously selective.

The particular Radical pattern of titles becomes evident only when compared with the whole provincial political press.[136] Such an apparently conservative title as "patriote" was used by two Radical papers; such an apparently left-wing title as "travail" was used by three right-wing papers. Some symbols were acceptable to all. "Réveil," which has only vague political connotations, was adopted by six Radical papers, nine right-wing papers, four republican papers, and six Socialist papers. On the other hand, some symbols were too clearly associated with one party to be acceptable to others—"socialiste," "radical," "ouvrier." As a rule, the Radicals' titles were much more strongly political than the moderates', though less so than the Socialists'.[137] They neglected, as did the whole press, the hallowed symbols of the Revolution. "Liberté," "libre," and "libéral" had become exclusively right-wing, though even there little used. "Gauche" was almost as outmoded as "droite," with only one Radical paper adopting it. Among non-political titles, Radicals favored "dépêche," whereas the conservatives preferred "journal," "écho," and "gazette."

Radical papers showed a curious reluctance to proclaim their Radicalism; I came across only five that used the word "radical" in the title (whether as a noun or an adjective)—about 3 per cent of the total. This can be compared with 29 Socialist uses of the word "socialiste," or nearly 50 per cent of the total; among the parties of the right, there was no party identification. Explicit party attachment declines as one moves from left to right. It has been claimed that the Radicals were committed to the general concept of "petit," and this is reflected to a limited extent in the press—*Le Petit Savoyard,* for example. Of 23 political papers with the word in the title, eight were Radical, eight moderate, and seven republican.[138] The Radicals tended to reject titles indicating action, such as "action," "éveil," "cri," "rappel," "volonté"; only "progrès" and "réveil" had any currency. They preferred the pure, austere, abstract, and static. The two great symbols for them were "républicain" (31 times as noun and adjective), "république" (11 times), "démocrate" and "démocratique" (11 times), "tribune" (eight times). "Démocrate" was, indeed, used only by Radicals.[139] This narrowness of what might be called essential interest pervades not only newspaper titles, but the whole ideology of the party, as the next chapter will show.

CHAPTER 2

The Nature of Radicalism

What was Radical doctrine? For an answer to this question, one usually turns to the writings of Alain,[1] whose hostility toward state authority is taken to represent Radical attitudes in general.[2] The Radicals themselves, however, seem to have paid little attention to Alain's writings. According to Jacques Kayser, who was active in the party from 1923 to 1939, "Never did I hear references to Alain . . . even though his *Eléments d'une doctrine radicale* appeared in 1925."[3] Although Alain wrote a weekly newspaper column, it was carried in only one of the hundred local papers I examined; although he published prolifically, I never saw his books in the homes of the party workers and deputies I visited. Even the systematic mistrust toward the state and toward industrial organization that he emphasizes so frequently was little in evidence in parliament. Those deputies who were most hostile to the "trusts" and the "money powers" were generally the most in favor of strong state intervention. Admittedly, there was a certain suspicion of the authorities among provincial voters,[4] but the exercise of power and responsibility had long since weakened, if not removed, such feelings among Radical parliamentarians.

The books Radicals did read were, above all, Herriot's *Pourquoi je suis radical-socialiste,* and Jammy Schmidt's *Idées et images radicales* and *Les Grandes Thèses radicales,* and, to a lesser extent, Bayet's *Le Radicalisme* and Archimbaud's *L'Heure des jacobins.* These works were to be found on every bookshelf, and presumably struck a responsive chord. Yet the search for any system of Radical thought in this literature is singularly fruitless. The dominant impression it imparts is not Alain's anarchic defiance, but a rather sentimental and unsystematic eighteenth-century belief in progress. The symbolism is all derived from the Revolution. The writers naïvely identify with all the good people of the past and reject the bad.[5] Herriot's *Pourquoi je suis radical-socialiste* is not an exposition of doctrine, but an autobiography practically devoid of doctrinal content. He did not choose to become a Radical, but grew into one; Radicalism was the natural spiritual home for a young academic of the last years of the nineteenth century.

Whatever "theory" was contained in these works is unimportant. Ultimately, the ideas of individual politicians, however naïve and confused, form the crucial link between theory and action. Since this is a study of parliamentary history, the half-formed, incoherent attitudes and clichés of the average deputy are the only expressions of ideology that need concern us. Indeed, it has been questioned whether this was really an ideology or merely the verbal expression of a pattern of behavior, a "cultural pattern."* It is possible, in any event, to speak of a dominant style of thought that transcended conflicting groups within the party; they all shared the same symbols, although they may have applied them differently. The Radical style had both method and content.

The method was shown in the touching belief expressed by Albert Chichery that "from the ideological point of view, Radical doctrine best embodies the Cartesian spirit of our country. . . . In the words of President Herriot, Radicalism *is the political application of rationalism,* that particularly French quality."[6] A conservative wrote, "Proceeding from critical and constructive rationalism, [Radicalism] manifests itself in the quest for progress in the political and social spheres, in letters, in the arts, and in the sciences. It has a part in all intellectual currents."[7] "What is Radicalism?" asked Albert Bayet, an extreme left-winger. "Above all, a method. What is this method? Science applied to politics."[8] Such statements were common in Radical literature.

This Cartesian rationalism was to be applied to purely liberal goals.

---

* Alroy, Chap. 2, pp. 14, 21. This chapter was written before I had a chance to read Alroy's excellent thesis. His findings have led me to alter the terminology in this paragraph while retaining the body of what I had written. Alroy shows that the Radical party was the crystallization of a larger Radicalism in the country, the most important political expression of a "cultural pattern"; he discusses Radicalism as a functional expression of French social structure. My concern is with the Radical party not as a cultural pattern, but as the dominant political party in parliament. Thus I do not consider generalized Radical sentiment in the country except as it directly affected the behavior of Radical deputies. The only pattern of thought that directly concerns this study is that of the deputies themselves.

As Maurice Sarraut, a moderate, put it: "Men are born—and remain—
free and equal in rights. This formula is the starting point for all the
social doctrine of the Radical party."[9] Liberation of the individual
was to come through the realization of the "Republic" and of "Democracy," concepts that were more specific and absolute than is common in Anglo-Saxon thought. "Faithful to the republican ideals that
we regard as sacred, [we] have, by means of liberty, secularism, and
social progress, sought to achieve Democracy, the end toward which
the Republic is directed."[10] Democracy was not simply a form of government, but an ideal society, a "continuous creation," whose end was
the good life. For this reason the secular school was of central importance, since its purpose was not merely to guard republicans from the
error of clericalism, but, more ambitiously, to mold the citizen.[11]

For Radicals, both "Republic" and "Democracy" had specific, narrow meanings. A republican had to be anti-clerical; a democrat had
to believe in the salvation of the individual by a "continuously created" state. This has to be remembered in order to understand the
extremely specialized way in which Radicals use the word "republican"; when three left-wing deputies wrote of "a broad democratic
majority consisting of all the members of the great republican family,"
what they meant was an alliance between Socialists and Radicals.[12]
When Léon Blum spoke to the Radicals in the Chamber above the
interruptions of the center and right-wing deputies, he said to his in-
terrupters, "I am speaking to republicans, and to them alone."[13] Radicals played on this general sense of "republican" to exploit the diffused
republican sentiment in the country for their own ends.[14]

The chosen instrument of the new democracy was the Radical party
itself. Here are two typical statements. "From the republican point of
view, [I] am absolutely convinced that [the party] embodies the very
essence of democracy."[15] "Radicalism is something broader and deeper
than a simply organized party with a doctrine, a program, and members; Radicalism truly embodies the soul of French democracy."[16] This
was a nice theoretical structure: the party applied rationalism to politics to create a new democracy, which in turn was created in the image
of the Radical party.

The concept of the "Republic," with all the peculiarly French connotations that had accrued during the nineteenth century, retained its
hold more or less intact on the average Radical at the beginning of
the 1930's. The Republic, so narrowly conceived, was always in danger

of being overthrown by "reaction," and the concept of "republican defense" was one of the few vital sources of political action. This concept was never clearly defined. Like "left" and "right," it was liable to infinite variation. Yet, for all its vagueness, it was very real. Radical behavior throughout the 1930's is inexplicable if this deeply held principle is forgotten. The Republic could be realized only by allying with republicans, and this alliance—first the Union des Gauches, then the Popular Front—was the most constant aspiration of the average Radical until the time of Munich. Yet, throughout the eight-year period from 1932 to 1940, other forces and new allegiances gradually eroded the Radicals' devotion to the Republic—the capitulation of February Sixth and the hysteria of Munich ultimately led to complicity in the murder of the Republic itself in July 1940.

Two fundamental conditions for the Republic were private property and public order. Private property, which meant peasant proprietorship and small business, was sacrosanct. Radicals do not believe in the abolition of private property, wrote Maurice Sarraut, for it is the necessary condition of human dignity.[17] Herriot became a Radical rather than a Socialist for precisely this reason.[18]

The importance of "order" in Radical petty-bourgeois sentiment cannot be overestimated. "Order is both the first requirement and first responsibility of democracy."[19] "As a party of social and parliamentary action," runs the program of 1907, "[we] repudiate any violent demonstration that is not justified by a serious attack on the republican constitution and the national will."[20] According to Bertrand de Jouvenel, the key to the whole inter-war period was "hatred of the use of force."[21] The fear of disorder was constant: it drove the Radicals into the Doumergue government, then into the Popular Front, and then out of it.

The practical means by which the Republic was to be realized are set forth in a bewildering array of detailed programs. The Radicals indulged in grandiose social fantasies. The party officially favored the nationalization of private monopolies—the railways, electricity, insurance, and so on.[22] It supported what was called the "directed economy." One favorite scheme was profit sharing, which was to abolish at a single stroke that antithetical social manifestation, the class. The social class and any theory built upon it were a defiance of revolutionary universalism, specifically *fraternité*. The party disliked the class war. A typical statement is Daladier's "the party does not rest . . . on class interest, but attempts, on the contrary, to reconcile the classes in a general harmony under the rubric of justice and brotherhood."[23] Yet classes existed; therefore, they had to be eliminated, and the way to do this was for everyone to share in profits and become a stockholder. "The hour must come—let us do everything to hasten it—when the legislature will institute compulsory profit sharing and cooperative industrial management, a peaceful revolution that will *assure the fusion of classes* and social justice."[24]

There was, indeed, a certain ambivalence in the Radicals' attitude toward class, since on a practical level they claimed to represent the petty bourgeoisie. After the Popular Front, in an effort to gain the same kind of strength that the Socialists and Communists derived from the CGT, they formed a Confédération Générale des Classes Moyennes—a dismal failure. Profit sharing and working-class stockholding at once satisfied the requirements of solidarism, and defended a class structure that favored Radicalism against the inroads of a growing Marxist proletariat. Abolishing the working class by making all workers capitalists would create Radical voters.[25] Profit sharing therefore remained the great goal. According to the manifesto of a small left-wing group, the Radical party "favors abolishing the class of wage earners, since by this means the liberation of man will be achieved."[26]

Finally, most Radicals were in some degree hostile to industry. Whereas the rural conservatives were silently hostile, the left-wingers loved to indulge in tirades against the department stores, the chain stores, the "money powers," and the "trusts," particularly the grain importers and the fertilizer combines. This was often accompanied by a virulent anti-capitalism. One critic wrote: "I greatly fear those republicans who go preaching moderation to the masses with regard to the money powers. This moderation is weakness, even lack of faith." And he continued: "Every time that the liberty, happiness, or independence of our country is involved, we find capitalism in conflict with the national interest. Capitalism is a public danger!"[27] According to a perceptive contemporary German observer, "[The Radicals'] whole existence is based on a political outlook that vacillates between partly conservative, capitalist interests of a petty-bourgeois sort, and aversion to large-scale capital, between the narrowly circumscribed, rather philistine individualism of the average Frenchman, and a certain sentimental socialism, which, if not progressive, at least wants to appear so."[28]

In all this, Radicals were acting with the typical insecurity of petty bourgeois, whether Nazis, Poujadists, or, with modifications, American small businessmen. The Radicals differed from these groups in that they interpreted this program in the light of the French Revolution. Bayet proclaimed an "economic 1789" the great goal, and spent forty pages showing how the "general will" was to prevail over the "great vassals" (modern industry), in an all-inclusive application of revolutionary symbolism to modern economics that leaves one breathless, and whose clearest lesson is that eighteenth-century ideas adapt only with difficulty to twentieth-century problems.[29] In fact, the whole revolutionary nostalgia of the Radicals was beginning to look rather jaded. "Let's admit it," said Campinchi, "without being afraid of words or things: the ideas of 1789 no longer rouse the masses."[30]

The function of the Radicals' doctrinal extremism was undoubtedly psychological. For some, it was an outlet for their accumulated exasperation at the inroads of modern capitalism; for others, it reconciled an anachronistic progressive ideology with social conservatism. The less likely it became that the articles of the creed would ever be translated into action, the more tenaciously they were held to. Thus, profit sharing as a plan for "freeing the wage earner" had long been demonstrated to have no practical liberating effect in the few places in which it had been tried. There is no indication that any Radical ever seriously considered implementing it in any way.[31] Yet it continued to be advocated. At the end of the 1931 Congress, the following pathetic exchange took place:

PARTY WORKER: Don't you think it would be advisable to state somewhere in the text that we want the worker to hold shares in industry? (*Applause.*)

PRESIDENT: That can be found, I am sure, in preceding declarations; that has always been the doctrine of the Radical party, which does not consider the condition of the wage earner a definitive state. . . .

M. HERRIOT (*a presidential pronouncement*): I would like to add that the right of the worker to shares in industry is expressly defined in the report of our President Godard, which is printed in the pamphlet we were given.[32]

An omission in the creed was quickly spotted by the faithful.

Since the function of the program was psychological rather than practical, it was subject to no material limitations. On the contrary, the more provisions the better. The basis of the program was that adopted at Nancy in 1907;[33] this was supplemented by the so-called Daladier Program of the Congress of 1931.[34] In addition, the party accepted the complete program of the CGT, along with numerous minor accretions. The result was an inexhaustible source for anything at all. The program contained all the elements necessary for a drastic transformation of society. When Léon Blum proposed a working alliance with the Radicals in 1932, it was simply on the basis of proposals drawn from the Radicals' own program.[35] Chautemps claimed that "all the measures [of the Popular Front] were, we are proud to say, drawn from our own program."[36] On the other hand, one might choose to find nothing there at all. The very conservative president of the Federation of the Haute-Garonne, Béluel, maintained that nothing had been added since Gambetta's Belleville program of 1869.[37]

Contradictions did not cause the slightest concern. On the question of the "directed economy," three official pronouncements were made: "[The party has] always defended the principle of a directed economy at home"; "The directed economy . . . will lead only to the dictatorship of one class, the dictatorship of a gigantic bureaucracy"; and "It is possible to have a regime with an 'oriented economy.'"[38]

Despite the fertility of the party's program, it is difficult to find any clear exposition of its content.[39] To Radicals it was simply "The Program." "My program is the party's program," said one Radical candidate; "to discuss it in detail in the course of several lines is impossible."[40] When Herriot, during the elections of 1932, was asked what he stood for, he replied by inviting "all those who believe in the necessity of a reasonable and continuous evolution to rally to the Radical-Socialist program."[41]

There is no indication that any Radical during the 1930's ever envisaged putting a single reform into effect.* Such behavior was, of course, in keeping with Stanley Hoffmann's model of the stalemate society, in which the "state's function was an ideological one," and the traditional mode of politics had been to occupy power rather than to govern.[42] The Radicals had occupied power with great effectiveness, but now that the time had come to govern, their attempts to make

---

* With the exception of Jean Zay, as Minister of Education in 1936. Another possible exception is Daladier, who introduced a financial bill in October 1933. This bill, however, which included some measures of control over the arms industry and a monopoly of petroleum importing, was used chiefly as a bribe to get the Socialists to accept reductions in the fonctionnaires' salaries.

positive proposals were stupefyingly banal. After the crisis of 1934, the party decided to establish a practical economic program, which resulted in the so-called Roche Plan, presented at the Congress of May 1934; its author, Emile Roche, modestly considered that it "would put an end to the economic crisis."[43] The Plan consisted of reducing the labor force (by expelling foreigners, lowering the retirement age, extending compulsory education, etc.), shortening working hours, watching prices, encouraging small businessmen, establishing popular credit houses, guaranteeing bank deposits, and changing the system of public works. "If we vote purely and simply for the Roche Plan," said a delegate, "we shall seem to be applying fragmentary expedients to a profound crisis."[44] The Congress, however, happily voted the Plan, and it was promptly forgotten; it became another item in "The Program."

The Radicals simply did not like concrete proposals. At the Congress of 1937, the report on social policy was made by Dr. Rosenthal. Contrary to all precedent, he made a very detailed examination of a plan for pensions for retired workers, without mentioning the other social categories. He made a series of specific proposals, demanding, moreover, that the Congress adopt them without referring to committee, so that a bill could be immediately enacted into law.[45] As one writer described such situations: "In order that this play may retain its self-sufficiency at the level of pure form, the content must receive no weight on its own account; as soon as the discussion gets businesslike, it is no longer sociable. . . . The form of argument may occur, but it must not permit the seriousness of the momentary content to become its substance."[46]

Rosenthal had violated the rules by making a serious proposal, and his colleagues were profoundly disturbed. Maurice Rolland rose to restore propriety. The report, he said, concentrated too narrowly on one aspect: think of the unwed mothers, the orphans, the tubercular, and the sick—all of them should be reassured. Furthermore, what was important was not detail, but great principles like the following: stopping the class war, putting an end to speculation and exploitation of the consumer, and drafting proposals for the emancipation of the worker.[47]

Such vapid verbalism was widespread, but not universal. At the beginning of the 1930's there was a strong movement for reformism within the party. Indeed, the Radicals seemed to be the only party that reformists could readily join. Neither of the two other major parties of the left, the Communists and the Socialists, constituted a serious alternative. The Communists were, of course, revolutionaries, which made them the enemies of reformism. They were, in addition, weak in France, and severely hampered by Russia's economic failures. As late as 1928, Bertrand de Jouvenel wrote: "After comparing the USSR with the USA, . . . the proletariat has come to the conclusion that the capitalist system is the one that at present leads to the greatest production and the greatest general prosperity."[48] The party was plagued with dissensions that were not finally ended until 1930–31. At the beginning of the 1930's, therefore, Communism had no attraction for would-be social reformers. The Socialist party was a more likely haven for reformists, and a few, like Marcel Déat, strayed into it. But they were handicapped by a strongly entrenched bureaucracy, and by a verbal Marxism that was the more dogmatically affirmed the less plausible it became, and the less it accorded with the party's social base.

For those who sought in a political party a means of action rather than a psychological crutch, there remained the Radicals. Although the Radicals were never admired, they were not yet despised. The party had failed miserably in 1926, which was a portent; but for a while it was plausible to argue that it had learned its lesson. In 1928, at the Congress of Angers, it had performed an act of heroic self-abnegation by voluntarily withdrawing from the government, and it had remained in opposition for three and a half years. There was a new president, Daladier, who was relatively young and seemed open to new ideas. There was no bureaucracy to bar the way to those with talent.

Thus, in spite of the party's sorry reputation, young men entered for sound reasons.[49] The newspaper La République, founded in 1929 by Daladier and Emile Roche, provided a forum for the discussion of political and economic issues, and printed four or five doctrinal articles daily. Moreover, L'Oeuvre, the left-wing daily of national importance, published many articles by Radicals. The young Radicals were not tied to any traditional social or economic order: Pierre Cot was to become a near-Communist; Bergery was extremely open-minded; Bertrand de Jouvenel was to become first a fascist and then a well-known political theorist. There were solid practical innovators like Pierre Mendès-France and Jean Zay, who were to show their worth later. All the Young Turks were original, capable, and willing to consider new departures. The party was unequaled for its potential talent.

The reasons these men gave for joining the Radical party were sensible and explicit. One wrote that he considered the Radical party, "because of its composition and ideology, the most apt and qualified to readapt democracy to the prodigious . . . development of capitalism."[50] Pierre Cot said: "Our ideas roughly corresponded to those that were taken up several years later by the American New Deal; we were convinced democrats, who thought we could solve the social and international problems inherited from the war by the world-wide extension of the principle of democracy. Today, I can see that this notion was more idealistic than practical."[51]

All members of the party, even the old guard, were haunted by the realization that they had to prove themselves. If the party succeeds in overcoming the crises of the 1930's, said Daladier, "it will prove to the world that free men can freely resolve the most serious problems without resorting to dictatorship."[52] "No one can be unaware of the extremely serious political crisis that would follow if the Radical party failed in its effort," stated Maurice Sarraut.[53] And Jacques Kayser, on the left, wrote: "Governmental failure in the face of crisis could spell the doom of reform. If this happens, we will be forced to admit the facts and our resounding failures, and to pass from reform to revolution. . . . But we are not at that pass yet!"[54]

Yet all these aspirations led to nothing. The immense doctrinal efforts filled the pages of La République and L'Oeuvre with interminably tedious, empty, and irrelevant thought. The young men with original ideas—Gaston Bergery, Bertrand de Jouvenel, Henri Clerc— left the party. Bergery gave his reasons: "Gaston Bergery is leaving the Radical party in order to remain faithful to the party's doctrine, to remain faithful to the promises he made his electors in 1932."[55] Later he was more explicit:

The idea that "today we are in a narrow pass where combat is impossible, but tomorrow we shall see the plain stretched out before us where we can deploy our troops" is . . . an illusion, the effect of a mirage. Only revolutions give history access to the "plain." Reformism is but a succession of narrow passes; to refuse to open fire there is to refuse, forever, to fight, and reformism without fight is reformism without reform.[56]

Apart from the fact that it would have been extremely difficult to transform the inert mass of the party, the renovators themselves were incapable of shaking free of the old ways.

The Radicals abandoned their reformist vocation to the Socialists. Some of the reformers remained with the party and struggled successfully to bring it into the Popular Front. But the Radicals' role there was sullen and derivative. Pushed by the need for action, the party lurched forward, borrowing attitudes and policies where they could be found—on the left, the plans of the CGT, of Henri de Man, and of the Popular Front; on the right, pro-fascism, anti-parliamentarianism, spurious pan-Europeanism, and a veiled anti-Semitism.

The Radical party in the 1930's was open to all possibilities. Of all French parties it was the most likely to adapt to moderate progressivism. Yet it did not. This failure to translate progressive slogans into action was serious, since the party gradually became incapable of acting at all unless stimulated by a crisis. The party's doctrinal sterility, however, had one useful effect: renouncing reformism, the Radicals became a buffer, moderating the extremism of right and left. They were able to accept first the deflation of the Laval government, then the audacities of the Popular Front, and finally the financial austerity of Paul Reynaud; indeed, not only to accept these policies, but to claim them as their own. Having no unequivocal ideas, they presented no great obstacle to positive programs, once the complete control of events had slipped from their hands in 1934.

As we have seen, the Radicals claimed that their doctrine was "the political application of rationalism." Yet there is no evidence of analysis in their reactions to any of the major problems of the 1930's. Jacques Kayser maintains that the characteristic mode of Radical thought was the historical parallel.[57] During the 1930's, Herriot and Daladier, at least, thought primarily in historical terms. There were two types of historical thinking. The first was the relatively harmless habit of describing contemporary people and events in revolutionary terms— Daladier, for example, was commonly called a Jacobin, although it is hard to imagine what was meant by this. More dangerous was the insistence on assimilating each new situation to a precedent in the Third Republic: Doumergue's constitutional reforms were discussed in terms of Marshal MacMahon; the problems of 1932 were treated in terms of 1926; Hitler in terms of Bismarck; all estimable political behavior in terms of Waldeck-Rousseau. Combined with the general disinclination for analysis, this habit ensured that every new situation was essentially misunderstood.

This intellectual approach to special problems makes a case study of considerable interest. Examples could be drawn from several areas —for example, foreign policy, where partial explanations became absolute dogmas, or the Popular Front, which was founded on misunderstanding and the anachronistic attribution of revolutionary symbols to twentieth-century phenomena. This chapter, however, will deal with the Radical approach to economic and financial problems because these were the most constantly present and the most widely discussed.

With regard to economic and financial matters, the Radicals had little experience. All but five of the deputies had grown up before the First World War. Their education had been humanistic, and the context of their formative years had been Boulangism, the Dreyfus Affair, and the anti-clericalism of Combes—all purely political issues. Only three Radicals in the 1930's had any facility with financial and economic questions—Caillaux, Bonnet, and Mendès-France. The first two, however, were instilled with the conservative financial orientation of the Inspectorate of Finance, and Mendès-France, though much more up to date, was only 25 in 1932.[58]

In spite of Herriot's "vast culture," which was the wonder of the political world, his financial incompetence was notorious. Both Gaston Bergery, who was his adviser on the reparations question in 1924 and disliked him, and Julien Durand, who was his Minister of Commerce in 1932 and respected him, told me how when they talked to him about economic questions, he would hold his head in his hands in despair and tell them to do what they thought right.[59] In 1932 he chose Germain-Martin, a man of orthodox financial views, as his Minister of Finance in order not to be bothered by the banks.[60] His was not simply the helpless ignorance of the politician faced with technical problems, but a disruptive force. Herriot had the knack of coining phrases that caught on and obscured the issue. The "Mur d'Argent" was his, as was "either budgetary deflation or monetary inflation," the false dilemma that condemned the 1932 legislature to impotence.

He was, moreover, haunted by his ignominious capitulation to the banks in 1926; according to Paul-Boncour, whenever a difficult question arose during a cabinet meeting, Herriot repeated that he did not wish to live through 1926 again.[61] Although the parallel with 1926 was not valid, Herriot's belief in it forced him to follow a false majority in 1932. His fear of the banks caused him to bar a Popular Front government in June 1935, and to delay an attack on Laval's Ethiopian policy until it was too late. His financial ignorance infused him with a primitive terror of the mysterious powers of the banks: "Finally, let us consider financial difficulties. I counsel—I repeat—utmost caution. I do not want to make positive, general promises. You must know how to proceed slowly, if you do not want to walk backward. Don't fall into traps. No one suspects me of devotion to the economic interests, but let me tell you, in the interest of France herself and of your cause, be cautious!"[62]

Daladier, too, was an economic illiterate, and, realizing his deficiencies, he went, as he put it, "to night school"[63]—with unfortunate results. Seeking a way out of the economic impasse, he was prompted to develop, in his only major economic speech of our period, the lessons to be learned from the "melting money" of Woergl. Woergl was a small town in the Austrian Tyrol that achieved prosperity by issuing paper designed to lose 12 per cent of its value each year, a measure that stopped hoarding and prompted frenetic economic activity. "They say at Woergl that saving bank notes belongs to a bygone stage of civilization."[64] The horror that this provoked among the party workers, who were more accustomed to the party's "demanding the protection of the *bas-de-laine français*,"[65] comes to us in the discreet indication "Mouvements" in the record of the proceedings. "Melting money" disappeared from the Radical economic repertory as quickly as it had appeared, with the sole result that Daladier's assault on Herriot's presidency of the party had to await Woergl's oblivion, and the more congenial platform of the Popular Front.

Other Radicals had as little grasp as Herriot and Daladier. Marcel Régnier, who as Finance Minister was the architect of the Laval deflation, discussed the concepts of deflation and devaluation at a meeting of the Radical departmental Congress at Vichy. If the deficit reappeared, said Régnier, it would mean bankruptcy and revolution.* "Devaluation?" he continued. "The franc has already been devalued by 80 per cent; can one go any further without its falling to zero?"[66] Or take the statement of Julien Durand, Minister of Commerce in the Herriot government, who set out to restore order to the economic chaos:

* The budget, though balanced on paper, was, like every budget since 1930, deeply in deficit.

What had to be done, therefore, was to restore domestic consumption by making money circulate, and to promote foreign trade while protecting national production. . . .

I did not plan a dogmatic system; I felt it necessary to diminish manufacturing costs and the cost of living, to preserve the consuming power of the masses of the people, to give new life to national production, to develop credit, to protect savings, to favor industrial cartels. . . .

These proposals were admitted in principle, but would require persistent effort to be put into effect.[67]

These "proposals," with the exception of the unfortunate idea of government-sponsored industrial cartels, were simply a description of the symptoms of the crisis. In short, Durand had no program. As one deputy put it, "The worst of it is that those who have the responsibility give one the impression of not knowing exactly what they want or where they are going."[68]

The dearth of competence among the Radicals was partly compensated by talent imported from other parties: only four of the eight Ministers of Finance who served in Radical cabinets were Radicals— Georges Bonnet, Marcel Régnier, Paul Marchandeau, and Lucien Lamoureux.[69] Unfortunately, though, many others had a finger in the pie: the Minister of Commerce, the Minister of the Budget, the presidents and *rapporteurs-généraux* of the Finance Committees of the Chamber and of the Senate, the members of the Finance Committees, and, finally, the Premier himself all had a chance to assail the French economy.

In view of the limitations of the Radical leaders, it is not surprising that the Radical members of the Finance Committee of the Chamber were unimpressive. Whereas Thorez represented the Communists, Blum and Vincent Auriol the Socialists, and Reynaud and Georges Mandel the moderates, only Bonnet among important Radical leaders was ever a member, and then only for six months. The Radical members were characterized by a striking lack of professional preparation.[70]

Even more harmful than the incompetence of most Radicals was the financial skill of Joseph Caillaux. Caillaux was extremely talented, and, as we have seen, he dominated the Senate through its Finance Committee. His financial principles were orthodox, and he used his senatorial power to prevent, or at least hinder, attempts at economic innovation. If an imaginative program had been put forth, it would have had to overcome his formidable opposition.

The consequences of the Radicals' being in power at this time of economic crisis were, first, a misdirected and incoherent policy, the result of a general misunderstanding of the situation; and, second, since the few competent men in the party were financiers rather than economists, a total subordination of the broad needs of the economy to the narrower needs of the Treasury.

Given this personnel, the Radicals were naturally susceptible to the financial and economic myths that governed the politics of the 1930's. The first myth of the Radical financial experts was that the balanced budget was immediate to God. They had generally been trained in the school of communal and departmental finance, where the chief virtue was parsimony, and they transferred their principles to national finance, unaware that they no longer held. One expert, Georges Potut, a journalist by profession, wrote: " 'You are following a grocer's policy,' Jacques Duclos said one day to Camille Chautemps, president of the Council. This was intended to be scornful, coming from the Muscovite leader, but he was only stating the simple truth. Yes, indeed! Methods do not differ, whether one is running a small business or managing the finances of a great nation. Two and two makes four."[71] The same sentiment was expressed by Joseph Caillaux at the 1933 Congress: "The French State must behave like a good housewife. Basically, finances are not so complicated as they seem. You must align your receipts on one side, and your expenses on the other. (Vigorous applause.)"[72]

Although these two were conservatives, they were fully representative, since, with the exception of Mendès-France, the Radicals' would-be financial experts were all conservative.[73] Moreover, the left wing of the party, as well as the right, accepted orthodox economics; there was no dissension on financial doctrine. Dezarnaulds, for example, an extreme left-winger who indulged in demagogic anti-capitalism on occasion,[74] could piously say, "At present, the re-establishment of a balanced budget seems to me an absolute necessity, for the future of our country and for the normal and desirable development of its domestic and foreign policy."[75] Jean Zay proclaimed his entire confidence in Daladier, Bonnet, and Lamoureux to put an end, at last, to the financial deficit.[76] Léon Archimbaud wrote: "We shall not hesitate to make massive and indispensable cuts in the budget. Commerce and agriculture cannot take a single new tax!"[77] And Gaston Martin: "Balance the budget or die!"[78] Thus, when even the most stridently left-wing Radical deputies publicly insisted on maximum deflation, there could be no effective opposition to the official policy.

In the years 1932 to 1934, therefore, there was almost total unanimity within the party on the primacy of the balanced budget. This unrealistic policy was specifically Radical. "When you talk to [the Radicals] of Roosevelt's daring," wrote Charles Laurent, "you should see their eyes widen, and they talk about the need to balance the budget, and they add in a horrified tone, 'Monetary devaluation!'—as if the policy they advocate will not as surely lead there after causing ruin and unemployment."[79]

As we shall see, the Radicals fought the elections of 1932 on this issue of the balanced budget. Surprisingly enough, they even saw themselves as the watchdogs of orthodoxy against the depredations of Tardieu, Flandin, and Reynaud, although these represented "the parliamentary faction that is most clearly identified with the controlling elements of the economy—the banks and finance."[80] One left-wing deputy wrote: "Taxpayers! Watch out for your pockets! Watch out for the Cartel des Droites . . . who have already drained the Treasury dry! ! !"[81] Another wrote: "Caution and financial austerity scarcely had any defenders for twenty years except Poincaré and the Radicals, principally the senators. The Radicals wanted to govern like thrifty petty bourgeois; the conservatives with the sumptuousness of aristocrats."[82]

The hope for a balanced budget maintained itself intact despite its obvious unreality. Although 16 billion francs were cut from the budget between 1932 and 1935, including seven billion by Radical governments,[83] the deficit continued to increase. In all, the deficit was 35 billion francs during these four years.[84] A balanced budget under such conditions was impossible, and to concentrate on it to the exclusion of all other policy was folly.

The most disquieting aspect of this policy was the way in which it was directed toward an entirely peripheral matter—the reduction of fonctionnaires' salaries—which became the focal point of all political activity for more than a year. One advocate wrote: "The first and most urgent measure—one that must take precedence over all others, one that will give the whole French economy the forward thrust it needs, the only measure that can really lead to economic equilibrium in a short time—is the general reduction of salaries and pensions in state and public services."[85] It will be seen that this obsession came to dominate all politics. Eventually, even Radical deputies began to find the fantasy of public policy disturbing: "They have tried to create a mystique of a balanced budget achieved by means of the simple reduction of public expenditure, as well as the mystique that the remedy for the economic crisis is the simple reduction of salaries."[86] Yet the mystique was too widespread to be easily eliminated. Henri Clerc wrote a surprisingly perceptive analysis of the way this attitude had created an impossible political situation:

It seems a priori impossible that the [Sarraut] government will not make the same attempt to balance the budget that led to the fall of the Daladier ministry. . . . This is the imbroglio arrived at by a campaign that has been carried on for 18 months by the opposition, and by the government itself, in favor of a measure which is *economically very questionable* if not downright harmful, and is *politically* impossible to pass, but has become *psychologically* indispensable in the present state of opinion.[87]

It is hard to imagine how anyone could drift so far from reality as to believe that a reduction of 10 per cent in civil servants' wages would solve the problem of the Great Depression. Yet this was believed, and believed by Radicals whose banner was human liberation by means of Cartesian rationalism.

Fear of the apocalypse faded when it became clear that life could continue relatively normally with a deficit. By the beginning of 1933, one conservative deputy could write: "Economizing means deflation, that is to say, an aggravation of the crisis, which in turn means that less tax money comes in; what point, therefore, in increasing taxes? . . . A nation can very easily live with a deficit."[88]

It was relatively easy to give up the idea of deflation, but much harder to accept the full consequences of deficit financing, a concept that was so alien to Radical thinking. A typical reaction to this uncomfortable situation was utterly to deny the logic involved, and to support the most contradictory policies provided they appealed to the voters. The following electoral statement of Léon Meyer, a man of considerable ministerial experience, is typical of the way issues were presented to the voters:

It is essential that receipts and not needs should determine expenses. Otherwise, it would mean continuing to borrow, which hampers economic life and leads to bankruptcy of the state and devaluation of the franc, which I consider unthinkable.

I voted against the [deflationary] decree laws: I am resolutely hostile to them because they are unjust and hit blindly. . . . I want their abrogation. . . . These decrees have had the consequence of reducing purchasing power and slowing down business.[89]

The void created by abandoning the myth of deflation, however, was easily filled by the creation of a second great myth—that devaluation of the franc was a sin.

The catastrophic reluctance of the French to consider devaluing the franc between 1930 and 1936 has become a classic example of wrong-headedness.[90] The Radicals shared this reluctance, although there were a few exceptions. It is hardly surprising, with the Socialists and Communists against devaluation, that the left-wing Radicals should entirely misconstrue Paul Reynaud's arguments in its favor:[91] Reynaud's devaluation proposals are reactionary;[92] Reynaud wants to promote speculation;[93] Reynaud proposes it to annoy Flandin.[94] Daladier summed up the Radical position: "How should we proceed? By Paul Reynaud's devaluation? That will resolve nothing. When the value of the currency is reduced by half, a day will inevitably come when two new bank notes will be needed to get what today you pay for with one. I add that it is an injustice."[95] According to Sauvy, "The first and most important error was to *confuse devaluation and inflation*."[96] Within two critical years, reality once again overcame a mythology too flagrantly opposed to it, and the franc was devalued.

The Radicals promptly accepted yet another vision to deceive themselves: that exchange control was the work of the devil and would destroy liberty. Georges Bonnet claimed that not only would it be ineffective, but it would require a government monopoly of foreign trade and censorship of the mail and of the press. "Could such a regime," he concluded, "succeed outside of a dictatorship?"[97] Then came the war, and with it exchange control.

These three monetary myths were fairly commonly held by Frenchmen of all sorts—the Radicals shared the illusions of their time. The function of a simplistic monetary slogan such as "Either budgetary deflation or monetary inflation" was to make an extremely complicated economic situation appear uncomplicated. The slogan's inadequacy became apparent only in time, but meanwhile it served as an effective, if rudimentary, economic theory that permitted consensus. The role of the slogan as a unifying myth was no less important than its role as an economic program, so that when the program inevitably broke down, it was imperative to find a replacement. The new myth did not arise from a new economic analysis, but from the need for psychological reassurance. The construction of these myths was as natural as it was pernicious.

CHAPTER 3

Two Local Examples

In a general political history the special character of a historical experience may disappear, since so many particulars have to be suppressed. When we speak of individual deputies, it is generally to identify them with one faction or another. Yet the reactions of Radical deputies to a given situation were not the automatic responses required by a certain ideology. Each deputy belonged to a particular generation, represented specific interests, and had a personal outlook on foreign affairs and economic policy. In this chapter, a close look at one Radical deputy, Michel Geistdoerfer of Dinan, and at the contingent of Radical deputies from the Charente-Inférieure* will give us insight into the general development of the party in the 1930's.

I

Michel Geistdoerfer was the Radical deputy for the first district of Dinan in the Côtes-du-Nord. He has been chosen for study because he ran a newspaper in which, every week without interruption, he wrote an unusually frank editorial. This journalistic dedication is atypical, but the results are very informative. Geistdoerfer was intensely interested in local politics and published not only his own minute account of every important event, but often large extracts from the opposition press. He had collected many personal papers, which he showed me, for the whole period. I interviewed three deputies from the Côtes-du-Nord, Geistdoerfer, André Lorgeré, and André

---

* The name Charente-Inférieure was disliked by the more sensitive inhabitants, who considered "Inférieure" deprecating; a long campaign finally succeeded in changing the name to the present Charente-Maritime. The former is used here, however, since it was the official title before World War II.

Cornu, and Lorgeré provided me with large sections of his unpublished—and unpublishable—memoirs, upon which much of what follows is based.

As the throwaway reproduced on p. 80 shows, Michel Geistdoerfer was a third-generation republican from a family of some note in the region. He had married into a prominent local family. His grandfather had been an important Mason; his father was a Mason; Geistdoerfer himself was not a Mason, but was sympathetic to the cause. He was a civil servant of modest success, and the proprietor of a local newspaper. In short, he was a notable of the classic type, whose family history was comparable to that of most Radicals.

The department of the Côtes-du-Nord is in the northeast corner of Brittany, and is divided sharply into French-speaking and Breton-speaking sections. Dinan is French-speaking, and was in a state of constant hostility to the Breton-speaking region of the department; it was the second city of the department, but with no more than 15,000 inhabitants and scarcely any industry. The vast majority of electors consisted of poor farmers who owned their own land.[1] Dinan is in a part of Brittany where the power of the landowning aristocracy was insignificant.[2]

Brittany is a Catholic region, and the lines of political division were drawn on the clerical issue. One was not right or left so much as clerical or anti-clerical. Michel Geistdoerfer maintained his anti-clericalism to the finish. When, near the end of our period, certain Radicals were trying to get the party to repudiate anti-clericalism in order to broaden its centrist appeal, Geistdoerfer would have nothing of it. Guernut, he wrote, "continues to shock the Radical party worker in me when he reasons (for he is a master reasoner) about the opportunity for the Radical party to stop practicing anti-clericalism."[3] In 1959 he was involved in publishing an ambitious serialized exposé of Church politics entitled "The Vatican As It Really Is."[4] Regularly, throughout the 1930's, *Dinan-républicain* would return to the attack:[5] Geistdoerfer wrote of education and clericalism, the Spanish Civil War and clericalism, the Saar plebiscite and clericalism, agrarianism and clericalism, fascism and clericalism, the merchant marine and clericalism, the Boy Scout movement and clericalism. Just as "the priests run everything in Dinan,"[6] so in the world. The worldwide conspiracy weighed heavily on Michel Geistdoerfer.

The electoral divisions of the first constituency of Dinan reflected

Michel Geistdoerfer, Républicain de Gauche, candidate
in the legislative elections,
Councillor-General of the Côtes-du-Nord,
Licensed in Law,
Officer of the Academy,
Decorated with the Croix de Guerre,
Graduate of the Ecole des Sciences Politiques,
Former head of the Secretariat for Municipal Affairs
at the Prefecture of the Seine,
President of the Cantonal Delegation
of the eastern canton of Dinan,
President of the section of the Wards of the Nation
of the eastern canton of Dinan,
President of the Dinan Pigeon-Lovers Society [*société colombophile*].

———

Michel Geistdoerfer was born in Dinan, April 14, 1883. . . . His great-uncle founded a republican newspaper entitled *Le Sentinel du peuple* in Dinan in 1851, which was suppressed after the coup d'état. . . .

In 1910, after passing a competitive exam, Michel Geistdoerfer entered the Prefecture of the Seine, where, until last June, he headed the secretariat for municipal affairs.

It was then that the death of his brother-in-law, François Rames, Councillor-General, whose colleague he was, caused him to leave his administrative post for active politics.

His brilliant election victory and his very clear stand in favor of the Union des Gauches marked the republican revival in the Côtes-du-Nord.

For a long time Michel Geistdoerfer has been respected as a journalist. At 20 he joined *Le Petit Bleu de Dinan,* created to support the candidature of Dr. Baudet. He wrote for *La Grande Revue, Le Progrès civique,* and various regional papers such as *La Bretagne touristique* and *La Bretagne à Paris.* . . . He founded and directs *Dinan-républicain.*

For a long time he was secretary-general of the Bleus de Bretagne.

He founded the Society of the Friends of Lamennais, which has organized numerous demonstrations in Paris and the provinces in support of the great Breton democrat; he is its secretary-general.

He belongs to the Society of Men of Letters and has published several novels and plays. He had a philosophical play performed in Paris last year.

Michel GEISTDOERFER, because of his *competence,* his *breadth of culture,* his *political* and *administrative connections,* and his *achievements,* as well as his *unpretentiousness* and *generosity,* is the best candidate that a constituency can choose if it wishes to *prosper.*

THROWAWAY
From Geistdoerfer's personal papers, sent out during the 1928 elections.

the clerical issue. Elections were fought by the clericals against the anti-clericals, with more central twentieth-century issues scarcely considered. Thus, in 1932 Michel Geistdoerfer received 6,300 votes; his right-wing opponent, 5,456; the Socialist, 35; the Communist, 56. Class consciousness did not reach Dinan until after the Second World War, but the ideological battle within the communes was fierce. Although there was a fairly even distribution between right and left within the constituency as a whole, there were sharp divergences within individual communes. Geistdoerfer obtained as much as 65 per cent of the recorded vote in Trevilar; as little as 14 per cent in St.-Maden. The nature of the conflict that divided these villages can perhaps best be savored by citing an anonymous letter from a party worker in a rural commune:

We believe it is unnecessary to tell you that the commune of Evran is a nest of reactionaries [Geistdoerfer 26 per cent, right wing 59 per cent, 1932]. However, there are several good republicans who have decided to organize a Committee of Republican Defense.

The Committee, which is very small, and for good reason, will have to act with extreme caution so that our adversaries are not alerted too soon. We must all be prepared to begin the fight on the right day and hour. The battle, you told us at Tréfumel [the second commune to the southwest, Geistdoerfer 48 per cent, right wing 31 per cent], must begin after one election and with a view to the following one.

The municipality of Evran, which is extremely reactionary and Dorgerist, must fall; but if we are to succeed we must take it by surprise without giving its members time to collect themselves. Hence the need for great tactical caution.[7]

From this, it is not clear whether the intrepid party worker was planning to lay siege to the town hall or merely the electors' hearts. Naïveté shines forth from every line. This man was in politics not to promote his interests, but to defend good against evil. Such was the inspiration of the average Radical in the Dinan of the 1930's.

Geistdoerfer belonged to the Radical Group in Paris. His relations with the party were extremely casual, though not unusually so. In his electoral propaganda he called himself not a Radical, but a Républicain de Gauche. The fact that Flandin's group in Paris had the same name and Geistdoerfer's opponent in Dinan also called himself a Républicain de Gauche seemed to confuse no one. Geistdoerfer's local committee was called the Comité Républicain, with no mention of

Radical-Socialist. According to the party statutes, all committees were supposed to be affiliated with the local federation and hold party cards from Paris. The Comité Républicain of Dinan did neither. In spite of this, Martinaud-Déplat, as secretary-general, admitted that the Committee was Radical.[8] The party never sent any directives or propaganda to Geistdoerfer. There was, therefore, no contact between the central party and the Dinan party workers. Outside contact came through visits of dignitaries on Geistdoerfer's invitation—Herriot, Chautemps, and Cot all visited Dinan. These were great occasions, replete with banquets and dedication ceremonies.

Geistdoerfer's relations with the Federation of the Côtes-du-Nord were much less cordial. This organization was born uncertainly in 1933, and led a tenuous existence.[9] Its first president was André Lorgeré, the deputy from Guingamp. According to Geistdoerfer, the purpose of the federation was to undermine his own position by creating a rival organization in Dinan. When the federation tried to create a Radical committee in the second constituency of Dinan, Geistdoerfer wrote, "Since its foundation, this pseudo-federation, apart from several insignificant meetings of its Bureau, has shown only inertia, impotence, and ineptitude."[10] The decisive break between Geistdoerfer and the federation came in 1938, during the disastrous senatorial elections. Geistdoerfer's intense hostility toward the federation came from the threat it represented to his own position. The Comité Républicain was his own creation, but certain councillors-general had independent ambitions. Geistdoerfer quarreled with them in 1928 and again in 1938, when two of them openly fought him in the senatorial elections.[11] Geistdoerfer's hostility toward the federation was natural enough.

The pattern of friendships in the department was confused, and did not follow doctrinal lines. Of the deputies elected between 1932 and 1936, five were Radical, two Gauche Radicale, and one right-wing. André Cornu and Pierre Michel, the two deputies from St.-Brieuc, the major city in the department, were Geistdoerfer's great enemies.[12] They were Radicals of very recent vintage, having joined the party in 1933. Before that they had been Gauche Radicale. They were both moderate to conservative. André Lorgeré inclined to the left, but he and Geistdoerfer disliked each other. Yves Le Gac was also fairly far to the left, and Geistdoerfer seems to have remained on tolerably good terms with him. Le Vézouet, one of the Gauche Radicale deputies, was closer to Geistdoerfer, and in intra-departmental skirmishes, these two would often ally. Geistdoerfer was most devoted to the only local deputy of national consequence, Louis de Chappedelaine, leader of the Gauche Radicale, who was notorious as the most opportunistic of deputies. Traditionally de Chappedelaine's second constituency of Dinan was reactionary, whereas Geistdoerfer's was progressive.[13] Geistdoerfer was on the extreme left of the Radicals, and de Chappedelaine on the right of the Gauche Radicale. In parliament they could never conscientiously support the same policies, yet they were great friends and allies in the department against the Breton-speaking western section, whose deputies, in turn, were equally unhomogeneous, and yet united in opposition to the pair from Dinan. In the fall of 1933, de Chappedelaine was working hard to replace the left-wing Daladier government by a majority of the center, a policy known as Concentration. Geistdoerfer was absolutely against Concentration, yet closely involved in a peripheral local intrigue with de Chappedelaine.

None of the senators was of national importance; Geistdoerfer disliked most of them on personal grounds.

In the summer and fall of 1933 an incident occurred that belonged to what the French call *la petite histoire*, but nonetheless touched on *la grande histoire*, and illuminates it. This incident was the sort that shook dozens of similar provincial circles throughout the period—the life-blood, the battle, the overwhelming preoccupation of the political man. The affair can be briefly summarized. The new president of the departmental federation, on being elected, had said that "he was going to conquer the department by flawless organization,"[14] and set about establishing a committee in de Chappedelaine's constituency. Counterattacking, Geistdoerfer and de Chappedelaine planned a joint function in late August consisting of a banquet at Plenée-Jugon in de Chappedelaine's territory and the dedication of the Ecole Pratique du Commerce et de l'Industrie at Dinan. Such an event called for a cabinet minister; Anatole de Monzie was chosen, and he accepted the invitation.

The Breton-speaking deputies put great pressure on Daladier to prevent de Monzie's appearance, since if he came, power and patronage would seem to rest with the old guard rather than the new organization. "If de Monzie had come," wrote one of the conspirators, "it would have been regarded as a slap in the face of the Radical party, its deputies, and its party workers."[15] Geistdoerfer himself unwittingly provided de Monzie with an excuse for withdrawing—a series of typically immoderate attacks on de Monzie's educational policies.[16] De Monzie telegraphed his refusal. The other camp was delighted: "We could have announced this refusal. We counseled it before it was official. We waited—with a smile—for it to become a fait accompli."[17] Geistdoerfer reported that political circles had been gravely shaken by de Monzie's refusal.[18] The banquet was gloomily held in the "deliberate absence" of the four western deputies, Lorgeré, Michel, Cornu, and Le Gac. De Chappedelaine and Geistdoerfer denounced their adversaries in a river of print.[19] The whole departmental press was filled with interminable postmortems.[20] Echoes of "the de Monzie incident" reverberated as far as Morocco. An obscure Paris weekly, *Le Petit Bara*, wrote to congratulate Geistdoerfer and to ask him to contribute an anti-clerical article. No other event in Brittany had achieved such fame since the summer of 1932, when the autonomists tried to blow up Herriot's train during his visit to Geistdoerfer.

The incident had surprisingly far-reaching consequences. Locally, the Socialists openly broke with Geistdoerfer; they had accused de Chappedelaine of undermining the Union des Gauches in parliament, and they now denounced Geistdoerfer as his accomplice. This conflict lasted until the war.[21] Nationally, de Chappedelaine, as leader of the Gauche Radicale in parliament, intrigued more violently than ever against the Daladier government, helping foil Daladier's scheme for achieving Concentration. When Albert Sarraut came to form his ministry, the perennial problem of finding a Breton minister became more complicated than ever; de Chappedelaine and Geistdoerfer violently opposed Lorgeré and Cornu, so Sarraut finally opted for Senator Fernand Le Gorgeu of Finistère. This action not only irritated the western Radicals from the Côtes-du-Nord,[22] but was violently opposed by the Finistère deputies; the five deputies from Finistère accounted for half the Radical abstentions on the vote that overthrew the government.* A few months later, Geistdoerfer remarked that one of the incoherencies of Daladier's second government, one of the most

---

* *Le Temps,* Nov. 25, 1933. The Breton problem was difficult, since for some obscure reason there were very few Breton deputies capable of being ministers. During the 1930's there were only seven Breton ministers, two of whom—Le Gorgeu and Alphonse Gasnier-Duparc—were there simply to give Brittany a representative; of the others, only de Chappedelaine, La Chambre, and Pierre Mazé were in any way outstanding. Five governments—those of Herriot, Doumergue, Flandin, Bouisson, and Laval—had no Breton in them. And once in the cabinet, the Breton was normally just an undersecretary of state.

poorly constructed of the period, was that both de Chappedelaine and Lorgeré were in it.[23] As a final distant result, the animosities aroused in 1933 helped lose two senatorial seats for the left in 1938.

The de Monzie incident is only one example. The Daladier government was overthrown in October 1933 on a measure for redressing the French economic and financial situation; Hitler left the disarmament conference on October 15; French democracy was challenged at home and abroad, and de Chappedelaine helped overthrow the government because de Monzie had not come to dinner. By itself, the incident was not serious; but when we remember that there were ten or a hundred such incidents for each ministerial crisis, we can at least glimpse the complexity of the French governing process.

The basis of Michel Geistdoerfer's local power was the Comité Républicain. Its membership fluctuated around 250. Practically all the members came from the town of Dinan. In addition to the Committee, Geistdoerfer had a network of supporters throughout the communes, two or three to a commune, ranging from mayors to one mere "poster-placer." In all, he had a respectable 159 declared supporters in the villages, including 12 mayors; only in St.-Maden, where he had received just 14 per cent of the votes, was this support reduced to a poster-placer.

The role of the Committee was to meet before legislative, municipal, cantonal, and senatorial elections to choose Geistdoerfer as its candidate.[24] It provided the participants for the banquets that were the great social and political events of the department, especially since the Tour de France had decided to bypass Dinan. It regulated the nomination of lesser candidates, municipal councillors particularly.[25] Otherwise it did nothing. Since it exercised no control over Geistdoerfer, its members were mere ciphers, content to shout "Vive Michel!" The only time national policy came before them was when Geistdoerfer indulged in a marathon harangue "before their rapt attention." He was thus free to adopt whatever position pleased him on national issues without worrying about local pressures. Any opposition to Geistdoerfer had to find expression outside the local organization; from this situation derived the local support for the intrigues of the departmental federation.

Geistdoerfer's attitude toward his followers was a fairly typical aspect of Radicalism. Officially the party claimed to be a party of free

discussion and dissent; in practice there was a broad hint of Bonapart-
ism in its attitudes. Geistdoerfer's greatest pleasure was to be acclaimed
by the crowds from the balcony of his home or carried in triumph
through the streets.[26] He rejected criticism and silenced his opponents
ruthlessly and with relish, tolerating only yes-men in his entourage.
He was a demagogue, who preferred invective to discussion. An example will demonstrate his attitude. During a debate on the communal budget, the Socialists in the municipal council accused him of having sold the town a piece of land for 135,000 francs when it was worth
only 80,000; the land belonged to his mother-in-law. His response was
characteristically not an explanation, but an attack: "You have never
understood anything at all, and you wish to throw mud at your colleagues. What you say proves that you are unworthy of being municipal councillors." "Certain councillors have lost all common sense."
After Geistdoerfer got the appropriation put to a vote, the opposition
cried, "Look at the sheep! Go ahead! Vote!" Geistdoerfer replied,
"You, you are donkeys!"[27] He then launched an investigation into a
drain contract in which one of the opposition councillors was involved, and he tried generally to discredit the opposition with accusations of corruption. For the rest of the year, whenever his opponents
tried to speak, Geistdoerfer refused to give them the floor and turned
the meeting into a secret session; he ended by not inviting them to the
meetings at all.[28] They called him "tyrant" and "Hitler." He accused
them of being drunk. His articles related with obvious relish the cheers
from the public benches as the mayor once again silenced the opposition. His 19 supporters never said a word, and voted when he told
them to.

It is interesting to compare Geistdoerfer's relations with the Radicals with his relations with the Socialists and the right. With the departmental Radicals, as we have seen, he was engaged in continual intense polemics; his own followers were treated with Olympian condescension. Although he was dependent upon Socialist votes for election,
and was further to the left than the average moderate Socialist, he expended any hostility left over from his anti-Radical forays on the Socialists.[29] He was in the midst of one of his vendettas with the Socialists
at the time of the cantonal elections of 1934, so they, not unnaturally,
voted for his opponent in order to defeat him. He managed to patch
up relations just in time for the municipal elections (March 14, 1935),
which he won, and the truce continued for the legislative elections of

1936, but broke down utterly and completely at the end of that year in the municipal council fracas described above.

Geistdoerfer's attitude toward the right was more subtle. On one level he indulged in the same genial invective. "M. Bazin [his opponent in the 1932 elections] has managed, as far as we know, only one intelligent act—that is, to stop attending the meetings of the municipal council of Dinan"; at the last meeting at which Bazin had been present, "he had the air of a sheep that had been dipped in mustard."[30] But between electoral campaigns, he polemicized less against the right than against the left.

At first Geistdoerfer maligned the right-wingers in the traditional way. They were the "hucksters of the Rue de l'Horloge," or the "men of the bishopric," "enfeoffed to the bank and to industry"; he denounced the "citadels of reaction" and the Chamber of Commerce.[31] Nuances appeared in this traditional vocabulary as he began to notice the existence of fascism, and he occasionally came near to calling them fascists: "Fascism and dictatorship have all the sympathy of M. Thoreux and M. René Pierre."[32] But he was always of two minds about whether or not they really were fascists or simply old-fashioned reactionaries and scoundrels. On the national level, however, he had no hesitation in unqualifiedly denouncing February Sixth as fascist, and in believing that an abstract fascist force was hovering somewhere on the right.[33] Agrarianism was the one form of right-wing extremism that was close to home. Henri Dorgères, who was very active in Brittany, demonstrated against the constitutive meeting of the Radical federation, making things distinctly unpleasant for the deputies.* The Dorgerists were a serious political threat in a peasant community, their opposition often taking the form of physical violence. Geistdoerfer's continual denunciations of them had more justification than his usual polemics.[34] The right, therefore, appeared to Geistdoerfer in several guises: reaction, the traditional enemy; the abstract threat of fascism; and the concrete threat of the awakening peasantry.

The great intellectual pressure groups seemed to have little importance in Dinan, or at least in Geistdoerfer's representation of Dinan. He never mentioned the Ligue des Droits de l'Homme, or the Ligue de l'Enseignement, and virtually ignored Freemasonry. There was a

---

* *La Démocratie bretonne,* March 18, 1933. Gordon Wright tells of Dorgères's Greenshirts locking up a deputy in a pigcart, and reports Dorgères's claim to have manhandled some thirty deputies (p. 52 and n. 23, p. 219).

group called the Bleus de Bretagne, a regional left-wing confraternity, whose relative prominence in *Dinan-républicain* may be explained by Geistdoerfer's being its president. The agricultural societies and credit unions were never mentioned. The Ligue des Contribuables attained a certain importance for a while, but that was, of course, confined to the right wing.

Geistdoerfer was a politician. He was deputy, mayor of Dinan, and, until 1934, councillor-general from Dinan. He was also parliamentary representative for St.-Pierre and Miquelon, on whose behalf he made, during Prohibition, a trip to Washington to try to straighten out the difficulties caused by smuggling. In parliament he belonged to two committees and 21 groups, including those for the defense of agriculture, commerce, maritime interests, veterans, and colonies. In parliament he spoke very rarely, never in a general debate; occasionally he defended the merchant marine. He considered that his duty as a parliamentarian was "to defend the Republic and contribute to the prosperity of the region." More specifically, he wished to end unemployment; promote secular education, public hygiene, public assistance, housing, and unions; improve the condition of the artisans; and lower taxes.[35] As mayor of Dinan he delighted in erecting new public buildings, and, if one is to believe the Socialists, in enrolling the unemployed on various projects during the six weeks preceding elections. There were, however, only seven unemployed men in Dinan.

His "contribution to the prosperity of the region," if one can judge from his editorials in *Dinan-républicain,* consisted of defending agriculture with torrents of print. The two aspects of agriculture particularly dear to him were potatoes and cider; for the latter, he established an annual Good Cider Air Show (Fête Aérienne du Bon Cidre), which usually required the attendance of a cabinet minister and provided newspaper copy for the uneventful summer months. Toward the end of the thirties he became a vehement defender of the home distillers as well. His other major interests were the deep-sea fishing industry and the merchant marine,[36] for which he made his one major parliamentary intervention. As late as April 1940 he wrote, "Deep-sea fishing is in danger!"[37] This was a curious interest for Geistdoerfer to be defending, since although there were Bretons who were fishermen, they did not come from the first constituency of Dinan. By the 1930's deep-sea fishing had almost vanished from the north coast of Brittany;[38] furthermore, Dinan had no ports. The interest group for which he expended most of his parliamentary energy could have comprised no more than a handful of voters; perhaps a few men who sailed out of St.-Malo lived in Dinan. There were undoubtedly some retired fishermen among his voters, but they were scarcely comparable in number to the overwhelming majority of farmers. Probably his impassioned defense of a nonexistent voting bloc satisfied the Bretons' image of themselves as a seafaring folk, and was therefore an effective political stance.

We have, then, a fairly clear picture of one Radical deputy; it is instructive to observe the development of his political attitudes. He was profoundly ignorant of economic matters and almost completely indifferent to them. Apart from his various defenses of local interests, he turned his attention to the larger economic scene only rarely. He attacked protectionism three times, but this issue was closely linked with the interests of his department whose farmers hoped to sell potatoes to the English.[39] On general matters he wrote two articles, one, as early as 1933, espousing the forty-hour week as the solution for unemployment,[40] and the other, also well before the formation of the Popular Front, supporting an increase in purchasing power as a solution for the depression.[41] Otherwise he threw in the occasional petty-bourgeois invective—as harmless as it was vague—against the "haute banque" and "grand commerce,"[42] but he never seriously analyzed any economic problems.

On non-economic questions, he showed a very interesting development. At the beginning he was indifferent to national questions. The only general policy that aroused any response from him was what seemed to him the dangerously anti-secular measures of Anatole de Monzie as Minister of Education.[43] The one event of the Herriot ministry to excite his interest was the defeat on the war debts.[44] Throughout 1933 he regularly devoted one article to each ministerial crisis;[45] but, except for an occasional worried article about fascism and Hitler,[46] he was entirely wrapped up in his domestic quarrels and the defense of local interests. February Sixth brought a brief flash of anger; the Republic must be defended, as at the time of Boulanger and Dreyfus, by a regrouping of left-wing forces.[47] But he was in a false position, unsure and vacillating, a week later defending Radical participation in the Doumergue government,[48] and thereafter concentrating on the cider problem in order to avoid the issue.[49] 1934 was a year of local political setbacks, with the defeat of his candidate in a cantonal by-election in May and his own defeat in October. Not once from 1932 to 1934 did he discuss foreign policy.

His great awakening came in 1935. From the early spring his articles concerned national issues more and more frequently. He was particularly alarmed when Paul Elbel, a fellow Radical deputy, had his eye knocked out.[50] He became fully conscious of fascism.[51] The Popular Front came slowly to the Côtes-du-Nord; there was no parade on July Fourteenth, but in November there was a mass meeting with 4,000 present.[52] The issue that most aroused Geistdoerfer was the Ethiopian Affair.[53] This was the first time he had shown any interest in foreign affairs. It catapulted him into the main political stream, and, throughout the fall and early winter of 1935, cider and deep-sea fishing, the local Radicals and Socialists, were all put aside for fascism, Ethiopia, the right-wing Leagues, Laval, and the Popular Front. Occasionally he even attained a certain nobility of sentiment.[54]

The high point in his political involvement was undoubtedly reached in 1936, with the overthrow of the Laval government. Never again did he have the assurance that unqualified opposition bestows. The hard world of compromises obviously dimmed his enthusiasm. The Sarraut government got his qualified support; he grudgingly approved inaction on the occupation of the Rhineland. He was honest enough to say that the results of the elections appalled him; although he himself scarcely suffered—his share of the vote fell from 42.5 per cent to 40.5 per cent—the three western Breton departments lost seven Radical deputies. He must have been secretly pleased, however, when three of the four enemies to the west—Lorgeré, Le Gac, and Cornu— were defeated, and a friend of his, Pierre Serandour, elected. Geistdoerfer was curiously indifferent to the Blum government. The strikes and the Spanish Civil War aroused some interest, but were soon dropped. By October he was saying that the government was enfeebled,[55] and he made some veiled criticisms of the Communists.

By spring 1937 he was definitely disillusioned.[56] He attacked the Socialists: "Even at the grass-roots level, in the provincial branches, Socialism is led by young incompetents who have no experience or authority, and who too easily confuse the general interest with personal interest or ambition, democracy with demagogy, doctrine with method."[57] While the Blum ministry was falling, he wrote advocating the use of the little colonies as air bases (St.-Pierre and Miquelon?

Against whom?), describing the view of France from New York, and paying tribute to Lamennais. If Blum was neglected, Chautemps was utterly ignored. His only mention came with his fall.[58] For the rest, Geistdoerfer remained uninterested in national affairs. He seemed to think some sort of Union Nationale was necessary following the Anschluss,[59] but Daladier's government did not win his allegiance. At first it, too, was ignored for cider, potatoes, and the merchant marine.[60] Munich aroused him, and he opposed the settlement.[61] And after the Reynaud decrees, the visit of Ribbentrop to Paris, and the crushing of the general strike of November 30, 1938, Geistdoerfer's opposition to the Daladier government became total.[62] "For those who want to remain faithful to the traditional policy of the Radical party, it is impossible to follow the government . . . on foreign or domestic policy."[63] "The decree-laws of the Daladier government were improvised, poorly studied, and poorly conceived, and they are disorganizing the national life."[64] By summer 1939, opposition to the government could not be carried on by any patriotic Frenchman, and so gradually he lapsed once again into simple regionalism.

The war came, and Dinan was occupied; in December 1940, Geistdoerfer was ousted as mayor. After the war, he continued to publish his newspaper, but he no longer had any effective political power. His bitterness now focused on René Pleven. He claimed that if he were still in politics, he would be a "progressiste" of the Cot variety—that is, a near-Communist.

II

The Charente-Inférieure was another Radical world entirely from Brittany; the embattled anti-clericalism of a Catholic region is here replaced by the tranquility of a local Radicalism whose battles had been won by Emile Combes at the turn of the century, and whose politicians were serenely furnishing France with her governors. Here, 52,000 Radical votes were cast in 1932, making it the fourth strongest Radical department in the nation, surpassed only by the Seine, the Rhône, and the Seine-Inférieure; five out of six deputies were Radicals; the department boasted the largest federation in France of the Ligue des Droits de l'Homme, with 8,000 members;[65] and it was a stronghold of Freemasonry, three deputies, André Hesse, William Bertrand, and Théophile Longuet, being Masons.[66]

The Charente-Inférieure is a long, diversified department whose major city, La Rochelle, is in the far north, whose southern extremity, Jonzac, is closer to Bordeaux, whose eastern extremity looks inland toward Cognac. The deputies of the department reflected this diversity. James Sclafer and Maurice Palmade were conservative, Bertrand and Hesse moderate, and Longuet extreme left. Because of the superabundance of talent, the federation was not dominated by any single figure. There were five strong personalities—the senators Gustave Perreau and Fernand Chapsal, and Hesse, Palmade, and Bertrand. Chapsal was never a member of the Radical party in Paris, but belonged to the local Republican Committee of Saintes. The Federation of the Charente-Inférieure usually met twice a year, more often in election years. Its primary functions were to endorse the decisions made by the local committees and to give the more important party workers the feeling that they were participating in decision-making. The local organizations were not impressive; there was no official Radical committee in Saintes until 1937; in Jonzac there was only a Committee of Republican Action that apparently was not directly affiliated with the party.[67] In Saintes and Marennes there were a few strong personalities among the party workers—Pérault, Jean Hay, and Castanet—who stood out from the mass, but in general the deputy was in complete and unchallenged control of his electoral situation. The Radical party in the Charente-Inférieure was essentially a confederation of autonomous committees. One body, though, had considerable power—the gathering of Radical senatorial electors who met before each election to choose a candidate. Since the Radicals had an absolute majority, this group's choice was equivalent to election. The purpose of these meetings was to prevent mistakes in the always tricky senatorial elections.*

The characters and positions of the deputies differed markedly. Hesse and Bertrand were smooth professionals. Hesse was a Parisian lawyer who before World War I had come down to La Rochelle to win a seat. This he managed by endearing himself to the members of

---

* Senatorial elections were settled by a complex three-ballot runoff between rival lists of candidates. Between the ballots the least successful candidates withdrew. Since the election took place at the Prefecture of the department, and since tickets could be split and all the several hundred electors were present and milling about between ballots, if the first ballot was not decisive for all or part of the list, frantic on-the-spot maneuvering took place. In many departments where the majority of electors were Radicals or related sorts of Republicans, it had become the custom to hold a preliminary election among these electors so that animosities could work themselves out harmlessly and the Senate seats would be safeguarded from the reactionary opposition.

the powerful rural cooperative movement, acting as their lawyer without charge. He was vice-president of the Chamber of Deputies and had been minister twice. Bertrand, as one of Chautemps's favorites, was the only deputy in the department to be openly associated with any of the leaders; he was first undersecretary of state and then minister frequently. Both inclined very gently to the left.

Palmade, too, held cabinet posts, but was conservative, especially on financial questions. A professor at the University of Bordeaux, he was the first Radical to be faced with the problem of balancing the budget in the 1932 Chamber. He apparently wielded a great personal authority over his Charentais peasants.

Sclafer, also very conservative, was a deputy of the fourth rank. He never made any stir in the Chamber; the only remarkable fact about him was that his behavior in Paris was much further to the left than his outspoken anti-Communism and anti-Socialism at home, a discrepancy for which he was occasionally attacked. Sclafer had an admirable organization within his constituency and managed to keep a close hold on it.

Longuet, in contrast, was a peasant and an intransigent left-wing Radical of the old school—he was 66 in 1932. No Radical in the Chamber had a more consistent left-wing voting record. He opposed Doumergue, Laval, and Daladier with an equally dogged persistence. Daladier, in return, used against him the most terrible of ministerial weapons, one we have already seen employed in Brittany: he forbade the Minister of the Navy, Campinchi, to go to St.-Jean-d'Angély to dedicate a monument to Emile Combes.[68] All these deputies were elected by 1924 at the latest, and thus dominated the inter-war period until, at the very end, many of them were moved up to the Senate in a general shift to make room for younger men in the Chamber.

The Radicals of the Charente-Inférieure drifted into the 1930's with the complacency of a party sure of its pre-eminence. The left-wing opposition was desultory and declining, the right was easily bested, the issues were old, and the only causes of conflict were personal antagonism and the traditional rivalry between the provinces of Aunis and Saintonge. Sclafer and Palmade were outspoken conservatives (the Socialists claimed that Palmade was supported by the Union des Intérêts Economiques[69]), Longuet was very far to the left, and Hesse and Bertrand were in the middle; yet all got along well in a smoothly functioning federation. The electoral graphs for all five deputies are

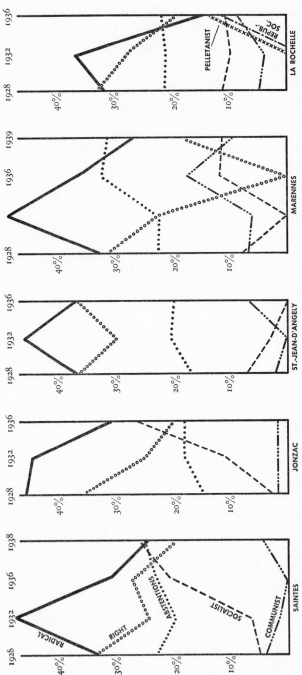

These graphs represent the election returns in the Charente-Inférieure in the 1930's. The graphs for Saintes and Jonzac illustrate the dilemma of the Radical deputy who chose the conservative alternative. In Saintes, from 1928 to 1938, the Radicals lost 21% of the electorate to the Socialists and gained about 12% from the right. Similarly, in Jonzac, the Radicals lost 25% of the electorate to the Socialists and gained roughly 15% from the right. St.-Jean-d'Angély, by contrast, is typical of constituencies with extreme-left-wing Radical deputies. From 1928 to 1936, there is little change; they defended their position well against the parties to their left, and the voters they had momentarily gained from the right in 1932 were once more pared away. Marennes's record shows a combination of the two above trends. Bertrand was a moderate, so the evolution from 1928 to 1936 is similar to that of Saintes and Jonzac: his electorate is well displaced to the right by 1936. In 1939, however, Bertrand is replaced by the left-wing Hay, and the right-wingers that Bertrand had won by his conservatism return to the right-wing candidate. Hay wins back about half the left-wingers who deserted in 1936, but he is far from re-establishing the Radical domination of the left that existed in 1928. Neither the right-wing nor left-wing alternative was attractive enough to maintain the Radical position. La Rochelle, finally, exemplifies the disastrous impact on the Radical vote of a split in the party. The triangular Radical pattern, peaking in 1932, of four of the five examples was repeated in the great majority of Radical constituencies throughout the country, and illustrates as well as anything the real electoral resurgence of 1932 at the expense of both right and left, followed by the electoral decline of 1936 chiefly in favor of the left, but often in favor of the right as well.

remarkably similar (see opposite); with the exception of Sclafer, all of them gained considerable numbers of votes in the 1932 elections. The first two years of the legislature that followed were politically prosperous: Palmade and Bertrand were ministers, and Hesse was a vice-president of the Chamber. The principal form of political activity was banquets. There was little unemployment, and social unrest was nonexistent.

The Stavisky scandal and February Sixth shattered this peace. The Federation of the Charente-Inférieure was torn apart, with schisms and exclusions engendering a rapid evolution of local Radicalism. After 1934, the electoral destinies of the five deputies diverged sharply.

The effect of the Stavisky scandal was profound, since André Hesse, as one of the principal political culprits, was expelled from the party at the Congress of Clermont-Ferrand in 1934. He was never expelled from the local federation, and was even to run as the official Radical candidate in the elections of 1936, with the endorsement of national headquarters, which had officially expelled him. His influence, none-theless, was diminished.

The Federation of La Rochelle had always been the most democrati-cally run of all those in the department; Hesse had not been a dictator, and, indeed, was not even president, that being the position of Senator Perreau. With Hesse in disgrace, two party workers, of equally un-pleasant character, emerged to take his place: Declie on the extreme left, and Miaux on the extreme right. The ideological division be-tween these two gentlemen was confused by a purely personal one: Miaux supported André Hesse; Declie opposed him. Hesse, on the other hand, had such a pleasant personality, in comparison with the two leading party workers, that left and right preferred him to the two faction leaders. Such is the nature of local ideological groupings. The tensions between these two leaders resulted in the Radicals of La Rochelle lurching first to the left, then to the right, and finally split-ting right down the middle.

The riots of February Sixth profoundly shocked public sentiment in La Rochelle, and the left-wing Radicals, under the leadership of De-clie, promptly joined two massive demonstrations at La Rochelle, the first on February 11 with 5,000 participants, and the second on Febru-ary 12 with 2,000 participants. The report of the Radical Committee meeting that month ran: "Important decisions were taken about com-mon action with all the organizations of the left, without exception,

. . . that is to say, with the Socialists and the Communists, all for the defense of the French Republic."[70] A grass-roots Popular Front emerged as an immediate response to the riots, 16 months before the real thing. The newly united left organized frenetically, sent teams of orators throughout the department—18 on one occasion—broke up meetings of the Jeunesses Patriotes, and generally showed a degree of political vigor quite exceptional in the provinces. For the Radicals, this period ended with the Congress of Clermont-Ferrand, which endorsed "the Truce" the national party had concluded with the right after February Sixth and encouraged the right-wingers within the federation to counterattack. The forces were essentially stalemated by the beginning of the summer, with the Popular Front Radicals unsuccessful in their attempt to drive André Hesse out of the federation.[71] The attitude of these left-wingers toward the Doumergue government is very interesting: at the beginning, although they demonstrated with the Communists and Socialists against the Leagues and February Sixth, at the same time they praised Doumergue; it was only later that they began to identify him with the Leagues.[72]

In September 1934, the two forces met again, and after a turbulent discussion the left was strong enough to have a motion voted against the Truce.[73] By February 1935, however, the right-wing Miaux forces had seized control of the federation. The left-wing Declie forces established their own committee. The departmental federation, under Longuet, tried to conciliate the two rival camps. Finally the party in Paris sent out Ernest Perney to arbitrate; the Miaux forces legitimately triumphed in a face-to-face vote—87 to 64—and Declie immediately seceded from the party to form a local section of the Parti Camille Pelletan.[74] The two wings continued to battle each other until the election of 1936, although by the fall of 1935 the Popular Front impetus within the party was sufficiently strong to bring even the Miaux committee to uneasy terms with it.[75]

The internal strain was not so severe in the other arrondissements, where the deputies' honor and vigor were intact, but they all now headed off in their own directions. Sclafer seemed pleased by February Sixth; his paper said that the Socialists bore the responsibility for the riots, and, anyhow, the budget could at last be balanced.[76] He continued to be a faithful supporter of right-wing governments until the end. He was henceforth labeled a Lavalist, and was an unquestioning anti-Popular Front Radical. Palmade followed a somewhat similar course, although not quite so intransigently, since he voted against Laval at the end of December 1935. Longuet, on the other hand, opposed Doumergue, Flandin, and Laval to the limits of his ability. Bertrand was in a more ticklish situation: he was not, initially, nearly so conservative as Palmade or Sclafer; his newspaper was surprisingly hostile to February Sixth[77] and even published the protest of the Young Turks. Yet he himself went into the Doumergue government and remained there until Herriot withdrew in January 1936. His position as one of Doumergue's ministers, however, forced him more and more to the conservative side.

The elections of 1936 reflected these divergences. Longuet fought with the Popular Front, Palmade and Sclafer against it. (These two had Socialists against them on the second ballot, and the right withdrew in their favor.) Bertrand had no candidate of the right opposing him, so his campaign was run strictly against the Socialists, though it was much more restrained than the vocal anti-Communism of Palmade and Sclafer. Bertrand and Sclafer complained about left-wing violence breaking up their meetings. La Rochelle was again the most interesting constituency. Hesse was, as he said, a "Radical anti-fascist" candidate, but the three other candidates to his left solemnly declared that they would not withdraw in his favor under any circumstances. There were a Socialist and a Communist, and a candidate of the Declie Pelletanist federation, René Château. Here the full incoherence of the Radical situation came out: Hesse, expelled from the party, was its candidate; Château, a left-wing renegade from the party, elected against the official Radical candidate, went to sit with the Radical Group in Paris. Hesse had not even campaigned for fear of the violence he might run into. Nonetheless, he still managed to come first out of five candidates on the left on the first ballot, which shows the remarkable hold that the man had over his followers; he had no chance, however, against the Popular Front forces, and withdrew in favor of Château.[78]

After the elections of 1936, the same general drift occurred within the federation as within the party generally. There was considerable alarm over the strikes.[79] The Miaux federation in La Rochelle turned to an ever more voluble anti-Communism, and formed a section of the Jeunesses Radicales in February 1937.[80] The Radical awakening of 1937 aroused the Charente-Inférieure, and a vast series of demonstrations and lectures took place throughout the spring. Then, since everyone seemed to feel that Radical demonstrations were tiresome, the

Radicals reverted to the more congenial semi-annual banquet-meeting pattern.[81] Bertrand moderated the anti-Popular Front drive and managed to keep the federation from openly breaking with the Front on the occasion of the cantonal elections of 1937, despite the emphatic hostility of the professional anti-Communists.[82] But by the following spring the federation was in open rebellion.

The by-election of Saintes in 1938 was one of the milestones in the disintegration of the Popular Front. Palmade had moved up to the Senate and had to be replaced. On the first ballot, the Socialist outdistanced the Radical, but the Radicals refused to withdraw, by a vote of 157 to seven. The Socialists in Paris put pressure on the Radicals, and so the Bureau of the party officially ordered the Radical candidate to withdraw, an action that the federation refused to consider. It was an open fight between Radicals and Socialists, the right-wing candidate withdrawing in favor of the Radical. The executive committee of the Radical federation voted to maintain the candidature, adding, significantly, that it had noted the invitation of the Bureau of the Executive Committee to withdraw, and that the Bureau's "benevolent tone" had not been overlooked.[83] The Radical won. Two other Radical deputies followed Palmade into the Senate in 1938 and 1939. Bertrand was replaced by the left-winger Hay, in a clear triumph of personality over the conservative tendencies of his federation, which was unanimously hostile to his politics (he had been one of the seven who voted to withdraw in favor of the Socialists).[84] Sclafer was not replaced because of the coming of the war.

By the end of the period, the Radicals had generally been transformed into a party of the right. Only Longuet remained a traditional representative of Radicalism, and he was consequently driven out of the federation in 1939. His letter of resignation shows the fate of traditional Radicalism in the dying years of the Republic:

I find it unthinkable that the question of discipline should be raised against a republican who has never wavered, against a Radical-Socialist who is faithful to the doctrine of Emile Combes [a Charentais], who has never allied with the right, and never bargained with it, while the same question of discipline has never been raised against the so-called Radicals who, under the Doumergue and Laval ministries, allied not only with reactionary parties, but even with the friends of the rioters of February Sixth. Among those who accused me, or who saw fit to make excuses for me, at the Congress of Saintes, I cannot forget that there were some who, according to circumstances, were now ministers of Union Nationale, now ministers of the Popular Front [Bertrand], and who are prepared to become at any moment ministers of any other government that will have them. . . . I can no longer conceal by my presence in this federation the failure of Radicalism or its increasing fusion with the forces and doctrines of reaction.[85]

This last lament by Longuet concludes the examination of the structure, thought, and style of the Radical party. What follows is an account of the party in action, a term that suggests a more coherent pattern of behavior than there really was. Decisions had to be made, so in one way or another politicians usually got around to making them; but these decisions were often of singularly little importance, even for the politicians themselves. Michel Geistdoerfer was far more disturbed by a snub from the Minister of Education than by half a dozen governmental crises. Political action was fragmentary, incoherent, unplanned. Purpose was generally lacking. Politics was a day-to-day business whose form was more important than its content, and the Radicals were the businessmen of French politics.

The Radicals were a collection of politicians masquerading as a party. Their behavior was anarchic; their thought anachronistic. They claimed to represent the country, but in the relatively unarticulated political structure of the time their representative role was small. They claimed to defend the little man, but were compromised with the big. They claimed to embody progress, but they defended the most archaic elements of society and resisted modernization. They claimed to be rationalists, yet their action was unreasonable. Their politics had little to do with the great issues of the time. For most Frenchmen, politics meant a system of spoils, and at best a public commitment to a view of life, but not action in the world. The Radicals shared this attitude, and in the narrative that follows, the Radical party must not be taken for more than it really was.

PART TWO

The End of the Radical Republic

CHAPTER 4

The Enjoyment of Power, 1932–34

The period beginning with the elections of 1932 was brought to a violent end in February 1934. The riots of February Sixth transformed French politics, inaugurating a period of uncertainty that has not yet ended. The riots are justly regarded as a decisive event in French history, yet few historians have paid much attention to their political origins. John Marcus rightly stresses that the riots acted as a crystallizing agent for a diffuse public frustration, but claims that this frustration was caused by the economic crisis; the many political causes he cites all date from January 1934. Goguel asks what caused the riots, but ends by discussing only the intentions of their organizers.

However, the habit of concentrating upon immediate causes has recently shown signs of giving way: René Rémond, in an excellent article, observes that it is necessary to go back to the elections of 1932 to understand the riots: "The right did not like being kept out of power: it had decided to do everything to get back in. It could do so only by disrupting the majority of the left, by separating the Radicals from the Socialists, as it had in 1926."² The right certainly was the most obvious agent of the assault on the parliamentary majority: first, by systematically obstructing the majority within and outside of parliament for twenty months; second, by organizing or supporting the riots themselves. Yet, as we shall see, the greater responsibility lies with the left—and, within the left, with the Radical party. The problems of the legislature of 1932 were such that, given the nature of the Radical party, a violent solution was scarcely to be avoided.

The riots themselves came as an overwhelming surprise to almost everyone, even to their organizers. They seem to epitomize the unforeseen, catastrophic event. Yet, for the few who cared to analyze the nature of the legislature, they were the logical denouement of the elections. In June 1932, an anonymous former minister made this startling prediction:

[Herriot] is always helpless in the face of reality. He plays up to the public; but the cascades of ministries will begin: ministers of finance will be changed like shirts,* and all this will finish up heavens knows where, . . . *in riots,* in [a coup d'état]. . . . Let's not joke. In 1924, I was not ready for this sort of thing. In 1932, I will be the first to call for decisive action, *for a Doumergue ministry.*[3]

Such a prediction did not take place in vacuo, of course, being part of the very skillful campaign of the right to promote Doumergue, and up to a point, therefore, a self-fulfilling prophecy. Even aside from the role of the right, however, a violent solution was to be expected. The riots fulfilled a necessary political function, permitting the contradictions that the parliamentary system had created, but could not solve, to be overcome, and providing the psychological shock necessary to bring to an end the twenty-month incoherence produced by the elections of 1932.

The elections returned a majority dominated by the Radicals and the Socialists. These two parties were incapable either of working together or of renouncing alliance. The difficulty was particularly pronounced among the Radicals. In the conditions created by the elections, the Radicals were obliged, by the very nature of their party, to ally with the Socialists and at the same time to practice a policy unacceptable to them. Because the crises of the 1930's made immediate solutions necessary, something had to give. The normal instrument for the resolution of such a contradiction was the governmental crisis; yet, since five traditional crises had proved too weak to overcome the ingrained habits of the Radicals, it clearly required a super-crisis, the violence of February Sixth, to force them to choose between incompatible policies. If Daladier had resisted the rioters, the contradiction would have been resolved, for the Socialists would have entered the government, and political, rather than financial, problems would have dominated—not an impossible outcome, but, as we shall see, rather improbable given the character of the Radical party. Daladier did not resist, and the impasse was broken by bringing the right into the ma-

---

* There were to be six ministers of the budget in 18 months.

jority and driving the Socialists into opposition. The alternation between stalemate and traumatic transformation through crisis, a condition that has since become so familiar in French politics, was just then becoming established, and so the psychological impact of February Sixth was profound.

I

All the problems of the legislature derived from the composition of the Chamber. The elections of 1932 returned a left-wing majority of unprecedented strength. If the left had not won, there would have been no February Sixth; even if the Radicals' victory had been less decisive, they would have been able to escape graciously from the suffocating alliance with the Socialists. But the numbers of the several blocs within the Chamber made the search for a viable majority at once the dominating concern and impossible to achieve. The problem can best be illustrated graphically: on page 106, A shows the composition of the Chamber; B, C, and D show the three majorities that were formed at various times.

The majority of the left, called the Cartel des Gauches, and the majority of the right, called the Union Nationale, were both large enough to ensure a stable government, while the majority of the center, known as Concentration, was not. Whereas the two comfortable majorities were incapable of reaching agreement on a coherent policy, the majority of Concentration, which could have done so, remained so narrow that it never became a real political force.* Yet because the center parties were in basic agreement on key policies, the legislature continued to place great hopes in a majority of Concentration, hopes that transcended even the crisis of February Sixth. This unfortunate political situation resulted from the elections of 1932, not only because of the new power distribution within the Chamber, but also because of the positions taken by the principal blocs during the electoral campaign.

It was not then understood that election results are extremely equivocal, and consequently the elections were generally misinterpreted. It was agreed, first, that the country had massively repudiated the right

---

* Although the Radicals agreed with much of the center and right on financial policy, and although their foreign policy did not differ strikingly, they felt, at least, that it was incompatible with the foreign policy of the right.

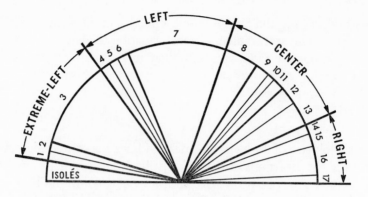

A. COMPOSITION OF THE CHAMBER

Extreme Left
  1. Communists
  2. Unité Ouvrière
  3. Socialists

Left
  4. Parti Socialiste Français
  5. Parti Républicain Socialiste
  6. Gauche Indépendante
  7. Radicals

Center
  8. Gauche Radicale
  9. Indépendants de Gauche
  10. Républicains du Centre
  11. Démocrates Populaires
  12. Républicains de Gauche
  13. Centre Républicain

Right
  14. Action Economique, Sociale, et Paysanne
  15. Parti Républicain et Social
  16. URD (Fédération Républicaine)
  17. Indépendants

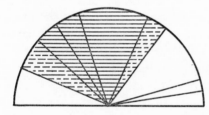

B. CARTEL MAJORITY

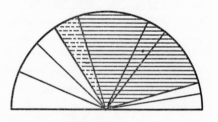

C. CONCENTRATION MAJORITY

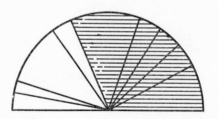

D. UNION NATIONALE MAJORITY

and, second, that the Radicals and Socialists had been mandated to work together.[4] When they did not, there was a widespread belief that the verdict of universal suffrage had been ignored. Were the people's wishes not heeded? What, indeed, were the people's wishes? What did the electors pronounce upon?

There were two campaigns, quite distinct and almost unrelated: the national and the local. The national campaign consisted of oratorical jousts between the leaders of the great blocs. The other parties tried to force the Radicals to take a position. Both Tardieu and Blum wanted the elections to be an unequivocal pronouncement one way or the other. Blum demanded an alliance between the Radicals and the Socialists on a limited program. Tardieu, for the outgoing government, proposed that the Radicals join with the right to oppose Socialism.[5] But Herriot was too skillful a politician to accept such utopianism, however statesmanlike it might seem. These demands annoyed him and the Radical party. Such unambiguousness was not only alien to their way of thinking, but politically unrealistic. At first, Herriot ignored the challenge, but finding the silence embarrassing, he produced a number of justifications. At La Tour du Pin he said: "I have not expressed myself on the parliamentary formations of the future. No one has the right to mortgage the decisions of universal suffrage at this point. . . . When universal suffrage has spoken, we will have a month to examine . . . the results of the battle."[6]

This had the political philosophy of Burke's Bristol speech behind it, of course, and it would be unjust to say that Herriot was not sincere. There were, however, other considerations: first, the loosely articulated structure of the party meant that any commitment made by Herriot would not greatly affect the local arrangements made by the deputies. If he had committed himself to an alliance with Tardieu, he would have been placed in an impossible position: "If we had listened to [Tardieu's] appeal," Herriot said, "does he think that our troops would have followed us? They most certainly would not."[7] The spontaneous and almost universal alliance between the Radicals and Socialists following the first ballot, without any clear instructions from Paris, amply demonstrates the point. The overtures from the Socialists were more important than those from the right, since it was clear that most of the local elections would find the Radicals and Socialists allied. Why, then, not accept a consequent governmental alliance, as Blum proposed? Herriot's personal attitude and his estimation of the election results led him to reject such a scheme. It seems clear, above all, that the victory was greater than anyone's expectations,[8] and it was on lesser expectations that Herriot's calculations were based. He antici- pated, it would seem, around 130 Radicals and perhaps 100 Socialists, not a majority even when the left-wing splinter groups are included.[9] With such figures, the center's support would be required for an Her- riot ministry; and in the interview in *La Volonté* cited above, Herriot said he would need 350 to 400 votes—that is, most of the center—for a workable government. This centrist vote would obviously not be forthcoming if Herriot agreed upon a program with the Socialists. All these calculations were undone by the magnitude of the left-wing majority.

The second factor in Herriot's reluctance to commit himself to the Socialists was personal. He was terrified, as we have seen, by the finan- ciers, and was willing to do anything to placate them, which meant keeping the Socialists out of the government. He disliked the Social- ists, moreover, from his experiences in Lyons, where they were his principal opposition, and from the 1924–26 episode. He stated publicly during the campaign "that if he were given the opportunity to form a government supported only by the Socialists, he would refuse, and would counsel his party to refuse."[10]

Apart from a between-the-ballots appeal by the party to observe "re- publican discipline," there was nothing, therefore, in the national cam- paign that committed the party to any post-election alliance.

What of the local campaigns? Do they offer any ground for claim- ing that the electorate had given the party a mandate?* The programs are characteristically vague, noncommittal, and inconclusive. They are

---

* Two principal sources have been used for the campaign: on the one hand, the local press; on the other, the collection of programs—the *Barodet*—and the analysis of the programs in *Journal officiel, Documents parlementaires, 1932.* The newspapers have the advantage of explicitness, the programs of completeness. Programs were phrased in conventional language which requires a considerable expertise to decipher, but which, nonetheless, generally reveals the attitudes of the deputies. Newspapers were far more straightforward. I have used 53 local papers roughly covering 76 constitu- encies; these illuminate the nature of the conflicts within the individual districts. There are, in addition, a number of sociological studies covering relevant districts; but, with the exception of Barral's study of the Isère, these are of limited value for the political historian, for they do not succeed in relating sociological forces to the accidental fea- tures of politics; thus, such an extraordinary election as that of 1932 is almost entirely overlooked. Finally, the nature of the withdrawals can be determined from the figures in Lachapelle, *Elections législatives, 1er et 8 mai, 1932.*

phrased in conventional language and tend to refer to the past rather than the future—i.e., the services the deputy had performed, the speeches he had made, the misdeeds of the outgoing parliament—the future being generally covered in a vow to protect the interests of particular groups.*

A few specific issues, however, are included. Only 41 of the 157 statements omitted programmatic content altogether. Of the rest, only 15 made concrete proposals, the remainder contenting themselves with generalities like promising to "fight the economic crisis." It might be expected that the content of the programs would relate to the political views of their authors, and that a left-wing deputy would produce a more radical program than a right-wing one. Such is not the case. Of the four deputies who specifically adopted the socializing program of the CGT, for example, one was conservative and three were moderate. The proposal that the state control monopolies was advanced by eight conservatives, six moderates, 12 moderate-lefts and nine left-wingers, figures roughly proportional to the total strength of these four groups. Two deputies said they accepted the Radical program, and about a score wanted public works. The most frequent economic proposal was the traditional Radical farm policy of credit, cooperatives, and tariffs; but again there was no clear preponderance of any one political group. The study of the newspapers reinforces these findings; nowhere was there emphasis on social or economic reforms, even when it was considered worthwhile to include something about them in a program; the left wing demanded economic reforms no more often than the

---

* The following list for 1936, though even more heterogeneous than the average 1932 list, gives an idea of the campaign material:

> Industriels, Fabricants, Armateurs; Eleveurs et Cultivateurs
> Commerçants, Marchands ou Représentants Hôteliers, Cafetiers
> Restaurateurs ou Détaillants, Artisans, Employés;
> Ouvriers, Marins et Pêcheurs, Fonctionnaires
> ou Agents des services publics, Retraités
> Pensionés et Rentiers, Propriétaires
> Locataires, Combattants, Mutilés
> Veuves et Victimes de Guerre
> Vieillards et Orphelins
> Blessés et Infirmes
> Victimes du Travail!

I remain entirely devoted to your aspirations to establish among all Frenchmen more solidarity and goodness, more harmony and justice.

Eugène Canu, candidate [unsuccessful] in the Pas-de-Calais.

Le Républicain du Pas-de-Calais, April 15, 1936.

right. The Radical electorate, in short, did not speak clearly on these matters.

Two issues, however, were mentioned in most campaigns: finance and foreign affairs. In the latter, 109 deputies favored Herriot's Geneva Protocol: peace was to be maintained by international arbitration and progressive, controlled disarmament.[11] Although substantially different from the Socialist proposals of simple disarmament, the Radical stand clearly reflected left-wing internationalism. In retrospect, proposing disarmament in 1932 may seem foolish, yet, from all appearances, it was an issue about which Radicals felt strongly; it was over disarmament that the left wing of the party revolted in June and July 1932.

As for finance, the deputies' pronouncements are particularly important in view of the tyranny the financial question was to exert over the legislature. Ninety statements were made in favor of budgetary deflation of one sort or another; not one was made against it. These ninety reflected the following support: 68 per cent of the conservatives, 55 per cent of the moderates, 59 per cent of the moderate left, and 39 per cent of the left.[12] Forty-four deputies wanted immediate budgetary equilibrium: 35 per cent of the conservatives, 34 per cent of the moderates, 22 per cent of the moderate left, and 21.5 per cent of the left.[13] What is remarkable in these figures is not that there is a slight decline in enthusiasm for the balanced budget as one moves to the left, but rather that such a large proportion of the left wanted deflation at all. Ignorance of the effects of deflation can scarcely be pleaded, since Germany's experience had been carefully watched, and the pressure groups, particularly the fonctionnaires' union, kept the politicians informed. For example, the fonctionnaires sent a delegation to the government in June to point out the vanity of deflation, "a policy that has not succeeded in any country."[14] It is unclear, therefore, whether the divergence between left-wing sentiments and right-wing policy among the left-wing deputies was caused by an inability to understand elementary economic facts, a need to coddle an electorate whose material interests were opposed to their political beliefs, or some other factor. But it is clear that the Radical electorate, if it demanded anything, demanded a left-wing foreign policy and a right-wing financial policy, a contradiction that was to be the source of many troubles.

If we look beyond programmatic content to the question of alliances and the atmosphere of local campaigns—matters that were, undoubt-edly, in the minds of voter and candidate of much greater weight—we find an almost total absence of any clear pronouncement in favor of forming a government with the Socialists. In fact, only three depu-ties mentioned the Socialists by name, all vituperatively. Thirty-nine others mentioned some sort of formula for a government: 11 against the right, or reaction, or dictatorship; eight for a Union des Gauches; eight for a union of republicans; four for a union of democrats; and two for Concentration. This meant very little. Yet, if we look at the campaign material in the newspapers, the pro-Socialist bias is unmis-takable. There were, of course, a few constituencies—notably in the Aude—where the Socialists were the enemy; but everywhere else, the campaign was right versus left, with neither of the terms defined, but, in context, understood. Even such conservatives as Pierre Cazals in Ariège and Charles Bedu in Cher attacked only the right.[15] This una-nimity, in striking contrast to the divisions of the 1936 elections, pro-duced an impression of leftward orientation which, though unspecific and contradictory, was of fundamental political importance. In spite of subsequent claims that the election results implied no consequent political formation*—claims which, technically, were correct—there was the widespread conviction, extending even to the conservatives, that they did just that. This is, of course, one of the dilemmas of elec-tions: the parties and candidates speak obscurely and with many voices, but the electorate's response seems so starkly unambiguous that it conveys the irresistible impression that a program has been endorsed.

The elections were an extraordinary victory for the Radicals; for the first time in many years they lost no votes to the Socialists, and they gained 200,000 from the moderates. Although the Socialists picked up 260,000 Communist votes, they were concerned by the strength of the Radicals, who seemed to be about to consolidate themselves as a pow-erful, left-wing liberal party.[16] This trend toward moderation within the electorate during a period of acute economic crisis is rather sur-prising.† Can it be explained by the crisis within the Communist

---

* Chautemps, for example, asserted that "universal suffrage has not called for a politi-cal formation of social warfare, agitation, and impotence"—i.e., a majority of the left —in a speech at Maves, Loir-et-Cher, reported in *Le Temps,* July 25, 1932.

† Some electoral studies have shown considerable local suffering from the crisis com-bined with a shift of votes from the Communists and Socialists to the Radicals: Phi-lippe Bernard, p. 228; Peltier, p. 49.

party?[17] By the long opposition of the Radical party, during which a new image may have been created? By the charisma of Herriot? One can only speculate.

The high hopes raised by the elections were quickly frustrated. Why? According to Alexander Werth, the 1932 election was "a sterile victory, since the Socialists, led by the extremely doctrinaire Léon Blum, would on no account enter into a government coalition with the Radicals."[18] Such a judgment is one-sided at best. The Socialists' responsibility need not concern us here, since the absurdity of their attitude toward participation is well-known; it need only be noted and regretted. Their role was, in any case, of only secondary importance, since Herriot, the only possible Premier-designate, had no intention of offering them participation on any terms. Would the situation have been different had another man, Daladier for instance, been leader of the Radicals at that time? Herriot's policy was personal, and it disappointed even some conservatives within the party; by the time Daladier came to present the left-wing alternative, eight long months had passed, and a vicious exchange of recriminations had begun. Yet Daladier's attempt to bring the Socialists into the government in January 1933 was so easily thwarted that it seems likely that no greater success at achieving a viable Union des Gauches could have been expected in June 1932.

In any event, no attempt was made. Between the elections at the beginning of May and the adjournment of parliament in the middle of July, a complex maneuver took place that clearly defined the political possibilities and foreshadowed the impotence of the legislature.

Herriot had fought the elections in anticipation of a majority of Concentration, but unexpectedly a strong Cartel majority had been returned. This made Concentration unlikely, but not numerically impossible. The month of May was spent in one vast, unpublicized intrigue in which the three blocs—the Radicals, the Socialists, and the center—fought among themselves about what was to be done.

More interesting than the Socialists' division into participationists and anti-participationists is the division among the centrists. One wing, led by Flandin and François Piétri, wanted to entice the Radicals away from the Socialists, a course which, according to Piétri's later statement, "seemed, in fact, to correspond closely to the secret wishes of most Radicals, who rather wanted to free themselves from the insolent tutelage of the Socialists."[19] This wing quickly initiated a press campaign that blandly asserted the elections had decided nothing. "And now it is up to the victorious party to declare its preferences: either with the republicans of the center left, or with the revolutionaries of the extreme left."[20] They buttered up the Radicals: "If the Radical party alone were concerned, no doubt its desire [for financial prudence] would suffice to calm the fears that the electoral campaign may have caused. Among its members are technicians whose authority is recognized, and whose arrival in power would certainly give no cause for anxiety. . . . [The uneasiness] results from the confusion that persists in the relations of the Radicals with the Socialists."[21]

The deputies in the other wing of the center, led by Tardieu, rejected this tactic flatly. They felt that unwavering opposition on their part would finally force the Radicals to break with the Socialists. The principal center group, the Républicains de Gauche, was evenly divided on these tactics at the time of the presentation of the Herriot government, and the Tardieu faction seceded to form a new group, the Centre Républicain, dedicated to intransigent opposition. This detachment of some thirty votes was to make a workable Concentrationist majority impossible.[22]

The Radical Concentrationist wing supported the Concentrationists wholeheartedly. Edmond Pfeiffer, an influential party worker, wrote, "Any majority that is supposed to be 'Cartellist' seems improbable."[23] Le Quotidien proclaimed: "Concentration, which we have unswervingly supported, . . . is today shown to be an inescapable necessity."[24] During this barrage, most of the left wing of the party showed itself totally unaware of what was happening; none of the fifty provincial papers consulted for this crucial period indicates any understanding that the electoral victory was being sabotaged. Toward the end of May, the left-wing deputies belatedly organized an ineffectual opposition, but they never made any contact with the participationist Socialists.[25] The left was decisively outmaneuvered by Herriot.

Herriot's problem was to keep the Socialists out of the government without splitting the Radicals, annoying the electors, or letting the Radicals appear responsible. He succeeded in all three. By convention, it was his duty to offer the Socialists participation, since Radicals and Socialists had fought the election together. He did not want to offer anything, for fear they might accept; he wanted them to submit conditions, which he would then refuse. To accomplish this, he did two things: first, he scrupulously avoided any contact with the Socialist leaders; second, he managed to arrange for the Radicals' Executive Committee, which was to have met before the Socialists' Congress to discuss the conditions of participation, to meet after it. The original date set for the Executive Committee's meeting was May 25, so the Socialists scheduled their Congress for May 29. Then, at a meeting of the Radical Bureau on May 20, the Executive Committee meeting was postponed until May 31. The Socialist Congress was too cumbersome a body to adapt itself easily to this game of "you-first," so it was stuck. The motive for the adjournment was obvious at the time: "The conservatives claim that the Socialists will insist on their program," wrote Bergery, the most ardent of the Radical Cartellists, "and that is the reason my friends and I insist, as strongly as possible, that the Executive Committee meet before the Socialist Congress. And it is also the reason why the 'Concentrationists' are moved to put off, as long as possible, the meeting of the Radicals."[26]

Reports of the Bureau's meeting, which lasted three and a half hours, indicate that it was Herriot who pushed through the adjournment. Herriot himself wrote, "The Socialists who favored participation hoped that we would take the initiative on the resolutions that they were considering. I showed my friends that this procedure seemed dangerous for us, that it would make us seem responsible for the Socialist decision."[27] This postponement was unquestionably the crucial decision. Only after the event, on May 24, did Paul Faure publish his explosive anti-participationist article, which is sometimes blamed for the failure. The left-wing Radicals, aroused too late, published a futile little manifesto,* to which Herriot accurately replied, "The publication of this motion will really change nothing in the internal situation of the party."[28]

The end was simple. The Socialists were forced to make fairly strong demands, or be accused of abandoning their program, and the Radicals had no difficulty in rejecting their proposals. The Socialists sent a delegation from their Congress, which was still in session, to meet with a delegation of the Radicals' Executive Committee. In spite of the fact that the Radical delegation was ultra-conservative in its make-up (Caillaux, Maurice Sarraut, Renoult, and Herriot), Herriot

---

* The authors of the manifesto considered "profoundly disappointing any tactic that, on the morrow of the victory, would attempt to revise the alliance that permitted it, and to include the party whose policy of isolation abroad and deficit financing the people have just condemned" (*Le Temps,* May 29, 1932, p. 6).

permitted no discussion, and when the Socialist proposals (known as Cahiers d'Huyghens) were received,* he apparently refused to let the Radical delegation even consider them. He personally wrote the reply, which he delivered before the Executive Committee, rejecting the Socialist conditions point by point. At no time, therefore, did he negotiate.[29] The Socialists, particularly the participationists, were outraged at such treatment, delegating one of their leading reformists, Pierre Renaudel, to edit their communiqué, which laid the blame squarely upon the Radicals. Since Concentration was impossible, Herriot had to form a purely Radical government, to which the Socialists grudgingly gave their support.

Herriot's strategy was successful, so successful, in fact, that the Socialists have generally borne the onus for non-participation. The immediate disappointment at the failure of the negotiations was softened by the existence of the first "republican" government since 1926.† Nonetheless, there seems to have been a general feeling of regret. The left-wing Radicals were subsequently to lay the blame on their own party,[30] and many moderates concurred. Bertrand, a moderate, wrote: "The Congresses held by the two parties concerned did not, of course, reject [collaboration], which would have been an inconceivable betrayal of their followers, who were still worked up over their common fight, but the parties—*the one and the other*—used so much formalism and reticence and showed, let it be said, so little enthusiasm, that collaboration was not achieved."[31] Similarly, Delbos, another moderate, blamed both parties equally.[32] Even Marchandeau, who was to lead the conservative Radicals from 1934 to 1938, seems to have supported a Radical and Socialist government.[33]

A study of the local press reinforces the impression of disappointment. Of 51 papers examined, eight ignored the issue, and six were equivocal. Of the 37 remaining, 25 favored a government of the left or opposed Concentration; eight were against the Socialists, or in favor of Concentration; and only four blamed the Socialists for the failure.

---

* The Socialist demands were: (1) massive reduction of defense spending; (2) the nationalization of the arms industry and the prohibition of trade in arms; (3) a balanced budget without reduction of social services; (4) measures for control of the banks; (5) creation of national wheat and fertilizer boards; (6) nationalization of the railways; (7) nationalization of the insurance companies; (8) establishment of a forty-hour week; and (9) a general political amnesty. These demands were much stiffer than the program Blum had originally offered the Radicals. See p. 269, note 35.

† Excepting the brief Chautemps and Painlevé governments in the 1928–32 legislature.

Herriot, apparently, was more opposed to Socialist participation than were most of the Radicals, so it can be argued theoretically that he undermined the legislature from its beginning. But, as we shall see, it would have been extremely difficult for the most pro-Socialist Radical to conduct a financial policy acceptable to both parties. The contradiction within the French political system was too profound for a single leader, however perverse, to bear more than a small responsibility for the ensuing chaos.

II

The twenty months following the formation of the Herriot government saw the last genuine manifestation of the Radical Republic. The six governments of this period were so predominantly Radical in composition that the history of the party is inextricably entangled with the broader history of France.[34] The party workers basked in the favors of a recaptured Ministry of the Interior, unaware that their world was coming to an end. The deputies were only a little more conscious of the predicament of their party and of France. The ministers went about diligently applying outmoded remedies to minor problems. All, in short, seemed perfectly normal.

Yet, curiously, the large left-wing majority was even more impotent than usual. During the first six governments of the 1932 legislature, less was accomplished than during any comparable period in the Third Republic. True, eight financial bills, all essentially alike, were presented to the Chamber, and the three most harmless passed; but three governments were brought crashing down merely for trying to cut the salaries of the fonctionnaires, and two others would have suffered the same fate if other matters had not intervened.

The political record is drearily monotonous: no bills that were not financial, no ministries that were not reshuffles, no legislative action, no reforms, no ideas—only stagnation and the endless repetition of tired speeches. Yet such repetition did not happen by chance: the men involved knew what they were doing. The bill survived unscathed, though the governments perished. Politicians are supposed to avoid difficulties, yet here they kept patiently attacking the same difficulties in the same way, like a man repeatedly crashing his head against a closed door. That a dreary little measure of pay-cuts dominated seven separate bills is more surprising than if each bill had presented a different solution.

The context of this comedy was the Great Depression, which demanded immediate action. In an extraordinary example of mass inconsequence, the nation's whole political effort was concentrated on reducing the pay of the fonctionnaires, with a tenacity that implied this was the crucial issue. No alternative policy, indeed, was offered. In fact, the deficit was so enormous that such minor deflationary measures could have had little effect, yet they were demanded so insistently, by such a large section of the Radical party, that they were politically necessary. But since the Radical ministries required Socialist support, no solid deflationary measures could get passed. Such was the dilemma that hamstrung the legislature.

The period from 1932 to 1934 can be best understood as an unstable equilibrium of conflicting forces, all of which manifested themselves within the Radical party. On the one hand was the indefinable commitment to the left—whether electoral or ideological. This mystique of the left, in spite of its infinite contradictions, was a very strong force. In its most intense form, it pushed the Radicals toward the Cartel alliance. In its more attenuated form, it prevented the alliance of the Radicals with the clerical right in a Union Nationale majority. Herriot, for instance, was anti-Cartellist, but he flatly refused to ally with the right, which was separated from the Radicals, as he said, "by the whole abyss of secularism."[35] The mystique was materially supported by the pressure groups that stood to suffer from measures of financial austerity—the veterans and, more important, the fonctionnaires.

On the other hand were the conservative forces that were trying to break the Cartel. They demanded financial orthodoxy from the Radicals, and had two formidable weapons to enforce it: financial crisis—which had proved itself in 1926—and the Senate, under the indomitable leadership of Caillaux. The right was able, moreover, to use the conservative Radicals in the Chamber to excellent effect—the Radical finance ministers, we have seen, were all conservative, as were the president and *rapporteurs-généraux* of the Finance Committee, Malvy, Lamoureux, and Jacquier. The history of the period from 1932 to 1934 concerns, essentially, the interaction between the mystique of the balanced budget and the mystique of alliance with the left.

Once the Socialist obstacle had been overcome, Herriot was able to form his cabinet, which had probably been settled even before the "negotiations" at the end of May.[36] He had had his way with little opposition until now, but his very success weakened him. His cabinet was poorly constructed, including four members from the previous right-wing government; the 19 Radicals were also predominantly right-wing.[37] The Minister of Finance, Germain-Martin, was orthodoxy itself, and was said to be the nominee of the banks.

Herriot deliberately created this imbalance, in the hope of winning a centrist majority.[38] But, failing in this, he succeeded only in raising considerable difficulties for himself within his own party. The massive entry of the competent moderate Radicals into the government permitted the whole parliamentary apparatus to fall into the hands of the left-wingers. Before the formation of the government, seven out of eight members of the parliamentary Bureau were moderate and conservative;[39] the new Bureau had four left-wingers, including its president, François Albert.[40] Herriot had, therefore, created a cadre for the opposition that was to plague him during the following weeks—a difficulty he could easily have avoided had he neutralized the principal left-wingers by giving them minor cabinet posts. Again, although almost every moderate ministrable was pulled into the government, those few who were left out—Bonnet, Lamoureux, Malvy, and Nogaro—were potentially highly disruptive in their inordinate desire to do anything to become ministers. Blum, when later faced with the phenomenon of Georges Bonnet in search of a portfolio, showed greater sense than Herriot, shipping Bonnet to Washington as ambassador. The conjunction of these two forces resulted in the immediate passage by the Group of a motion that was rather hostile to the government and warned against any attempt at Concentration.

When the government first met the Chamber, its hopes for a centrist majority were quickly shattered by Tardieu's hostility and by some skillful maneuvering by Blum.[41] So Herriot had to manage a Cartel majority with a cabinet more appropriate to Concentration. The already immense difficulties facing any left-wing government at this time were thus compounded by quite unnecessary internal distortions.

Thenceforward, the Herriot government was the object of continual harassment—from the left for being too conservative, and from the conservatives for being too lax. In the process it was reduced to helplessness. Though Herriot chose to fall nobly on the question of repayment of the American war debt, if he had not, he would have fallen ignobly, like all the others, on the financial question.

The principal question now, as for the next 19 months, was the elimination of the deficit. The Finance Minister, Germain-Martin, and the Minister of the Budget, Palmade, chose the orthodox policy of reducing expenses, thus nearly provoking a crisis on June 10, three days after the presentation of the cabinet. When the first measures, including reductions in the pensions and salaries of fonctionnaires, were brought before the cabinet, Daladier, as spokesman for the left, objected so strongly that the two ministers threatened to resign.[42] A bill to balance the budget, which included a 5 per cent reduction of salaries, was placed before the Finance Committee of the Chamber on June 30. Within two days, it was demolished by a coalition of left-wing Radicals and Socialists. Herriot rushed back from the international reparations conference at Lausanne and, by personal magnetism, dissolved the opposition in both the Group and the Finance Committee, and had the crucial measures restored. But the moment he was gone, the bill was amended out of existence. In the end, Herriot was quite unable to get the necessary financial measures past the Chamber and had to resort to borrowing.

Another thread of opposition concerned foreign policy and defense. Immediately after the presentation of his government to the Chamber, Herriot had left for Lausanne, where his rigid attitude on reparations was repugnant to a large number of Radicals. Throughout June, with Herriot abroad, the Chamber was left without anything to do, and the deputies fell to mischief. There was a meeting of the Radical Group on June 28, in which François Albert, Bergery, and Nogaro made inflammatory speeches against Herriot's foreign policy. Bergery went so far as to propose that a delegation be sent to Switzerland to express the party's disapproval of Herriot's behavior. An adjournment and a hasty rally of all loyal deputies prevented this act of treason, but the Herriot forces were unable to elicit a motion of confidence in the government's policy. The forces within the Group were reported to be roughly 50 for Herriot, 50 against, and 60 on the fence.[43] No other Radical Premier of the 1930's was to suffer such widespread opposition from within the party.

The most serious explosion occurred when the two strands of foreign policy and financial policy came together in one of the budgetary provisions. On Blum's suggestion, the Finance Committee had agreed to compensate for the elimination of the salary cuts by suppressing the credits for training the army reserves, thus substituting a very left-wing measure for a classic right-wing measure. This created a ticklish situation, since Herriot was apparently under strong pressure from the Senate and the army not to accept the suppression.[44] Apparently, a face-saving compromise was being worked out when the bill came before the Chamber. In what one moderate Radical called a "coup de théâtre,"[45] Herriot made the restoration of the army credits a matter of confidence. The majority split. The Socialists voted against the government and, more important for us, 33 Radicals abstained and 11 voted against Herriot. Because the Flandin center supported him, Herriot squeezed through with 305 votes, a pure majority of Concentration; but, as Pierre Cot wrote, "It is clear that if it were a matter of creating a [permanent] majority of Concentration, 50 Radicals at least would cry, 'No!'," and the majority would no longer exist.[46]

This disintegration of the Cartel majority was profoundly shocking. Although the Cartel reappeared shortly afterward in a vote on a bond issue to provide the money refused in the budgetary cuts, the left was discouraged. "As I write these lines at the end of this exhausting session," wrote Bertrand, "I cannot but be sad to think of the shock to which the majority was subjected."[47] The provincial press generally passed the matter over in silence. Only two papers dared blame the Socialists. The rest expressed their disappointment. Charles Bedu, a conservative, had a motion passed by his federation in which he "regretted that the question of confidence posed by the government . . . on the army reserves had put disciplined members of the party in a delicate situation with regard to their electoral promises. He respectfully begs President Herriot . . . to conform, in the future, to the decisions of the party Congresses in matters of general policy."[48]

The two-and-a-half-month period between May and the middle of July had decisively tested the opposing parliamentary forces. Herriot had consistently pushed the party as far to the right as he could, temporarily creating the majority of Concentration that he really wanted; but in doing so, he split the party, created mistrust in the regular majority, and proved by the way he achieved it that Concentration was chimerical. And, in spite of all this effort, the financial problem remained unsolved. It seems as if this experience discouraged Herriot from pushing the left again. He was to become lax and feel the consequent wrath of the right. Meanwhile, as La Lumière wrote, the country was "menaced neither by the Union Nationale nor by Concentration, but by the risk of confusion and impotence."[49]

The conflict of factions within the Radical party during the eleven-week period just described shows where the real centers of power within the party lay, and how the party, as an institution, made decisions. Of the five principal bodies, the Conference of the Presidents and Secretaries-General did nothing. The Bureau of the Executive Committee played only a limited role: when Herriot decided on his electoral tactics, he presented them to the Bureau, but did not permit discussion; when he wanted to postpone the meeting of the Executive Committee in May, he had to get the Bureau's consent, but met with no very strong opposition. The third body, the Executive Committee, met once, for the negotiations with the Socialists. Surprisingly, in view of its composition and its later behavior, it offered only minimal resistance to Herriot's schemes. The Congress met only later. Only within the parliamentary Group did Herriot encounter difficulties. On the non-parliamentary party organization, the discontent that Herriot's policy aroused among the Radicals' supporters had not the slightest effect.

The real centers of interest in the struggle within the party were the parliamentary Group, the Finance Committee, and the Senate. The left-wing opposition worked through the Group and the Finance Committee. This opposition was always ad hoc, ephemeral, and only temporarily effective. In May, the crucial month, it was dormant, and after the parliamentary adjournment it dissolved. The deputies dispersed to their arrondissements, and tended to forget the outrages of July in their enjoyment of the tangible benefits of a Radical government in power. The grouping in June and July was an unselfconscious coagulation. There is no evidence that there was anything but the most accidental contact between the various Cartellists during the summer and fall, and it was not until January that there was any comparable regrouping. While the opposition existed, however, it could easily obstruct any positive measures from the government, but was unable to impose its own policies.

The Senate Radicals, on the other hand, were a fairly coherent, constant conservative force, having an enormously effective instrument for imposing conservative policies in their own Finance Committee, presided over by Caillaux. The few Cartellist senators—Emile Lisbonne and Léon Perrier are the most prominent—were without influence. The pressure of the Senate was usually discreet; in July, it defined, for the first time, the permissible limits of laxity.[50] Later it was not to be so polite.

The Finance Committee of the Chamber was the instrument for destroying the government's financial bill in July, yet was also the instrument of conservative pressure on the government in the fall. But more of this apparently contradictory character later.

Finally, among the institutions of the party, there was the annual Congress, which met only after the events so far described.[51] There is no better illustration of the incoherence of the party than this Congress. Yet the façade was impressive enough for *Le Temps* to write on its conclusion that the Radical organization equaled that of the Socialists, and that the party "had thus arrived at a power and effectiveness that must frankly be called impressive."[52]

It is difficult to say what was settled at this Congress. Four main questions were debated, but only on foreign policy was the party's voice clear. Herriot had made a rapid enough swing to the left since the preceding June to be able to accept the two foreign policy reports made by the left-wingers Cot and de Tessan, and there was no opposition.[53] The government's financial policy of deflation, however, was roundly denounced by Mendès-France and Bonnet, without anyone's attempting to defend it—not even Caillaux, who was explicitly called on to speak.[54] A move inspired by Herriot to enforce discipline on the Group was rejected after a concerted defense of parliamentary rights by Zay and Guernut.[55] The most interesting of the four debates was the attack on the government's general policy made by Kayser and Bergery on the first day. Kayser's speech was soberly critical. Bergery's was an aggressive, logical attack on all aspects of the government's policy.[56] The debate never got further than that, for Herriot rose in his wrath to reply to Bergery, who "is not one of those vulgar beings who allows himself to be overwhelmed by the weight of services received."[57]

Herriot's speech deserves study, for it is characteristic of his style, and illuminates the party on which such a style made an immense impression. Its gist was as follows: If he remained silent, he said, it would look as if he were afraid of criticism (applause). Kayser had made a fair attack (which Herriot did not answer), but Bergery had brought in personalities. Were the electors whom Bergery described as discontented perhaps not Radicals, but Communists? (Wild applause.) The cares of government were heavy; and he thought that he was above criticism because of what he had done in 1924.(!) Then, belligerently: it was not he who was responsible for the breakdown of the negotiations with the Socialists. (!) And then:

I am a Radical-Socialist; I follow the policy of the Radical-Socialist party!
. . . I look neither to the right nor to the left, but straight ahead. My beliefs
are reflected in my acts. The Parliament votes as it wishes, now for me, now
against. It sometimes happens, even in my own party, in spite of decisions
in favor of discipline, that certain deputies abandon me. I have never complained about it, I do not complain now [but he will next month]. I do my
duty, let everyone else do his!

All of this was irrelevant. Herriot protested against being called an
enemy of the secular school (which no one had accused him of being)
and his remark was greeted with cheers. Bergery had accused him of
ruining international relations by extracting a partial payment of 18
billion francs; he replied that, on the contrary, he was proud of the
promise won from Germany, and if Germany did not pay, as Bergery
had implied, why France would withdraw its renunciation of the
rest.(!) Finally, he said (finishing on a grandiloquent note), how
painful it was to hear only criticism of France (i.e., of Herriot); the
country must strive ever higher and higher. He was given a standing
ovation; the party workers were so carried away that the meeting had
to be ended forthwith.[58] This was Herriot's greatest party triumph,
and the opposition dissolved before this extraordinarily eloquent tissue
of irrelevancy.

Yet the discontent continued to exist, and it inevitably reappeared
when the magic of Herriot's presence wore off. In fact, as one commentator reported: "The essential work of the Congress was to applaud Herriot."[59] Or, as a more naïve party worker put it, "One feels
all the friendship that is shown by this crowd, their genuine affection
for this great leader, who was able to put into words what we were
thinking and feeling."[60] This was "Herriotisme." The more independent had their misgivings: "If we understood it properly," wrote
Cot's paper, "it was not around a program . . . that the Radicals were
united, but around a man, a man whose great intelligence, profound
honesty, and power of thought we do not contest, but who is only a
man, no matter how eminent."[61]

Thus the Congress came and went. Did it mean anything beyond
the momentary ascendancy of Herriot over the mind of the party
worker? It certainly settled no problems, saw no showdown of right
against left; and it left all the contradictions unresolved.

As Bergery had said in his speech, "Don't think you will resolve the crisis simply by crying 'Long live Herriot!' " The budgetary crisis remained and the government was paralyzed before it. Although the principal outlines of a measure were made known in October, by the time the government was defeated on December 14, systematic discussion of the budget had not yet begun. There was, apparently, considerable right-wing pressure on the government to practice deflation. Bertrand de Jouvenel wrote that if the Radicals' program "is not being put into effect, it is because most of the members of the government have individually been subjected to a discreet, but efficacious, campaign, which claims that the application of the Radical program would endanger international security and budgetary equilibrium."[62]

But Herriot, evidently chastened by the left-wing opposition to his measures in the summer, seemed in no hurry to resurrect that opposition, and his reluctance to enact orthodox measures annoyed the conservatives. Malvy and Lamoureux, president and *rapporteur-général* of the Finance Committee, threatened to go on strike and intrigued continuously against the government.[63] The Senate was volubly discontented.[64] There was no compensating support from the left, for although the measures were too mild for the conservatives, they were too harsh for the Socialists and, particularly, for the fonctionnaires' union.[65] After Herriot's fall, Charles Laurent, head of the fonctionnaires' union, wrote: "We will not shed a tear over Herriot's ministry. The brutal fight between him and us was becoming every day more inevitable. . . . [The government] did not intend in any way to modify its attitude toward us. Its fall cannot therefore sadden us."[66] Since the government's projected measures satisfied no one, and since no resolution to the conflict was in sight when the government fell on the question of war debts, we can conclude from subsequent experiences that the Herriot ministry was inexorably doomed to be defeated the moment it presented its budgetary measures, no matter what they were.

These considerations reduce Herriot's fall on the American debt question to a magnificent diversion, an excellent find in the traditional governmental search for a favorable issue on which to fall, but an issue only incidentally related to the problems of the time, and one whose success would have changed nothing.[67] We can ignore it, therefore, except for two incidental observations. First, although 137 Radicals voted for Herriot on December 14, it is clear that the majority of them no more wished to pay the debt than did the deputies who voted against him. There was a proliferation of public statements by deputies of all complexions to the effect that they were really against payment, though they had voted for it.[68] Second, because Herriot insisted on repayment as a condition for his entry into the cabinet, he voluntarily excluded himself from the subsequent governments.

We can also ignore the Paul-Boncour government. It was a government for the Christmas holidays, little more than an academic exercise—the budget was to be balanced by cuts of five billion francs and by five billion francs' new taxes, the most orthodox measure of the period. Whatever grandeur such austerity had was destroyed by the weakness of the Finance Minister, Henri Chéron, who abandoned the whole bill the moment it was opposed. Paul-Boncour compounded difficulties by choosing this moment to introduce his own corporatist theories, which, in the event, involved winning the support of those groups whose interests were being attacked in the elaboration of the bill. Needless to say, idealistic corporatism was crushed by pressure-group practicality, and the whole affair was a rather sorry spectacle, whose principal importance was to contribute to the disaffection of the French people from their parliament.

III

A most interesting parliamentary combination occurred during the Paul-Boncour ministry, when the left-wing Radicals revolted and made the most concerted effort in this period to work with the Socialists. The minor Radical deputies gained temporary control of the party's policy, but the conservative Radicals rallied and, aided by the uncertainties of the left-wingers, managed to abort the revolution. The episode has been virtually forgotten, for it was without consequence. Yet this, the only unequivocal confrontation of forces in the period, serves to demonstrate that any positive alliance between Radicals and Socialists was now—and probably had been from the beginning—impossible.

The revolt occurred simultaneously within the Group and within the Finance Committee. The exasperation at the failure of left-wing cooperation was becoming acute, and the divisions within the Radical party became public. Within the Group, the factions neutralized each other. At the first meeting in the new year, the conservatives tried to oust François Albert as president of the Group, and although the attempt failed, only about half the deputies voted in his favor.[69] At the second meeting, the left tried unsuccessfully to condemn the Paul-Boncour financial bill in toto.[70] This second meeting was venomous, and afterward prominent Radicals publicly expressed their fear of a party schism.[71] Neither side was able to dominate the Group.

The revolt was more successful in the Finance Committee. On the same day that the government presented its Draconian ten billion franc measure, the Socialists produced a positive alternative. Rejecting new taxes and salary cuts, they claimed to have found some nine billion francs through certain financial manipulations, and through the nationalization of the insurance companies, whose profits would be used to finance social-welfare benefits.[72] For left-wing Radicals, this was a godsend, and they seized upon it enthusiastically. Largely by chance, the eleven-man Radical delegation to the Finance Committee was more left-wing than the Group as a whole, six of them being ardently pro-Socialist.* These six consistently voted with the Socialists to make, with the representatives of the other small left-wing groups, a total of 20 solid left-wing votes out of 44. This in itself was not a majority, but it became one when three of the five right-wing Radicals joined with the left to bring about consideration of the Socialist bill.[73] Malvy and Lamoureux, on the other hand, did their best to defend the government's bill.

In three important meetings of the Finance Committee (January 18, 19, 20), a solid, positive left-wing majority was formed. The Radicals and Socialists established a four-man committee to work out compromises between the two parties, and the government's bill was forgotten. The enthusiasm was intense at the beginning, but gradually cooled before the facts. When the key provision, nationalization of the insurance companies, was discussed on January 24, Herriot, in the Group, attacked the left-wing committee members. The left wavered, the conservatives gained heart. We have already seen the role played by insurance company money in the party. When the moment of decision came, the moderate Radicals who had ensured the majority balked. The precise vote is not known, although even Deyris, it ap-

---

* Members tended to be chosen with little regard to their political coloration. Three members were left-wingers and remained so throughout the period (Archimbaud, Dezarnaulds, Jammy Schmidt); three others I have categorized as moderate-left, since, by 1938, they had softened considerably; but in 1933 they were indistinguishable from the first three (Deyris, Lassalle, Jaubert). In addition, there were two moderates (Nogaro and Jacquier) and three conservatives (Lamoureux, Malvy, Palmade).

pears, switched sides when the Committee rejected nationalization of insurance by 17 to 14; nationalization of petroleum importing was defeated by 16 to 15. These votes emasculated the Socialist bill.

It had been an open, stand-up fight between the conservatives and the left. To destroy a right-wing bill, the left could assemble 24 votes, nine of them Radical; to advance a positive left-wing policy, it could gather, at most, only 20 votes, six of them Radical. The first was a majority, the second was not. In all this, the Paul-Boncour government had played no role. The government appeared, finally, before the Chamber, and, rejecting the wholly negative bill the Committee had produced, it fell.

Although the Socialist bill was defeated in the Committee, the momentary cooperation between the Radicals and Socialists had awakened hopes for their cooperation in a government. Daladier, apparently, had been seriously negotiating with the Socialists for this purpose during the last days of the Paul-Boncour ministry.[74] He seemed to offer the Cartel a way out. Bergery wrote afterward:

Then suddenly a name arose: Daladier. A name charged with a mystique. He is the man credited with breaking the Union Nationale in 1928; it was forgotten that up to the last day he voted for the Poincaré ministry, that during the Congress of Angers he was opposed to the violent break, and that the finishing touch was put on this break the last day by a "declaration of the party" that he had not wanted. He is the man who offered participation to the Socialists [in 1929]. It was forgotten that after their refusal he tried to form a ministry of semi-Concentration. After the sorry spectacle of Paul-Boncour-Chéron, he seemed to be the only one who could bring the left back to life. The mystique was so strong that he himself believed in it.[75]

So Daladier offered the Socialists participation with five important ministries,* which was expected, but the Socialists accepted, which was not. At the end of a frantic day, however, the entente dissolved, and the Socialists and the Radicals went their separate, futile ways.

The event revealed the real structure of power within the Radical party and the nature of its commitment to the parliamentary alliance with the left. Yet the episode was completely forgotten. It plays such a small role in the collective memory of a decline, many of whose events have remained symbols to this day, that one might wonder if it was

---

* Finance, Agriculture, Public Works, Commerce, and Post, Telegraph, and Telephone (PTT).

not simply a phantom crisis. Nonetheless, the defeat of Socialist participation in January 1933 was, at least on the surface, the decisive act in the decline of French parliamentary government and deserves careful analysis.

After the Radical Cadillac Committee had come out strongly in favor of participation on January 29, Daladier offered the five portfolios to the Socialists on the morning of January 30.[76] His one stipulation was that he could not wait for them to call their customary national council to decide on the matter. After consulting with their group for three hours, the Socialist delegates returned to accept the offer in principle, demanding only that the program of the preceding June, which was theoretically mandatory, should "inspire" the government's action. As Bergery later wrote, "it was scarcely possible for them to go further along the path of opportunism without denying their own past."[77]

The Radicals were stunned by this acceptance. Daladier asked for time.[78] The grandees of the party—Maurice Sarraut, Herriot, Milhaud —converged upon him. He talked with Bonnet, Lamoureux, Nogaro, and Delbos. The left-wing Radicals—François Albert, Bergery, Mazé —tried to stem the tide. Daladier met a third time with the Socialists. "The presence of the Socialists," wrote Blum, "which was considered so desirable in the morning, by evening seemed almost embarrassing."[79] The initial enthusiasm was destroyed by the accumulation of quibbles and hedgings. In the end, the Socialists saw that they were not wanted, so that, released from the enormity of their commitment, they sank happily back into irresponsibility. What had happened? Only a tentative reconstruction can be made.

First, was Daladier's offer sincere? There were rumors, even before he had been called to form his government, that his plan was first to remove the unsettled question on the left by making an unacceptable proposal to the Socialists, and then, armed with their refusal, to make a strong government of Concentration.[80] In view of his later gyrations, such an easy transition from left to right was quite consistent with his principles. If such a scheme was planned, it was thwarted by the Socialists' untimely acceptance. Thereafter, it became impossible to lay the blame on them, and Daladier had to wriggle out of their participating as best he could.

The foregoing is supposition. There are more solid grounds for doubting his sincerity. Daladier had offered the Socialists the Ministry of Finance, and since the negotiations were not finished until ten in the evening, this post should have remained open. Yet we know from Lamoureux's memoirs that by five in the afternoon, Daladier had offered finance to Bonnet and the budget to Lamoureux, both of whom had accepted.[81] *Le Canard enchaîné* described the denouement of the crisis as follows: "M. Lamoureux, who had been held in reserve in the washroom, made his entrance, rubbed his hands, brought out his little story about the respect due the credit establishments and acquired wealth, and, with an automatic gesture, opened the door for the Socialists to leave."[82] Whether or not it happened just that way is not very important. *Le Canard* saw the essential, which even the protagonists did not try to hide: the threat of financial panic had determined Daladier's action. Lamoureux was a symbol of the triumphant orthodoxy. Daladier's own official biographer accepts Blum's version of the negotiations. Blum wrote, "There no longer remained the slightest trace of democratic reform or democratic will in the measures that M. Daladier judged himself forced to take. . . . He was obsessed in turn by the urgent needs of the Treasury, by the need for 'confidence,' by the obligation of reassuring the suppliers of the Treasury, large and small."[83]

The key pressure was probably applied by Herriot and Maurice Sarraut, who had been hurriedly summoned following the Socialist acceptance.* Herriot said the next day to the Group that the state of the Treasury did not permit experiments "whose consequences from the financial and budgetary point of view would be incalculable."[84] He added the incredible, though characteristic, consideration that accepting Socialist participation would have been an intolerable censure of the policy of his government in June. Bergery wrote of the decisive day: "The truth is that Edouard Daladier was assailed all day by the emissaries of 'confidence.' By six in the evening he was beaten, cowed by the responsibility he no longer dared to take, that of facing up to the money powers. He was a man now ready not to fight, but to reassure. There lies the drama, and not elsewhere."[85]

The decision was taken by the party bigwigs, in defiance of the

* Herriot, typically and preposterously, denied to the Group the next day and in a published statement that they had talked about Socialist participation (*La France radicale,* February 1933, report of the Group meeting, Jan. 31); but Maurice Sarraut's paper, whose political editor was Yvon Delbos, says the contrary (*La Dépêche de Toulouse,* Feb. 1).

Group. The Group remained in session, however, and in order to gain the necessary time for preparing a fait accompli, it was decided to dupe the parliamentarians. The Cadillac Committee met at 6:00 P. M., and again at 10:00 P. M. Herriot told the second meeting that the negotiations were progressing famously, so an enthusiastic endorsement of Daladier's action was voted. On leaving the room, the committee members discovered that Socialist participation had been scuttled. The left wing was outraged, and sent a delegation consisting of François Albert, Gaston Hulin, and Bergery to protest. Daladier managed to turn their wrath by giving the first two men ministries. Their double-dealing broke the back of the left-wing opposition. Bergery left the party shortly thereafter, understandably convinced that the party was hopeless.

The Radical newspapers published the spurious motion of confidence the next day, implying that it meant an endorsement of the breaking off of negotiations, instead of the reverse.[86] There were a few protests from the provinces, but the event was soon forgotten.[87] Daladier did his best to look like a left-wing Premier, which reconciled the recalcitrant. At a moment of decision the Radicals had forsworn the left, and sold out their electorate for a respite from financial difficulties. Hitler had come to power the previous day.

IV

Daladier, like Herriot, had failed in his attempt to create a real majority. Parliament was henceforth patently unworkable. The parties could now only maneuver within ever-narrowing limits and hope that time would bring change. Yet the Radicals characteristically refused to recognize that they were in an impasse, so no real attempt was made to break out of it. The average Radical stolidly maintained, and even reinforced, his belief in the necessity of two incompatible policies— budgetary deflation and the alliance with the left. This belief, as we shall see, found its most explicit formulation at the Congress of Vichy in October 1933.

In the meantime, there was the Daladier government, which illustrates the marvelous confusion possible when the logic of a political situation has been deliberately obscured, and when a basic decision appears to be offset by a number of secondary decisions. The basic decision was Daladier's initial capitulation before the financial threat. The secondary decisions consisted of appointing a number of left-wingers to the cabinet—in part a result of buying off the left-wing opposition with ministries—mouthing left-wing slogans, and introducing minor left-wing social reforms to win over the Socialists. The secondary decisions were compensatory crumbs, yet they provided the government with the agreeable façade of reformism. In this way, Daladier hoodwinked the whole nation into believing that its political problems were solved. The façade was sufficiently convincing for Le Temps to write sourly that the government might just as well have had the Socialists in it,[88] and for the entire Radical party to rally enthusiastically behind Daladier: the left-wingers were happy about the proposed social reforms, and the right-wingers about having Bonnet and Lamoureux in control of finance.

Unviable though it was, the Daladier government was permitted to exist for ten months by a conjunction of favorable circumstances. First, Lamoureux and Bonnet were very adroit, balancing the budget in steps rather than all at once, playing the Senate off against the Chamber, and initiating token measures that temporarily appeased the deflators without seriously hurting the deflated.[89] Second, the Socialists, always more logical than the Radicals, were busily engaged in tearing their party apart on the issue of reformism—a long-drawn-out schism that occupied them for ten months. Daladier initially benefited from the reformists' support.[90] Third, the left-wing opposition in the Radical party once again evaporated, since most of the leaders were now in the government, Bergery had resigned from the party,[91] and the focus for party discontent was now Herriot, who had no appeal for the left. Fourth, the Senate had little room for maneuver, the most apparent replacement for Daladier being Herriot, who had highly acceptable conservative ideas but who was anathema to Caillaux.[92] Finally, the country was becoming exasperated at the frequency of crises, and the parliamentarians sagely decided to let up for a while.

All these factors gave the government support enough to exist and to pass two weak bills,[93] but the favorable conditions did not last, and the basic contradiction was not resolved. Deflation in stages had permitted the easy solutions to be passed first, but when these were exhausted, the same old problem, that of hitting the fonctionnaires hard, once again came to the fore. The Socialists finally split, creating a new situation, this time unfavorable to the government. Herriot fell sick, so Caillaux was no longer inhibited by fear of aiding him. The country's exasperation had been dissipated in ten months without a crisis.

Only the left wing remained pretty much the way it had been in the late winter, quiescent and harmless.

Daladier was very conscious of the difficulties that lay before him in the fall. He tried to counter the threat by constructing a majority of left-Concentration, which, in his scheme, meant making anti-deflationary concessions to the right-wing Socialists. In order to round out a solid majority on the other side he hoped to get the support of the left-wing centrists.[94] But the opposition from both sides was too strong. Although a majority of Socialist deputies had supported the Daladier measures in the spring, only a minority were willing to leave their party over the question of participation.[95] Once this minority had departed, the internal balance of the Socialist party itself tipped strongly to the left, and the Radicals were less likely than ever to get help from that quarter. The difficulties from the right were different, but even more serious. Lamoureux, Minister of the Budget, continually consulted with the conservatives Caillaux and Régnier while working out his projected measures. His financial orthodoxy was rigid, and he would make no allowances for political circumstances. When Daladier tried to make him go easy on the fonctionnaires, he threatened to resign. He insisted on enunciating the strong deflationary principles of his policy in a speech in late August despite Daladier's entreaties to desist.[96]

Faced with this situation, Daladier was, in Lamoureux's words, "incapable of choosing firmly between a political solution and a financial solution, which made it impossible to get a majority in the Chamber."[97] So, in spite of an exhaustive search for a compromise between Radicals and Socialists in the days between the meeting of the Chamber on October 17 and the fall of the government on October 23, no solution could be found. The government was overthrown by a combination of the Socialists on the left and the moderates on the right.

The Daladier government fell essentially because the Radicals were unaware of the incompatibility of their aims, and so made no attempt to alter them. Before the Chamber met, the annual Radical Congress was held at Vichy. Two important debates took place, one on financial policy and the other on general policy. The decisions taken were mutually contradictory. The Bureau had rigged the financial debate so that it would be dominated by the conservatives—Potut, Régnier, and Caillaux.[98] Although the discontent among the party workers with the official policy was so great that 12 of the 13 speeches from the floor attacked the government,[99] Caillaux managed to quell the assault, and the Congress voted a motion favoring rigid deflation. The next day, however, in the debate on general policy,[100] the party declared itself, without opposition, fully in favor of the Cartel des Gauches, and against Concentration or the Union Nationale. The party's declaration blandly affirmed both points.[101] It is tempting to suppose that this contradiction was a conscious compromise of incompatible positions for the sake of unity within the party. There is no trace, however, of conflict in the elaboration of the declaration, which was adopted unanimously;[102] moreover, the same contradiction was embodied in the report of Jammy Schmidt published a month before the Congress opened.[103] There is every indication that the overwhelming majority of Radicals did not yet realize that deflation and the Socialist alliance were incompatible.[104] It was not until the dark days of the post-Stavisky era that reality forced them to choose.

This fuzzy thinking made the Radicals deeply resent the Socialist overthrow of the Daladier government. With one exception,[105] the deputies and the provincial press praised Daladier and blamed the Socialists. Jean Zay, who within two weeks was at the head of the left-wing opposition to Concentration, published the one manifesto of his career addressed to his electors, attacking the Socialists bitterly.[106] The defeat of the Daladier government inspired a degree of political unity in the party that would never again be attained.

The fall of the Daladier government let loose the flood of political incoherence that partial success had temporarily held back. The fate of the Sarraut government illustrates unequivocally the pressures from both sides that made all movement impossible. The left attacked the moment Albert Sarraut was named Premier-designate; since he had a reputation as a Concentrationist, the Group flatly refused to vote the expected motion of confidence in him.[107] Yet Sarraut was no doctrinaire, and his sole concern was to get a majority, no matter where. Since the left had attacked, the left had to be appeased. The easiest way to do this was to promise to do nothing unpopular, and to give away lots of money. So Sarraut went before the Cadillac Committee immediately,[108] and said he would reduce taxes and create a vast program of public works. He tacitly abandoned all cuts in the budget. The deputies were elated by the way this scheme avoided all their difficulties: one of them went so far as to claim that "Sarraut has scored an unprecedented personal success. He has made a speech of unparalleled loftiness of thought and eloquence."[109] But such a policy was politically impossible. Quivering with outraged orthodoxy, the Senators who had been at the Cadillac Committee hurriedly assembled the full senatorial group, La Gauche Démocratique, and passed a motion stating that all questions of economic development and social reform must be subordinated to the immediate establishment of complete budgetary equilibrium. A few left-wing senators—Alexandre Israël, Maurice Violette, and Lisbonne—vainly protested that this was unprecedented and illegitimate pressure on a government as yet unformed, but the conservatives, led by Régnier, had an easy victory. Sarraut capitulated before the massed ranks of the Senate, and issued a statement asserting that his speech in the earlier meeting had been misinterpreted.*

Since the Senate would not permit a left-wing policy, Sarraut then tried to form a government of Concentration. Flandin's centrists were particularly receptive to such a scheme. Flandin proclaimed on October 28, "If one day the Radicals should say to the center, 'Now that we think the way you do, help us!' it would be wretched to refuse them."[110] But this hope was also vain. After a particularly difficult gestation, Sarraut managed to bring forth a cabinet scarcely different from the others, with the exception of two men from the center, Piétri and Jacques Stern. The Ministry of the Budget was taken from Lamoureux and given to the even more conservative Gardey.[111] What sort of support could this government obtain from the Chamber? At the end of the initial debate, the Neo-Socialist Pierre Renaudel asked Sarraut what majority he anticipated. Sarraut, as a good Radical, was indignant at having conditions submitted, and refused to commit himself.[112] Dissatisfied, the Neo-Socialists abstained, the Socialists abstained, and a small number of Radicals abstained. Fragments of the

* This denial, of course, raises the question of whether Sarraut actually did use the words attributed to him in the earlier meeting. Le Canard enchaîné, Nov. 1, 1933, indeed claimed that the rumor was spread by Sabatier of Le Journal, as a service to Daladier who had given him the Legion of Honor. This seems unlikely, since Daladier had no interest in scuttling the government, and indeed did it considerable service. The reports in the press all concur with the interpretation given in the text, and they seem to have been established independently. Sarraut's own paper, La Dépêche de Toulouse, Oct. 27, gave the essence of his speech, except for the part about public works. If Sarraut did not say these words, then why did the senators who were present feel obliged to call their emergency meeting to reject such a plan? Indeed, it would have been a gratuitous insult to a sympathetic politician. We can assume, then, that the official denial was a strategic retreat.

center voted for the government to make a precarious support of 307, which was a majority of Concentration.[113]

Concentration, however, was anathema to the left-wing Radicals, who called a protest meeting.[114] A delegation under Zay went to see Sarraut. The whole Group met next day, and although vigorous speeches by Daladier and Chautemps prevented an embarrassing motion from being voted, the limits of the government's advance to the center were staked out. According to one well-informed provincial journalist, the measure was protested "very strongly at the meeting, . . . which most of the newspapers reported incorrectly. In spite of the presence of several ministers and the interventions of Chautemps and Daladier, the great majority of the 80 Radicals present let the government know . . . that they were not yet willing to remain in an irregular majority."[115] The government, therefore, was helpless to enact any positive policy, but it would not have fallen at once without Sarraut's political bumbling. (The Christmas holidays were fast approaching.)

The same helpless alternation between placating the left and appeasing the right characterized the program the government was forced to produce. Gardey brought forward a rigorous financial measure, which satisfied the right, but this was immediately amended out of recognition by the left-wing majority in the Finance Committee. Sarraut capitulated before the latter, giving the curious explanation that he did not wish to be accused of not collaborating with it.[116] This inconstancy lost him respect, but it was his incredibly sordid bargaining when the measure came to the floor of the Chamber that finally brought him down.[117]

The merry-go-round began once again, and Chautemps was Premier. He benefited from public exasperation, from his own considerable political skill, and possibly from the fact that he was a Freemason.[118] He achieved the signal distinction of finally forcing the Socialists to permit the fonctionnaires' salaries to be cut—by a scant 275 million francs, clearly of little weight in a deficit that was optimistically estimated at six billion.[119] The Socialists tried to save face in their capitulation by a shoddy theatrical march out of the Chamber when the vote came to be taken.[120] Chautemps had a comparable victory in forcing the bill through the Senate over the protests of Caillaux, who felt that the measures were too weak. No important problem, of course, had been solved.

Yet the passage of the Chautemps bill marked the end of an epoch.

Ten days after it became law, the Stavisky scandal broke, and politics were henceforth drastically altered; financial problems were dethroned from their central position.

In retrospect, the history of the Radical party from 1932 to 1934 strikes one as a perfect stalemate between the unthinking left and the outmoded right. The conservatives knew what they wanted, but were not strong enough to get it. The left, on the other hand, had the necessary strength, but was simply too confused to pursue a coherent policy. Behind the conservatives, however, was the decisive force of the financial circles, a force that ultimately triumphed.

The money powers were a great bogey, but that should not prevent their being taken seriously. The financial circles wanted, as they always do, to maintain a sound currency; and to ensure this, they felt they had to keep the Socialists out of the government. Since the budget was always out of balance, the government had to borrow to finance itself. Control of the money market, therefore, gave the financial world a weapon of great subtlety and strength: when the financiers were discontented, the market for Treasury bonds suddenly dried up, the Bank of France placed conditions on advances to the Treasury's account, and gold began fleeing the country.[121] Some of these symptoms were, undoubtedly, induced by the economic situation, but one student of the policy of the Bank of France has written that in the period following 1919, psychological motives tended to replace economic motives in the movement of gold, and that "every economic or political event had its repercussions on the Bank's holdings."[122] One example of the close control exerted on governments will suffice. Before Chautemps formed his government in November 1933, he met with Bonnet, who insisted that the budget be balanced, and then with the Director of the Mouvement Général des Fonds, the Director of the Caisse des Dépôts, and the Governor of the Bank of France. When they had given their blessing to the new combination, he started meeting the usual politicians.[123] Financial pressure was exerted most effectively in the crisis of January 1933, when the Socialists were kept out of the government, and in the autumn of 1933, after the fall of the Daladier government. This pressure persisted until the passage of the Chautemps measure.

In alliance with the financiers were the rural, pre-capitalist senators. The link between these two worlds was Caillaux. Most of the rural senators could not understand financial matters, but a balanced budget was, for them, a self-evident necessity, moral and material.[124] This alliance, between two Frances in two stages of economic development, was unfortunate. Because of their traditional political attitudes, the senators were incapable of joining the modern urban conservatives of the Reynaud or Tardieu brand to create a viable conservative policy. The Senate opposed action by the left in 1932 as it had opposed action by the right from 1929 to 1932. Roy's speech in July 1932, Jeanneney's warning to Paul-Boncour in January 1933,[125] the obstacles to the financial bills in February and May 1933, the manifesto during the formation of the Sarraut government, the constant consultations of the ministers with Caillaux, and finally the defeat of the Chautemps bill in the Senate Finance Committee in December 1933, which was disavowed later by the Senate itself—all these were in the name of an outworn conservatism.[126] Perhaps the most revealing indication of the nature of the Senate's pressure on the government is given by the unchallenged statement in the Chamber by the Socialist Albert Bedouce: "When we offered to procure for M. Lamoureux [as Minister of the Budget] the sum equivalent to the amount he would lose if he rejected [the reduction of the fonctionnaires' salaries], he told us: not only am I committed to the figure, but I have specified to the Senate what means I would use: it is essential that the fonctionnaires give up 500 million on their salaries."[127]

The third factor was the uncomprehending left with its ideological void. Each time the moderates and conservatives within the party tried to break with the Socialists—in July 1932, January 1933, and the fall of 1933—the left interposed its veto. Yet it did nothing to create an alternative policy. This incomprehension stemmed in part from the fact that the left-wing Radicals shared most of the economic conservatism of the right. But we should be giving the Radicals undeserved credit for fidelity to their ideas if this explanation were overstressed. True, the party had unanimously fought the elections on the theme of balancing the budget, but by the time of the Sarraut government most Radicals would willingly have adopted any policy they could have got passed. In the long run, deflation came to be little more than a question of pressure politics. The Socialists, indeed, said that deflation was self-defeating, since it cut purchasing power and tax returns, but they applied this doctrine only in favor of the interests who voted for them. When the rentiers, for example, were hit by the conversion of the debt in September 1932, no one protested, although the amount of deflation that resulted dwarfed the paltry 275 million that Chautemps finally managed to lop off the fonctionnaires' salaries.[128] The Radicals were better able to withstand this pressure, and indeed to vote every deflationary measure with surprising unanimity,[129] only because they were more susceptible to pressure from financial threats.

The failure of doctrine was important, however, since it meant that no alternative to deflation was presented. The Radicals might very well have accepted such an alternative, since they were later to accept the financial fantasies of the Popular Front with surprisingly little difficulty. As it was, the right wing chose deflation, and the left wing prevented the right from finding a majority that would permit it. Yet the left proposed nothing in return. Thus every Radical government was caught in a vise, from which the only escape was to break one of the jaws; that break came with the Stavisky affair and the riots of February Sixth, and it was the left that was broken, and with it, France.

Throughout this period of Radical governments, the action of the party as such was minimal. We have seen that none of the party organs, except the Group, played more than a minor role during the spring and summer of 1932, a role that did not essentially change in the following months. The two Congresses were festive outings, and had no noticeable effect on the political situation. Only the Group and the senators were entities independent of the leaders. We have noted in Chapter 1 the extent to which the parliamentarian was the ultimate locus of sovereignty within the party, and this sovereignty was successfully maintained in the one attempt by Herriot to enforce discipline on the deputies. Although the Group was capable of imposing a few general restrictions—such as calling Sarraut into line—on the whole, the leadership was able to hoodwink it fairly successfully. The most striking example of this was the way in which the Group was tricked out of the alliance with the Socialists in January 1933. On the whole, one might say that the parliamentarians had to pay very little attention to their constituents—except in matters of local interest— and the leaders relatively little to the parliamentarians. Although the policy of the party seems generally to have affronted its local supporters, the only time the parliamentarians had any difficulty in this respect was when they voted the highly unpopular payment of the American war debt installment. In the crisis of January 1933, Daladier clearly had to pay more attention to what Herriot, Maurice Sarraut, and a few others thought, than to the Group. In this sense, the Group could be dangerous only when one of the leaders chose to use it.

Toward the end of the period, however, the left wing in the Group was becoming more self-conscious, and the separate meeting of left-wing Radicals in November 1933 was a presage of the greater role they were to play in the period that followed. With Stavisky and February Sixth, moreover, the traditional power structure of the party was shaken, and during the next two years the party as an institution became a factor of considerable importance in French politics.

CHAPTER 5

Stavisky, February Sixth, and the Great Disgrace

The twenty months preceding February Sixth had left the legislature in a predicament that the traditional governmental crisis had served to aggravate, rather than transcend. Clearly, a super-crisis was needed to break out of an intolerable situation. The super-crisis was February Sixth, which played a role comparable in this respect to the inflation of 1926 and Munich. Yet though the crisis was called for as a precipitating agent, there was nothing inevitable about its form—it might have been another financial panic. The particular form of a scandal and riots, in fact, had surprising implications. The scandal and the riots are so obviously connected that they are generally regarded as moments in the same event; yet their effects, though connected, were almost contradictory, and must be examined separately.

Taken by themselves, the February riots were the greatest piece of good luck for the left. In one stroke they ended the paralyzing fixation on finance; the old theme, the defense of the Republic, was once again predominant, and no Radical could have equivocated on this fundamental creed. The enormous latent popular sympathy for the Republic was suddenly tapped to sustain a discredited regime. The most important political issue since the law of separation of Church and State, one that was to inspire the greatest burst of popular enthusiasm in twentieth-century France, had fortuitously, but implacably, forced its way into a primary position. Moreover, it was the very issue whose absence had permitted the divisions of the Cartel in 1924 and 1932. The stupidity and violence of the right was such that it succeeded in uniting the divided and quarreling left. The riots of February seemed to be a providential event to save the republicans from themselves. In fact, they did nothing of the sort, for the impact of the Stavisky affair wiped out the effects of the riots. Since the scandal came first, it inhibited the political rebirth of the left.

I

The Stavisky scandal itself was bizarre, melodramatic, and grotesque. The affair became public on December 28, 1933, and within a few days it came to absorb public attention. The details of Alexandre Stavisky's career have been related many times; he was a second-rate confidence man who juggled inflated bond issues. He benefited, however, from judicial treatment so benign as irresistibly to suggest illicit political interference. Stavisky had, in fact, bought the influence of two Radical deputies, Joseph Garat and Gaston Bonnaure, and he had managed through his political lawyers, including the prominent Radicals André Hesse and René Renoult, to procure no fewer than 19 adjournments of a trial pending for years. With revelation after revelation, the web of involvement came to include cabinet ministers, superior court judges, police officers, and newspaper owners—with Radicals and Freemasons predominating in all categories. The climax of public indignation was reached when Stavisky was found dead on January 8, in circumstances that suggested police complicity and perhaps even instructions from the Minister of the Interior and Premier, Camille Chautemps.[1]

Although not spectacular as scandals go, the affair assumed such monumental proportions in the popular imagination that the Radicals were discredited even in their own eyes. This moral crisis undermined their capacity to defend the Republic. The Chautemps government was compromised, first, because a minister, Albert Dalimier, was involved in the scandal; second, because Chautemps refused to appoint a commission to investigate the affair, and even appeared personally responsible for Stavisky's death; and, third, because a second minister was found to be involved in another scandal.[2] The image was disagreeable, and disgust with the government unanimous. Even Radicals were indignant. It was, in fact, a demarche of the Young Radicals, inspired by Jean Zay, that precipitated the resignation of the Chautemps government on January 27, after a month of crisis.[3] Chautemps here established a precedent of resigning at difficult moments, a course he was to follow under more tragic circumstances in 1938.

The crisis which now began showed that control of events was slipping from the hands of the leaders, even within the party itself. Zay's action on behalf of an informal group of left-wing Radicals strengthened the centrifugal forces that had manifested themselves during the Sarraut government. The traditional channels of action having proved inadequate, new ones came into being. The Young Radicals published a manifesto demanding "pitiless punishment of all misdemeanors" and a cabinet comprised only of "forceful men above suspicion, who are resolved not simply to stay in office, but to govern as men of action."[4] This was the first unmistakable disavowal of the old guard within the party; a second came with the choice of Daladier to succeed Chautemps.

Herriot felt it was his turn; on learning of Daladier's designation as Premier, he was infuriated, and threatened to resign as president of the party.[5] He did nothing to help Daladier during the critical days that followed, remaining silent even during the debate in the Chamber on February Sixth; and he later joined the Doumergue government, an action that was an affront to Daladier. Daladier, on the other hand, deliberately humiliated the party. He neglected to make the customary appearance to request the endorsement of the Cadillac Committee, and when a delegation was sent to protest, he replied he was too busy to be bothered.[6] He did not even consult Herriot personally. In retaliation, the Cadillac Committee refused him a motion of confidence, and the discontent among the Radical deputies was extreme.[7] Such haughtiness was possible only because Daladier was planning to break the Cartel and form a government of Concentration, or even of the Union Nationale—from Frossard (Socialist) on the left to Jean Ybarnégaray (Fédération Républicaine) on the right, as the formula went. However, the initial enthusiasm for this scheme quickly cooled, and all that was produced was a Radical government with mild Concentrationist overtones; it included three centrists, Jean Fabry, François Piétri, and, as an undersecretary of state, Gustave Doussain.[8] Any hope the presence of these three may have inspired for a Concentrationist majority was dashed when Tardieu's Centre Républicain expelled Fabry for his action.[9] Since the Radicals were irritated and the Socialists hostile,[10] the Daladier government had no political foundation. It was to establish this foundation that Daladier fired the prefect of police, Jean Chiappe.[11]

Chiappe was the bait offered to the Socialists, who, regarding him as a reactionary, had been calling for his head for months and were delighted when they got it.[12] That it was the necessity of finding a majority which drove Daladier to do this cannot be doubted. During the formation of the government, he had promised Fabry and Malvy not to touch Chiappe.[13] When Concentration was demonstrated to be impossible, Daladier could renege, and he did. The eternal search for a majority led to the firing of Chiappe, which in turn touched off the riots of February Sixth.

The riots of February Sixth were the most serious public violence Paris had seen since the suppression of the Commune in 1871. It is true that the preceding month of January had been filled with a series of noisy right-wing demonstrations, inspired mainly by the Action Française, which certainly increased tension; but the violence of February Sixth was infinitely more serious than these. Calls were made by the right-wing Leagues for mass protest demonstrations on the occasion of the presentation of the Daladier cabinet before the Chamber. Around six in the evening of February Sixth the greater part of the leaguers, joined to their later embarrassment by a number of Communists, converged on the Place de la Concorde across the Seine from the Palais-Bourbon. While the frightened deputies within debated motion after procedural motion, the crowds outside stormed an improvised police barricade on the Pont de la Concorde. The police finally held after several desperate hours, but only at the cost of an appalling number of dead and injured on both sides. Although the government was repeatedly given overwhelming votes of confidence by the Chamber, Daladier's nerve was broken, and when the cabinet met during the night to consider what should be done there was only confusion. The next day Daladier resigned under the threat of a resumption of the preceding night's violence. The extent to which this apocalyptic event transformed the conditions of politics is simply demonstrated by Léon Blum's spontaneous offer to join a Daladier government to defend the Republic.[14] Daladier, of course, refused Blum's offer, on a technicality. He exhibited an almost indecent haste in resigning, without even consulting his cabinet.[15] Although on February Sixth parliament repeatedly confirmed its confidence in the Daladier government, this government was overthrown by the use of force; February Sixth was an explicit repudiation of parliamentary supremacy. Like Chautemps before him, when faced with the task of defending the Republic, Daladier chose to abdicate.

The key political fact in the three changes of majority in the inter-war period was, in each case, the Radicals' break with the Socialists. The capitulation in 1934, however, was entirely different from Her-riot's capitulation to the banks in 1926, since the issue was now a cen-tral part of Radical doctrine—the preservation of the Republic itself. In 1926, the crisis had been financial, and Radical doctrine supported Poincaré's conservative solution. If the Radicals had broken with the Socialists in 1933 on the question of deflation, this, too, would have been doctrinally justified. February Sixth, however, did not concern finance, but, rather, the basic issue of the sovereignty of parliament versus the efficacy of force. When Daladier ignominiously refused to defend parliament against the street, it became clear that something vital had vanished from the Radicals' conviction that they alone were the true defenders of the Republic. February Sixth marks the end of the Radical Republic.

Why did the Radicals capitulate? The most obvious reason is that Daladier was afraid.[16] Yet there was more. If Daladier alone were re-sponsible for betraying the covenant of the party, there should have been the protests, demarches, and delegations that proliferated in eas-ier times. Now there was tacit acquiescence, or even positive support. Not only had Herriot refused to back up Daladier in the Chamber on February Sixth, but on February 7 he urged him to resign. It is often said that certain young ministers—Cot, Mistler, La Chambre, and Martinaud-Déplat—advised him to remain in power.[17] Yet Daladier later maintained, without refutation, that even these four had told him to resign.[18] Herriot's request for authority to enter the Doumergue government was granted by the Cadillac Committee without opposi-tion. The capitulation, then, looks more like the collective failure of the party than the sole responsibility of Daladier.

Excuses were found. The police were weakened by injuries and sym-pathized with the rioters, and they were not fully controlled by the new prefect.[19] The army's reaction was not certain. Although Max Be-loff's conjecture that a military plot lay at the roots of February Sixth seems farfetched,[20] to use the military to maintain order would have been risky; Paul-Boncour had made one of the conditions of his entry into the Daladier government as Minister of War that it not be so used.[21] Yet such reasons are only symptoms of a more profound mal-aise. The police, though weakened, were physically capable of suppressing the Communist demonstrations of February 9 efficiently.* Any opposition to the government that may have existed within the police or army was passive and unorganized. Although the riots had been violent, the Leagues at this time were numerically weak and un-unified. With firmness, the government could have suppressed the rioters and established its majority on a sounder basis.

It was clearly a generalized moral failure that caused the Radical capitulation. Three reasons should be noted. First, as we shall see, the Stavisky scandal undermined the moral position of all Radicals. But one wonders if their behavior would have been different even without the scandal. One cannot imagine a Combes, Pelletan, or Clemenceau capitulating in terror before a few thousand rioters because several deputies had been corrupted. A second generation was now in power, and its fiber was not so strong. Leon Trotsky wrote:

Only the most superficial people can think that the capitulation of Daladier and the servility of Herriot before the blackest reaction are caused by fortui-tous or temporary factors, or by the lack of character of these two sorry leaders. No! Great political phenomena must always have profound social causes. The decadence of the democratic parties is a universal phenomenon that has its causes in the decadence of capitalism itself. The French bour-geoisie is saying to the Radicals: "The time for joking has ended. If you do not stop flirting with the Socialists and the masses, promising them moun-tains and marvels, then we will call out the fascists. Understand that Febru-ary Sixth was only a first warning!" After which the Radical camel gets down on his four knees. There is nothing else left for it to do.[22]

Although Trotsky leaves much to be explained, his contention that Herriot and Daladier were acting representatively, and that the party they represented was decadent, is difficult to contest. One can scarcely imagine a Radical leader at this time who would have been capable of taking a determined stand, since the very qualities that had promoted him would have militated against decisive action. Other Radical lead-

---

* It may be objected that the police, under Chiappe, had always preferred to club Com-munists rather than Patriots; while this is true, it is also true that this preference never involved disobeying orders, which a refusal to suppress a right-wing disturbance on February 7 would have. There is no indication that a sufficiently developed philosophy of the police's anti-Marxist mission, necessary for such disobedience, existed. The point here is that the personnel injuries adduced as a reason for capitulating on February 7 were no longer a significant factor by February 9.

ers—Chautemps at the time of the Anschluss and Albert Sarraut during the Rhineland crisis—were quite as incapable of action. For the Radicals who equivocated, there were, as always, extenuating circumstances. As often happens, the real nature of the capitulation was befogged, and the issues confused. For months the principal Radical leaders had been trying to break with the Socialists, and now it became very simple. They did not realize that to accomplish this at the cost of an abjuration was disastrous.

Second, whereas for the Communists, and to a lesser degree for the Socialists, the Doumergue government was, a priori, fascist or protofascist, the Radicals saw it as composed largely of old republican friends. The benign figure of Gaston Doumergue, an old Radical Freemason, was singularly reassuring, and the man most responsible for his being called was Maurice Sarraut himself.[23] It was not until the following November that the statesmanlike image current in February was replaced by that of a vicious old man playing apprentice-dictator. Both images, of course, were constructed to fit the needs of the moment—Doumergue was a mediocrity. But his arrival in February was as much the work of the Radicals as of reactionary forces, and the Radicals regarded him as a providential rampart against the new and terrible phenomenon of what were taken to be fascist bands. That his government's existence was founded on a violation of parliament was easily overlooked. We have already noted the Radicals' passionate attachment to order. When order suddenly dissolved, they were filled with consternation. "This horror of violence," wrote Bertrand de Jouvenel, "appeared in a striking fashion on the day following February Sixth. The public and moral stakes in the February onslaught were forgotten because blood had been shed. Nothing after that mattered so much as stopping the flow of blood."[24]

Finally, the composition of the Chamber made the Radicals a necessary part of any majority. Once Doumergue had been called, the Radicals had to decide whether or not to defeat him, and if they did, with whom to replace him. There was no left-wing Radical leader to inspire a Socialist-Radical alliance; Herriot was the only leader who was not discredited, but to defeat Doumergue for the sake of a similar government under Herriot was too sordid and dangerous to consider. The alternative was chaos with no government, but even that could not have lasted, and was scarcely a positive counter to the threat of the armed Leagues. Once Herriot, president of the party and of the Group, was installed as Minister of State, the opposition within the Party was necessarily vitiated by elementary loyalty; when a Radical heard the cabinet described as fascist or reactionary, he was forced to deny the charge, or, in accepting it, to condemn his own party. These considerations make it clear that, given the situation on February 7, some Radicals had to support Doumergue. They do not excuse the resignation of Daladier that produced Doumergue, nor do they condone the equivocation of those Radicals who opposed him.

The Doumergue government was accepted with extraordinary ease by the Radicals. Without exception, all clung to the label "the Truce," which became the current substitute for the discredited formula "Union Nationale." True, there were consistently about thirty Radicals voting against Doumergue, but the reasons given for this opposition were not what one would expect. No one denounced the anti-parliamentary foundation of the Doumergue government. Two deputies did say they regretted that parliament had been attacked, but even they expressed their confidence in Doumergue himself.[25] The other explanations for opposition all bear on secondary points, almost as if the deputies dared not examine the true nature of their party's capitulation. Some deputies felt, for instance, that the extreme differences of political beliefs within the cabinet would paralyze positive action.[26] Some were annoyed when, in March, the government demanded what they felt were undemocratic powers of legislating by decree.[27] A few rebelled at the reactionary nature of the financial decree laws;[28] unlike the subsequent Laval decrees, however, these aroused surprisingly little opposition from the left. Some members of the left were even fully in favor of Doumergue, as were, more understandably, the conservative Radicals.[29] I found no Radical newspaper that came out against the political configuration of the Doumergue cabinet.

The extent of the Radicals' misunderstanding of their capitulation is illuminated by the statement of a leading left-winger and self-styled theorist of the party, Jammy Schmidt: "The Truce has been adopted for clearly defined objectives. The goal once reached, the Truce ends. The parties return to their road once again, with their program, their natural allies, their traditional policy. Otherwise, the Truce is a trap. And, if this were the case, many of us would not have consented to it, nor let it pass."[30] As if history were reversed so easily! Given such reasoning, it is not surprising that Herriot's entry into the Doumergue government was authorized at three successive meetings of the Cadillac Committee, on February 7, 8, and 9.[31] There was no opposition in the February 7 meeting, and only a few protests on February 8, which Herriot easily quieted.[32]

The Radicals' abdication is all the more striking when contrasted with the reaction of the Socialists and Communists. These parties fought the government not because of its composition, or its demands for full powers, but because it was founded on what were, for them, fascist riots. One need only compare Blum's fighting speech in the Chamber on the night of February Sixth with Daladier's collapse and flight. The implications of the Radical collapse are not generally understood. Thus André Siegfried could write: "The answer of the left [to the riots] was rapid and efficacious, the traditional reaction of 'republican defense' operating according to the rules, but with the nuance that revolutionary forces were associated with it."[33] In fact, it was precisely the "traditional reaction" that failed when the Radicals collapsed in fear, and it was the revolutionary "nuance," drawing its inspiration far more from the peculiarly twentieth-century phenomenon of anti-fascism than from republican defense, that was decisive. Republican defense was to become an important factor once the storm had passed and the Radicals crept out from beneath their beds, but by that time what was left of the Republic had already been defended.

II

The Stavisky scandal, the riots, and the capitulation shook the Radical party to its foundations. Mendès-France, for example, recalls: "In 1930, 1931, 1932, I was still a young man full of illusions of a happy future; what shook me very badly for the first time was, of course, the 6 février rioting in the Place de la Concorde."[34] The Radicals had been living on the illusions of a vanished Radical Republic, and these illusions were now shattered by a catastrophe from which the party was never fully to recover. During the next two years, the customary domination by a few men was replaced by a leadership vacuum, the customary unanimity by intense internal strife, the customary quiescence of the federations by grass-roots activity and initiative.

One of the most striking effects of the 1934 crisis was the simultaneous eclipse of all the important Radical leaders. Herriot was a prisoner in the government, a Minister of State without function, bound to defend a government for which he had no enthusiasm. Albert Sarraut was in a similar position. Chautemps was too busy trying to establish his innocence of corruption and murder to be available. Daladier, who, because of the riots, was regarded as an executioner by the right and a capitulator by the left, was politically sidelined for more than a year. Bonnet was discredited by his inept evasion of the accusation that one of his associates, Guiboud-Ribaud, had been connected with Stavisky. Only the reputations of Maurice Sarraut and Caillaux were intact, and their talents and inclinations did not permit them to fill the vacuum. This unnatural situation left the organizations of the party, the minor deputies, and the party workers with unprecedented freedom of action.

The first manifestation of this new independence was a serious, but rather obscure, outburst of irritation from the provinces, which threatened to disrupt the party itself. Political news in the post-February period is difficult to come by, since the proceedings of the two investigating commissions filled every available inch of the newspapers. A manifesto seems to have been drawn up on February 8, which, according to a leading left-wing party worker, received hundreds of signatures in the provinces. The president of one of the departmental federations "let [the secretary-general] know openly that he was immediately taking the initiative to alert a certain number of committees and federations, and to have them meet at once in an assembly."[35] A separate assembly risked creating an open break, and heading off this unheard-of initiative exacted all the skill of the extremely adroit secretary-general, Albert Milhaud. Milhaud was a devoted follower of Herriot, a bearded Radical of the old school, defiantly petty-bourgeois, cultured, a graduate of the Ecole Normale Supérieure, and universally respected. In the midst of the party chaos, he took the step—without even consulting Herriot, as he proudly noted—of calling an emergency meeting of the Bureau to discuss the crisis within the party. This diverted into regular channels the potential dissidents, who now insisted that a national Congress be held immediately.[36]

Milhaud gave ground and agreed to a Congress, but managed to have its meeting delayed until May, on the well-founded calculation that, given time, the passions of the moment would cool. He accomplished this by concocting an extraordinary assembly—composed of the hitherto dormant Conference of Presidents and Secretaries-General, combined with the Cadillac Committee—and at the same time suppressing all meetings of the Executive Committee, which normally had jurisdiction. The purpose of this move was to supplant a left-wing assembly by a right-wing one, since, in Milhaud's words, the Executive Committee would have permitted "its strictly Parisian influence to corrupt the whole fabric of French Radical thought."[37] Milhaud then had no difficulty putting off the Congress till the middle of May.[38]

The sudden outburst and subsequent gradual waning of party indignation deserves further investigation. What was the party's attitude toward the February crisis? There were two principal strains—the effects of the Stavisky scandal, and the effects of the riots—which acted in different directions. The result was collapse.

One outraged deputy could protest about the Stavisky scandal, "Are we going to lose the benefit of the confidence placed in us by the electorate simply because there are two or three bad ones in our party?"[39] Public opinion seemed to think they should. The full extent of the party's corruption is not yet clear. Six men were excluded from the party in May, and probably more should have been; but Tardieu's charges against 14 members of the party, made in his testimony before the Stavisky Commission in July, seem unwarranted.[40] Among the six excluded were an honorary president of the party, René Renoult, a vice-president of the Chamber, André Hesse, and the president of the Comité Mascuraud, Louis Proust. The extensive involvement of Freemasons,[41] the curious connections of the Chautemps family with the scandal, and the impression that much was being concealed, resulted in the party as a whole being condemned. Bayet wrote: "All this news suddenly bursting upon the heads of the party workers has provoked first stupor, then disgust. Many at first considered leaving a party they reproached for becoming rotten. I have received countless letters from individuals and groups announcing such an intention."[42] Right and left happily threw mud at the Radicals, the most sensational instance being the poster put out by Henri de Kerillis showing a six-million-franc check signed by Stavisky for Radical electoral expenses.[43]

The chief effects of these attacks were felt not in Paris, but in the provinces; locally, the charges of corruption were meant and taken personally, so that most of the deputies found themselves occupied in defending their own rectitude. The extent of such charges cannot be measured accurately, since the Radical press did everything in its power to ignore them. However, the difficulties faced by some deputies apparently uninvolved in the scandal were considerable. Pierre Cot, in Chambéry, was accused by both the Socialists and the right of being corrupted by Stavisky. From the later testimony of his own paper, his credit had sunk very low, and he began to defend himself only in March. This possibly accounts for his initial failure to oppose the Doumergue government.[44] Lamoureux had to list his personal properties and divulge their origins to defend himself against charges of corruption.[45] Léon Courson wrote to his enemies, "You say that *the whole of my party* is sunk in the ignoble swamp, and that for the last elections it was copiously furnished with the millions stolen by Stavisky."[46] Jean Hérard said, "I have known so much injustice, so much evil, so much hate, that I wish to express my gratitude to those who never lost their faith in me."[47] Paul Elbel was defeated in a cantonal election in October 1934, in which the chief weapon in the campaign against him was Stavisky.[48] Geistdoerfer, Liautey, Girard, and Leculier also were attacked for being elected on Stavisky's funds.[49]

These men were all unconnected with the Stavisky affair. It made no difference whether they were right- or left-wing; they were attacked simply because they were Radicals.

It can be assumed that such attacks were widespread, if not universal. The assault was effective. The membership of the Federation of Finistère dropped from 2,500 in December 1933 to a figure so low that it was not published again until it had climbed back to 1,200 in 1936.[50] Raoul Aubaud wrote later of his department, the Oise: "Little by little, life and activity are returning to our cantonal committees. The shameful exploitation of the Stavisky scandal succeeded for a time in throwing our troops into disarray."[51] The effect was all the more serious because the attacks came not only from the right, but from the Socialists, who intended to profit from the situation, as well. "The Socialist party, in particular, is living in electoral fever. It counts on the profound discredit into which the Stavisky affair has plunged the Radical party, and it imagines that this time the electorate will give it a majority among the parties of the left."[52] Thus assailed, the Radicals were evidently not inclined to devote their full energies to the defense of the Republic.

The other ingredient in the crisis of 1934 was the riots with all their implications, and these, as well as the Stavisky scandal, found their echo in provincial France. There, as in Paris, the numbing effects of corruption dampened the vigor of the Radical riposte. The Socialist and Communist protest strikes and demonstrations of February 12 in Paris were paralleled by smaller demonstrations throughout France,[53] in which the Radicals were generally asked to take part. The Radicals' reply was usually silence by the press and abstention by the deputies. The burst of indignation that so stirred the party organization in February 1934 was not widespread. Of the 42 local papers examined on this question, only eight reported Radical participation in the February 12 demonstrations, and 24 either had no information or reported Radical refusal. In the Jura, for example, both the deputy Raoul Girard and the senator Marius Pieyre were asked to attend the demonstration, and both refused.[54] Girard's refusal caused him to lose the elections of 1936. Pierre Cot, who later became the leader of the Popular Front Radicals, abstained from demonstrating at Chambéry and urged the Radicals to support Doumergue.[55]

Even those few instances when the Radicals did participate in the counter-demonstrations illustrate the volatile and ephemeral nature of the Radical opposition. In general, those who at first protested did not maintain this attitude consistently, whereas those who were to promote the Popular Front originally acquiesced in the Doumergue government. In the Gers, Camille Catalan's committee enthusiastically demonstrated on February 12, but refused to join a similar demonstration in April on the grounds that it was anti-governmental.[56] The same thing happened in Grenoble, the Landes, and La Rochelle.[57] There were exceptions—the deputies of Loiret, for instance, who from the first consistently opposed the government[58]—but it seems safe to say that these initial protests were a republican reflex not particularly suited to the new conditions. Albert Milhaud himself noted that the first rush of opposition was not sustained.[59] The significant growth of support for the Popular Front within the Radical party came only when the shock of February Sixth and Stavisky had been absorbed.

This impression of uncertainty and incoherence in the initial opposition is confirmed by the behavior of the deputies in the Chamber. Twenty-eight deputies refused to support Doumergue on his presentation to the Chamber on February 15. There were two other important political votes during the winter and spring,* in which 30 other Radicals voted against the government. Yet only 14 of the 58 dissenters voted consistently in opposition. Many of them drifted into supporting Doumergue after an initial opposition.[60] Some of the hardcore Popular Front deputies at the beginning voted for the Doumergue government.[61] Indeed, nine men who ultimately turned out to

* The vote granting full powers on Feb. 22 and the vote on an interpellation by the Socialist Frossard on May 18.

be staunch conservatives opposed Doumergue on one of the three occasions.[62] This erratic behavior is in sharp contrast to the clear-cut divisions that developed during the next two years. It seems to indicate an
uncertainty of attitude and lack of conviction which over the long run
undermined the strength of the protest that had first shaken the party
structure.

The opposition was further weakened by a series of by-elections that
demonstrated both the sorry electoral position of the Radicals and the
popularity of the Doumergue government. Sometimes the Radicals
were simply wiped out in traditional strongholds; or the Socialists refused to withdraw in their favor, thereby defeating them;[63] or the Socialist withdrew only on condition that the Radical vote against the
government;[64] or the Radical vote split, with a large number supporting the right, on the occasions when the Radicals allied with the Socialists.[65] The election that justified the new government, however,
and reconciled most Radicals to the new majority was that of Mantes.
Gaston Bergery had resigned his seat as deputy to protest February
Sixth, and was now running as a test. He had the same opponents as
in 1932. Although he was no longer a Radical, the Radical Federation
of the Seine-et-Oise supported him, as did the Socialists and Communists. His defeat seemed to show that the electorate was happy with
the Truce.

This campaign was particularly important to the Radicals in its
effects on intra-party politics. Between the first and second ballots,
Albert Milhaud, as secretary-general, appealed to all Radicals to vote
against Bergery, although the federation, which was technically sovereign in these matters, supported him. A number of left-wing Radicals thereupon drew up a manifesto denouncing Milhaud. Both the
appeal and the manifesto were widely distributed in the campaign.
The Bureau and the Group met, and both emphatically disavowed
Milhaud's action and forced him to resign as secretary-general.[66] This
election was an interesting prelude to the Congress of Clermont-Ferrand, which finally met two weeks later.

Between February and July 1934, the party virtually withdrew from
politics. It gave Doumergue no trouble. As already mentioned, the
Executive Committee ceased meeting, and there were no important
meetings of the Group. In fact, the only manifestation of life was this
extraordinary Congress of Clermont-Ferrand. The original purpose
of the Congress was to cleanse and revitalize the party. It was to ex-

amine the new political situation, purge the party of its unworthy members, and establish a positive program for the future. Yet it did little more than applaud and refurbish its tarnished leaders. There was a minor purge. Eight deputies were accused of corruption, and the six who were absent were expelled.[67] The two who were not expelled, Malvy and Hulin, won the Congress over by the usual pathos, which the party workers could not withstand. The economic debate never took place; only an exceptionally unimaginative report, drawn up by Emile Roche, was adopted without discussion. Daladier, Chautemps, and Herriot all made emotional speeches vindicating their actions and stressing their spirit of self-sacrifice. Herriot managed to provoke a warm unanimity when an opportune fainting spell briefly overcame him during his peroration. But the enthusiasm was no longer there, and such histrionic devices were not able to conceal the despondent character of the Congress.

Extraordinary events had called forth an extraordinary Congress, wrote Kayser, "but at no moment is there any allusion to these extraordinary events."[68] Although the Congress was a complete disillusionment to the left wing, and despite a minor schism led by Cudenet (the founder of the ephemeral Parti Camille Pelletan), the rest of the left-wingers remained "to make their views triumph within the party."[69] Mendès-France wrote that they would eventually win because—and this is very interesting—they had the party workers with them.[70] Their first success was to displace Milhaud and to put in his place Raoul Aubaud, who was on the left. Within a year, they were to convert the whole party to the ideals of the Popular Front.

CHAPTER 6

"Concentration" and the Popular Front

I

Two events in July 1934 abruptly shoved the protesting Radicals back into the mainstream of French history: for the moderate Radicals, the illusion of the Truce was shattered by Tardieu's vicious indictment of the party, made before the Stavisky Commission on July 18; for the left-wing Radicals, the illusion of a residual Cartel was shattered when the Socialists deliberately turned their backs on the Radicals to form the Common Front with the Communists on July 15. The Radicals were isolated in a hostile world. These untoward events pushed the extremes of the party toward the center, and for the next six months there was a surprising consensus within the party in favor of the only remaining solution, Concentration, or, as it was now dubbed, the Third Party.

Tardieu's attack on Chautemps was a great shock to weary politicians preparing for vacations after six months of crises.[1] A painful week-long crisis opened. The most disagreeable part for the Radicals was that their pathetically affirmed "Truce," which justified their sharing office with the reaction, was shattered. Blum wrote, "After such a blow, who could still speak of mutual sacrifice, of appeasement, of national reconciliation?"[2] The Radicals wanted anything rather than a governmental crisis which, besides risking another riot, would not permit, in Herriot's words, "without prejudicing the future, the normal course of the vacation."[3] So, swallowing their pride and forcing Chautemps to swallow his, they accepted the insult, slightly mitigated by Doumergue's censure of Tardieu. In doing so, however, Herriot grimly announced "the rupture of the Truce," and promised that the Radicals' position would be reconsidered at Nantes, where the Congress would meet in the fall. Newspapers began speaking of a governmental crisis for the fall.

The summer crisis of 1934 opened a period of schizophrenic behavior on the part of the Radical party that has been a source of confusion ever since. The left and right followed two parallel lines of development for the next year and a half, with the party playing on two boards, to the great exasperation of friends and enemies. In the beginning, however, the left-wingers were inhibited by the necessity of digesting the Common Front and accustoming themselves to working with the Communists. The initiative lay first with the central core of the party, which had to work out a new political order for itself.

After an initial period of serious disorganization following the Tardieu attack,[4] the party pulled itself together remarkably well. The Herriot faction within the party wanted to rid itself of Doumergue and substitute a government of Concentration. The accomplishment of this program was the most technically brilliant political operation of the 1930's; Doumergue was overthrown with impunity and replaced by an enthusiastically supported dynamic Concentrationist government under Flandin. Flandin's subsequent failure resulted not from political maladroitness, but from the inherent impossibility of Concentration in existing conditions.

Concentration was, nonetheless, the most natural form of escape for the Radicals following Tardieu's attack. A great, spontaneous controversy arose over its theoretical formulation and the attempt to supply a Concentrationist majority with a program. Concentration was rebaptized the Third Party, and during the late summer the press was filled with an extraordinary number of doctrinal articles.[5] For sheer bulk, no comparable controversy involving the Radicals in the interwar period equaled this one.

The Third Party was similar in composition to the majority of Concentration,[6] its novelty being that, whereas Concentration was only a parliamentary coalition, the Third Party was to have a program and fight elections. Its purpose was to exclude the right from the majority and prevent electoral disaster for the center and the Radicals. Conditions were so propitious for such a formulation that it was proposed almost simultaneously by Jean Mistler, a conservative Radical, Emile Buré, centrist editor of the political newspaper L'Ordre, and above all by Emile Roche, spokesman for Caillaux, editor of La République, and a power within the party. The discussions remained vague. The proponents underlined all that united the Radicals to the center, defense of parliament, defense of the currency, progress, and all that divided them from the extremes, clericalism, socialism, revolution. Roche felt that the economic program he had proposed at the Congress of Clermont-Ferrand would be a good working basis for the new coalition; but, not surprisingly, no one showed any enthusiasm. Even the composition of the Third Party was vague. On September 5, Roche suggested that the boundary to the right should be fixed by the question of secularism, but by September 7 he was forced to consider admitting the Popular Democrats, a Catholic party. The whole discussion faltered when any economic solutions were proposed, since the major center party, the Alliance Démocratique, espoused liberal economics, and the Radicals were supposedly interventionists. As Kayser said, the Third Party was an "association of contraries in inertia," and as Emmanuel Mounier put it, "The formula 'neither right nor left' falls to the level that it tried to transcend, introduces a 'Third Party' as summarily political, as intellectually confused, as spiritually impoverished, as the positions of right and left."[7]

The practical aspects of Concentration were more serious. The inspiration came from Herriot. His motives are obscure, although he certainly began with a sense of personal humiliation at his treatment by Doumergue during the July crisis, a feeling that he never completely repressed. "During the parliamentary vacation," he said at the Congress during the fall, "a serious incident occurred. Its settlement cost our pride a great deal."[8] The issue, of course, on which the government was to fall was not injured feelings, but Doumergue's proposals for constitutional reform, which were publicly announced in two radio addresses.[9] There is no doubt that whatever Herriot's original motives were, by the end of October he had wholly projected himself into the role of defender of the Republic against a Doumerguian tyranny. The essence of Doumergue's reform was to give the Premier effective power to dissolve the Chamber. During the fall this proposition was seized on by the Radicals, who were so successful in interpreting it as a dangerous attempt at the promotion of "personal power" that by the time Herriot felled the government on November 8, a large part of public opinion was convinced the country had been within an ace of succumbing to dictatorship. Constitutional reform was, of course, an utter irrelevancy, since February Sixth and the decree laws had given the executive all the authority it needed to carry out any reform it could think of; the trouble was that it could think of nothing, and so launched this diversion, which eventually absorbed political attention to such a degree that people thought they were living through great events. Through it all, Doumergue was masterfully outmaneuvered by Herriot.

To achieve this victory, Herriot had to overcome a number of difficulties. First was the unfortunate fact that in the spring the Radicals had voted in the Committee for the Reform of the State for texts that were rather similar to those proposed by Doumergue; the Radical *rapporteur* on the question of constitutional reform for the Congress of Nantes was slated to be Paul Marchandeau, who had already prepared a report advocating that the Premier be granted the right of dissolution. The providential murder of the King of Yugoslavia permitted Marchandeau to ascend to the higher functions of Minister of the Interior, replacing the delinquent Albert Sarraut. He was to be replaced in his turn by André Cornu, who could be counted on to do the politically expedient, and who demonstrated to the Congress that effective dissolution was immoral.[10]

The second problem was that no great popular opposition to dissolution existed within the party. The left-wing Radicals opposed Doumergue for entirely different reasons—his indifference to the armed Leagues and his regressive economic policy, but not especially constitutional reform.[11] Many conservative Radicals later said they would have happily supported the project.[12] Toward the end, a number of middle-of-the-road Radicals raised objections to the proposal for dissolution, but these may have been orchestrated by Herriot himself. The most difficult of Herriot's obstacles was that everyone wanted to preserve the Truce. A normal warlike posture in overthrowing the government, therefore, was out of the question. Herriot had simultaneously to slay Doumergue and defend the Truce. For this he used the Congress of Nantes.

By the time the annual Congress met at Nantes at the end of October, a considerable amount of opposition to the Doumergue projects had been generated. At the same time, however, the party was agitated by a deeper ferment that was essentially unconcerned with Herriot's little schemes. There was a real grass-roots attempt to get control of the party apparatus, which caused Herriot a certain amount of difficulty.[13] The Young Turks were well organized and emerged for the first time as a force in the Congress. They complained about the continued economic stagnation, retrograde social policies, and the Radicals' electoral isolation. This was a deep-seated anti-ministerial opposition, but the Young Turks were not concerned with constitutional reform, which they regarded as a diversion from the real problems. As Daladier wrote, "Others present [constitutional reform] as a desirable remedy to the economic crisis. . . . Give a single man the right to send the deputies before their electors and prosperity will be restored. . . . The present government has had all the necessary power and has done nothing."[14]

Herriot had to resort to offering his resignation to overcome the disaffected party workers' attempt to gain control of the party Bureau. In overcoming this opposition, he posed as the defender of the government and the Truce.[15] At the same time, he happily let the Congress vote a motion hostile to "measures, under any form whatsoever, that might favor attempts to gain personal power to the detriment of republican liberties," which was the text on which he overthrew the Doumergue government.[16] The Congress closed on a surprising note of unanimity, since everyone agreed—although for different reasons —on tossing Doumergue out.[17] The situation was left so thoroughly confused by Herriot's at once defending the government and attacking it that Léon Blum said he was "totally incapable of choosing" among three interpretations: (1) that the Radicals had decided to come to an understanding with Doumergue; (2) that they wanted to make Doumergue take the initiative for the break; and (3) that they had adjourned the question.[18] This was exactly how Herriot wanted it. As Marcel Déat concluded, "The Congress of Nantes . . . from the technical point of view must be acknowledged as a sort of masterpiece."[19]

Herriot could indulge in such maneuvers only because Concentration for the first time was a practical alternative to the majority of Union Nationale, and because Flandin, a bright, unjaded alternative friendly to the Radicals, was eager for the job of Premier. On the eve of the overthrow of the government, Flandin said, at the Congress of the Alliance Démocratique at Arras:

I am happy to note the almost cordial relations that we now have with the Radical-Socialist party. . . . On the occasion of the last cantonal elections, I asked our secretary-general to undertake conversations with the secretary-general of the Radical party. For the first time, too, this party's Executive Committee has referred to us without calling us reactionaries. ("Very good!" —smiles—applause.) I have constantly upheld the idea that a stable governmental majority must be established in this country resting on these two pillars, the Radical-Socialist party on the one hand, the Alliance Démocratique on the other.[20]

Such a statement amounted to posing his candidature for replacement Premier. Herriot had only to complete the overthrow of the government, which he did when Doumergue was rash enough to request three months of provisional financing in case he should decide to dissolve the Chamber. Herriot worked over his reluctant Radical colleagues in the cabinet night after night. "Among [the five Radical ministers]," Lamoureux wrote, "there was not one who was really convinced by Herriot's projects, not even Queuille, who was extremely attached to him."[21] Finally, he persuaded three of them—Bertrand, Queuille, and Berthod—to resign with him, and the cabinet collapsed.[22]

The heat and fury over Doumergue's designs had been considerable, and when Flandin was called to be Premier, he was enthusiastically greeted even by the left. No Premier of the period except Herriot was so unanimously endorsed by the Radicals. The motion of confidence in him was written by the leader of the Young Turks himself, Jean Zay, who later intimated as did others that this might be a new Waldeck-Rousseau.[23] All factions of the party showed an equal enthusiasm. Herriot and Caillaux effusively praised him in public; the right admired him; the left—Jammy Schmidt—said it was its duty to support him.[24] The Flandin government was explicitly regarded as a centrist, parliamentary alternative to the right-wing formula of Doumergue. The budget was voted with dispatch. Laws on wheat and wine were passed, and a bill for the general reorganization of industry was introduced. Flandin fearlessly faced up to the major problems of the moment. That was his mistake. By the end of May the Radicals' unanimous support had dwindled to a mere 45 votes in his favor, and he fell unwept, his great experiment in democratic government dissolved in a demand for full powers.

What had happened? The change was not sudden, but rather the final term in a progressive deterioration. The deterioration was not inevitable; Laval was to do far more unpopular things, trick his friends and deceive his enemies, and yet retain his majority to the end. The decline of Flandin was the natural fate of a center government that tries to reconcile opposites. On the problems it faced, there was a solution of the right and a solution of the left, neither of which was satisfactory to the opposing faction. When, for example, the first of the numerically deficient war-born classes of recruits came of age, rather than accept the smaller army the majority of Radicals preferred, Flandin chose to increase the length of service, which was a right-wing measure. Then, should Flandin attend or ignore the service in memory of the dead of February Sixth? His presence irritated the Radicals[25] without placating the right. Should he tolerate or suppress the right-wing Leagues? He did not suppress them, which annoyed the left yet gained no credit with the leaguers, who did not forgive him for replacing Doumergue. Probably the key factor in the erosion of his popularity was his bill to reorganize the wheat market.

The existing situation in the wheat market had been created by Queuille's decree in the summer of 1933 fixing a minimum price for wheat; because it lacked any means of enforcement, an untenable situation had resulted, whereby the farmer was paid less than the legal price, which was nonetheless used for charging the consumer. By a law passed on December 13, Flandin abolished the legal price, which immediately lowered the price of bread in the cities. Such a move entirely accorded with his liberal economic ideas.

This "spectacular and opportune" gesture[26] caused one of the few violent protests from the Radicals' constituents. The disastrous surplus of the 1934 crop and the end of price control combined to drive wheat prices to unprecedented lows. When the bill was before parliament, Jean Piot reported that a rural deputy had complained about it as follows: "The government's bill? Don't talk to me about it. What a nightmare! It has brought an avalanche of letters from my constituency."[27] When the deputies went home for the Christmas vacation, they were apparently deluged with complaints, and those who had voted the measure rapidly backtracked. The conservative Charles Bedu was quite happy about the law in December, but in January had talked to the farmers and changed his mind. Raoul Aubaud, a left-winger, underwent the same transformation.[28] Deputies, left, right, and center, who had opposed the measure were applauded. One deputy wrote, "We warn the government against a situation that cannot last any longer and is of a catastrophic character."[29] There was no support whatsoever from the provinces for the Flandin measure. As soon as they returned to Paris, the agitation of the rural deputies in the Group was a constant source of trouble for the government.[30] The only protest in the whole period comparable to this one was the outcry against Herriot's desire to pay the war debts to the United States.

Another factor sapped the strength of the Flandin government. Flandin had posed as the champion of normal parliamentary forms, which meant that he had to accommodate the demands of the parties, which, in a period of deflation, were incessant. The Radicals were the chief party in the government coalition and one of the pillars of the cabinet, but Flandin's wheat policies and his deflationary finance spawned Radical meetings, motions, and delegations. One example should suffice. On January 11, the Radicals threatened to join with the Socialists to demand a revision of the decree laws. Delegations were sent to confer about this with Flandin on January 17, January 24, February 5, and February 8. Under such a barrage, he was forced to give in to some of the Radicals' demands. Each such conflict eroded the fund of good will and made a mockery of the government's desire to work through parliament. When the crisis came in May, the two parties who had joined together so happily in the fall parted without a backward glance. They were entering a new political era.

The defeat of the Flandin government ended all independent moderate Radical action. Henceforth the moderates were either to drift silently with events or to solidly attach themselves to the camp of Pierre Laval. The Concentrationist solution had proved a dead end and was not heard of again. The other strand of Radical action, that of the left wing, must now be traced.

II

The formation of the Common Front in July 1934 came as a blow to the left-wing Radicals, for it seemed to block a possible regrouping of the left. The intransigent left-winger Jammy Schmidt, who earlier in the year had been talking of a united left with a common program, now said that the Common Front could lead only to revolution.[31] Henri Guernut said that it had ended forever any possibility of an electoral Cartel.[32] When the Communists in the fall proposed to support the anti-governmental Radicals electorally, which was the first step toward the Popular Front, the overwhelming majority of the party did not consider an alliance with them a serious possibility. Although the Communist proposal was public and the subject considerably debated in the Paris press, 42 of the 53 local Radical newspapers examined for this period did not even mention it; of the rest, seven rejected it outright and four showed interest, but none accepted. Included were the newspapers of the most outspoken Popular Front Radicals—Cot, Zay, Aubaud, Archimbaud. The analysis of the proposal in a local paper sympathetic to the left shows what the Radicals thought separated them from the Common Front: there was no money for the social reforms demanded; independence for the colonies and autonomy for Alsace-Lorraine were unacceptable; so were the abandonment of national defense, the systematic offensive against the decree laws, proportional representation, and the immediate dissolution of parliament.[33]

Refusal to consider the Common Front constructively did not mean, however, that the left-wingers abandoned their positions. On the contrary, they opposed Doumergue and all his works, and attacked the Leagues and the decree laws. This was the opposition of the Young Turks, trying to infuse life into their party. But no one faced up to the issue of whether an alliance with the Communists was possible, although, if it were not, all left-wing talk was empty. Thus, in the Loiret, for instance, the campaign continued hot and violent against "reaction" and "fascism," but not a word about the Common Front. In the Loire, the Radicals were called on "to organize the fight against reaction."[34] Similarly, in the Paris press the supporters of the left wing took a negative stand against the government, against Concentration, against the right, against fascism, but not for the Common Front.[35] The alternatives to the Common Front were unpleasant for men of the left, but it was difficult to see how the obstacles to an alliance with the Communists were to be overcome.[36] In most Radical districts in the provinces, it was simple to talk of the "left" and all its concomitant abstractions, since there were so few Communists that working with them was not a real possibility, and Paris and national problems were far away. But a national alliance was something else again.

The first real tug toward the Common Front came with the cantonal elections in October 1934, on which occasion Maurice Thorez launched his celebrated "Popular Front" formula in extending Communist support to Radicals hostile to Doumergue.[37] Herriot grandly replied, in the Group, that the Radicals, being a very great party, did not have to concern themselves with whether or not they should follow in the wake of less important parties. There were some secret negotiations with the Common Front, and more serious ones with the Alliance Démocratique; but the Radicals generally fought the elections alone.[38]

They were hurt at the polls by the Common Front. According to the published figures, the Communists won 16 seats and the Socialists two, whereas the Radicals lost 17; since the Radicals kept 486 seats, the defeat was not serious on the surface. Herriot writes, however, "that despite the clever presentation of the statistics by the Ministry of the Interior, . . . I estimate that we lost almost 50 seats."[39]

Since the peculiar nature of the cantonal elections prevented big changes, the national pattern of alliances occurring only rarely, the significance of slight shifts in returns was greatly magnified. There were only 324 second ballots out of 1,512 constituencies. An examination of the second ballot withdrawals gives some disheartening results for the Radicals: in the few places where electoral alliances were meaningful, the Cartel between Radicals and Socialsts functioned successfully only 18 times; in 55 other cantons, the Cartel might have won but for disunity between the two parties or a split in the Radical vote; in 34 cantons, the Common Front operated against the Radicals. If such a pattern were to hold in the legislative elections, the Radicals faced serious difficulties.

Disabused comments in the local press reinforce this impression of defeat—the worst in years, according to Pierre Cot.[40] The left-wingers were particularly frustrated since the exclusiveness of the Common Front transformed all Radicals into right-wingers. This dilemma can be understood from a proclamation of a Radical candidate in the Drôme: "Against the Union Nationale, against the decree laws, against fascism, against war! For unity of action!" It was signed "Candidate of the Red Bloc"; yet this wild revolutionary was fought and beaten by the Common Front.[41]

The results of the cantonal elections were not conclusive, for if the Radicals suffered, the Common Front was no great success either; the right did best of all.[42] The electoral pressure these elections presaged took another six months and the municipal elections to become compelling.

After the cantonal elections there was scarcely any apparent movement toward the Popular Front in the Radical party. Everybody seemed absorbed in the Flandin experiment. During the winter of 1934–35 the dearth of doctrinal discussion among Radicals about regrouping the left is almost complete, in striking contrast to the plethora concerning the Third Party the previous summer. In December 1934, a few articles in *La République* discussed the possibilities of a Popular Front.[43] Zay and the other deputies from Loiret were among the few provincials actively interested.[44] Even these discussions were soon balked before the insurmountable hurdle of the Communist rejection of national defense; how could the Radicals accept disarmament in the face of Nazi Germany? At a meeting in Orléans, Zay was asked by a left-winger: "How can you be an anti-fascist and vote money for national defense?" Elsewhere there was a doctrinal void. One exception was the extremely left-wing Federation of the Seine, which met on February 2 to discuss tactics for the coming municipal elections. After a long argument about allying with the Communists, they ended by voting a measure that definitely favored a left-wing alliance, although it did not mention the Communists specifically.[45] The federation had made contact with the other groups of the left in a proto-Popular Front as early as January 10, 1935, and held a joint meeting later in the month.[46] Until late May 1935, however, there was no widespread doctrinal preparation in the party for the extraordinarily bold step of allying with the Communists.

The alternatives of Concentration and the Union des Gauches were given a crucial test in the municipal elections of May 1935. These saw the one positive attempt by the party, under the inspiration of the Minister of the Interior, Marcel Régnier, to establish Concentration on a firm electoral basis in the country.[47] The criterion for acceptable electoral allies was set forth by Herriot as including those who supported "republican defense and national defense"[48]—which, curiously, only one week later with Stalin's declaration, included the Communists, surely not Herriot's intention. At the time, this meant in practice that widespread alliances were formed between the Radicals and the Alliance Démocratique in the larger towns.[49] These alliances were made not only in conservative and moderate Radical areas, but even in some of the most left-wing strongholds: in Grenoble the left-wing Perrier faction was overcome by the right-wing Belmont-Vallier faction, and the Radicals and center took the municipality from the Socialists; in Rouen, the left-wing mayor George Métayer declined to run on a centrist ticket, and temporarily retired from municipal politics; in Meaux, the left-wing de Tessan joined the centrists in the municipal elections. There were Radical-centrist alliances in such left-wing towns as Auch, St.-Dié, and Agen.[50]

According to the official figures, the policy of the center alliance was a success; the Radicals sustained their position in 222 major municipalities and lost only four; the Communists won 43, it is true, but the Socialists lost six.[51] Behind the façade, however, Concentration had failed. The principal mark of municipal elections is their extreme confusion; no other French election can equal their extent, since nearly 38,000 communes each had a list of councillors to be elected, most of whom did not have explicit party affiliations. Generalizations about such an election are extremely hazardous, since no adequate study has ever been made of any one of them. A few remarks, however, may be made. Within the limits of a single department, every conceivable alliance might exist.[52] Serious divisions were widespread within the Radical party itself—a fact that went relatively unnoticed at the time; in perhaps a quarter of the towns studied there were Radicals fighting each other, some on a list with the Alliance Démocratique, and others with the Socialists and Communists. In perhaps another quarter, the Radicals went it alone. In some towns they allied with the Socialists. The election was, in short, chaos.[53]

The most striking characteristic, therefore, of the centrist alliance was the failure of the two main component parties to enforce the agreement made in Paris. The Alliance Démocratique was even more a phantom party than the Radicals. One journalist wrote that he had read in the papers that there was a local alliance between the Alliance Démocratique and the Radicals, but that in reality, neither of these parties had any organization.[54] Only the victories and defeats in the cities could be analyzed by the parties in Paris because of the complexity of the elections, and, on the balance, the moderates concluded that Concentration had met with a check.[55] According to Goguel, however, the real results of these elections did not become clear until 1938, when the municipal councillors, who were the great bulk of the senatorial electors, voted very conservatively in the senatorial elections, showing that the centrist electoral tactics had really worked without anyone's realizing it.[56]

This interpretation may be correct, but it is rather surprising that the deputies, who were apparently pushed into the Popular Front from below, were not aware of this current. According to an analysis by Jean Zay, the Alliance Démocratique, though it represented something in the towns, where the most publicized alliances took place, was nonexistent in the villages, where politics were absolutely polarized between right and left.[57] It would require an exhaustive analysis, commune by commune, to determine whether, in fact, the centrist tactics had failed; but in the minds of the strategists, they were universally interpreted as illustrating the electoral bankruptcy of Concentration, and henceforth nothing more was heard of it. When the results of the elections were known, the quick string of events that led to the Laval government and to the Popular Front began.

III

Between May 12, the date of the second ballot in the municipal elections, and the end of July, the conditions of French politics were completely altered. On May 13, gold began fleeing the country in the financial panic that was to bring down the Flandin government two weeks later. On May 15 came Stalin's declaration supporting French national defense, removing the major obstacle to the Popular Front. On May 22, the government announced it was going to ask for full powers to stop the financial panic, and on May 31 came the defeat in the Chamber. After the longest crisis of the 1930's, Pierre Laval formed his government on June 7. June 17 saw the formation of the Committee of the Popular Front, July 14 the great Popular Front parade, and July 16, as if in reply, the Laval austerity decree laws. In these two months, most of the confusions that had plagued the legislature from its beginning were clarified, and the broad political questions of the next three years introduced. All that was missing was the crucial decision on foreign policy, which came two months later with the Ethiopian crisis. 1935 was the critical year of the 1930's, and these months the turning point.

The Flandin-Laval crisis destroyed the remaining illusions of the Radical party. They had had convincing rationalizations for their participation in the Doumergue and Flandin governments. Their support of Doumergue, they said, had spared the country civil war; their support of Flandin had preserved the constitution and prevented a Doumergue dictatorship, and, moreover, had the blessing of the Socialists. Then, during a week of painful crisis, it gradually became clear that the Radicals were prisoners; and when the Laval government was formed with the votes of half the Radicals, they supported him for reasons no nobler than that the financial crisis had forced them to do so, and that they were too frightened and too weak to prevent this naked affront to their own principles.

The Flandin government's demand for full powers for enforcing deflation in May 1935 was the final demonstration of the inability of a center government to please either left or right, even within the Radical Group. The right-wing Radicals wanted a return to a government of Union Nationale that would effect a thoroughgoing deflation; the anti-Flandin offensive within the Group was led by the arch-conservative Malvy, supported by Bonnet. The left-wing Radicals, on the other hand, insisted that Flandin was trying to impose a right-wing policy on them.[58] The government was dispatched, with two-thirds of the Radical deputies deserting it.[59]

During the final appearance of the Flandin government before the Chamber, Maurice Thorez, for the Communists, declared, "We are ready to bring you our support, President Herriot, if you or any other leader of your party wish to take over the direction of a Radical government . . . that would really apply the policies of the Radical party."[60] With this startling proposal opened a curious week of feverish negotiations. The Delegation of the Left was revived and met constantly. The Communists shamelessly deferred to the Radicals, who were delighted by the contrast to the sticky Socialists. The Communists went so far as to offer to enter a government that included some of the more republican moderates like Laurent Bonnevay, and whose only program would be "a government struggling to protect democratic liberties and fight the crisis."[61] The Socialists were appalled by such opportunism.

In the meantime, however, the ministerial class of the Radical party was playing on another board, and while the negotiations with the left were just getting under way, it was announced that a cabinet led by Fernand Bouisson had been formed. As Blum commented, "[The Radicals'] conversations with us were only a curtain behind which they pursued their negotiations with Bouisson."[62] This interpretation postulated a nonexistent Radical unity of action. Aimé Berthod wrote more accurately, "The two negotiations were carried on simultaneously with an equal good faith and an equal interest"[63]—a fact that scarcely made the Radicals' conduct any less exasperating. The left-wing deputies were decisively outplayed by the old guard. That might have been all there was to the crisis of June 1935, but for the sorry end of the Bouisson cabinet.

This government was an interlude in the greater crisis. The cabinet was hastily and badly formed. The presence of Caillaux was a real detriment, both because of his rivalry with Herriot and because his deflationary proclivities were notorious. The war veterans immediately sent all deputies letters warning them to vote against him, which had a certain effect. Bouisson tried to undo the effects of this pressure by publicly assuring the veterans that their interests would be safeguarded; yet the threat was undoubtedly effective, since a number of deputies, including one who never otherwise voted against a government, used the veterans' letters to justify their opposition.[64]

More serious, however, were two other factors. First was the deplorable effect that Bouisson's speech to the Chamber had on everyone—M. Louis Aubert: "Don't make deals in the Chamber! That's what the lobbies are for!" M. Plard: "Your words don't suit the occasion!"[65] Second, the cabinet had been arbitrarily imposed on the mass of the deputies by the old guard before the possibilities opened by the Communists had been exhausted. During the much longer second half of the crisis, Herriot avoided this mistake and permitted the left to negotiate itself into an impossible situation.

The Communists wanted to form a government of Popular Front on the spot, and some of the Radicals were willing to go along with them. But there was nothing the Socialists wanted less. Among the Radicals, the two sets of negotiations continued as before, but this time the left wing dominated. At two critical meetings of the Delegation of the Left on June 4 and 5, the parties of the left got down to discussing programs. When the Radicals became serious enough to submit to the Socialists a detailed questionnaire, the Socialists reacted by spelling out their minimum program. Nathan Leites has written of the Fourth Republic:

Precision can be used for the purpose of sabotage, for instance to prevent the conclusion of an agreement which one does not desire to reject out of hand. Thus . . . in the course of the crisis, . . . a group (the Socialists) wishing to "torpedo" a candidate for the premiership . . . sent him a thick file of concrete demands, whose full acceptance was to be a necessary condition for the group's participation in his government.[66]

The Socialists, on this occasion, wanted, in addition to the Communists' minimum demand of dissolution of the Leagues, the nationalization of the key industries (electricity, insurance, and possibly the Bank of France); measures against tax fraud; improved unemployment insurance; introduction of the forty-hour week; a great public works program; an overhaul of commercial conditions; agricultural reforms of various sorts; and price control. All this was to be accomplished without using full powers. And as if this were not enough to discourage the Radicals, the Socialists added a demand for the immediate dissolution of the Chamber of Deputies and new elections to be held according to proportional representation—both of which were known to be anathema to the Radicals.[67] It is not surprising, then, that, as Blum put it, "From the first words uttered by the representatives of the Radical Group [in reply to the Socialist program], all those present had the same impression. The Radical Group—if not its representatives—judged the agreement impossible."[68] They did not think "that the Socialist plan corresponded to the needs of the present time in any way," and, at their joint meeting at the Mutualité three weeks later, Daladier said pointedly to Blum, "This is not the time for presenting detailed plans that end up as useless encyclopedias. This is the time for action."[69]

Faced with the Socialist refusal to join a government, the left-wing Radicals had no choice but to return to a right-wing majority. This time, however, the point was made unmistakably. After a mysteriously abandoned attempt by Piétri to form a Flandin-type ministry, the President, Albert Lebrun, offered the job to Herriot and to Delbos, who both refused. Herriot reported this to the Group, and then cruelly asked if there were any Radical volunteers, for he would be quite happy to suggest their names to the President of the Republic. No one replied, and Herriot noted in his diary that Daladier left the room.[70] The Laval ministry was formed immediately thereafter. The Radicals therefore had no more illusions; they could not form a government on the left and they could not form a government of their own; they could not decently complain about Laval.

In spite of the unpopularity Laval's deflation and foreign policy soon gained for him, at the time he was not disliked by the Radicals and no great outcry arose from the provincial press. The left-wing paper La République de l'Oise wrote that Laval was "one of the politicians most suited for holding the reins of government." There was some embarrassment at having refused full powers to Flandin and to Bouisson and then having voted them for Laval. Laval had cannily given the Ministry of Pensions to a Radical, an action that quieted a number of fears about the veterans. A number of deputies had optimistically taken Laval's promise of a limited application of the decree laws as precluding any severe deflation. The real motive of those who changed their votes, however, was probably that frankly given by André Liautey: he voted for Laval simply because a third crisis in a week would have been catastrophic. "My vote . . . signifies in no way that I trust the Laval cabinet or that I approve its policy of deflation or of special powers."[71]

IV

The left was vanquished in the Laval crisis, but within two weeks the Radical party had entered the Popular Front. The conversion was rapid and simple. On June 18, Herriot was invited by the organizers of the Popular Front to join the July 14 parade. On the following day, the Bureau met and approved participation without opposition. On June 21 the first meeting of the Committee of the Popular Front was held. Then on June 28 Daladier irritated Herriot greatly and almost upset the works by appearing on his own initiative at the first public meeting of the new formation at the Mutualité with Blum and Thorez—thereby firmly establishing himself as the unchallenged leader of the Popular Front Radicals. The movement was too strong to be reversed, however, and on July 3 the party's participation was accepted with one vote short of unanimity by the Executive Committee.[72] The enthusiasm for the new formation increased as the great day of the parade approached. Paganon, the Radical Minister of the Interior, facilitated the material arrangements to the best of his ability.[73]

The decision to join the Popular Front and to parade on July 14 with the Communists met with almost unanimous approval from the provinces. Herriot, indeed, had his Radicals parade separately in Lyons, but of all the local papers consulted, only two were against Radical participation, four were noncommittal, and six ignored the parade. Thirty-three, however, were enthusiastically in favor. Those who approved included the most conservative Radicals, some of whom were to lead the opposition to the Popular Front—Lamoureux, Ducos, Thiébaut, Girard; even old Jacques de Chammard, who was to be defeated by the Popular Front the following April, felt deeply touched by the crowds singing the Internationale. Radical participation was accompanied in the left-wing districts by the first formations of local committees for the Popular Front. The Radicals joined the Popular Front spontaneously and almost unanimously, but never again was the Popular Front so popular with them as at its very beginning.

Why did a petty-bourgeois liberal party noted for its timidity suddenly find its most venerable members parading under the hammer and sickle, crying for bread, liberty, and peace? How could they talk themselves into it? Could it happen again?

Certainly one of the principal motives was electoral. The legislative elections were less than a year away, and the municipal and cantonal elections had demonstrated that the Radicals were losing ground and

electorally isolated. Since the party's goal was to elect as many deputies as possible, the most profitable course had to be taken. Still, electoral opportunism alone cannot generate enthusiasm as great as the
Radicals' for the Popular Front.

There was the economic crisis, which was at its most severe in 1935.
The crisis affected individuals principally by unemployment, bankruptcy, and the collapse of agricultural prices. The Radicals were relatively unaffected by the first factor.* There was almost no mention of
unemployment in the local press—some at Gien, St.-Dié, St.-Etienne.
Presumably the party's commercial and agricultural clientele suffered
from the last two factors, which increased the discontent of the Radical
electorate and pushed the deputies toward extremist solutions. Agricultural discontent had fatally weakened the Flandin government.
Under the best of circumstances, however, it is very hard to relate such
factors to political behavior with any precision. Given the nature of
French statistics and the purposes of this study, no attempt will be
made to do so here. It should be noted that economic discontent was
seldom cited to justify joining the Popular Front.

The principal reasons for the Radicals' easy and rapid acceptance of
the Popular Front seem to be pride, fear, and ignorance: pride enough
to be annoyed at insults, fear of the Leagues—or, as they were called,
fascism—and ignorance of the Communist party.

The Radicals were pushed into the Popular Front by the right, some
of whom stupidly vented most of their taste for vituperation on the
party. From de Kerillis' poster of the Stavisky check through the Tardieu attack on Chautemps, to Charles Maurras's violence against those
who supported Ethiopia, ending with de Kerillis' calling Herriot in
the same breath Public Enemy Number One and a "big fat bull from
the Nièvre,"[74] the abuse was as puerile as it was self-defeating. Compare this heavy-handedness with the Communists' silken treatment:
"We have never thought for a single moment of pressuring the Radicals to adopt . . . our program in order to fight jointly with us." Or
the somewhat blunter: "[The Communists] salute in you the great republican party whose roots are in the very body of the great French

---

* Unemployment in France was relatively light, although serious in certain non-Radi-
cal districts. Of the ten departments worst hit, Radicals were important only in the
Rhône and Seine-Maritime, where about 4 per cent of the working force was out of
work (Letellier, pp. 116-19); in the first they were electorally shattered, in the second
they turned to the extreme left.

Revolution and in the purest Jacobin traditions of this country. You are the party which, in the past, has always been the most ardent defender of republican liberties."[75] By 1937 the right, too, had learned how to get its way with the Radical party: "There is scarcely a meeting in the Chamber when, profiting from the thousands of occasions offered by a debate, the parliamentarians of the right do not appeal to the wisdom of their Radical colleagues, to their spirit of moderation and thoughtfulness, which ought to separate them from the Popular Front and lead them perfectly naturally toward those who have the . . . same qualities."[76] In 1934 and 1935, however, the right-wingers seemed intent on forcing the Radicals to break their alliance with them out of simple self-respect.

With someone as thin-skinned as Herriot in control of the party, the effect of abuse cannot be underestimated. But the real pressure for entering the Popular Front seems to have come from the base, not the leadership, and the preoccupations of the rural Radical must therefore be considered. These Radicals were frightened by the armed Leagues. Whether the Leagues were or were not really fascist is entirely immaterial here.[77] It is doubtful whether a rural Radical would have known a fascist if he saw one. He knew the leaguers, though, as the most outspoken, active, and vituperative of his local enemies, who had taken up the alarming habit of riding around the countryside on motorcycles, breaking up his meetings, threatening and committing armed violence. It was against them that he was reacting. If, incidentally, he called them fascists, the word may have added to his apprehensions, but it did not create them.

The Radicals were devoted to keeping the public peace. When thousands of Colonel de La Rocque's activists in their black leather jackets converged on a quiet provincial town, the Radical deputy felt that public order was being transgressed. It must be remembered that in 1935 the Communists and Socialists were behaving themselves very decorously in the streets; the threat to order came from the right. "Citizen Corsin dreams neither of disorder nor of destruction; he wishes to assure internal peace by the dissolution of the armed Leagues, which constitute a threat to the Republic." "All violence is hateful." "The Popular Front is far from being a revolutionary movement, for today the troublemakers and those who want civil war are on the right."[78] February Sixth had been an act of violence, and the memory of that burning bus in the Place de la Concorde remained etched in the mind of the average Radical until it was erased in 1937 by the violence of the Communist riot of Clichy. 1935, however, saw the full flowering of de La Rocque's little army games, which reached a climax in the crucial pre-Popular Front month of June 1935.

The Leagues really passed all bounds when they began beating up the Radical deputies. Even before February Sixth, the wife of the deputy François Cadoret had been attacked by the Action Française in her home in Brittany. Crutel had been assaulted in the train when he was returning to Rouen from the crucial meeting of the Chamber on February Sixth. Dezarnaulds was warned by the Jeunesses Patriotes that his continued anti-governmental demonstrations "will bring acts of violence against your person."[79] The climax once again came in the spring of 1935, when Paul Elbel had an eye knocked out at a political meeting in March, and acid was thrown at the face of Pierre Cot at the end of May.[80] As will be seen, the Radicals were almost unanimous in opposing the Leagues, and it was their most constantly reiterated grievance against Laval that he had done nothing about them. It was surely not just coincidence that the first time the Radical Group were sufficiently disturbed to send a delegation to Laval protesting the violence of the Leagues was on June 25, the very eve of the formation of the Popular Front.[81] "There would have been no Popular Front without the fascist menace," wrote Aubaud. "Let the Republic be re-established, and the normal life of the parties will begin again."[82]

Finally, the Radicals' eagerness to join the Popular Front can be partially attributed to their ignorance of their new allies. They knew the Socialists, but, as Aimé Berthod wrote, they and the Communists "had different hunting grounds."[83] In 65 per cent of Radical constituencies, the Communists were less than 5 per cent of the registered voters in 1932. Parties in the Third Republic began to be taken seriously only when they had more than 10 per cent of the vote, and the Communists attained this in only 14 per cent of the Radical constituencies. Real rivalry arose only with more than 20 per cent, which occurred just once or twice.[84] In most of the Radical constituencies where the Communists were strong, the Radicals were strongly anti-Communist— Martinaud-Déplat, Meyer, Bonnet, Potut. The contrast between the average Radical's attitude toward the oppressively present leaguers and the benignly absent Communists can be appreciated in the reply of one deputy to an attack on alliance with the Communists: "Does the Communist peril even exist in Eure-et-Loir?" he asked. "Even if it did, it would not [like the Croix de Feu] mass thousands of individuals at the very gates of Chartres."[85]

In the normal rural constituency, the local Communists were no threat. "At La Rochelle," wrote one enthusiast, "we do not have *that sort* of Communism to fight; and even if our local Communists were to accept in theory their Communist goals, in practice they act quite differently."[86] Another claimed that the Socialists were much more dangerous than the Communists, that the Communists were building a fine country in Russia, and that if the Socialists would work as nicely with the Radicals as the Communists did, then things would get done.[87] Few were quite so naïve, but essentially the Popular Front, for the local Radicals, meant simply the traditional good fight—right versus left—only with a new name and a new éclat. One Radical wrote from the depths of the most distant province: "The Popular Front, which represents the alliance of all the democratic forces, is no novelty. Ever since the founding of the Republic, the Popular Front has functioned. In spite of the diversity of doctrines, republicans since 1877 have, on the great occasions, formed a bloc against the adversaries of the regime. . . . Then there were reds against whites, and from that point of view nothing has changed."[88]

Such anachronistic thinking was encouraged, and perhaps even shared, by the leaders of the party, possibly because it was comforting to be buttressed by the past, possibly because it made the alliance easier, possibly because they themselves did not have the courage to analyze fully what allying with the Communists meant. Chautemps was quoted as saying, "From the electoral point of view . . . the Popular Front is nothing but the old republican discipline that has operated for forty years."[89] And even Jean Zay, on the far left of the party, did not hesitate to minimize the significance of what was being done: "In the past few months, a sort of regrouping has been reproduced across the country, which you may call whatever you want, but which always occurs in times of danger or crisis with the same spontaneity; it is only its name that, through the ages, has changed."[90]

This happy innocence was reinforced by the Communists' behavior toward the Radicals. The Radical deputies were naïvely impressed by the Communists' attitude during the Laval crisis. Maurice Delabie wrote of Thorez's "sensible declarations" during the crisis, and contrasted them with the unreasonable demands of the Socialists.[91] The bad conscience at having betrayed their left-wing origins resulted in a general uneasiness that all but the most conservative in the party felt about their alliance with the right, particularly in an election year. Berthod, a moderate of moderates, generalized this sentiment following the Laval crisis: "The fact is . . . that governmental combinations like those we have put up with since February Sixth—no matter what respect or what sympathy we may have for their leaders, no matter what understanding we may even have about their momentary necessity—can only be reluctantly accepted as a provisional evil by the greater part of the Radical parliamentarians and their followers."[92] The moderates did not as yet have any firm ideological ground on which to build an alternative to a left-wing alliance, and so they drifted with prevailing opinion into the great adventure of the Popular Front.

The Radicals entered the Popular Front ignoring the nature of their allies and lacking doctrinal preparation, by an instinctive reflex and a sort of nostalgia for the Revolution. They believed that they were once again participating in the old Union des Gauches, which, in an electoral sense, was true, but which left them quite unprepared for dealing with the erratic tactics of a parliamentary ally that took its directions from abroad. This Union des Gauches was not going to behave like its predecessors.

CHAPTER 7

Laval

The initial Radical enthusiasm for the Popular Front was deceptive. The conservatives who joined in it felt that it was nothing more than a holiday parade. Probably the almost unanimous support for joining the Popular Front was primarily due to a misunderstanding of what such a step implied. Lucien Lamoureux, for example, who repeatedly supported the July demonstrations, in the same breath supported rigorous budgetary deflation, and found the Laval decree laws completely to his taste.[1] Yet the two policies were technically incompatible.

The Popular Front, in fact, introduced into local Radicalism an entirely new element—ideology—and a partisanship that was as novel as it was disruptive. "There are some of us in the Radical party who consider the party's fidelity to the Popular Front a condition of our own fidelity to the party itself."[2] The Radicals were, of course, famous for their internal divisions, but hitherto these were divisions among groups in parliament, each deputy being supported by a more or less united local committee. If conflicts reached the federations, it usually concerned rivalries of personalities devoid of doctrinal content and easily settled by a promotion in the Legion of Honor. In the period of the Popular Front this all changed. The suddenness of the conversion to the Communist alliance took people quite literally by surprise; but, on reflection, even the staid locals eventually realized that the new alliance was more positive than the former contentless Union des Gauches. Even for a Radical, a commitment was involved in being pro- or anti-Popular Front. The new acceptability of the Communists, moreover, gave the conservative wing within the Radical party a program for the first time. Before 1934, there was no mention of anti-Communism within the party, for it had no meaning; by 1936, anti-Communism had rallied a considerable number of Radical deputies; and by 1938, it had swept aside all other issues within the party.

In the period from 1934 to 1938, local Radicalism was rent, federation by federation, by a great debate. At first, dissidents inspired by anti-fascism disrupted the normal tranquility of committee life; after 1935, the troublemakers were more often the anti-Communists. The extent of these divisions is extremely difficult to evaluate. They were, naturally, hushed up by the local Radical press whenever possible, and largely ignored by the Paris press. Yet they erupted into open breaks in the municipal elections of 1935 and the legislative elections of 1936. The number of dissident deputies elected in 1936, despite the opposition of the local federation, probably did not exceed half a dozen; but even an unsuccessful dissident candidate could wreak havoc by splitting the vote. It is almost impossible to ascertain the number of such candidates. Yet I have found no fewer than 42 instances of open local schisms involving over 50 constituencies represented by Radicals in the years 1934 to 1936, a figure equivalent to at least one-third of the Radical deputies. This is an enormous number, considering the paucity of documentation and the fact that it was possible to examine less than half the constituencies. It seems indisputable that the party was almost universally divided against itself.

One example will show how the divisions affected a local federation. In January 1936, there was a confrontation of the opposing forces when the Federation of Lons-le-Saunier in the Jura met to designate its candidate for the coming elections. A conservative received 63 votes, a moderate 151 votes, and the Popular Front man 356 votes, who was therefore officially designated. Among the party workers, at least, the Popular Front was clearly ahead. But the moderate candidate left the party and ran as an Independent Radical against the official Radical. A number of Radicals and the entire clerical right supported him, so that at the end of the normally complex election, whose details need not be gone into, the dissident defeated the official Popular Front Radical on the second ballot. He went to Paris and sat with the Gauche Radicale. The federation was shattered, for it had lost control of a safe constituency.[3]

Such conflicts were repeated in most Radical constituencies, and, for one of the few times in its history, Radicalism came to life as a broad popular party. Everywhere party members discussed and debated questions of national import. The Radical plunge into the Popular Front may have been a political maneuver on the part of Daladier, but, for the party as a whole, it was a strong popular movement, capturing the enthusiasm and allegiance of the party workers.

The Radicals had entered into an alliance with the Socialists and Communists as partners, and for the next three years they worked closely together. In the fall of 1935 they were in constant contact during the interminable overthrow of the Laval government. The mutual attitudes of the three parties should, therefore, be considered.

The Radicals' relations with the Socialists were never close. Many left-wing Radicals were further to the left than many right-wing Socialists; they had comparable voters in many instances, and comparable programs. This similarity went so far that Kayser once seriously proposed an amalgamation of the two parties: "On all critical and constructive points there is no opposition in my opinion between the Radical program and the Socialist program. I would like to see a grouping of the two parties: the elements of the right of the Radical party and of the left of the Socialist party would be excluded."[4]

Such an idea could be entertained only on abstract grounds, for the mass of the members could not share it. The two parties, which electorally were the closest of all in the early years of the 1930's, were temperamentally antagonistic. I asked one member of the Federation of the Seine, a Radical of the far left, why he had not become a Socialist. Startled by the question, he said that there had never been any question, since the two parties represented incompatible ideas: Marxism versus eclecticism, dogma versus free thought. They had different temperaments.[5] Ideas unconnected with conservatism or radicalism in practical matters separated the two parties: the one was bureaucratic, the other disorganized; the one accepted the tradition of Marxism, the other that of the French Revolution. The contrast is extreme between the Socialist congress with its doctrinal debates, its precisely worded mandates and enumerated votes, and the Radical congress, with no mandates, no doctrinal debates, only the overriding desire to applaud its leaders and vote unanimous motions. Boris Mirkine-Guetzévitch wrote that the differences between the programs of the two parties were not great. "However, the difference in soul, spirit, and emotion between the two parties was considerable; it was the difference of tactics, of men, of leadership, of the atmosphere of congresses and meetings; it was the difference of 'climates.' "[6]

Not only were their temperaments incompatible, they were contemptuous of each other. Blum once wrote of the Radical party: "[It is] a party which does not know how to choose, which does not dare take an unequivocal position, which seems ashamed of itself, which, nonetheless, taking shelter in ministerial intrigues and hypocritical statements, denies its traditions and its principles—that is the show the Radical party has just given."[7] And Herriot replied: "It appears that we are fascists, or proto-fascists; who says that? The very men who have openly included in their program the destruction of parliamentary institutions and the dictatorship of the proletariat, supported by well-endowed plutocrats, revolutionaries in dinner jackets, or by generous publicists, who, in their chateaux, compose touching works on the misery of the masses."[8]

Daladier was continually on bad terms with the Socialists after October 1933, and this led to innumerable complications. The antagonism between Socialist and Radical leaders, rather than the disparities in their programs, was cited by François Albert as the reason for the failure to form a stable majority at the beginning of the 1932 legislature.[9] If the Socialists treated the Radicals as vulgar politicians, the Radicals, rather more surprisingly, said the same of the Socialists: "The Socialist party is, on its side, a fighting formation for electoral battles only, and nothing more; its members are without convictions and without avowed doctrine."[10] The anti-Socialism of the Midi, where Socialists were regarded as synonymous with Communists, could go to extremes—one federation president feeling so strongly that he wished to strike the word "Socialist" from the name "Radical-Socialist."[11] When the two parties came to collaborate in government under the Popular Front, their mutual dislike was increased. Paul Bastid, who was Minister of Commerce in the Blum government, spoke to me very slightingly about the utter incompetence of the Socialist ministers—with the exception of Blum—during this government.[12]

Perhaps the best index of the mutual incompatibility of the two parties was that, although the 1930's was an era of schisms and withdrawals in both parties, there was no interchange of personnel. Paul-Boncour, Frot, Frossard, and the Neo-Socialists preferred to remain isolated, or to form their own party, rather than join the Radicals. Left-wing Radical dissidents in 1934 formed the splinter "Pelletanist" party rather than join the Socialists; a party worker driven to quit a federation in despair might join a desultory formation, the Socialistes Français, but not the SFIO.[13] Bergery formed the "Frontist" party. Bertrand de Jouvenel moved to the Parti Populaire Français (PPF). Pierre Cot and the whole extreme left of the party, which quit following the Liberation, jumped over the Socialists to form the "progressists" on their left. I have found only one instance of a party worker or deputy from either party leaving to join the other—Alexandre Varenne, who quit the SFIO in 1933 and joined the Radicals after World War II. This mutual impermeability surely indicates an incompatible political temperament, which may have been more important than doctrinal differences. When a district turned toward Socialism, and the same voters sent a moderate Socialist rather than a Radical to parliament, the new deputy might have the same program as a left-wing Radical, but he would also have an entirely different style.

In contrast to their always testy relations with the Socialists, the Radicals and Communists always got along well personally, even during the doctrinal anti-Communism of the last years. Blum commented on the Radical-Communist flirtation in the early days of the Popular Front: "This attitude was astonishing, and it is not astonishing that it was astonishing. . . . The Radicals have even gotten the impression, shown by some of them without dissembling, that an entente was easier with our Communist comrades than with ourselves, or, at least, that they made less trouble for the Union des Gauches than we did."[14]

The impression was not a fleeting one. The Communists worked hard to flatter the Radicals. In the Committee of the Popular Front, if one is to believe Jacques Kayser, it was generally the Radicals and the Communists who teamed up against the Socialists.[15] This collaboration was most pronounced in the early days of the Front, but as late as October 1937, the highly respected political journalist Raymond Millet could seriously report rumors of a Radical-Communist collaboration behind the backs of the Socialists which might even lead to a governmental alliance.[16] Whereas the Radicals were on the electoral defensive against the inroads of Socialism,* they were, except in a few isolated instances, not threatened by the Communists. The Socialists were in competition for votes with both the Radicals and the Communists, with all the consequent tensions. The Radicals were impressed by the Communists' opportunistic departures from doctrine, while they were exasperated by the Socialists' punctilious dogmatism. In addition, Herriot's dislike of the Socialists and admiration for Communist Russia must be mentioned. In the legislative elections of 1936—particularly in Lyons—and the cantonal elections of 1937, the Communists were far more correct than the Socialists in their application of republican

* Electoral competition between the two parties was severe: in 50 per cent of Radical constituencies, the Socialists gained more than 10 per cent of the registered vote in 1932, and in 21 per cent they were serious rivals with more than 20 per cent.

discipline.* Such antagonisms and affinities accentuated the pendular movement of the Radicals; they had helped drive them to the right and away from the Socialists between 1932 and 1934, and they helped attract them to the Popular Front in 1935.

During the summer and fall of 1935, there was considerable fear that the party would actually be split by its internal conflicts over the Popular Front and the Laval government. The Congress of 1935, held in the Salle Wagram in Paris, was anticipated with apprehension.[17] The Congress pulled two surprises: it did not overthrow the government, and it unanimously endorsed the Popular Front. The Communists and Socialists were startled.[18] The agitation against the Leagues dominated this Congress to the exclusion of all else. The question of the Popular Front more or less slipped in sideways. The proposals for a program for the Popular Front were unbelievably anodyne.[19]

This was one of the delightful prewar Radical Congresses that are still spoken of with nostalgia. The "war of the two Edouards" raged mercilessly. Laval had cannily issued some decrees on the eve of the Congress prohibiting the right-wing leaguers from carrying arms, and in the Committee on General Policy Herriot dutifully defended them. Daladier called them "laughable," "a shabby political maneuver," and so on. According to Le Temps, "the debate became so heated that the Minister of State [Herriot] decided to leave. . . . 'I understand now: I am being assassinated!' he exclaimed. . . . After a quarter of an hour of discussion, M. Chautemps succeeded in bringing him back to his colleagues, who warmly applauded him."[20] This battle went on for three full days. The political world was held in suspense by the possibility of a new Coup d'Angers, which would have occurred if Daladier had succeeded in imposing his demand that new stringent measures against the Leagues be taken by October 31, that is, within a week's time.

After interminable closed sessions and threats of an utter break-

---

* See particularly the way the Socialists made not voting for right-wing Radicals in the cantonal elections of 1937 a national question of principle, which unnecessarily irritated the Radicals. The Communists supported the Radicals in principle on this occasion, and then locally voted against the right-wing Radicals, which was normal and evoked no protests from the Radicals. (Paul Faure, Le Populaire, October 14, 15, 16, 17, 24, 26, 29, 1937; Daladier, Congress, October 28, 1937, pp. 188–92.) The Communists' and Socialists' action here was identical in fact, but differed totally in form, which is, in politics, the essential.

down, the Congress closed, as usual, with a motion that was unanimously approved. "Let me express my joy, my dear President Herriot," said the arch-foe Daladier, "at seeing this unanimity of our party, which presages the necessary rebuilding of the Republic that you, better than anyone, are in a position to accomplish."[21] The government was saved. In all the fury over the Leagues, which were the Radicals' bête noire, the Popular Front was somewhat forgotten. Both Daladier and Zay actually uttered the words "Popular Front" in the public debate,[22] but the final declaration contented itself with an awkward circumlocution about those parties associated in the "great popular demonstration of July Fourteenth," and asked that these parties establish a common program.[23] The Popular Front was accepted unanimously. Everybody was happy. The conservatives were not unduly disturbed, since the Radical proposals for a program of action were weak; the clauses on financial policy, positively benevolent toward the Laval government, received the full approbation of no less a conservative than Lucien Lamoureux.[24] The Congress ended, in the words of a left-winger, "in indescribable enthusiasm."[25]

The Radicals' desire for unity, be it at the cost of all clarity of thought, was extraordinary. Their often derided, unanimously voted "nègre-blanc" motions resulted from this desire.* So did the fact that they were able to enter the Popular Front as a united party despite the vehement opposition of many party members—an achievement that testifies to their remarkable capacity for serving as a buffer between blocs.

Above the happy enthusiasm hung one great, familiar cloud. What was going to happen when the "Mur d'Argent" fell on the aspiring social reformers? The Radicals were not much as economists or financial specialists, but they could add, and they had been severely battered in 1926. In a nationally publicized controversy, Lucien Lamoureux asked Blum how he contemplated financing a Popular Front government. Blum replied (not unreasonably) that like all the other governments, his would be financed by bank loans until the revived economy brought in more taxes. And if the banks refused? The Socialists, "rather than capitulate, would not pay the government's installments; they would proclaim to the people that their wishes were being at-

---

* The "nègre-blanc" motion, in which the Radicals specialized, incorporated two mutually contradictory provisions. Unanimous approval was thus achieved, with half the party endorsing each provision.

tacked by the financial oligarchies. They would point out those responsible, or rather, those guilty, to the state's creditors. They would ask
the fonctionnaires to help in the common struggle, and to continue
their services without pay and with the fighting, self-sacrificing spirit
of striking workers."[26]

Such an idea appalled even the most pro-Socialist Radicals, and undoubtedly contributed to their extreme hesitation in overthrowing the
Laval government.[27] With this discussion obviously in mind, César
Campinchi rather ominously said, shortly before the Congress, "The
question arises: is there an incompatibility between a left-wing policy
and healthy finances?" If such an incompatibility were demonstrated,
the Radicals would rally to the moderates, "be it at the cost of their
own destruction."[28] Eventually, of course, they were to do just that.

Of all the governments of the 1930's, Laval's is the most instructive.
From October to January it was under constant attack, which for once
permitted every issue to be squarely faced and voted upon, after being
discussed at such length that no misunderstanding could remain. This
is the only time that the left and right within the Radical party stood
up against one another and permitted themselves to be counted. Four
major issues stand out: the armed Leagues, the financial and economic
policy of deflation, Ethiopia, and the coming elections.

The political situation was, as always, intricate. The position of the
Radical party was more ambiguous than usual, for it was at once in the
government and in the opposition, the keystone of the Popular Front
and of the Union Nationale. On his presentation to the Chamber,
Laval had obtained a symmetrical 72 Radical votes in his favor, seven
votes against, and 72 abstentions, with six absent. The degree of Radical opposition, moreover, varied from issue to issue, from a low on
financial policy to a high on the Leagues, which permitted Laval to
maximize his advantage by arranging the order of business. A con-
summate politician, he shamelessly deferred to the Radicals' sensibili-
ties while outraging their principles;[29] in this he showed a skill as
marked as Doumergue's clumsiness the year before. The ambiguity
of the Radicals' position was magnified by the fact that the ministers
responsible for dealing with two of the three major irritants, the
Leagues and deflation, were Radicals—Paganon at the Interior, and
Régnier at Finance. The positions of the leaders themselves were contradictory. Herriot was appalled both by Laval's foreign policy and

by the prospect of a Popular Front government that might result if the government were overthrown; this internal conflict drove him to the most erratic acts. On the other hand, Daladier, who had staked his future on the Popular Front, was quite sympathetic to Laval's foreign policy. There were a few minor complications, such as the vicious but self-destructive attack on Herriot by the right-wing press, led by Henri de Kerillis, which goaded him into a prolonged fury and hastened his departure from the government.

The fall of the Laval government occupied three full months, during which time the threads of action became so tangled that, in the end, it became quite impossible to say why it was overthrown, or, indeed, how it was overthrown. As we shall see, even the principal actors became hopelessly confused about what exactly had happened and why they had acted the way they had. This confusion has pervaded almost all analyses of this crisis, and it is therefore useful to examine it in some detail.

With the possible exception of the Communists, no one really wanted to overthrow the Laval government. If Laval were defeated, he would have to be replaced by one of three alternatives: a government like his own, which would be incoherent; a government of Popular Front, which the Socialists and Communists hesitated to accept, because they wanted to fight the elections unencumbered by a governmental past; or a Radical government, which everyone approved of except the Radicals. Yet all the anti-Lavalists had to pretend that their sole aim was to get rid of this infamous government with dispatch, and a good deal of deliberate obfuscation was the result.

Clearly, it was the Socialists' attitude that was decisive. Did the Socialists want a Popular Front government? Publicly, they seemed to accuse the Radicals of preventing Laval's defeat: "It can be considered settled that the leadership of the Radical party does not think it desirable to form a government of Popular Front at the present time."[30] Herriot, on the other hand, reports a series of conversations with Léon Blum: on July 11, Blum was worried by the possibility of a premature Popular Front government in the fall; on October 31, he wanted to overthrow the government immediately; around November 15, he had changed his mind.[31] On November 11, Marcel Déat reported that the Socialists would collaborate in a government only if it immediately dissolved both the Leagues and the Chamber of Deputies; the second condition was known to be unacceptable to the Radicals.[32]

The Socialists continued, nonetheless, to attack the government with might and main, presumably hoping to force the Radicals to take over by themselves. "As for the Radicals," Déat wrote, "they consider with some perplexity and emotion the development of these warlike humors. They wonder, not without reason, what experiments are going to be conducted on them if they are left to lead the battle alone, if it should begin, against the Leagues and the 'money powers,' the moment the ministry is formed."[33] Jean Zay, who was leader of the Radical opposition to Laval, indignantly rejected the Socialists' scheme, declaring that with the stock exchange trying to bring about a government of Popular Front in order to discredit it for the elections, and the Communists and Socialists refusing to participate in such a government, the Radicals refused to take power simply to test the right's intentions. "Please excuse them for having no taste for suicide!"[34]

Yet to leave the government undisturbed had three unthinkable consequences: the Leagues would be permitted to flourish and endanger the Republic; Laval's Ethiopian policy would be permitted to wreck the League of Nations and destroy the British alliance; and a Laval government would be permitted to preside over the Popular Front elections. To overthrow Laval, on the other hand, was to risk a new February Sixth and a financial panic.

In spite of their tactical embarrassments, all the Radicals except the extreme right-wingers disliked the Laval government, but in varying degrees. The Laval deflation was opposed, but not very seriously. An occasional deputy vehemently attacked it. "Many of these decree laws are unjust, and certain ones, I do not hesitate to say, border on dishonesty."[35] Usually, however, the decrees only added fuel to already existing discontent. What is surprising is the extent to which such unpopular measures were approved within the party. When the deflation came to a vote on November 29, 63 Radicals voted in Laval's favor, which was a loss of only nine votes from June, and some of those who voted against him were such reliable Lavalists as Cornu, Michel, Martinaud-Déplat, and Castel, who did so only when they knew it would do no harm.* Moreover, the motion of confidence in Laval was presented by Briquet, Potut, Chichery, and Baron, all Radicals. The conservative Radicals waxed positively rhapsodic over the government's uninhibited deflation.[36]

---

* Judging from a vote the preceding day, the full number of supporters of deflation was probably 74, or more than supported him in June.

The left did not care to press its attack on this issue. In early November, when the Radicals and Socialists in the Finance Committee were hacking up the government's budget with such gusto that a governmental crisis threatened, the Bureau met to consider strategy. "It decided unanimously to ask its representatives in parliament and in the government to make every effort to bring about a reconciliation of the latter and the Finance Committee."[37] The unanimity meant that the following left-wingers consented or were absent—Zay, Mendès-France, Archimbaud, Lorgeré, Kayser, Lallemant, and Lange. *Le Temps* concluded: "In all, it is clear that the Bureau refused to have a hand in provoking a ministerial crisis over the budget." The unanimity in favor of supporting the government was reaffirmed at a meeting of the Group on November 15: "The Group unanimously confirmed the actions undertaken and the decisions made yesterday by its representatives,"[38] a startling statement, since the majority of the Group was hostile to the Laval government. The debate at this meeting was dominated by Herriot, Lamoureux, and Malvy, all financially orthodox; the left wing did not peep.

The Laval government's financial austerity program clearly had little to do with alienating the Radical party. The question of the armed Leagues was more serious. All Radicals were hostile to the Leagues. Laval was in a delicate position, since the bulk of his supporters favored the Leagues. It was on the matter of the Leagues that the opposition concentrated. Blum, with his usual candor, discussed in *Le Populaire* the most propitious ground for defeating the government; rejecting the decree laws because of the Radicals' ambivalent attitude, he selected the Leagues as being the only sure position.[39] Dislike for the Leagues had dominated the Radical Congress at the end of October, and fear of them was intensified by a serious clash between the Leagues and the extreme left at Limoges in late November. Not even the most conservative Radical could afford to be indifferent to the threat.

In this strait, Laval decided to give in all along the line. He gave Herriot carte blanche to settle with the Radicals as he saw fit; to make doubly sure, he staged a little comedy in the Chamber on December 5, the so-called national reconciliation, whereby a spokesman for the Leagues, Jean Ybarnégaray, spontaneously offered to disarm, to the utter astonishment of the left and the annoyance of most of the equally surprised leaguers.[40] Laval even refused to oppose a left-wing bill for complete control of the Leagues, the Thiolas amendment. By agreeing to everything demanded, he disoriented the opposition. Admittedly, some people no longer trusted him with anything. Gaston Martin, for example, said he would not trust Laval even if he "brought us the most radical declarations conceivable about his changed methods of government,"[41] but enough were won over to keep him in power. He did nothing, of course, to implement the new laws. He had succeeded, however, in tricking a majority into existence, and he was to apply the same tactics successfully on foreign policy.

The major issue was Laval's Ethiopian policy, on which no consensus existed within the party. Some deputies were deeply interested; some paid no attention.[42] Some were anti-Italian; others were not so sure. A few conservatives were even enthusiastic about Laval's scuttling the League of Nations—"Neutrality is security," or "Laval, c'est la paix!"[43] Even among the Radicals who supported the League of Nations, the arguments were blunt and unidealistic, in marked contrast to those of the British. The standard sanctionist argument had nothing to do with international law and morality. The British, the argument ran, were forced by their imperial commitments to oppose Italy's justifiable need for expansion. Since France needed the British alliance more than the Italian for defense against Germany, France had to support the League of Nations.[44] Most Radicals showed no concern for the Ethiopians as such. Lucien Lamoureux, a sanctionist, wrote: "If the conflict could have been limited to Italy and to Ethiopia, and if there had been no repercussions outside of these two countries, we might have considered sympathetically the effort of a great neighboring country to develop its national expansion and to assure its colonial power."

Even such an internationally minded deputy as Pierre Cot argued the case from power realities. "Attacking sanctions," said Cot, "is a crime against France, because such arguments would deprive us of British support, without which we could not resist German aggression, if such aggression were to occur."[45] Virtually all Radicals were fully convinced that Italy had a real need, and a right, to expand because of her exploding population.* On the other side, almost alone, was

---

* Among those I have read, only Julien Durand, ordinarily not noted for prescience, remarked that Italy already had Eritrea for her excess population and only 5,000 had settled there (*Le Petit Comtois,* December 30).

Edouard Herriot, who, all through the period from August to December, spoke for the League of Nations, legality, and humanity, and gradually awakened similar sentiments within the party.[46] Raoul Aubaud, secretary-general of the party, who proposed in September that the matter be settled by giving Italy some of Ethiopia, was, by December, moralistically denouncing the Hoare-Laval pact for doing just that.[47] The right-wingers in the party tended to be more pro-Italian, and the left-wingers more pro-Ethiopian, but this correlation was far from perfect. The most striking divergences were in the positions of Herriot and Daladier, with the former being the champion of the Ethiopians and the latter apparently approving Laval's policy. Herriot was passionately concerned with the survival of the League of Nations and with justice; at no other time in the 1930's did he come so close to statesmanship.

After Laval's success in the debate on the armed Leagues, there was no possibility that he would be defeated by parliament without help from Herriot. The positions in the party had become too fixed. Herriot could either break up the ministry by withdrawing, as he had done with Doumergue, or he could try to have it regularly defeated in parliament by putting pressure on his supporters to vote against it. Although he first took the latter tack, he was so torn between supporting the government's financial policy and attacking its foreign policy that he was reduced to almost abject incoherence. His financial apprehensions were reinforced by an ominous flight of gold in November and December,[48] which several times led him to save the government from being overthrown.[49] On the last occasion he declared to a group of Socialist and Communist leaders that he was "very hostile to the formation of a government of Popular Front, which, at the very least, might be forced into a devaluation."[50] Once again bold Edouard was successfully terrorized by the "money powers."

Since Herriot was everybody's choice to replace Laval, his repeated statements that he would neither preside over, nor take part in, the succeeding cabinet buttressed the government.[51] Thus, he was the government's most useful defender. Yet, at the same time, the Ethiopian policy infuriated him, and the insults of Henri de Kerillis in L'Echo de Paris were unbearable.

De Kerillis detested both Herriot's pro-Ethiopian policy and his pro-Communism—Herriot had just spoken at a Lyons meeting of the

Friends of the Soviet Union, which provoked the de Kerillis assault. In article after article, de Kerillis heaped invective on the hapless, hypersensitive Mayor of Lyons.* The Group voted motions reassuring him. Laval published statements reassuring him. Herriot complained publicly, and de Kerillis, delighted, quoted him as saying, "It is Laval who is putting de Kerillis up to it. . . . It is odious! . . . It is atrocious! . . . They are trying to raise the street against me; they wish to have me assassinated!"[52] When Herriot resigned from the cabinet in January, he told Laval that he could no longer remain in the government because of the insults of the right.[53]

Yet Ethiopia was his main concern. The Ethiopian affair reached a climax in December, when the Hoare-Laval plan for partition became known. Herriot replied by a speech at Montbéliard on December 15, which was so pro-Ethiopian that it was invoked by Ethiopia at Geneva in refusing the Hoare-Laval agreement. Herriot's statements were so contrary to the government's that it would be difficult to conceive of his staying in the cabinet, if not for the peculiarly hypocritical relationship he had with Laval. With the publication of the Hoare-Laval agreement, it seems clear that Herriot finally concluded that the government had to go, or, at least, that he had to leave the government. His move did not have the decisiveness of the resignation of Sir Samuel Hoare in Great Britain; it took no less than a month for Herriot to get out.

Herriot's first tactic was to try to get the Chamber to overthrow the government, while voting for it himself. This approach failed in the memorable debate on December 27 and December 28. Before this debate, when Maurice Rolland as usual asked for Herriot's advice on how the deputies of the Rhône should vote, Herriot's answer was characteristic: "Rolland, do your duty!"[54] So the Herriot contingent voted against the government for the first time. Yvon Delbos, president of the Group, made one of the three key speeches against Laval. Laval barely squeezed out a majority by reversing his own policy and coming out moderately in favor of sanctions against Italy—a method

---

* "Herriot is Public Enemy Number One," he wrote November 6. "He is very erudite, very cultivated, very much a musician, very artistic. He is reassuring. He speaks agreeably, smoothly, placing his fat hand on his fat chest, shaking his head gently, like the fat white bulls of the Nièvre when you stroke their nostrils. And, I assure you, he frightens no one."

he had already used on the matter of the Leagues—and probably by some tinkering with votes.*

The moderate Radicals, apart from Herriot's immediate circle, voted for Laval. If they had not, he would have been beaten. The Delbos motion of nonconfidence was defeated by only 296 to 276 with 20 abstentions and 18 absent; 37 Radicals voted for Laval, 14 abstained, 93 voted against, and eight were absent. Herriot had not been followed by his conservative troops, who now looked to Laval for leadership. Herriot himself, as a member of the government, had to vote against the motion, and this provided an excuse for some, who maintained that "political probity itself" required their voting for the government.[55] As Malvy had said earlier before the Group, if any minister were unhappy with the government's policy, he had only to resign.[56] But Herriot had wanted the government to be defeated in the Chamber, not overthrown by an irresponsible act of a minister or of the party.

Laval had proved himself invincible under the most difficult parliamentary circumstances. He had forged the most loyal and effective majority of the entire legislature. His Radical supporters were more faithful to him than to their party. Yet he fell within three weeks. The explanations for his resignation are extremely obscure. The most common interpretation is that "Laval had been forced to resign after the Radical-Socialist party had finally brought about the withdrawal of its ministers from the government."[57] This interpretation is more or less accepted by Edouard Bonnefous: "The Radicals hostile to the government's policy rose to 88 this time [January 16]. In these conditions the resignation of the Radical ministers became inevitable. It was hastened by the vote of the Executive Committee of the Radical party, which, according to the commentators of the right and center, was another Coup d'Angers."[58]

* Herriot wrote, "The result was fixed" (*Jadis*, II, 635). Elbel said he had never seen such faking of votes (*La Gazette vosgienne*, January 11, 1936). Crutel reported that the vote was rigged: Legions of Honor, Palms of Agricultural Merit and Public Instruction were handed out by the ministers in the lobbies; the deputies in difficult electoral situations were promised that they would not be opposed by right-wing candidates; subsidies were granted for bringing water to rural communities, and agricultural credits were widely distributed; and during the vote in the Chamber, the ballot boxes were stuffed (*L'Eveil*, January 5). See also *Marianne*, January 15, and *La Lumière*, January 4.

Bonnefous, however, adds in a footnote the explanation given in Lamoureux's memoirs, which is radically different: Herriot, ill at ease in the cabinet and wanting to escape, found a good excuse in the plan put forward by the right and welcomed by Laval for prolonging the mandate of the deputies by two years. "Herriot immediately seized on this. He had found the issue on which to fall, and he was determined not to let it go by."[59] Goguel explains the fall as follows: "To force the government to resign, it was necessary that the Radical ministers, conscious of the danger of a foreign policy that threatened to deprive France definitively of the diplomatic and military support of Great Britain, decide to abandon the Laval cabinet. They resigned in the middle of January, following a motion hostile to the government voted by the Committee of the Rue de Valois."[60]

All interpretations but Lamoureux's agree on the decisive role of the Executive Committee; Bonnefous adds the opposition of the 88 Radical deputies; Goguel cites the preoccupation with foreign policy, without making it clear whether it was the ministers or the members of the Executive Committee who were the decisive agents. The responsibility of the Executive Committee was emphasized by the conservative Radicals. Charles Bedu wrote that the crisis was the result of the decision of the Executive Committee, and that "it was the first time that an assembly without a parliamentary mandate, composed of irresponsible elements belonging almost entirely to the Paris region, had overthrown a ministry."[61] Yet assigning primary responsibility to the Executive Committee clearly distorts the causal sequence.

After Laval's victory in the foreign policy debate, the Chamber went on vacation, having given final approval to the budget. It returned to work on January 14, and the first major debate was held on January 16. The left-wing Radicals wanted to turn this debate into an interpellation on general policy, before Laval left for Geneva, with the manifest intention of overthrowing him. In another political move of exquisite finesse which evoked the grudging admiration even of his opponents,[62] Laval decided that he preferred an agricultural debate; the price of wheat had fallen again and, agriculture coming before all things, the left was beaten before it started unless they could enforce discipline within the Group.

On January 14 and January 15, what were probably the most heated debates of the 1930's took place in the Group. The left wanted discipline. Some wanted to exclude those who continued to support Laval.

"If they could not accept the vote, they did not have to remain Radicals."[63] The Bureau met; the Federation of the Seine met. No one wanted to take the extreme step of enforcing unity. Discipline, as we have already seen, was not accepted.[64] Laval went before the Chamber and won by a handsome majority of 62. Immediately thereafter came the announcement that Herriot intended to resign from the government.[65] With typical inconsistency, he asked his fellow Radical ministers to remain. (According to Lamoureux, however, Herriot really worked them over daily to try to make them resign, as he had under Doumergue.)[66] Bertrand immediately announced that he would resign also, as did Paganon the next day. Bonnet seemed likely to agree, and Herriot reported that Flandin would probably follow.[67] Laval desperately dispatched the Governor of the Bank of France to tell Herriot about the difficulties of the Treasury, but for once to no avail. La Dépêche de Toulouse on January 17 concluded that the government was lost, and L'Oeuvre wrote on January 19 that "the crisis has virtually begun."

This all took place before the Executive Committee meeting on the evening of January 19 which voted the motion hostile to the Radicals' presence in the government. The decision had clearly been taken by Herriot himself; the vote in the Executive Committee was a helpful formality. The four ministers who had announced their intention to resign prior to the meeting were the same four ministers who did resign after the meeting. The other two Radical ministers, Maupoil and Régnier, did not resign in spite of the motion. After Herriot's and the others' announcements, it was apparently decided, after endless discussions,[68] that the best strategy would be for the ministers not to resign on their own, but to have the support of an announcement by the Executive Committee, which has since been taken as responsible for the decision. The right-wing Radicals felt betrayed by this maneuver and met separately to protest. The majority faction also met separately, and each side talked of schism. Pierre Cot declared that "Those who oppose the Laval ministry are the only true Radicals. . . . Let us then form a true Radical party."[69] Laval might have survived even the resignation of the Radical ministers if the conservative Radicals alone had been concerned—they were a surprisingly devoted bunch. They met twice, and the second time voted a motion protesting the decision of the Executive Committee.[70] But Laval would have had to reconstruct his ministry and there were rumors that Flandin, Mandel, and even Marin were ready to withdraw. Laval threw in the towel and resigned.

Herriot had been the inspiration of the final overthrow of Laval. Why had he done it? Because of Ethiopia, certainly, and simple weariness, but also because of the upheaval within the party. The crisis of the Laval government coincided with Herriot's replacement as party president by Daladier and the final consummation of the Popular Front.[71]

Herriot had resigned as president in a moment of irritation at the meeting of the Executive Committee on December 18. At the end of the meeting, during which Laval's policy had been denounced but no decision taken, a left-wing party worker, Charles Addé-Vidal, came forward: "There are 78 deputies in our party who voted against the government; we must know what we want and adopt a motion that frankly decides one way or another. We are not here to support a policy of horse-trading."[72] Herriot: "[In this speech] there are arguments and an insult! No! No! No! . . . This is the first time since I have been among you that anyone has said such a thing to me. . . . In every horse trade, there must be at least two, . . . he who proposes and he who accepts. . . . If I was not the one who proposed, I must have been the one who accepted, mustn't I? . . . This cannot continue! It is over, you hear, it is final, I resign!"[73]

Was this the fruition of a Daladier plot? Probably not. The resignation caused universal surprise. If there was a plot by the left-wing Radicals, Addé-Vidal was not a part of it. According to him, his reason was a spontaneous feeling of disgust at this cover-up of the international capitulation on Ethiopia.[74] Kayser claims that Herriot's resignation as president had nothing to do with the Popular Front, but derived entirely from his false situation in a ministry opposed by a majority of his own party.[75]

Left and right, however, immediately drew the consequences, the one side to push Daladier to the presidency, the other to try to get Herriot to change his mind or promote Chautemps as an alternative.[76] To ensure Daladier's election, the Federation of the Seine packed the Executive Committee and demonstrated against Herriot at the meeting in the Hotel Continental on January 19, 1936. The change in presidents was marked by the conversion of the party to the Popular Front. The program of the Popular Front was published on January 10, 1936. The Bureau confirmed that the Radicals who had participated in its formulation were duly mandated by the party, and the same Executive Committee that asked the ministers to leave the government and elected Daladier as president of the party explicitly accepted the Popular Front program and the Radicals' participation.

Yet have the real reasons for the successful overthrow of the Laval government been discovered? Was it simply an accumulation of discontents and a change of party leadership? If Herriot was concerned only about foreign policy, why did he wait until the debate on interpellations of January 16 instead of resigning immediately after the foreign policy debate on December 28? Again, if the Radicals were really so concerned about the League of Nations, the armed Leagues, and deflation, why did they not change these policies in the Radical-dominated Sarraut government that replaced Laval? The Sarraut government again rejected England's demand for the petroleum sanction against Italy. It did nothing about the Leagues until the assault on Blum forced it to take measures against the Action Française. It retained Laval's Finance Minister, Marcel Régnier, and with him his decree laws. On all these matters, not a peep was heard from the Radicals, left or right. Yet these were the questions that had provoked turmoil throughout the fall and early winter.

Laval's government had begun to disintegrate immediately following his successful repulse of the attack on January 16. The motives for the new assault on the government had been only marginally connected with the issues raised earlier, a point emphasized by Blum in his brief, blunt speech in the Chamber:

In a few minutes you are going to cast the vote that will decide whether the government will preside over the elections. . . . If the government is not overthrown today by a republican majority, the elections will take place in a state of confusion, trouble, and political improbity that will compromise their result. . . . A party like the Radicals cannot . . . go before the electorate at the same time as a party of opposition and as a party participating in the government. . . . This contradiction would affect the entire coming electoral campaign. It would weaken by disappointment, worry, and suspicion the movement of the Popular Front . . . on which liberty in this country and peace abroad depend. You will do something more, something that is so grave that I ask you to reflect for a moment about it: you will compromise the fate of the coming legislature in advance. . . . You risk condemning the coming majority to impotence if you permit the elections to be equivocal, if you Radicals return here with deputies representing two irreconcilable states of mind.[77]

At the Bureau on January 15, Jean Hérard was reported as saying to the general approval: "The whole problem is whether we can tolerate a Laval government presiding over the elections."[78] When the Sarraut government was formed, and when it got the support of the Communists and Socialists, somewhat to its own surprise, the equivocation that Blum feared had been resolved. Henceforth nothing was done about other problems. Whether Herriot was finally moved to action by electoral considerations or simply by an undifferentiated exasperation at accumulated grievances cannot be known.

The defeat of the Laval government was a dreadfully inefficient political operation. It took so long that the issues that had first aroused the hostility to it were forgotten. The only real accomplishment was to change governments for the elections, which may be what underlay the opposition from the beginning. The elections shoved the threat to the peace from Italy and the (possible) threat to the Republic from the Leagues into the background. In all, it is a rather sorry tale.

With Laval overthrown, the delicate problem of his replacement had to be faced. The formation of Albert Sarraut's ministry was one of the most difficult of the period. Sarraut tried to form a ministry of the right, but ran into such sustained opposition from the disgruntled moderates—according to *La Lumière,* 52 moderates were offered portfolios—that the left rallied to his support. Sarraut's government became one of the left in spite of itself. The extreme left and extreme right of the party were equally unhappy about the new ministry. *Le Temps* wrote: "The situation created by the Radical-Socialist intrigues is so complex and confused that the malaise endemic among the Radicals has infected the neighboring groups."[79] The Socialists told the left-wingers to be sensible, and the Group decided to enforce discipline in favor of the Sarraut government. The government and the deputies then went home to prepare for their elections.

CHAPTER 8

The Decline of the Popular Front

I

The meeting of the Executive Committee on January 19, 1936, was the high point of the Radicals' affair with the Popular Front. Henceforth, one can only speak of a slow decline. Daladier completed his take-over of the party two weeks later when he replaced Herriot as president of the Group.[1] Now that he was in control, he had no more interest in being decidedly left-wing, for that would only weaken his party and would do him no good, and so he immediately began to show considerable reserve toward the Popular Front,[2] as did the party as a whole. The agitation that had filled the fall and early winter vanished. The Group rarely met. Apart from some slow-dying fulminations of the impenitent Lavalists, the divisions in the Group subsided.

The only excitement of a purely political sort came at the Committee of the Popular Front, when Vincent Auriol suggested that the candidates of all the parties be asked to sign the program of the Popular Front. "If [the program] is not going to have any practical usefulness," he asked, "if it is not going to be the link between the parties and the organizations and the basis for a joint undertaking, if it is to remain a dead letter, then why was it drawn up? Why did every party sign it?" The Communists saw at once that Auriol's proposal was a grave political error and dispatched a letter to the Radicals: "It would be, in our opinion, an unpardonable political error to involve the Popular Front to any extent in the campaign for the legislative elections."[3] The Radicals, of course, hotly rejected the Auriol plan.[4] The local Socialists, undeterred, seem to have submitted the Popular Front program to most of the deputies for signature, and to have voted against those who refused, thereby causing considerable resentment among the Radicals.[5]

The Sarraut government was kept from applying itself single-mindedly to its appointed task of preparing the elections by two events. First, Léon Blum was attacked in the street by the Action Française, a provocation that forced the government to ban the movement. The Radicals played no great role in the hullabaloo created by this attack, or in the Popular Front parade that followed, except that Sarraut insisted the marchers carry a considerable number of tricolors as well as red flags; since there were few Radical party workers to carry them, "it was the Socialist and Communist party workers in the end who themselves proposed that they carry the national standards."[6]

The second major event of the Sarraut government was the German occupation of the Rhineland. The Radicals showed no enthusiasm for taking serious action. The coup was passed over almost in silence by the local press, and those papers that did write about it supported a passive policy. Within the cabinet, only Sarraut himself, Henri Guernut, and perhaps Yvon Delbos,[7] among the nine Radical ministers, favored taking action, and it seems probable that Chautemps within the cabinet and perhaps Roche outside it were working hard against any positive measures.[8] The Radical president of the Chamber's Foreign Affairs Committee, Paul Bastid, refused to call the committee into session "in order not to alarm the French people."[9] The Radical Group met once, rather late (March 10), at which time Bastid was the only speaker and the government's inaction was approved without reserve.[10] There was, in short, no pressure from the Radicals for doing anything, and a good deal of support for doing nothing.

The party's main interest was the election. The national electoral campaign was quiet. Herriot did not speak outside Lyons; Chautemps refused to commit himself: "Because of my ministerial functions, and my wish to keep a great reserve and to leave the Premier the job of expressing the government's thought, I have voluntarily held myself aloof from the electoral campaign."[11] Daladier made an important speech at Beauvais, another at Orange in March, and as leader of the party, a radio speech just before the elections. The Executive Committee published a manifesto that no one paid any attention to. There was none of the excitement of 1932.

The Radicals ran into trouble from their left-wing allies; in the Landes, for instance, Robert Bezos, a member of the directing committee of the Popular Front, to his surprise found himself being treated by the Socialists as a member of the Croix de Feu.[12] Ducos's paper complained that his meetings were systematically obstructed by gangs of Socialists and Communists imported from Toulouse and armed with blackjacks.[13] There was scarcely any violence reported from the right.

On the part of the Radicals, the provincial campaign was very restrained, disturbed only by the conservatives' shrill anti-Communism. Now that the party was in the Popular Front, many left-wingers, like Daladier, became careful not to drive the conservatives out of the party. In the Federation of Indre-et-Loire, for example, a general meeting was held to consider the coming elections. Senator René Besnard announced his resignation as president of the federation because of "the increasingly accentuated tendency within the Radical party to form a general alliance with the Socialists and the Communists." A series of speakers immediately urged him to reconsider, assuring him of their "affectionate devotion." Finally the leader of the Popular Front faction within the federation likewise urged the staunchly conservative president to remain. His reasons? "What will happen," said the Popular Front partisan, "is that either the federation will name a Popular Front president and thereby surely lose a considerable number of its members [the conservatives], or it will name a president who shares the ideas of René Besnard, and therefore there is no reason that it not be he."[14] The federation entered the Popular Front and kept its right-wing deputy from Chinon, Léon Courson, as a reluctant supporter of Blum for a full year.

Another method of avoiding conflict was simply to keep quiet so that nobody could argue. "If the Radical-Socialist party does not participate in all the public discussions or all the meetings of the Popular Front, it is because it thinks that it is often a dangerous game to support political ideas in a public meeting that offend the opinions of one's associates, and might let the presentation of opposing political doctrines degenerate into painful controversy and conflicts in front of the audience."[15] Even those on the far left of the party seemed uneasy about what they were getting into and felt that they had to reassure their electors. A very pro-Popular Front deputy wrote, "I am faithful to the ideals of Radicalism, a firm supporter of the *principle of private property*," and only then did he add, "I abide by the program of the Popular Front."[16]

There was no such reticence on the part of the conservative Radicals. The full flavor of Radical anti-Communism was to be tasted not in Paris, but in the provinces. Auguste Chambonnet claimed that he would defend "the republican ideal against the domination of the Socialist-Communist dictatorship, which, behind the red flag, under the banner of Moscow, will lead us to bankruptcy, ruin, and civil war." Malvy claimed that the Popular Front advocated "a policy of *revolution* and *disorder* [while our program] is a democratic policy of order and consistent *progress* by means of wisdom and reason." James Sclafer tersely announced that "the choice to be made is between Socialism and the Republic." For Queuille, to vote for the Popular Front candidate would be to serve the USSR instead of the Republic.[17] Once in the Chamber, Chambonnet and Malvy openly went into opposition, but Sclafer voted for Blum even in 1938, and Queuille was Minister of Public Works in Chautemps's nominally Popular Front cabinet.

These statements were the product of prudent and responsible deputies; the party workers expressed themselves with less restraint. It is difficult to come up with a pure statement of aroused party-worker feeling, since, in the press, the party workers usually let the professionals do the writing. One authentic outburst of pure anti-Communism is cited here at some length, not only for the particular sentiments expressed, but also for its typically Radical historical outlook:

For more than thirty years we have followed Radical-Socialist policy with the certainty of preserving for the Republic the character defined by Waldeck-Rousseau, Clemenceau, Combes, and so many other great politicians.

Our ideal has been to continue the policy of our forebears, who made the Revolutions of 1789 and 1848 in order to give Frenchmen the status of citizens, that is to say, free men.

The great principles of liberty, equality, and fraternity are at the root of our ideas.

Faithful to the Declaration of the Rights of Man and Citizen, we regard property as an inviolable and sacred right, as the only one able to raise man to the state of a free citizen.

We have fought without a let-up. We have sacrificed everything to these ideas, to this ideal.

Now, we state that, under the influence of forces that we have not been able to define, our party has itself been drawn bit by bit toward ideas that today lead it in the wake of the collectivists.

Our ideal is dead!

Our dearest principles have been progressively annihilated by the extremists who, scoffing at the liberty that our fathers established, try to make the people believe that its future lies with collectivism, which is synonymous with slavery.

For a long time we were afraid of worse, and so we made concessions. Today the truth leaps to one's eyes. We must react with the same faith, with the same force that guided the steps of our fathers toward the Bastille in 1789, and to the barricades in 1848! . . .

Certainly, we want to alleviate the burden of the working classes! Certainly, we are determined to give all human beings the greatest well-being! But is it by delivering ourselves hand and foot to destructive Communism that this is to be achieved?

No! We do not want massacres.

We do not want the unthinking fury of the Revolution to ravage our France.

We Radical-Socialists, we are the patriots descended from those who, at Valmy, in wooden shoes and armed with pitchforks, fought the foreign armies that were coming to enslave us. We are still Radical-Socialists.

We will always be Radical-Socialists! Today betrayed by those in whom we placed our trust, we feel the soul of our ancestors revive within us.

We are free citizens, we are not tied by any contract. Our consciences are not for sale.

We are not defenseless animals to be slaughtered, sold to have our throats slit.

We protest and denounce the traitors who, having abused our trust in order to give free rein to their rancor and hate, do not hesitate to deliver the country to massacres.

Citizens:
Communism aspires to dictatorship.
We Radicals, as true republicans, aspire to liberty, equality, fraternity.
No killing! No useless destruction! Fight enslaving Communism!
Everybody vote! Under the folds of the tricolor!
For the grandeur of the French Republic!
One and indivisible!
Democratic and social!

VOTE AGAINST THE REVOLUTION! Vive la République!

[Signed:] A group of Radical-Socialists who do not wish to trail in the wake of Berlin, of Rome, or of *Moscow*.[18]

The reticence of the left and belligerency of the right during the campaign indicate that already the initiative had left the hands of the pro-Popular Front forces. They were to remain on the defensive thereafter.

In the 47 campaigns analyzed through the local press, ten Radical candidates opposed the Popular Front; 17 avoided the issue entirely; 20 favored the left, but only ten of these mentioned the Popular Front by name, and none made it a major point. This reticence pervades the declarations of the candidates, as collected in the *Barodet*. The ten anti-Popular Front candidates, on the other hand, dealt with it at length. Out of 101 declarations analyzed, 15 supported the Popular Front by name, and five, all conservative, attacked it by name.

If we shift our attention from alliances to specific programs, the Popular Front gets even less attention; only two left-wingers said they supported the program of the Popular Front. Of the items in the program, 29 candidates wanted to reform the Bank of France and 15 to control the arms industry. The other items were scarcely mentioned. Left and right were still moderately attached to their stodgy economic doctrines, with the left more hostile to deflation than the right. Twenty-two deputies still wanted deflation; only 11 attacked it. Nineteen mentioned devaluation, all opposing it. In the main, however, maintaining the currency was of less concern in 1936 than in 1932.

The party faced the elections sanguinely, some Radicals having predicted the previous October that they would win 150 to 160 seats, and Edmond Pfeiffer, immediately before the elections, wrote that it was generally thought they would lose only a few seats.[19] When they lost 400,000 votes and about fifty seats, the stupefaction was universal.[20]

The Radicals were the big losers in the elections. In 174 constituencies represented by Radicals in 1932 or 1936, the party lost votes in 140 and gained in only 34. No wing of the party was spared this onslaught, but the extent of the suffering varied. The moderates were crushed, dropping from 40 deputies to 23; the left wing maintained itself almost intact, only slipping from 28 to 24. The conservatives and moderate left fared about the same, the former dropping from 37 to 28, the latter from 53 to 37. The significance of these shifts is evident: the left and moderate left for the first time had a clear majority within the Group.[21]

The Radicals did not lose all their seats or all their votes to the left: they lost 30 seats to the Socialists, 12 to the Communists, seven to the center, and 26 to the right. They gained five from the Socialists, five from the center, and eight from the right. In 61 Radical constituencies, votes were lost to both left and right; in 50, votes were lost on the left, but maintained or won from the right; in 23 constituencies, votes were lost on the right, but gained from the left. Conservative and moderate deputies did somewhat better against the right, left and moderate-left deputies somewhat better against the left.

An examination of the electoral statistics for the Radical constituencies shows that the two categories of left-wing Radicals suffered considerably smaller losses of votes than the two right-wing groups. When a deputy lost over 20 per cent of the registered voters in his constituency, he was eliminated from politics, except in a few instances in which he had received more than 40 per cent of the registered vote in 1932. From the graphs on p. 204, the left's relatively successful resistance can be easily seen. Only 25 per cent of the constituencies where Radicalism was shattered were on the left, which accounted for 69 per cent of those where the loss was less than 5 per cent of the vote. The left-wing deputies apparently benefited either from their more plausible attachment to the Popular Front, or from their opposition to the unpopular deflationary governments, or both. The pattern is abruptly reversed, however, in those constituencies where the Radicals gained votes; here the strongest group is the conservatives, who were quite clearly the local heirs of the now vanished right, as a constituency-by-constituency examination demonstrates. This electoral situation presaged a novel kind of Radicalism, a new nuance of the right, and it gave solid electoral support for the conservative combativeness that almost immediately began to upset the old practices of the party.

II

With Blum's arrival in power in June 1936, the Radicals' role in French politics was altered. The intrigues in the corridors, in which the Radicals had flourished, were downgraded, and it took them some time to learn the new politics of mass demonstration, for which they had no natural talent. The personal quarrels within the party were now abated since Daladier was fully occupied with his Ministry of National Defense and Herriot had withdrawn into semi-retirement as president of the Chamber. Chautemps emerged as the dominant Radical, and he was content to groom himself as Blum's successor; Bonnet, indeed, caused a great deal of difficulty until he was appointed ambassador to Washington. The left was decapitated by the massive entry of six members into the government and of a seventh, Jammy Schmidt, into the Finance Committee as *rapporteur-général*. Of the former left-wing leaders, only Mendès-France remained outside, and he played a rather marginal role henceforth. The moderate and moderate-left Radicals were thoroughly chastened and subdued. In parliament, the deputies spoke so seldom that in the Congress in the fall, the reporter on the activity of the Group had to apologize for its "having

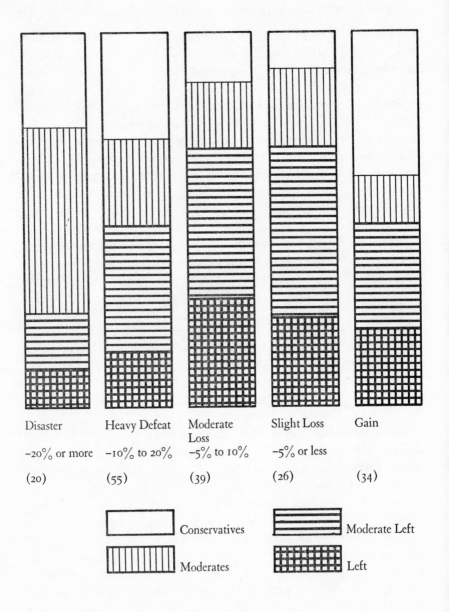

Disaster	Heavy Defeat	Moderate Loss	Slight Loss	Gain
−20% or more	−10% to 20%	−5% to 10%	−5% or less	
(20)	(55)	(39)	(26)	(34)

Conservatives   Moderate Left

Moderates   Left

Relative Losses or Gains of the Four Voting Groups (change in the percentage of the registered vote). The figures in parentheses indicate the number of constituencies affected.

withdrawn somewhat into itself."[22] Usually only Campinchi, as the new president of the Group, spoke (briefly) in its name. Meetings of the Group no longer caused governments to tremble, and often went unreported. Locally, meetings of federations ceased and newspapers stopped publishing. The only signs of life came from the conservative revival. The heroic days of the summer of 1936 are part of the Socialists' story, not that of the Radicals, who limited themselves to trying to restrain the enthusiasm of their allies, with only partial success. As Marcel Ribera said of the Popular Front, "Nous y sommes un peu les parents pauvres, nous autres, les radicaux."[23] The only initiative that really remained with them was to break the Popular Front, which some of them immediately set about doing.

Goguel writes that in the summer of 1936 "numerous Radicals shared the uneasiness [of the right and center] although, except for those in the Senate, they scarcely dared express it."[24] The numerical vagueness of this statement suggests that the government was not firmly supported in the Radical party. It was well known from the time of the elections that the conservative Radicals had no enthusiasm for the Popular Front, although all of them did not move immediately into opposition;[25] and Goguel's statement can scarcely be interpreted as including anyone else besides the 23 moderates, which still leaves the Popular Front firmly anchored in the Radical party. As we have seen, the elections shifted the balance in favor of the left wing of the party. Yet even the conservatives were willing, faced with the clear decision of the electorate, to permit the experiment to go on, "to be pushed to its very end, so that this end may be irrefutably shown to be quite bitter."[26] Lamoureux wrote in this vein:

If the experiment must fail, my wish is that it mark not only a failure in conception, but also a failure in action. I hope, that is, that the Radical party, which is involved in this enterprise along with the Socialists and Communists, lets the experiment be pushed to its limits, and that no chance is denied it that would have permitted it to succeed. . . . If . . . it fails, the failure must be certain, it must lead to no argument, and above all to no excuses; it must be entirely certain that the Socialist concepts failed in their aim and are bankrupt.[27]

Thus, although the ideological initiative passed from the left to the right in the early months of 1936, electoral support and parliamentary strategy ensured for a long time the position of the Popular Front within the Radical party. The moderate left and the left-wing Radi-

cals were, for the first year, firm supporters of the Popular Front.
When Lamoureux returned to the Chamber in January 1937 after his
successful by-election, he was struck by the way the Group was entirely
dominated by a number of left-wing deputies who "believed in the
Popular Front as if it were Santa Claus."[28] There were over sixty such
Radicals in the Group, which was sufficient to give Blum a majority
under the most trying circumstances. The moderates also were committed to the Popular Front, at least in June 1936. Thus a large part
of the Radicals' support for the Popular Front was perfectly sincere
and went considerably beyond the hypocritical opportunism that undoubtedly inspired some.

The eclipse of the deputies and their prolonged silence meant that
the Radicals acted efficaciously only in the Senate and in the cabinet.
The Senate forced the government to promise to prevent occupation
of the factories.[29] It was a Radical senator, the venerable Bienvenu-
Martin, who on July 7 summoned the Minister of the Interior, Roger
Salengro, to maintain order. The overwhelming majority of the Senate favored order, and the senators were determined to use their power
to enforce it. They were sufficiently wary, however, to know when not
to exceed their limits; so, in the summer of 1936, they contented themselves with warnings and with extorting the promise from Salengro.
So weak were the links, however, of most of the senators with the
party that it is much more correct to speak of a senatorial action than
of a Radical action in the Senate.

The activity of the Radical ministers within the cabinet is more
clearly a purely Radical affair. There were 13 Radical ministers in
the monster thirty-six-member government; of these, six were left-
wing, three moderate-left, and four moderate, there being no conservatives. Very early, apparently, the Radical ministers began withdrawing from cabinet meetings to work out a common position[30] (as did
the Socialists), an innovation that lent the party a more concrete existence in the government than it previously had. Ministers began assuring the public that ministerial harmony was really very good, which
probably indicated that it was not. The one issue on which the action
of the Radicals within the ministry is at all clear is the question of the
Spanish Civil War and the adoption of the policy of nonintervention.

The Radicals are generally allotted a major portion of responsibility
for the policy of nonintervention.[31] Léon Blum said, after World War
II: "The principal leaders of the Radical party had indicated to Delbos
how much they feared my proposal [to deliver arms to Spain]. I tried

to modify this position by a talk with Herriot, but I found that he showed great reserve on the Spanish question and forcefully advised me to do the same."[32] Blum also said, in his controversy with Jean Piot in 1939, that all the Radical ministers without exception supported this position. There is no question that a number of Radicals vigorously opposed intervention—Chautemps, Herriot, and, eventually, Delbos.[33] Combined with the President of the Republic, Lebrun, and the president of the Senate, Jeanneney, neither of whom was a Radical, they made a formidable crew and undoubtedly influenced Blum greatly. The other Radical cabinet ministers, however, are not easily disposed of. Pierre Cot, the leader of the left-wing Radicals in the cabinet, was perhaps the principal advocate of helping the Spanish Republicans.[34] Daladier's position is far more obscure, although as Minister of Defense and president of the Radical party he was a key figure. According to the American chargé d'affaires, "Our informant states that Delbos and Daladier even went so far as to threaten to resign if [nonintervention] were not adopted."[35] Yet, according to Jean Zay, "Daladier accepted nonintervention only with angry grumbles."[36] According to Paul Bastid, only three of the 13 Radical ministers in the cabinet supported nonintervention—Chautemps, Delbos, and, surprisingly, he himself.[37] Cot added Marc Rucart to the list of those sympathetic to the Spanish Republicans.[38] Probably the opinion of the less important ministers and the undersecretaries made little difference. Dezarnaulds was certainly very lukewarm; de Tessan and Liautey probably favored intervention, since both were directors of the committee for Franco-Spanish friendship later set up to prevent the recognition of the nationalist regime.[39] It seems fairly clear that as far as the ministers were concerned, the majority among the Radicals favored helping the Republicans.[40] What is interesting for a study of the party is that within the cabinet and, informally, on the highest level, the Radicals played a key role in the decision-making and, as usual, in contradictory fashions. It is also interesting to note that Herriot, despite his loss of the presidency and withdrawal from party affairs, seems to have played a role as important as Daladier's; Chautemps, for the first time in this crisis, ceased being a conciliator and emerged as a protagonist.

III

Much less attention has been paid to the decline of the Popular Front than to its rise. Most treatments grant it a moment of triumph during the great strikes and the rash of social reforms, but then it gradually fades away, until it is quite forgotten in the Anschluss, Munich, and the war. This is, of course, precisely what happened; as David Thomson says succinctly: "The Popular Front experiment neither failed nor was it overthrown. It was smothered by the looming clouds of international crisis."[41] It is quite impossible to date its end. Yet the Blum government did fail, and the majority of Radicals decisively and vocally rejected the Popular Front.

Why the Blum government failed is an interesting question, but entirely outside the scope of this study. What concerns us here is what turned the Radicals away from the Popular Front. The presence of the Radicals was essential, for without them there was no Popular Front, and their rejection of the alliance ended the Popular Front. Would they have departed if the Blum government's economic and foreign policy had succeeded? This is a basic question, since the Blum government and the Popular Front are often mistakenly treated as synonymous, and the survival of the Popular Front thought to be dependent on the success of the Blum experiment. Alfred Sauvy, for example, writes: "For the rational observer, the Popular Front had won in December 1936. . . . Only a few more months, and it would have attained the production levels of 1928. That would have been an unprecedented *political victory*." The failure to do so was "an unprecedented *suicide*."[42] Yet in October 1936 the Popular Front was assaulted, battered, and almost overthrown by the Radical Congress of Biarritz, long before the financial or economic failure of the Blum government was clear. The Radicals had joined the Blum government to fight for bread, liberty, and peace; after October, they remained in it simply because, for the moment, there was nothing to replace it with. The enthusiasm that had swept the party in the preceding winter was exhausted by autumn.

The reasons for this disaffection are numerous; the dreary tale of the vicissitudes of Blum's government is well known—the strikes of June 1936, the hurried social reforms, the hesitation over the Spanish Civil War, the embarrassed devaluation, inflation, economic stagnation, only to mention the high points. This list seems to give sufficient cause for the Radicals' estrangement. All these difficulties played a role, of course, but in very varying degrees, as a point-by-point examination demonstrates. The basic social reforms were the Matignon agreements on wages, paid vacations, the forty-hour week, and collective bargaining. Duverger blames resistance to these reforms among the Radical voters for the Radicals' growing coolness toward the Popular Front.[43]

Yet, whatever their secret feelings may have been, the Radicals never publicly protested these reforms. When the program was originally drawn up, it was generally recognized that it was as timid a manifestation of the revolutionary spirit as an aspiring social revolution had yet managed to produce.[44] The Radical program, Daladier immediately announced, was far more daring; Zay said that it would have to be complemented by "infinitely bolder measures."[45] After the reforms were enacted, the moderates joined the refrain. "The Radical party," said Chautemps, "does not flinch before any daring reform; all the measures adopted recently by parliament have been—we are proud to state—derived from our own program." He was, of course, in the government; what about the really conservative opposition? Paul Marchandeau said: "It is the Radicals' own program that has been followed"; Alfred Dominique, a real reactionary, found it "timid and insufficient."[46] The last two made these affirmations while bitterly attacking the Popular Front itself. Daladier, not to be outdone, claimed that all the measures had been included in the program of his 1933 government and would have been enacted if he had not been overthrown by the Socialists.[47] As time passed and memories faded, the Radicals' public attachment to the program, if anything, increased. When they had finally broken the Popular Front and had no more need to be mealymouthed, they claimed that "the program . . . in its broad lines did not differ from their own program and [it remains] more than ever the expression of their own ideals."[48] Even the Blum-slaying senators agreed: Abel Gardey, immediately after demolishing the Blum government, said that he fully approved of the social program of the Popular Front.[49] I have found no instance of the social reforms being denounced in the local press, despite all the subsequent discussion.

The only aspect of the social program that aroused hostility was the economically disastrous forty-hour week, which unquestionably hurt the interests of the Radical clientele.[50] Following its application at the beginning of 1937, the complaints became chronic. Campinchi, as president of the Group, in an important speech in the Chamber, said, "Everyone recognizes the principle of the forty-hour week as being just; but I think that its simultaneous application to too many areas—particularly to small and middle-sized enterprises—risks having effects that may hinder the economic revival we are all seeking."[51] Yet the Radicals never indulged in an all-out assault even on the forty-hour week. At the Congress of Marseilles, when it was no longer necessary to compromise with the parties of the left, Daladier said: "We have no intention of abrogating the forty-hour law . . . but it is indispensable that . . . it be made flexible, without useless formalities."[52]

Doubtless much of this reticence was simply political good sense, since the social reforms were enormously popular among the working classes. The essential point is that the Radicals never used the social reforms as a weapon against the Popular Front; their hostility was no doubt partially nourished by resentment of them, but their attack focused on a quite different issue—an issue which admitted of no such easy solution as rescinding the social reforms, and which warped the subsequent development of the Radical party.

In contrast to the social policy, the economic and financial policy of the government was a failure, everyone agrees. Yet economic issues never became very important in the attacks on the Popular Front within the Radical party. The Radicals were not concerned for long about the devaluation of September 1936, which was carried out in rather disreputable circumstances and generally regarded as detrimental to Radical interests. Devaluation had been fought over for more than two years, and, although the Radicals were against it as were all the parties, they seemed resigned to it. When it occurred, there was a certain flurry—Milhaud crowed that it marked the failure of the Popular Front,[53] and Bonnet denounced it in the Chamber. But this attitude was by no means universal. Riou, a conservative, acknowledged that it was inevitable.[54] Bertrand, a moderate, admitted that it was forced by circumstances.[55] At the Congress of Biarritz, the devaluation aroused a certain amount of hostility,[56] but after that the question was dropped. It may have formed a part of the underlying fund of discontent, but it never became a symbol.

The broader economic issues never became a very important part of the attacks on the Popular Front within the party. When Emile Roche tried to destroy the Popular Front at Biarritz, he did not mention economic matters once.[57] When the party finally broke with the Popular Front in 1938, there was not a word of complaint against Popular Front economics. It can even be questioned whether the average Radical was all that discontented with the Popular Front economic program. A local notable of the Gers, for instance, in an analysis of the decline of enthusiasm for the Popular Front in that region, denied that it had anything to do with economic discontent; on the contrary, people there were fully satisfied, since wheat prices were high, markets were good (because of the rise in workers' salaries), inflation was not severe, and the devaluation had not been followed by the anticipated catastrophe. The causes for discontent lay elsewhere.[58]

The economic reform that most profoundly affected the Radical clientele was the creation of the Wheat Board. It is said to have been strongly opposed by the Radicals and highly unpopular in general.[59] It profoundly altered the situation of the wheatgrower, since the free market was suppressed. The reform was carried out by the Socialist Georges Monnet, and was a reversal of the previous Radical policies of protectionism and piecemeal palliatives—easy credit, storage of surpluses, the abortive minimum price, and so on. The Radical program had been implemented principally by Queuille, the very conservative president of the important Société Nationale d'Encouragement à l'Agriculture. It is generally assumed that Queuille put Radical doctrine into practice and was supported by the party. Yet there were other currents of agricultural thought within the party. The agricultural committee of the party was headed by André Liautey, who generally made the reports in the Congress and was Undersecretary of State for Agriculture from 1936 to 1938. Liautey disliked Queuille's policy, which he claimed was dominated by the big landowners and the trusts. "The policy of the great landed-property holders," he wrote, "which aims only at protecting production, must be replaced by a democratic policy that aims at saving the small peasant from the ruin which threatens him."[60] He was not very happy with the Wheat Board, which he claimed was statist, but if forced to choose he preferred the Socialist policy to Queuille's, since it was positive.

The average rural deputy did not fully share either Queuille's or Liautey's ideas. He seemed fairly unconcerned with doctrine and was interested chiefly in higher prices. Since the Wheat Board seemed to bolster prices, it was greeted favorably and never really opposed. In 1938, the rural deputy Cabanis wrote: "The Wheat Board, in spite of politically inspired criticism, has contributed greatly to raising agricultural prices."[61] No opposition to the Wheat Board is to be found in the local press, and the Congress of 1938 endorsed it: "Once again, in

August 1936 the Radical-Socialist party made a reality of its ideal in voting the creation of the national Wheat Board, a lifeline thrown to an exhausted and discouraged peasantry."[62] The Wheat Board, far from weakening the Popular Front, economically buttressed it in one of the most crucial areas.

It would not be correct to say that the Radicals were unaffected by the economic floundering of the Popular Front. At times, they showed considerable concern, especially in the later years when French production was manifestly insufficient in the face of the German threat. But even then, economic discontent was a subordinate theme in the decline and fall of the Popular Front. In the beginning, it was negligible.

In considering the decline of the Popular Front, it must be remembered that its program and the problems it faced were out of phase. The program, drawn up in the fall of 1935, was preoccupied with social reforms and the fight against fascism. By the summer of 1936 the local fascists—if such they were—no longer were very frightening. The street disturbances now came from the Communists. The social reforms were passed in a spurt, and were regarded as something long overdue and inevitable. They were accepted even by the right. Campinchi said in the Chamber, without being contradicted: "As far as we are concerned, this social legislation is beyond dispute. Why? Because it was necessary! And so clearly necessary that we can be sure the opponents of the Popular Front will neither oppose it nor interfere with it, nor do they even express any intention of doing so."[63]

The program gave no satisfactory answer to the big problems of the next years. It had no solution for the perennial problem of the deficit. With the Spanish Civil War, foreign policy became dominant, and on this the Popular Front program said nothing, for although the Ethiopian affair was at its peak during the formulation of the program, foreign policy, according to Kayser, was scarcely ever discussed by the committee that wrote the program.[64] The few anodyne provisions about the League of Nations and disarmament were anachronistic. It was no longer a question of disarming, but of arming. By the time the Congress of Biarritz was held, the slogans of the Popular Front already seemed echoes from a distant past.

The right's attack on the Popular Front centered on two issues: the great strikes of June 1936 and the problems raised by the Spanish Civil

War. Nothing the government could have done would have mitigated the effects of these two events. The strikes came first and caused what Bertrand de Jouvenel has called "the great fear of June 1936."[65] Although not in themselves disorderly, the strikes created an overwhelming impression of the sudden disappearance of all public authority, surpassing, in this respect, anything the Leagues had done. The Radicals suddenly became frightened when they discovered that their Communist playfellows had turned into a mass of striking men. They were never to feel easy with them again. When Blum first presented himself to the Chamber, Campinchi was the only Radical who spoke. The kernel of his uncommonly short and cold speech was: "The government, suddenly beset by unforeseen events [the strikes], must not forget that the most urgent problem is not only political and economic, but also a problem of authority. A debilitated assembly of men grouped around a program will be a government only in name, and will be destined to rapidly disappear amidst the turmoil, if it does not know that to govern is not to exhort, but to act promptly and efficaciously."[66] Campinchi had been the Popular Front choice over Georges Bonnet for the presidency of the Group.

The transformation the strikes accomplished can be appreciated by comparing statements made before and after their occurrence. At the Executive Committee meeting of May 22, 1936, Emile Roche urged that the Radicals loyally collaborate in the government; at the meeting of July 1, he began his anti-Communist crusade. "We wanted to fight for peace and liberty; watch out that we do not have to defend them against the Communist party!" The shift in attitude was clearly inspired by the strikes: "I ask you to remember a certain Thursday. Everything in Paris was closed. There was an atmosphere of revolution. Imagine that in the place of partial strikes, a general strike had been decreed, and that the Communists had ordered out the masses at their disposition. That night, the revolution could have been made."[67] This speech by Roche, which was the manifesto of the right-wing attack on the Popular Front, caused a considerable stir in the Radical party. The same shift can be seen in the attitude of Gaston Thiébaut, a deputy. In May, he had been thoroughly pleased with the elections; in June, he warned of "the danger that will threaten France and her freely chosen regime if the real or pretended exaltation of the working classes continues."[68] The very first action taken by the newly reconstituted Radical Group within the Chamber was to send a delegation "to remind the Communists and trade unionists of their promise to support the government of Popular Front loyally and faithfully."[69] Chautemps made a speech calling for order.[70]

One qualification must be made about the effects of the strikes; although the deputies directly experienced them at their height in Paris, their voters in the provinces did not. There were very few strikes in Radical districts. Scarcely any were mentioned in the local press. The typical department had no strikes and read about them only in the newspapers. The effect there must have been considerably attenuated.

The strikes subsided temporarily, but in late summer began again, this time clearly directed by the Communists in order to force the government to help the Spanish Republicans. We have already seen that the attitude of the Radicals in the cabinet was at first sharply divided over what should be done in Spain. When the Communists began promoting strikes, parades, and public meetings to enforce intervention, the Radical reaction was uncertain. All groups within the party disliked the strikes, but Spain was a different question—a question that troubled the Radicals as it did all parties in France, creating a division that within the Radical party generally conformed to voting groups. The conservatives categorically condemned intervention; Riou wrote, "Without the desperate efforts of the Radicals—on three occasions I was their spokesman in the Foreign Affairs Committee—the West would have now been in flames."[71] In this, the conservatives reflected a trend, to become more and more marked in the next few years, of following the intellectual lead of the French right wing, and became fully assimilated to it. The left-wingers were sympathetic to the Republicans, but it was very difficult for them to demand arms for Spain since that was contrary to the government's official policy.[72] Most of the center deputies sincerely supported the government's policy while offering condolences to the Republicans.[73]

This pattern was not wholly consistent. The Spanish affair once again saw foreign policies cut across the traditional left-right spectrum. A minority of right-wing deputies favored helping the Republicans.[74] More left-wing deputies shifted the other way. Jammy Schmidt, for instance, attacked Bayet's left-wing criticism of the official policy.[75] Dezarnaulds and Delattre wanted neutrality.[76]

With the left in a false position or hesitating, the initiative unquestionably lay with those who actively sponsored nonintervention. Since the outspoken advocates of nonintervention in the government were Radicals, nonintervention understandably came to be identified with the Radicals. Rebuffing the Communists' attacks on nonintervention became easily associated with anti-Communism, which was thereby made more acceptable to the less hysterical deputies; anti-Communism, in the conjuncture of circumstances, thus benefited from the pacifism that was widespread throughout the party. The relation of the Spanish question to the strikes considerably strengthened the conservatives within the party, and made even the left-wingers uneasy. It permitted the accumulated anxieties over the foreign situation and the fear of disorder at home to be focused on a single scapegoat, the Communist party. The disorganized and uncoordinated anti-Communism of the elections of 1936 was suddenly crystallized in the summer of the same year into a forceful mystique.

By the time of the Congress in October, the conservative Radicals were clearly opposed to the Popular Front, and the moderates had lost all their enthusiasm for it. The new preoccupations transformed the average Radical's attitude. On June 6, Aimé Berthod exclaimed enthusiastically: "With the principle of republican defense accepted, which means that the dictatorship of the proletariat is impossible, we need not fear the boldness of any economic program." By autumn, he wrote that he no longer had faith in the Popular Front, not because of the social reforms, which he still endorsed, but because he feared the Communists for their role in the strikes and their attempt to force the Blum government to help the Spaniards.[77] Archimbaud, a thorough-going left-winger, asked for an end to strikes and the attacks on the rights of property.[78] The decline of enthusiasm was noticeable in all groups in the party, but was scarcely striking enough to prepare politicians for the shock of the annual fall Congress.

The Congress of Biarritz was a strange affair. The leadership of the party was entirely unprepared for such an outpouring of hatred for the Popular Front. Daladier commented at the outset that to his great surprise he found the Popular Front coalition questioned.[79] The first meeting opened tumultuously with the conservatives singing the Marseillaise and the left wing singing the Internationale, the left wing raising their clenched fists in the Popular Front salute and the right returning, to everyone's astonishment, something that looked very much like a fascist salute. The right easily drowned out the left, but its symbolic arm-raising seemed to have done it more harm than good.

Some tried to explain it away as the ancient Olympic salute; others said that it was a repetition of the Tennis Court Oath; but the gesture was altogether too compromising, so the next day they joined their hands above their heads, which was somewhat less equivocal, but which *L'Echo de Paris* claimed was the Freemasons' sign of distress.[80] In any event, the demonstration was hostile, and the leaders were shocked. Daladier had difficulty in making himself heard above the interruptions.[81]

The attempt to drive the Communists out of the majority dominated the Congress. The instigators were Milhaud and Roche; the troops used were the Jeunesses Radicales; the issue was anti-Communism; and the tactics, according to Jean Piot, were fascist.[82] Through two long days Roche insisted that he was going to present a motion of his own and have the Congress vote on it. "I am here to tell the government, in the name of a considerable number of Radicals, that we have had enough, and that we do not want to surrender to the orders of Moscow!"[83] Kayser rallied the left-wing supporters and found 37 departmental federations to sign a motion supporting the government. According to Kayser, the presidents of the federations declared, 42 to 14, in favor of the Popular Front.[84] The supporters of the government could point out very reasonably that ejecting the Communists from the majority would result in the overthrow of the Blum government, and that such an event was unthinkable since there was nothing to replace it with. The anti-Communists did not argue; they answered by crying, "A Moscou!"

The turmoil at Biarritz was somewhat artificial. The Congress was undoubtedly packed with conservatives from the neighboring southern federations. At the height of the crisis, Kayser demanded that if a vote were taken, only those with valid party cards for the past two years and registered as delegates since September 20 be allowed to take part.[85] The worst offender was apparently the Federation of Ariège, reported to have 120 delegates.[86] According to *La Lumière,* the six conservative federations of the Nord, Aude, Dordogne, Ariège, Pyrénées-Orientales, and Hérault, which together had ten deputies in parliament, had 479 delegates; whereas the 37 federations that signed Kayser's pro-government motion and had 53 deputies in parliament, had only 599 delegates.[87] (Of course, much of the disproportion may have resulted simply from the larger memberships of the conservative federations.) There are no official figures available. The rigging accounts for some of the hostility, but at the same time the Congress probably also reflected the party workers' tendency to oscillate further and faster than the deputies. The unpopularity of the Popular Front among a large part of the Radical party was undoubtedly a revelation to the leadership. What appalled the left wing most were the unheard-of tactics of violence and obstruction. "Either the Radical party has admitted unusual elements into its ranks, or those people were not Radicals but 'hired thugs.' "[88]

The Congress gave the defeated candidates of 1936 the first real opportunity to express their disgruntlement. The elections, which were a victory for the Popular Front, were a disaster for the Radical party. Torn between the desire to rejoice and to mourn, most of the local newspapers simply did not comment one way or another. They were, of course, fully aware of the magnitude of their loss, and a few people commented on it,[89] but no recriminations were made against the Popular Front because of the Radical defeat. Yet the Popular Front was an electoral formation that had failed the Radicals, and at Biarritz this was made clear. Daladier had to remind the aroused party workers that they would have lost more seats without the alliance with the Socialists and Communists—a comment greeted with hoots.[90] Possibly one reason that so little had been made of the loss until then was that the deputies in the Chamber had obviously not been defeated, and the losers were isolated and lacking a platform until they met together in the Congress. Never, however, neither then nor later, were losses at the polls made into an argument for breaking the Popular Front; on the contrary, electoral arguments in favor of the Popular Front were still used long after all the others had been forgotten.

The curious aspect of this initial opposition was that it distinguished very carefully between the Popular Front and the Blum government, and made a point of supporting the latter. Indeed, on the questions that most troubled the Radical soul—the strikes and the Spanish War—the government's policies pleased the conservatives and even brought the government their support. The Blum government's predicament forced it reluctantly to follow policies distasteful to the greater number of its real supporters, but agreeable to its lukewarm supporters and its enemies.

By the fall of 1936, the traditional domestic sources of controversy were definitively subordinated to foreign policy, or transformed into a dispute over anti-Communism that became progressively more detached from specific issues. In such conditions, the actual performance of the Blum experiment played a secondary role in the estrangement of the Radical party from the Popular Front.

IV

Feeding on fears of revolution and war, anti-Communism had burst upon the Radical party in full force for the first time at the Congress of Biarritz. Already its negativity was denounced: "Manger du communisme," wrote Geistdoerfer, "ce n'est pas un programme."[91] But it was used as one. This is the real significance of the Congress of Biarritz; it opened a phase in the history of the Radical party in which unadulterated anti-Communism gradually became the principal article of faith, perhaps filling the void left by the disappearance of anti-clericalism. At first it was subsidiary to fear of war and anxiety over private property, but by 1938 there was nothing else. Anti-Communism was the sole reason the Radicals gave when they officially ended the Popular Front: "[The party] declares . . . that the Communist party, by the unrest that it foments in the country, by the difficulties it has created for the governments since 1936, by its aggressive and destructive opposition of these last months, has destroyed the solidarity that united it with the other parties of the Popular Front."[92]

At the Radicals' last meeting with the Committee of the Popular Front, when they gave their reasons for withdrawing, they did not say a word about Blum, economic failure, the social reforms, or the devaluation. Fourteen of the 15 paragraphs, masochistically lingering over the insults the party had received, dealt with the misdeeds of the Communists.[93] After the Congress of Marseilles, Cot wrote, "The fight against Communism, and opposition to the CGT, are not a sufficient program to get France out of her present mess."[94]

To turn the party so sharply to the right was the substantial accomplishment of the conservative wing. Almost all the conservatives had a strong electoral base that pitted them against Socialists or Communists.* A number of them had been supported in the elections by the Croix de Feu.[95] They had the tacit support of the Senate. With the center of the party shattered by the elections, and the left occupied with its position in the new government, the conservatives were the only active force within the party.

---

* Le Temps published a list of 25 deputies elected without help from the extreme left; of these, all but five were conservative anti-Communists.

Just as the more extreme left-wing Radicals were further to the left than many of the Socialists, so many of the conservatives were further to the right than much of the center. The Radical party was not a simple center party with well-defined boundaries, but a party which, representing an authentic political subculture, embraced almost the full scope of political differences, excluding only Marxism on the left and clericalism on the right. There were two types of extreme conservatives, the old and the young. The old conservatives, like Régnier or Bienvenu-Martin, were positively regressive on social matters, far more reactionary than Tardieu, Reynaud, Mandel, or Flandin in the center, and even more than some of the right. The young conservatives, although not particularly retrograde on social questions, had far less sympathy for the Republic and democracy than the center and some of the right.

The young conservatives had an affinity with the French fascists, or at least with the Leagues. Although this affinity should not be exaggerated, for fascism remained anathema to the major part of the party, it was a precursor of the extreme right-wing Radicalism of the Fourth and Fifth Republics, typified by Martinaud-Déplat, André Morice, André Marie, and Albert Bayet. Articles by Jacques Doriot were published in Potut's *L'Echo de la Nièvre* in 1936, and Doriot was reported to have close ties with *La République*.[96] Following the cantonal elections of 1937, the Socialist Jean Lebas wrote in *Le Populaire,* "The Radical candidates profited from the public support given them by the Parti Social Français, whose leader is Colonel de la Rocque,"[97] and the eminently respectable political commentator Raymond Millet wrote about a possible fusion of the Radical party and the other center parties with the PSF and the PPF.[98] He also wrote that after the Congress of Marseilles, "people believed, said, and wrote that the Radical party was going to become nothing less than fascist."[99]

The conservatives were led by a number of senators and by Milhaud and Roche. Roche never managed to become a deputy; yet he was one of the most important members of the party. He was young, very intelligent, extremely cautious, and generally respected. His power had three solid bases: he owned the newspaper *La République*, which was influential in political circles and perhaps the publication most widely cited as representative of Radical opinion; he was president of the Federation of the Nord, second in size only to the Federation of the Seine; finally, and most important, he was recognized as the spokesman for Caillaux. Roche did much entertaining for Caillaux and ghosted many of his articles. Roche's own articles at crucial moments —for example, at the fall of the first Blum cabinet—were the unofficial statement of Caillaux's opinion. From 1936 on, Roche's role was of the first importance.

Within the Chamber, the men who now led the conservatives were Bonnet, until he left for Washington in January 1937, Lamoureux, re-elected in the same month, Marchandeau, and Malvy, and three former Young Turks, Mistler, Potut, and Riou. None of these had sufficient stature to be a possible Premier for a center or right-wing majority. For this role, surprisingly, they favored not Chautemps, Herriot, or Albert Sarraut, but Daladier, leader of the Popular Front. Already in 1935 he had begun to shift to the right on the Ethiopian question, at which time the right-wing paper *Candide* wrote that "Daladier seems to have been touched by grace"; he was no longer the revolutionary of a few weeks earlier.[100] It was probably Biarritz, however, that caused the crucial shift in his thinking. Gaston Riou (whose conservatism can be gauged by his accusing Cot of wanting to be the Stalin of the West) wrote that Daladier understood the meaning of the Congress immediately: "He has antennae. He has the wisdom to pay attention to them. Now he is at the head of the movement."[101] Shortly thereafter, Riou was calling Daladier "our leader."[102]

As Minister of War, Daladier collided head-on with the Socialists and Communists, who continually criticized the army's politics. Daladier defended the generals and continued the exclusion of *Le Populaire* and *L'Humanité* from the barracks. In return, he was attacked in the Army Commission of the Chamber, and then by a joint poster of the Socialist and Communist youth movements accusing him of being a reactionary. At the Executive Committee meeting of December, Daladier replied: "If the Jeunesses Socialistes does not like [the government's national security measures], let it take it out on its own leaders, who voted these measures, and let its leaders answer it." He added that he was totally indifferent to their accusations.[103] By 1937 Daladier had emerged as the leader of the anti-Popular Front forces within the party. Hippolyte Ducos, who was Daladier's Undersecretary for Defense from 1938 to 1940, wrote: "Those who definitely wanted to put an end to the Popular Front counted on [Daladier]. . . . From the beginning, Edouard Daladier, without renouncing the coalition to which he belonged, was opposed to the revolutionary excesses of the Popular Front, and appeared to be the only man capable of forming a government that would be upheld by a republican and national parliamentary majority."[104] He could not act openly, of course, since he was a member of the government. The crisscross in leadership had thus begun. It was not Herriot, as yet, who was looked to as the leader of the left, but rather Chautemps, of all people; he was closest to Blum and was regarded as his natural successor.

Beyond the activities of the leaders, the only grass-roots stirrings in the moribund party after the electoral disaster of 1936 came from an unexpected source—the youth movement called the Jeunesses Radicales. It is surely indicative of the tyranny of the fascist example over the minds of non-fascist countries that such a refuge for middle-aged respectability as the Radical party should produce its Radical Youth. It is even more surprising that this movement should be vigorous and successful.

Founded in 1933, by 1936 the Jeunesses was a force within the party. The Radicals had always been profoundly uninterested in youth as such; the arising in their midst of a youth movement clamoring for leadership and the applause awarded this claim by the veterans were clear signs of debility. Much information about this curious and obscure formation was first brought to light in Bardonnet's *Evolution de la structure du parti radical*.[105] Yet Bardonnet was making a structural study, and therefore tended to neglect the movement's significant, though minor, historical role in the decline of France. Its sudden vitality amidst the general decay is the vigor of a deadly growth in a disintegrating body; its toxins spread throughout the party, which was infected with hate, irrationality, and hysteria—all foreign to the Radical temperament and symptomatic of a Europe held in mimetic fascination by the rising Nazi power. The Jeunesses Radicales shows in a heightened form the generalized collapse of the optimistic, respectable, and in its own way almost admirable, Radical spirit of the old Third Republic.[106]

The formation of a youth movement had been proposed in 1930, but it was not until 1933 that the organization was established. At first it was nonpartisan and relatively obscure. The first president, Roger Huss, was left-wing in outlook; the secretary-general, Roland Manescau, was extreme-right. This neutrality did not last. One left-wing schism in the spring of 1934 shook the Paris area; another left-wing group was skillfully driven out of the national organization in the fall.[107] The right-wing Sableau drove the left-wing Huss out of the presidency. The movement was still very much an army of generals without soldiers,[108] and power struggles within a tiny organization are not in themselves very interesting, but for the fact that from the beginning, the Jeunesses Radicales attracted the benevolent attention of right-wing elements inside and outside the party:

It courageously proclaims its disdain for Marxism in all its forms, for historic and economic materialism, for the regimentation of human values in institutions worthy of ancient slavery. It has good and healthy basic ideas. Its philosophy is very French, and I must congratulate M. Marcerau [sic], the secretary-general of the Jeunesses Radicales, for having expressed it with an emotion whose vibrant sincerity brought forth the applause of an audience that was, unfortunately, a bit sparse.[109]

A very sympathetic special report in Le Temps in early 1935 gave it national publicity and many new members.[110] During 1935 and 1936, membership increased considerably; it claimed more than 20,000 members.[111] A number of federations, the most important being the Federation of the Seine, were uneasy with the direction taken by the new executive, and by 1936 had withdrawn from the national federation.[112] Apart from Roche's Federation of the Nord, the national federation's members were concentrated south of the Loire.

The Jeunesses Radicales was dominated by the two leading personages of the organization, Manescau and Marcel Sableau. Manescau provided the organization, Sableau the charisma. Each was an excellent orator, but there the similarity ended. Sableau was large, handsome, warm; even his enemy Eudlitz admitted that he had a "rather agreeable appearance," adding, however, that it concealed an "odious character."[113] Manescau, on the other hand, was small, delicate, precise, and cold as a fish. Even Sableau's worst enemies found something agreeable to say about him. A former Mason, he seemed to fit into the Radical tradition and image; but Manescau, a man who smiled only when he had made his point, did not.

The doctrine of the Jeunesses Radicales was confused and contradictory, but this only reflected its peculiarly twentieth-century disdain for thinking. Manescau said in 1937, "All those who equivocate on the colors of its flag, hesitate on its program, and fret over its doctrine inhibit Radicalism."[114] Sableau "was seeking orthodoxy," and Manescau reassured the older generation of the "sobriety" of the young.[115] Yet Manescau bitterly attacked the older members of the party, and Sableau's orthodoxy was of a rather peculiar sort: "What is the ideal, the aim of the Jeunesses Radicales? To infuse new blood into the party in spite of itself."[116] Sableau claimed it would never do anything that the Bureau disapproved; yet he was reported to have threatened to "take the Place de Valois by force to install new leadership there."[117] "Radicalism will be combative and dynamic, or it will cease to exist."[118]

Above all, the Jeunesses Radicales believed in anti-Communism. According to Sableau, "leper Marxism" had produced Mussolini and Hitler, caused the "enslavement of Austria, the Spanish butchery, and the division of Czechoslovakia." "The unnatural mating of democracy and Marxism—which is known in France under the name 'Popular Front'—produces this hybrid monster called 'fascism.' "[119] "We consider the Communist party as the present Public Enemy Number One."[120] Asked by a right-wing writer to outline their program in 1938, Manescau and Sableau demanded nothing but the dissolution of the Popular Front.[121]

The extent to which these young Radicals had rejected traditional Radicalism can be understood from the proclamation in the Jeunesses Radicales' newspaper of the motto, "Order, Authority, Nation!"[122] That a Radical should so openly repudiate "Liberty, Equality, Fraternity," and still remain a Radical, was clearly indicative of a moral transformation within the party. These men were seriously called fascists at the time.[123]

In its methods, too, the Jeunesses Radicales welcomed the violence of the 1930's. It terrorized—in a mild, Radical fashion—the left-wing opposition by beating it up, particularly at the Congresses of 1936 and 1937, which was a rude shock to the traditions of the party.[124]

Where the Jeunesses got its support is something of a mystery. It was no mean feat to find 20,000 young men to join such a staid old party. Millet reported in 1937 that many of the new recruits came from the moderate parties;[125] the left wing, not so generous, said they resembled, and probably had been, Doriot's thugs.[126] Others noted a certain interchange between the Jeunesses Radicales and the Leagues.[127] The left claimed that Sableau was working with Doriot, although this was denied.[128]

All of this is, of course, rather pallid—the Jeunesses Radicales was no Hitler Youth, but unoriginal, derivative, and stale. No one was ever seriously frightened by a Radical Youth. It was, indeed, exactly what one would expect from such an indifferent lot as the Radical party trying to imitate the Nazis. The appalling fact is that it tried. The Rights of Man are hard to reconcile with activism, with action for its own sake, with the adulation of youth, with the denial of rationality, with order and authority. And even the Jeunesses Radicales claimed it stood for the Rights of Man.

There is little doubt that the Jeunesses Radicales was inspired, used, and even financed, by some of the right-wing factions within the party, but who these were is not at all clear. The most commonly mentioned were a group of senators, Robert Belmont, Paul Maulion, and Jean-Pierre Rambaud. There is no agreement on the others, although Roche, Milhaud, and Bonnet were all mentioned. Manescau himself said that its support came from Milhaud, the senators, and the Sarrauts.[129]

The function of the Jeunesses Radicales, at which it worked tirelessly, was to spearhead the anti-Communist drive within the party. From November 1935 until October 1936, Manescau held 62 provincial rallies and Sableau 45, an enormous number for such a weakly articulated party. During 1937 and 1938, the formation of a section of the Jeunesses Radicales was an oblique proclamation of a shift within a federation from left to right. It was enthusiastically supported by the conservative parliamentarians, who attended the great rallies of the Jeunesses Radicales; the leaders were freely invited into conservative constituencies.[130] It formed the shock troops of the right wing that shook the Congresses of 1936, 1937, and 1938. Above all, it inspired the great series of banquets and demonstrations in the spring and summer of 1937.

The full weight of the conservative revival was felt only with this series of demonstrations. The most important was at Carcassonne in April 1937, but there were others as well: at St.-Gaudens on June 6, with 3,000, at Pau, on July 4, with 3,000, at Montauban on September 7, and at Vichy on September 12.

The great rally at Carcassonne was organized ostensibly as a simple political demonstration; but with the exception of Delbos and the Sarrauts and Henri Gout, the left-wing deputy from Carcassonne itself, the 30 parliamentarians who were invited and all those who attended were personally hostile to the Popular Front. Six thousand Radicals turned out,[131] certainly the largest assemblage in the prewar period, two-thirds being Jeunesses Radicales. Although the motions passed retained the insipid Radical form—affirming the party's doctrine and the Rights of Man—the speeches were hostile. It was a much smoother operation than the Congress of Biarritz, for there was no open denunciation of the government; yet the meaning was clear enough: it was a show of force—in an age when mass demonstrations were *de rigueur* —against the Popular Front.

According to the account of Hippolyte Ducos, who was the deputy from St.-Gaudens, Daladier supported these demonstrations. The banquet of St.-Gaudens, says Ducos, was part of the plan to overthrow the Blum government:

The purpose of the two great speeches made by the former Premier Albert Sarraut and by the party's president, Edouard Daladier . . . was to change the policy of the party. . . . When these courageous declarations were made public, and when it was learned that they had been approved and applauded by Maurice Sarraut and one hundred [*sic*] Radical deputies and senators, it was recognized that the demonstration of St.-Gaudens had tolled the knell of the Popular Front; before long, this demonstration, like several party Congresses in the past, brought about the overthrow of the ministry. That is what inevitably happened within two weeks.[132]

The passage of time has magnified the extent and effect of this demonstration; but it is hard to believe that the account does not accurately recall the hostility of those present to the Blum government.

These large demonstrations were the symptoms of a general, if somewhat artificial, resurgence of Radicalism throughout the country during the first half of 1937. An example may be taken from the Charente-Inférieure. In November 1936, a party worker wrote that it was no secret to anyone that the federation had shrunk to several hundred members scattered in perhaps twenty committees, and that its activity was nil.[133] By February of the following year, the situation was transformed. The federation had reorganized, and a great speaking campaign was plotted out, which blossomed in the spring in a substantial number of meetings.[134] The high point was a great meeting at Mirambeau with 1,500 present,[135] where it was reported that "the spirit of Carcassonne blew over the assembly," this spirit manifesting itself in the proclamation of the Radicals' independence from the other parties of the left.[136] Once the Blum government was defeated, however, the organization relapsed into its normal habit of having an annual meeting and banquet. This spirit of rebirth in 1937 was noted elsewhere, and was probably a general phenomenon among the conservative and moderate federations.

The Blum government's decline and fall need not be gone into at great length. Throughout the early months of 1937, the Radical ministers did their best to moderate the government's behavior, and were delighted when they succeeded in getting the "pause"—the return to a more cautious economic policy. In the Committee of the Popular Front, the Radicals steadfastly opposed the Socialist-Communist schemes for extending the program of reforms. The most upsetting incident of the spring for the Radicals was unquestionably the riot in Clichy in March; the Radicals were fully convinced that the Communists were responsible for the deaths involved. In the end Blum, although supported by the Chamber, was defeated by the Senate, when he was forced by a financial crisis, as all eventually were, to demand full powers. In the Chamber, there were 78 Radical votes for the government, 22 against, and nine abstentions. Only the conservatives were in open opposition. Since it was known that the Senate's vote, not the Chamber's, would be the decisive one, very little can be concluded from these figures about the real attachment to the government of those deputies who supported Blum. If they had not been assured that the Senate would do the job for them, the moderates probably would have refused full powers also. How far the moderate-left and left-wing deputies, still for the Popular Front, would have gone in upholding the government is impossible to say. It seems likely that they would have granted full financial powers to the government, but the moderate left, at least, was not ready to support an open fight with the Senate. Even among the left-wingers there was no bitterness against the Senate. Most deputies were apprehensive about what would happen when Blum was overthrown, and there was almost universal approval of the peaceful installation of Chautemps.

The right-wing assault on the government did not really affect the convinced left-wingers, but it undoubtedly weakened the attachment of the center, which was crucial. The continual difficulties of the government and the failure of its economic policy contributed to chilling enthusiasm; and the foreign situation increasingly pushed domestic questions into the background. The Popular Front was clearly in decline. Chautemps later claimed that during this period he was working toward a government of Union Nationale.[137] Alexander Werth quotes Mendès-France on the gradual erosion of confidence: "I was, in spite of everything, one of [the Popular Front's] most wholehearted supporters in the Radical Party; all the same, from 1937 on, I became more and more convinced that we were heading for disaster."[138]

CHAPTER 9

The Last Years

I

Blum was succeeded by Chautemps, and the Popular Front marched on—or so said its Radical supporters. The Socialists knew better; the right knew better;[1] but the Radicals liked pretending and said that nothing had really changed. They were, nonetheless, very pleased. The presence of Georges Bonnet as Minister of Finance altered the character of the cabinet so greatly that calling it a government of Popular Front may be misleading. Bonnet had, of course, been shipped off by Blum as Ambassador to Washington in order to keep him from disrupting things. Now that he was back, it might still have been hoped that participation in the government and the duties of his ministry would curb his destructiveness; any such hope was vain. Yet the cabinet had its contingent of Socialists and the solid support of the Communists, and Camille Chautemps declared firmly that his was a Popular Front government.[2] The Radicals praised Vincent Auriol and Bonnet in one breath.[3] Now logically, if one was happy to see Bonnet as Finance Minister, one could scarcely regret Auriol; if one liked Blum, could one be enthusiastic about Chautemps? On the surface, at any rate, everybody liked everybody.

Of all the governments of the Third Republic, there is perhaps none more dismal than this Chautemps government. It was stagnation after movement, a moment of immobility in a disintegrating world. It was all weakness, intrigue, and hypocrisy. Nonetheless, it managed one of the great structural reforms of the inter-war period, the nationalization of the railroads; but this reform, handled in a way that annoyed the Socialists and failed to inspire anyone else, had no political impact. For the rest, the government was a long wake for the Popular Front.

The slow expiration of the Popular Front is reflected in the language used to refer to it. The Radicals' conception of the Popular Front always differed somewhat from that of the two other member parties. The English term "Popular Front" translates two French terms, "Front Populaire" and "Rassemblement Populaire" which were apparently interchangeable. Ultimately, even in French, "Front Populaire" has prevailed; but such was not always the case. "Front" and "Rassemblement" have almost contrary connotations. "Front" excludes, opposes, draws a sharp line between friend and foe. "Rassemblement," on the other hand, draws together in an all-embracing grasp, and radiates warmth and good feeling. It embodies the old Radical notion of solidarity. It irresistibly calls forth the image of Edouard Herriot flinging his arms wide to welcome, like Abraham, the blessed to his bosom.

In retrospect, the image of conflict has dominated the memories of that time; yet for contemporaries, the great fact was the reunion of the left. The Socialists and Communists tended to use "Front," but the Radicals used "Rassemblement" almost exclusively. The only Radicals who used "Front Populaire" freely were the conservatives who wanted to frighten people with it; even the most extreme left-wing Radicals chose "Rassemblement Populaire," changing it randomly into "Rassemblement des Démocrates," "Rassemblement Anti-Fasciste," or even "Rassemblement des Hommes Libres."[4] This latter habit also indicated a disinclination to use "Populaire." When Herriot exclaimed, "Je suis peuple," he meant the unorganized sentimental people of the nineteenth century, of Michelet, not the proletarian "peuple" of the CGT. The most common substitute for "Front Populaire" was "Rassemblement des Républicains," which gained a certain currency under Chautemps's successor government. In 1935 Chautemps had already been quoted as saying, "*Front Populaire?* Wouldn't it be better to call it a *Rassemblement* of all republicans without exclusion?"[5] This had all the vagueness of a traditional French formula. Herriot had already used it in 1932 ("rassembler tous les républicains") to mean Concentration.[6] The Radicals managed to confuse the connotations so thoroughly that a Radical anti-Communist actually made the following profession of faith during the elections of 1936: "Either you will vote for the *Front Révolutionnaire* . . . or in a supreme and decisive effort you will rally [*vous rassemblerez*] from the first ballot . . . to effect with us, behind the incumbent deputy, Paul Richard, the rebuilding of the country, and thus preserve bread, peace, and liberty."[7] In a quiet evolution, the clear and definite "Front Populaire" was gradually to give way to Chautemps's contradictory and imprecise "Rassemblement des Républicains," a label that perfectly characterized the insipidity and inertia of the new cabinet.

The dissension within the cabinet, the cantonal elections, and the Congress of Lille all played a role in the disintegration of the Popular Front. All were closely connected. The chronic cabinet crisis naturally resulted from the incompatible financial and political conceptions of the Socialists and Bonnet. Xavier Vallat, a deputy of the extreme right, said when the government came before the Chamber: "If M. Georges Bonnet remains faithful to the reputation he has established, if he takes the country, by means of full powers, along the road of the 'Great Penitence,' you know very well that the Popular Front majority will not follow him, or not for long."[8] Bonnet's financial policy, embracing the most classical orthodoxy, was the antithesis of the ill-fated purchasing power theory.[9] It meant, among other things, the end of social reforms and of concessions to the wage demands of the fonctionnaires, as well as cutbacks in expenses, with the same implications as the Laval deflation of 1935. From the first meeting of the cabinet, rumors were abroad of a crisis between Bonnet and the Socialists; every week or so thereafter, a skirmish was reported.[10] Whether all the reports were accurate or not is not too important; for nothing could be clearer than Bonnet's conspiring against the government of which he was the key member. This can be seen from his actions at the Congress of Lille.

There was an underlying uneasiness about the Congress of Lille, induced by memories of Biarritz and the growing dislike of the Popular Front. The Congress, in theory, should not have worried the Chautemps government, since the desires of the right had been fulfilled in the overthrow of the Blum government, and the uneasiness of the left was quieted by the presence of the Socialists in the government and the support of the Communists. As Roche said, "there was nothing to fear from the Congress, because, after all, the government was Radical."[11] Yet Roche joined with Bonnet in a plot against the government that took place, contrary to all precedent, in the public session. In a normal Congress, the important business was carried on by the bigwigs of the

Committee on General Policy behind closed doors; the public meetings were reserved for the presentation of the compromises achieved there, acting as a safety valve for the frustrations of the party workers, who could hiss or applaud, or occasionally venture an inarticulate but sincere protest.

On the morning of October 29, a routine session on financial policy took place. As the Bureau had decided, there was no real debate, only speeches by three arch-conservatives, Potut, Roche, and Bonnet, after which the discussion was closed over the protests of the muzzled left.[12] So far, all was normal. But the motion produced by Roche and Potut included, among other admirably conservative provisions, the rejection of "so-called structural reforms," and asserted the necessity of changing the forty-hour week.[13] These clauses caused pandemonium. The clause on structural changes was the nub, and is a curious example of the dominance of reality by a myth. The Socialists were at this time busy spinning fantasies about the further reforms to be carried out by the Popular Front, reforms that included nationalizations, that is "structural reforms." No one with any grasp of political realities could imagine that Bonnet and Chautemps were the people to carry out further reforms, and it was extremely doubtful that the Radical party as a whole felt differently. Yet to admit this fact was impossible, and the anger the motion aroused demonstrated this impossibility; indeed, the phrase was doubtless introduced solely for the emotional effect it would produce, in an attempt to break, or at least weaken, the government. In the chaos of the meeting, the motion was passed, after Bonnet threatened that its defeat would have grave consequences and would jeopardize the nation's financial stability; the addition of the phrase "for the present" somehow made it more acceptable.[14] What happened then is not known precisely, but the general lines are clear. Did Blum actually call up from Paris to threaten Socialist resignation from the government unless the motion was withdrawn?[15] Whether he did or not, Chautemps let Roche know that the government would fall if the motion were maintained.[16] Daladier, as president of the party, insisted in the afternoon meeting that the vote be rescinded, and that the entire question be referred to the Committee on General Policy.[17] The final declaration of the party the following day made no reference to "structural reforms," but sagely reiterated over and over again its loyalty to the Popular Front.[18]

What happens in a Radical Congress is always confusing. One

searches for a thread of logic one thinks must be there, but always with the uneasy feeling that it may not be. Was the Congress a triumph for the Popular Front, because Bonnet had been beaten back? Or was it a triumph for Bonnet, because it had really pronounced in his favor while seeming to do the reverse? This was the same Congress that cheered, as though the rafters would break, Cot's defense of himself against the attacks of Sableau,* and then went on to elect Sableau, by a resounding majority, to one of the vice-presidencies of the party. The Radical party acted in devious ways. Did the profusion of affection for the Popular Front signal its acceptance or preparations for its demise? In a similar case, when Herriot praised Delbos, one paper said, "There is no mistaking it; he wants to kill him."[19] Although the Popular Front was explicitly reaffirmed at Lille, it had suffered some severe shocks. Kayser noted that after the Congress he felt the Popular Front begin to disintegrate.[20]

The cantonal elections that had just taken place were an immediate source of the heightened Radical discontent.[21] Only dubious conclusions could be drawn from the results. The Socialists and Communists claimed a victory because they had gained seats; but the opposition said they were defeated because they had not gained as many as they should have.[22] The Radicals lost seats, and it was said that they lost the elections,[23] but they themselves were pleasantly surprised and claimed a victory.[24] Yet, although the Radicals were delighted with their relative recovery, they complained about the behavior of the Socialists in the tender matter of republican discipline. The Socialists had an aversion for voting for conservative Radicals, and fairly generally accepted republican discipline only in favor of Popular Front Radicals.[25] Daladier said, "Such methods cannot be tolerated. If the Popular Front is to lead the other parties against the Radicals under the pretext that there is no reactionary peril, if class discipline is put ahead of republican discipline, then we will have to take our freedom of action with-

---

* One of the scandals of the Congress was Sableau's brutal attack against Cot's administration of the Ministry of Air, in which Sableau accepted the charges current in the right-wing press. His assault was replete with such remarks as "We are going to speak the truth; citizen Cot will answer," and "If you wish to hear Pierre Cot, it is in your interest to let me finish. (Numerous voices, no! no!) If not, M. Pierre Cot will not speak. (Applause and noise.) I ask my friends to remember this welcome and to reserve one like it to the others. (New interruptions.)" Such language was absolutely novel in Radical Congresses, where even the most vicious attacks were carried out under the guise of warmth, friendship, and unanimity.

out hesitation. (Loud, prolonged applause.)" The Radicals had lost 30 seats in 25 departments, Daladier claimed, because of the Socialists' indiscipline.[26]

Yet one wonders at the justice of these complaints. With few exceptions, those places where the Radicals were opposed by the Socialists were departments where the Popular Front had been only a sham if it had existed at all. And in such conservative departments as the Charente-Inférieure and the Rhône, discipline worked well;[27] if, in the Aude, the Socialists decided to oppose the arch-conservative Clément Raynaud, they supported the only slightly less conservative Léon Castel.[28] In 1936, the same breaches of discipline had gone unnoticed. The Radicals were probably now looking for excuses to bring about a break, and were beginning to look for alternative alliances. In the department of the Haute-Saône, for example, at the time of the cantonal elections the Radical parliamentarians sounded out the right unsuccessfully for an alliance and a truce against the extreme left, a truce that was consummated with difficulty the following March, and fairly definitively after Munich.[29] Doubtless a similar evolution was taking place in other middle-of-the-road federations. The electoral usefulness of the Popular Front was clearly being questioned by some within the party. This was serious, for electoral considerations were the groundwork of the original alliance. Around this time began a search for viable political alternatives to the Popular Front, the most consistently advocated being a system of proportional representation that would free the Radicals from the consequences of electoral alliances. The Radical electoral dilemma was not fully exposed, however, until the final break.

The Congress surmounted, the government uneventfully reached the end of 1937; within the party the only happening of note was the dissolution of the Jeunesses Radicales by the Bureau in reprisal for its attacks on Pierre Cot. Its leaders continued their agitation independently, with less effectiveness. The lull of 1937 was shattered with the new year. Henceforth the political evolution in the party and the country quickened. In four month' time, the final period of the Third Republic had begun. Only during these four months did the Radical Group regain anything like the sovereign functions it had enjoyed in its great days; before 1938 it was cowed by the whole mechanism of the Popular Front; after April, except on rare occasions, it was relegated to a purely formal role, as was the entire parliament, paralyzed by the fear of Germany and stripped of power. In this brief moment of activity, however, the Radical Group rendered one last, notable service to the French Republic: it kept Georges Bonnet from becoming Premier of France.

The crisis that began with the new year was the usual sort; a speculative attack against the franc meant that it was time to reconsider the majority. The Chamber was duly convoked; the lobbies were feverish; Chautemps went before his parliament. He made a curiously muddled speech whose precise significance was clear to no one, but whose purpose seemed to be to drive the Communists out of the majority. Most of it concerned the responsibilities of the trade unionists for creating the crisis; the remainder rejected the Socialists' preferred solution to the crisis, exchange control, it being stipulated that "conditions of monetary freedom" were to be maintained.[30] Since the Socialists had already accepted, in the cabinet meeting that morning, what Chautemps was now asking them to accept, they were puzzled. The Communists were irritated at being blamed for the social unrest. After a long day of negotiations, the Chamber met again and everything seemed settled, when, in one of those curious parliamentary incidents that overthrow governments in France, an exchange took place between the Communist Arthur Ramette and Chautemps, in which Chautemps made the famous statement: "M. Ramette demands his freedom; he has the perfect right to ask for it. As for me, I give it to him."[31] The Socialists took this as a disavowal of the Popular Front majority, and withdrew their ministers from the cabinet.

It was an obscure crisis; there was no apparent reason for it, since the problems had been temporarily solved, and it was no longer expected. Blum had to be gotten out of bed in order to resign. Bonnet wrote that he had talked with Chautemps after the cabinet meeting that morning, and he had not mentioned any crisis.[32] Chautemps himself is reported to have told the Group, "My departure was not premeditated. It was imposed by circumstances. France's prestige abroad required a strong reply to the remarks of M. Ramette."[33] Yet, accidental in its form, the crisis was not accidental in its basis. Daniel Halévy has brilliantly described the sitting of the Chamber in which a majority was breaking up, suspension followed suspension, and the labor of many hours brought forth a meaningless motion, which was demolished by a statement by Ramette and an outburst from Chautemps.[34] The Popular Front was clearly in decay. Roche wrote the following day in La République, "Is the economic, financial, and social recovery of France possible? Yes. With the present majority, that is, a majority that includes the Communists? No!"

The Radical Group had not been consulted. There was doubtless a fairly widespread feeling against the Communists, shown by the majority's vote against Jacques Duclos as vice-president of the Chamber.* Yet this vote was secret; and while it was one thing to irresponsibly express a dislike of the Communists, it was quite another to envisage coldly and openly a rupture of the Popular Front and an alliance with the right. For this the Radicals were not yet prepared, as Bonnet's attempt to form a government clearly shows.

President Lebrun turned to the Radicals to end the crisis. Chautemps, Herriot, Daladier, and Albert Sarraut all refused to form ministries; so he called upon Bonnet. Bonnet was, as we have seen, anathema to the Socialists. "If there is any politician with whom it is difficult for the parties of the left to come to an understanding now, it is M. Chautemps's former Minister of Finance."[35] They immediately let him know that he could not count on their participation, their support, or even their abstention. Armed with this information, which, it would seem, in no way dismayed him,[36] Bonnet asked for Radical authorization to continue his negotiations, thus indicating that he wished to break the Popular Front. This meeting of the Cadillac Committee was the one occasion when there was a clear confrontation among Radicals on the question of the Popular Front. As Delattre pointed out in the meeting, Bonnet would require 200 votes from the right in such conditions to obtain the Chamber's endorsement. A vote was taken: 32 were in favor of Bonnet's attempt and 26 against; there were perhaps 40 abstentions. "No one expected that M. Bonnet would be so completely abandoned by his friends."[37] According to an analysis in La Lumière, Sableau and Manescau, most of the senators present, and the right-wing deputies voted for Bonnet, while the Chautemps cabinet ministers abstained.[38] The left wing was led by young, little-known deputies, René-William Thorp and particularly Delattre. The vote indicates that as late as January the Popular Front was supported strongly enough for its partisans to brave Bonnet's vindictive head-counting. This majority was quickly to vanish. Bonnet was judged, in the words of one paper, to have conducted himself like a novice.[39]

* One hundred and two votes were missing from the ordinary majority of the Popular Front, and these must have come from the Radicals and Independent Socialists (J.O.Ch., Jan. 11, 1938, p. 3).

His failure was, indeed, the only time during our period that the Cadillac Committee had any noticeable effect on a government crisis.[40]

Bonnet's attempt was soon to be forgotten, and its interest is limited
to demonstrating which forces within the party were working against
the inevitable shift to the right. These deputies were the resistance that
prevented Chautemps from trying to form a government of Union
Nationale in February 1938.[41] A curious afternote to this crisis is the
personal myth that Bonnet has created to explain his failure. In an
article he claims is an accurate account of the crisis,[42] the following
explanation appears:

The Radical Group unanimously [sic] expressed its confidence in you [Bon-
net], eminent men supported you—in the Senate, Joseph Caillaux, president
of the Finance Committee, and Henry Bérenger, president of the Foreign
Affairs Committee.

But you declared to the President of the Republic that because of the gravity of the situation, a stable government was necessary, and this stability
could be assured only if the President permitted the dissolution of the
Chamber in the case of a new crisis, as is provided for in the constitution.
Unhappily, the President hesitated and refused.[43]

On being pressed, Bonnet told me that the majority in the Group was
perhaps 60 to 25 in his favor.

No sooner was the basis for the Popular Front thus reaffirmed within the Radical party by the Bonnet failure, than it was irrevocably
weakened by the Socialists themselves. Blum was asked to form the
government by Lebrun; to the astonishment of all, instead of trying
to form a normal Popular Front cabinet, he produced a new formula,
"From Thorez to Reynaud"—that is, an extension of the majority well
into the right. This proposal was the first official recognition that the
German threat had rendered the Popular Front obsolete.

When Reynaud refused to join the combination without Louis Marin, the endeavor was checked. Blum's attempt to enlarge the majority
meant that the Socialists could no longer reproach the Radicals for
doing the same thing, so that the Radicals experienced a great sense
of liberation. A few on the left regretted Blum's move.[44] Most were
pleased to be freed from the electoral compact. As one local paper
wrote, the formula of Union Nationale was now legitimate, and there
was no going back on it.[45] The Radicals' principal problem was therefore solved. In 1934, it had required the shock of the riots to make the
alliance acceptable; now, it had been justified more gently by Léon

Blum.* The rest of the crisis, which finally ended with the formation of another Chautemps government, saw no further attempts to change the majority, but concerned the more traditional intricacies of ministerial intrigues. After the Socialists refused to enter, the end product was a traditional Radical cabinet, not unlike the unhappy Chautemps government of 1933–34.

If the third Chautemps ministry was the most dreary in this period, the fourth was the most disgraceful. There was no question of its being a permanent solution, after the Blum coup had extended the parliamentary horizon. Whereas Chautemps's speech of January 13 had concentrated on the misdeeds of the unions to the annoyance of the left, his speech of January 21 spent no less than twelve long paragraphs recalling the misdeeds of the right since the riots of February. Chautemps then went on to praise the work of the Popular Front and attack the factory-owners, and even implied that the property involved in ownership was often nothing more than the result of a "lucky business deal." The right was outraged, the left delighted.[46] The words were as meaningless as those of the week before, but the tone had changed.

If social questions were still important in January, by March they were irrelevant. The rumblings of the coming Anschluss were heard throughout the world. From the middle of February, the intimations of the event, according to Ambassador William Bullitt, obliterated all other considerations. Delbos wanted only to resign as Foreign Minister, Chautemps only to form a government of Union Nationale.[47] In his speech to the Chamber on January 13 Chautemps had said, "When a man finds himself placed at the crossroads of duty by the chances of his career, it is not for him to ask whether or not he should serve; he must offer himself to the country on the single condition that he can be useful to it."[48] On March 10, Chautemps resigned as Premier; on March 11, Germany occupied Austria. Whether Chautemps knew that the Anschluss was about to occur has not yet been settled. He himself has always denied it; few others have been so certain. Chautemps said that he had no idea of the coming storm. If he had known, he would have stayed from "an elementary sense of duty." He had resigned so that the "psychological shock" necessary for the floating of a loan

* This is not meant in any way as a criticism of Blum's courageous attempt at national reconciliation in the face of the German threat; it is simply a statement of its effects on the Radical party.

could be administered.[49] Some of his former colleagues, such as Albert Sarraut, go so far as one can without documents in hand to accuse him of wanting to escape from a critical situation.[50] Dupuis wrote, "Nobody understood it, that is a fact. Let us hope that history will not be too severe on the former Premier."[51]

A number of facts are clear. There was no parliamentary danger—that had been surmounted by a marathon victory on a labor law at the end of February. There was no speculative assault on the franc. In fact, no one was expecting the crisis at all. Second, the imminence of a crisis over Austria was generally acknowledged.[52] And finally, Chautemps showed extraordinary haste to get out; Lebrun, Herriot, and Jeanneney had to insist that he go before the Chamber,[53] and even then he would not face a debate, but simply made a declaration and then left, in order to resign. The effect was deplorable. Had he done it for the purest of motives, the conjunction of his resignation and the German invasion would have inevitably imprinted the image of flight. France's reply to the Anschluss was another crisis.

This was the third time that Chautemps had resigned as Premier when the going got rough; at no time was he defeated. Chautemps was the average Radical writ large, with none of the peculiarities and sharp edges that made Herriot and Daladier personalities in their own right. He was all nuance, suppleness, and compromise. In this critical moment of the declining Third Republic, his action assumed an almost symbolic cast; his abdication was, in a very real sense, the abdication of the Radical party, and through the Radical party, the abdication of France.

With the Anschluss, a turning point was reached that drastically altered the conditions of French politics. Domestic affairs lost their significance; foreign affairs changed their focus. The Spanish question was now eclipsed by the immediate and total German menace. The Anschluss acted as a sort of February Sixth for the 1936 legislature.* Between January and March 1938, one passes into a new world. Thus, no valid comparison between the Radical attitudes toward the second Blum government and the first is possible. The fact that the second Blum government was constructed according to the political presup-

---

* The legislature of 1936 differed from those of 1924 and 1932 in having not one cataclysmic crisis, but at least two—the Anschluss and Munich. The mystique of the Popular Front was more profoundly rooted in the majority, and the foreign threat weakened divisive tendencies.

positions of the pre-Anschluss days, and thus was spiritually out of touch with the new political mood, accounts for its improbable nature and hopeless circumstances. The Radicals did not break the Popular Front; the Anschluss made it irrelevant. Thereafter, it existed only as myth. People were fully conscious of this transformation at the time. The deputy Emile Brachard wrote that everyone recognized the necessity of Union Nationale, which had nothing to do with the Popular Front, being concerned only with foreign policy.[54]

II

A cartoon in *L'Oeuvre* portrayed two politicians in the Palais Bourbon —the first: "Hitler has seized Austria!"; the second: "No! Ah! Ah! . . . and what does the Gauche Radicale have to say?"[55] An account of the attempt to form a cabinet ran: Blum poses a condition, the Radicals also; Blum insists, so do the Radicals. And then, "rumors begin to fly: Austria, the Hitler ultimatum. . . . Will Thorez take part without Paul Reynaud? If you accept Paul Reynaud, why not Louis Marin as well? Of course. But the news keeps coming. . . . Chancellor Schuschnigg gives way, the German troops enter, Chancellor Schuschnigg flees. . . . And France still has no government."[56] The psychological climate of intense disgust makes any discussion of the crisis from the traditional domestic point of view singularly inappropriate.

The full shift in Radical opinion became clear only during the second Blum government. Radical evolution went by qualitative jumps, and only during crises were decisions taken that forced the Radical deputies to fashion a new image from the uncertainty of their own minds. As late as February 1938, the Popular Front supporters were still sufficiently strong to prevent the conservatives Malvy and Lamoureux from entering the Finance Committee. By the time of the second Blum government, the left wing was in complete disarray. The Blum government was in an untenable position from the beginning, because it had insufficient support from one of its component elements.

Blum was called before the Anschluss was announced, and he sincerely wanted to form a national government that would include even the Communists. After lengthy negotiations he failed, to his intense disappointment, but he formed a government fairly closely in the image of the first Popular Front government, with the significant exceptions of Delbos and Chautemps (neither of whom voted for him). Blum himself was the first to proclaim the tentative and unsatisfac-

tory nature of the combination; he offered to enlarge it to Union Nationale on a moment's notice.[57] This unprecedented statement must
have given the ministers a sense of insecurity even more severe than
usual.* A government that proclaimed itself insubstantial as a shadow
could claim little consideration from the Chamber.

The Radicals, whether from contempt, impatience, or the sobering
effect of events abroad, for once seemed to feel little need for their
customary hypocrisy. The leaders did not conceal their opposition;
Daladier made it clear within the cabinet and the Group that he could
not accept some of the essential provisions of the financial program.[58]
La Dépêche de Toulouse criticized incessantly:

It is, it must be avowed, an unheard-of situation.

We have had no indication that those preparing the financial proposals
have discussed them at any time with the Radical members of the cabinet;
this is shocking. . . .

The government's bill is a collection of well-known measures whose principles have aroused polemics for more than ten years; moreover, they have
been continually rejected by parliament, although certain parties have used
them for electoral purposes; some of the other measures of more recent inspiration have been heatedly discussed recently and have even been officially
disavowed.[59]

Even more serious than these blasts from the big guns was the transformation of the hard-core Popular Front men. Delattre, who had led
the attack on Bonnet's attempt to destroy the Popular Front, now demanded a stable government without mentioning the Popular Front.[60]
Archimbaud called for a government of public safety.[61] Most striking
was the conversion of Kayser. Kayser had been one of the founders of
the Popular Front. He had been on the Committee of the Popular
Front; he had worked on its program. As late as January, he had

---

* A curious example of the certainty of rapid disintegration is the attitude shown by
William Bertrand and his newspaper, *Le Journal de Marennes*; Bertrand was a perennial minister, an intimate friend of Chautemps, who kept popping in and out of cabinets. His name was normally on the masthead of his paper, but when he became a
minister it had to be removed; when he ceased being a minister it was promptly restored. It was off in December 1933, on at the beginning of February 1934, off with
Doumergue, on with the fall of Laval, off with the third and fourth Chautemps ministries; but with the fall of the fourth Chautemps ministry, contrary to all precedent,
the name did not reappear, the spot remaining obstinately blank for a month; then,
with the formation of the Daladier cabinet, in which Bertrand was not included, the
name was back. He considered the Blum government so ephemeral that it did not
merit changing the type.

wanted to maintain the Popular Front majority. Now he denounced the Blum government in an article that had an enormous effect: "A government that declares itself without illusions about its possibilities of survival, but which does not know how to die. . . . When the essential concern is to reanimate France, it deliberates on financial measures, looking for what? For the most advantageous position on which to fall!"[62]

Thus, although the government won a majority of the Radicals' support when it finally presented itself to the Chamber, this majority was meaningless. The Radicals knew that the Senate would defeat Blum once again, and they felt that it might be necessary to have Socialist support for the Daladier cabinet to follow; therefore, it was better not to cause an open split in the Popular Front. There had certainly been traces of such an attitude in the defeat of the first Blum ministry; but if there had been a vote in the Chamber then in which it had been necessary to choose, it is probable that a majority of Radicals would have supported the Popular Front. Now such an outcome was unthinkable. The Senate promptly dispatched the Blum government.

There was no question about what was to follow. A Daladier ministry was universally anticipated, and probably already selected. The crisis came and went without difficulty. The Socialists remained outside the cabinet. The moderates entered in force. The Socialists and Communists reluctantly supported the new government. The equivocation about the Popular Front continued, for a myth as strong as the Popular Front takes a long time to disappear—thus the impossibility of dating its end.

The party had rejected the Popular Front and once again enjoyed full power. Yet this victory was self-mutilating. Those left-wingers who might have wanted to go into opposition were prevented from doing so by the Socialist and Communist support of the government. The right-wingers had achieved their aims; the Front was broken, the government was oriented to the right, one of their most diehard conservatives, Marchandeau, was Minister of Finance; and Bonnet, as Foreign Minister, ensured the most congenial foreign policy they could reasonably expect. Their victory was marked in the Chamber by the entry, at last, of Malvy into the Finance Committee, and the eclipse in the committee of the formerly dominant left-wingers. Since they could not reasonably hope for any more, any change would weaken their position, and they could make no trouble for Daladier.

The left wing could offer only a bankrupt Popular Front and dared opposition only when there was no chance of overthrowing the government. The party, therefore, as a party, could exert no pressure on the government. Meetings of the Group had no function but to occupy the deputies' time. The Bureau met occasionally, but did nothing. The Executive Committee met only three times during the two-year reign of Daladier.

Just as there was no alternative majority, there were suddenly no alternative ministers. Herriot was less and less representative of the Radicals, and he voluntarily withdrew. Chautemps was discredited by his behavior at the time of the Anschluss; Bonnet had had his chance too early, and the animosities were too great for him to form a government of Union Nationale. Albert Sarraut was no longer mentioned. Thus, Daladier was immune to combinations against him, except, in the waning days, one led by Reynaud.

Moreover, the foreign situation was much too dangerous for the luxury of ministerial crises to be lightly indulged in. Finally, the Senate had lost its sting by overthrowing the Popular Front, for it could not destroy a government whose majority it liked. It no longer exercised a preponderant influence. It was said that Reynaud, in working out his November decree laws, did not even consult Caillaux.[63]

Besides benefiting from this formidable tactical situation, Daladier systematically eliminated all traces of independent authority throughout the party. He had always personally disliked the formal aspect of the party; he had an authoritarian streak in him that he expressed freely when not too rigorously opposed. Just as in forming his February Sixth government he had entirely bypassed the Group, to the intense irritation of its president, Herriot, and in joining the Popular Front he had gone behind the backs of the Bureau and acted on his own initiative, so now he subverted the Group entirely. In the old days, the presidency of the Group had been a post of primary importance; Herriot had battled for it with François Albert; Chautemps, Delbos, and Daladier himself were presidents in succession. Daladier's president now was Chichery, and his function was reduced to reporting to Daladier the Group's opinion, gauging the temper of the Chamber, and transmitting Daladier's wishes to the Radicals. Chichery had a genius for such a role,[64] but he was in no respect the leader of the deputies. He was shot at the time of the liberation.

Daladier disdained to meet with delegations from the Group. At the time of the presidential election in 1939, when the deputies' opposition threatened Daladier's scheme for re-electing Lebrun, Chichery simply managed to prevent the Group's meeting until half an hour before the vote.[65] Meetings of the Group became infrequent; between January 1938 and April 9, I have noted 24 meetings; between April and December, only an additional 12. Complaints about Daladier's high-handed treatment of the Group were constant.[66]

There was no necessity to subvert the Bureau, for the Bureau was always more or less quiescent before the president of the party. Pierre Mazé, the secretary-general who replaced Aubaud in 1936, was a Daladier liege man. Daladier faced considerable difficulties from the Executive Committee, but he gradually overcame them. A meeting of the Executive Committee took place on January 26, 1938, to consider representation to a special congress that was to be held on the question of proportional representation. Daladier wanted a small congress, but in his absence, the committee, dominated by the Federation of the Seine, opted for some 2,000 delegates. The size would affect the outcome; it was thought that the small congress would reject proportional representation, whereas the large might accept it. Daladier had the Bureau revoke the decision of the Executive Committee, apparently by threatening to resign.[67] This disavowal greatly weakened the Executive Committee, but it was not brought fully under control until 1939.[68]

Other power centers within the party were likewise emasculated. The power of the Radical senators was greatly diminished. The vertical organization of the Jeunesses Radicales, which had placed considerable power in the hands of Sableau and Manescau (their local federations being responsible to the national federation, rather than to the local adult federations of the party), was transformed in December 1938 into a loose, horizontal, decentralized arrangement. The assault on Manescau's and Sableau's position was led by the left wing of the party; but it was aided by Daladier, certainly not for doctrinal reasons —he had drifted far from the left by the end of 1937—but because he did not wish to tolerate independent power within the party. The new organization imposed by the Bureau not only destroyed the power of the national federation but diminished the dynamism of the movement. With its authoritarian structure eliminated, its authoritarian appeal vanished, and it became one of the many shadow organizations that haunted the party.

One of the firmest bases of Daladier's support within the Chamber was his clique. He had a very strong hold over the minor deputies within the party. An agglomeration of these little-known provincials formed around Camille Perfetti. Who they were is something of a mystery. Frossard described them as "the soviet of the round table"— an active little group of deputies who had the habit of working together around one of the tables in the Chamber. They were modest provincial deputies, discreet, and scarcely known to the public. They ate together, lived in the same hotel, and finished by acting and thinking in the same fashion.[69] Lamoureux, less charitably, called them "a camarilla composed of a certain number of rather obscure deputies, whose mediocrity led them to call themselves deputies of the second zone. Their leader was a quaestor [of the Chamber] . . . named Perfetti. These deputies were called 'the Perfetti group.' "[70] They voted as a bloc for officers in the Group, the Chamber, and the committees. (Lamoureux blames them for his exclusion from the Finance Committee.) They were consulted by the leaders on all questions. Perfetti was devoted to Daladier and undoubtedly abetted the transition from the Popular Front majority by faithfully following him.[71] This clique was a unique power base within the party.

When the morbid fear of governmental weakness in the face of the German threat is added to these strategic advantages within the party, it is easy to understand Daladier's remarkably untroubled reign of two long years.

The spring and summer after Daladier's installation in power passed peaceably in parliamentary adjournments and vacations; these were suddenly ended by the Munich crisis. Munich traumatized French politics, decisively creating a new pattern of divisions that has confused the traditional formations ever since. The trauma came during the mobilization. Halévy described it as follows: "From the 24th to the 27th, in four days, France was touched to the very smallest of her hamlets. The separation that ordinarily exists between the public and private spheres dissolved."[72] Munich was a far deeper shock than the Anschluss; the Anschluss reversed the parliamentary majority, but Munich altered the very framework of political life. Munich turned the Socialist Paul Faure into a lifelong admirer of Bonnet,[73] and permitted *La Lumière* to seriously name as the leaders of the left-wing Radicals the old-guard moderates, Herriot, Delbos, and Maurice Sarraut.[74]

During the long development of the crisis, the party was divided inside and outside the cabinet. At the top, Daladier never fully favored capitulation and yet loyally defended it.[75] Within the cabinet, the defeatists were led, of course, by Bonnet, who was apparently supported by Chautemps, La Chambre, and Marchandeau; on the other side were Zay, Rucart, Campinchi, and Albert Sarraut. Outside the cabinet, Cot and, at first, Herriot wanted to resist, Caillaux, Roche, and Mistler to capitulate.[76] In the lobbies, the Radicals seemed at first to favor resistance. The resisters dominated a meeting of the Group on September 23 and sent a delegation to Daladier.[77] Bonnet called Lamoureux back to Paris from Vichy to work behind the scenes in favor of appeasement, furnishing him with official documents and maps. At two meetings Lamoureux lectured the Radicals, and felt he had converted a good number.[78] During this period, the traditional left and right partially disintegrated. Vincent Badie, a convinced conservative, was the most articulate resister. Albert Sarraut was a mild resister. Yet there was still a certain left-right division, since the most outspoken defeatists were almost all conservatives—Mistler, Lamoureux, Bonnet, and Marchandeau.

Then came the mobilization and the immense, overwhelming relief of the Munich agreement. Men changed overnight. Archimbaud, a resister, passed to the defeatists; Herriot withdrew his resistance at the same time.[79] Daladier returned from Munich in triumph. The enthusiasm within the party flooded over. The resisters were overwhelmed. "Hitler and Daladier, two veterans who had fought in the war, who know all its horrors and also its futility, have just found themselves face to face as they did twenty years ago, not to fight this time, but to come to an understanding."[80] "God Save Chamberlain," "The Miracle Happened," and above all, "Vive la Paix!" In the Indre, a team of deputies went out night after night to towns and villages proclaiming the good news, "How Daladier Saved the Peace!"[81] Such behavior was totally unprecedented. Meetings were held spontaneously throughout France. There was a great move for dissolving parliament, since the Radicals thought they would win 250 seats because of Daladier's triumph.[82]

There were few dissenting voices. Geistdoerfer refused to sign a joint poster with the other deputies and got soundly trounced in the senatorial elections partly, at least, because of it.[83] Cot noted that France had broken faith, but admitted that peace was a great good.[84] Long into the dismal year that led to war, Radicals recalled with nostalgia the moment of triumph that had been theirs. Miellet wrote that it had been a great moment, when Frenchmen finally had been united.[85] During an electoral campaign the following spring, a local Radical newspaper wrote, "From the cities to the smallest villages, we will proclaim the merits of our dear President Daladier, who, in the anguished hours of last September, saved Europe and the world from a fearful butchery that would have ravaged homes and hearts."[86]

As Potut remarked, Munich provided the necessary psychological shock for formally breaking the Popular Front.[87] A residual attachment to it had lingered even after the fall of the Blum government; the Communists and Socialists had supported the Daladier government, and the Committee of the Popular Front still met. Now the Communists fought the sacred Munich settlement, and all the Radicals' pent-up frustrations and guilt at having betrayed their ally Czechoslovakia poured forth on the Communists. The annual Congress, which met at the end of October in Marseilles, began as a triumph for Munich, but rapidly turned into an orgy of anti-Communism. When Bayet tried to defend the Popular Front, he was shouted down. Daladier was wildly cheered when he attacked the Communists.[88]

Daladier humbled the Congress as he had humbled the other party institutions. The Minister of Commerce, Fernand Gentin, made a very sensible economic analysis in a long speech; he advocated a national economic plan on modern lines, partially financed by the state.[89] The party workers were clearly delighted, and the Congress gave a clear mandate endorsing the Gentin plan. Two days after the Congress ended, there was a cabinet shuffle, and Paul Reynaud, the new Minister of Finance, forced the plan to be scrapped.[90]

One of the curious results of European humiliation was that Radicals began to seek compensation in the grandeur of empire. France's tenacious insistence on her colonies dates from 1938. For the first time, Radicals began commonly speaking of France as a nation of 100 million people. The connection between Munich and the myth of an imperial destiny is remarkably clearly shown in the report of Aimé Berthod at the Congress:

Now that [France's European system of alliances] no longer exists, ought we to try to reconstruct it on a new basis as some wish, or ought we deliberately to direct the nation's effort in a new direction. . . . Will we be accused of being petty and of accepting the "abdication of France," if we state that to the destiny of France as a western, maritime, African, and colonial nation, the development of a magnificent empire matters more than the thankless role of gendarme or even banker, which, in the elation of victory, we thought we were called upon to play.[61]

This connection becomes apparent again at the beginning of 1939. Mussolini had arranged a little demonstration demanding that France return Tunis, Nice, Savoy, and Djibouti to Italy. As a result, Daladier went off on a great junket through the Mediterranean empire. At the same time, the pro-Munich Berthod made a fire-eating speech in the Executive Committee against the Italians.[92] There was also a sudden burst of sympathy for the Spanish Republicans—the Italians were helping Franco. Defeatism with regard to Germany pushed these people toward seeking kudos in their empire, and when this also was attacked, it provoked an unwonted bellicosity from the defeatists themselves.

Even Munich had not made Daladier's victory within the party complete; the triumph on foreign policy at the Congress of Marseilles had been immediately followed by Reynaud's financial austerity measures and by the suppression of the general strike of November 30, which were both highly unpopular with the former Popular Front Radicals. Discontent within the party reached a peak on December 22, when the government obtained a majority of only 291 to 284 in a vote of confidence on Reynaud's decree laws. Twenty-four Radicals voted against the government, 12 abstained, and two were absent. With one or two exceptions like Delbos, this opposition was composed of the old core of Popular Front Radicals, but the Reynaud financial policy was unpopular even among the most conservative.[93] A relative majority of only seven votes was frankly frightening to the opposition as well as the government, since no one wanted a crisis; there was a second vote and the rebellious Radicals, after gaining some concessions, came back to the fold. On December 31 the Group managed to extort a few further concessions.

In this delicate situation, Daladier's political virtuosity prompted him to continue to defer to the Group, in complete reversal of his usual behavior. He had further to meet the dangerous Paris-dominated Executive Committee on January 15, which would surely have caused him trouble but for the unprecedented attendance of some 1,500 members from all parts of France, who overwhelmed the typical left-wing

Parisians.[94] Had the government rounded them up and financed their trip? It seems likely, but there is no proof. In any event, this often turbulent assembly was singularly quieted by the newcomers, and Daladier was given an ovation. A final left-wing stronghold remained, the Federation of the Seine, whose leadership was doggedly Popular Front and anti-Munichois; it normally dominated the Executive Committee and was a thorn in Daladier's side. The annual elections for its president took place at the meeting of January 25. The two candidates were Ernest Perney, a Popular Front advocate who apparently derived his support chiefly from the suburbs, and Lucien Bauzin, a Daladier man whose support came from Paris. The following account of the campaign was given by a Perney supporter:

The interest that the directors of the party felt in the outcome of the fight resulted in the general mobilization of the government's friends for yesterday's meeting. Up to the very last moment before the vote, certain federations purchased numerous membership cards, in order to increase their numbers. Transportation was provided for the delegates, the greater number of whom were new to the federation. In these conditions, the narrow victory of the government supporters was assured.[95]

Bauzin won by 226 votes to 164.[96] The issues were clearly the Popular Front and the policy on Munich. If Bauzin is to be believed, the Germans took such an interest in the outcome that Otto Abetz attended the meeting incognito.[97] The Perney forces were irreconcilable; the Committee of Asnières, for example, voted in March a motion of confidence in the former president and also expressed its intention "to remain independent of the new federation bureau."[98]

After these elections, Daladier had no more difficulty with any organized resistance in the party; the only failure he encountered was the refusal of the Executive Committee and the Group itself to impose discipline on the deputies, which Daladier desired but had no right to expect.[99] Throughout the spring and summer there was practically no life in the provincial federations, and the party seemed bent on discouraging any activity. The following press release was issued by the Federation of Boulogne-Billancourt: "Considering the present circumstances, and wanting to support the work of the government to the utmost, the Radical and Radical-Socialist Federation, which was going to organize a meeting on Thursday, March 28, at 9 P. M., Salle des Fêtes, has decided to postpone it to a more favorable period."[100] Quite clearly, the party had pressured the federation into abandoning the idea. Until the formation of the Reynaud government, the party played no apparent role. Considerable left-wing opposition to the government still existed within the Group and showed itself sporadically —for example, when Daladier asked for full powers following the German occupation of Prague—but it was never serious and did not even hope to succeed.

III

The Radical party did very little in the year following the occupation of Prague. Even its annual Congress was canceled because of the war. Domestic politics were largely forgotten and what continued was obscured by the thick screen of censorship.

Two last events, however, form a sort of epilogue to the history of the party in the 1930's: in March 1940, Radicals almost destroyed the Reynaud government; in July 1940, they participated in the liquidation of the Republic. The Daladier government was suddenly and unexpectedly overthrown on March 19, 1940, at the end of a secret session of parliament devoted to the Finnish war. On the question of confidence, Daladier received only 239 votes in his favor, with more than 300 deputies abstaining, and one opposed.[101] It was a curious vote, which showed the disarray of parliament; the Socialists were the only undivided group, and they abstained. The Radicals were unusually united, with only ten abstaining. All the other groups, from the Republican Socialists to the Fédération Républicaine, were divided.[102] The Radicals, irrespective of political outlook, were irritated at what seemed to be a plot.[103]

The Reynaud government was formed overnight, which only strengthened the Radicals' opposition—on its presentation to the Chamber, Lucien Galimand, a Radical, insinuated that such dispatch meant that Reynaud had plotted to overthrow Daladier. Blum tried to reassure the Radicals in the same debate that he had not been involved in any plot.[104] The government's presentation to the Chamber was upsetting. "I wish to express," wrote de Kerillis, "after the frightful day yesterday, my indignation and my feelings of revulsion. Parliament, the parties, and the press have done a frightful job."[105] Reynaud received 268 favorable votes, with 267 abstentions or hostile votes. The most striking aspect of this vote was the opposition of the Radicals; ten voted against the government, and 70 abstained. The vote was quite unique. The division was not entirely unconnected with the question of a hard or soft policy in the war—nine of the 10 hostile voters were conservative defeatists of the Mistler brand—yet defeatists and resisters mingled in the opposition. Four of the 11 Radical deputies listed by Tony Révillon as being on the *Massilia* abstained.* The traditional left-wing right-wing classification was now clearly meaningless, as can be seen by the table of votes by group:

	For	Against	Abstained	Absent
Conservative	4	9	12	—
Moderate	8	1	9	—
Moderate-Left	9	0	26	—
Left	11	0	13	2

(Twelve deputies could not be classified.)

If there was greater support among the left and moderate elements for Reynaud and more hostility from the moderate-left, the reason for this is probably that Daladier's firmest supporters were in the last group. It seems that the Radicals most hostile to Reynaud were Daladier and Bonnet.[106] Herriot supported the government. The question of personal loyalty to Daladier confused all existing relations; Daladier's friends and Bonnet's friends were both in the opposition, although they had scarcely anything in common.

The government decided to stay in power after the disastrous vote, with the Radicals Chautemps and Daladier giving it a provisional stay of execution. The period of grace was over when Daladier announced his resignation on May 9, but the German invasion the following day prevented the crisis from taking place. In this March crisis the Radicals were fighting to maintain a position they regarded as rightfully theirs, but that events and the other parties had bypassed. The Radicals were left with the power to destroy a government, which they did not hesitate to use, but they had no more power to construct.

In the chaos of the fall of France, the Radical party did nothing; Radicals as individuals worked in every possible direction. Chautemps and Lamoureux proposed the armistice; at the other extreme, 13 Radicals were on the *Massilia*.[107] During the Vichy meeting of the National Assembly, a number of Radicals were in the forefront of those

---

* Tony Révillon, p. 66. In the confused days of June 1940 before the armistice, a number of parliamentarians fled to North Africa aboard the steamship *Massilia,* in order to permit at least part of the government to escape the German advance. Most of those on the *Massilia* were resisters.

trying to block Laval's schemes; yet Mistler was one of Laval's most useful supporters. The Radical opposition was composed exclusively of minor deputies, many of whom had never been heard of before. Of the 14 Radicals who signed Vincent Badie's declaration hostile to Laval's projects, none had been so much as an undersecretary of state.[108] The consular figures consented in the new constitution. Herriot dithered about for a long time, and concluded with a crashing abstention.[109] In the end, no Radical managed to defend the Republic, although the only two parliamentarians who tried—Vincent Badie and Alfred Margaine—were Radicals.[110] Twenty-three parliamentarians voted against Pétain, eight abstained, 13 were on the *Massilia*, and 20 were absent.[111] The Radicals' behavior was scarcely worse than that of the others. Yet it had been their Republic, and they let it be replaced with scarcely a murmur. This was what Jules Romains called their "unpardonable sin."[112] It was a sad conclusion to their brave ideals and their boasts of two generations.

During the war, the Radicals did neither very well nor very badly; there were few actual collaborators, and as the great Masonic party, it was little favored by Vichy. A fairly creditable record was pieced together in a brochure published by Mazé at the end of the war. Daladier was the star of the Riom trials. Seventeen parliamentarians were deported; five were murdered by the Germans or by Vichy; at least one was assassinated by the Resistance. Jean Moulin was claimed as a Radical. All who had official dealings with Vichy—19 deputies and 15 senators—were excluded from the party (11 were conservative, two moderate, five moderate-left, and one left-wing). Among those excluded were Chautemps, Malvy, and Lamoureux, and the young conservatives, Mistler, Riou, and Potut.[113]

The party life which then was re-established was something quite different from that of the 1930's. The Radicals emerged chastened and diminished. They had a new role to play that has colored their retrospective image. In all probability, the leaders of the Fourth Republic were not the equals of the leaders of the Third. Queuille emerged as a first-rank deputy only after the war. Edgar Faure may have been the Chautemps of the Fourth Republic, but where is the Daladier, or the Herriot, or the Maurice Sarraut? The summer of 1940 ended an era.

The majority of 1936, like those of 1924 and 1932, had broken in the middle; the Radicals had shifted once again from the left to the right.

The superficial similarity invites a general law. Charles Micaud suggests that the Radicals "were in a convenient position to play the Left against the Right when at election time they appealed to republican solidarity, and the Right against the Left when, once elected, they appealed to the defense of the franc."[114] Only in 1926, however, was defense of the franc the central issue; in 1934, it was fear of the rioters; in 1938, it was fear of Germany. The 1938 crisis was in many ways quite different from the earlier ones. There was, indeed, the usual climactic event, this time Munich, which, however, unlike February Sixth, did not create a sharp left-right line, but divided every party and threw the deepest confusion into all traditional alignments. Then, the Daladier government was never so unmistakably a right-wing government as Poincaré's or Doumergue's;[115] nor was it faced with the same unremitting hostility from the left. Daladier was able to keep the right in hand by threatening to bring the Socialists into the government. After it was rumored on January 8, 1939, that the right, which now made up the bulk of the new majority, wanted its fair share of cabinet seats, Daladier had a private talk with Blum, and Chichery worked with Blum on trying to cooperate in the Chamber,[116] which quieted the unrest.

A more important novelty of the 1938–39 crisis was the downgrading of both parliament and domestic issues in the face of the overwhelming foreign threat. The French parliament had more or less ceased to govern by early 1939; its only function was the election of the President of the Republic and the periodic renewal of full powers; the rest of the time the Chamber of Deputies was faced with the choice of debating proportional representation or going on vacation. The eclipse of parliament in 1939 was far greater than in 1934 or 1935.

For the Radicals, the change was fundamentally different from the earlier ones. After 1926, according to Goguel: "The solidarity of the Radicals with the Socialists, cemented by the attacks they had undergone and continued to undergo in common, remained noticeably stronger than before 1914. Republican discipline remained their invariable rule in all by-elections; they even let the Communists, on certain occasions, benefit from it."[117] Between 1934 and 1936, republican discipline was not invariable, but it was at least frequent. After 1938, the traditional electoral foundations of the party were shattered. Communists were now beyond the republican pale, and since the Socialists generally continued to insist on a Popular Front alliance, the

Radicals were isolated, cut off on the right, too, by a resurgence of right-wing militancy.

Even before the 1938 crisis there was a gradual building up of electoral tensions quite unparalleled before 1926 and 1934; these tensions became critical following Munich. The by-elections of Lapalisse, Sète, Uzès, Saintes,[118] the cantonal elections of 1937, and the senatorial elections of 1938, demonstrated a progressive estrangement of the Radicals from their electoral allies. Instead of fighting the customary right-versus-left battle in the by-elections of the 1936–40 Chamber, the Radicals withdrew in favor of the right, got involved in a three-way fight, or simply withdrew in no one's favor; not once did they withdraw for a Socialist or Communist.[119]

The whole left was thrown into an electoral disorder from which it has not yet recovered. After 1938, the Communists began to lose ground.[120] Chichery, in a speech in 1939, commented that although the Socialists and Communists were falling back, the Radicals were not the beneficiaries.[121] An election in Aubusson to replace a Radical deputy turned senator clearly illustrated the left's new dilemma. On the first ballot the results were: Right, 4,082; Radical, 3,553; Socialist, 3,144; and Communist, 1,591. The Radical had run on a strictly pro-Munich, anti-Marxist program, which made the Socialists and Communists reluctant to support him as republican discipline demanded. The Radical did not want to permit the election of the candidate of the right, who was a clerical conservative. A three-way second ballot took place with the following results: Right, 5,589 (elected); Radical, 2,594; Socialist, 5,100. The Socialists blamed the Communists, the Communists blamed the Socialists, and the Radicals blamed them both for not withdrawing in the Radicals' favor.[122]

In such conditions, the Radicals' malaise was profound. The Radical association of Dax denounced "the domestic unrest resulting from the dislocation of the Popular Front, the increasingly accentuated demagogy of the parties of the extreme left, and the blackmail of the Daladier government by the parties of the extreme right."[123] Some saw the only answer to this electoral predicament in the adoption of a system of proportional representation, which they thought would end the necessity for electoral alliances.

The most far-reaching consequence, however, of the break in 1938 was that, for the first time, the principal enemy for the Radicals was on the left. In the past there had often been recriminations against the

Socialists, and occasionally outbursts against the Communists; but the latter had generally been ignored, and the Socialists were considered a difficult ally rather than an enemy. Anti-Communism had not captured the entire Radical party in 1938; but by 1940 even the extreme left-winger Bayet was talking of the "Communazis."[124] Henceforth the Radicals could no longer be a party of the left; that is the real significance of the protracted crisis of the years 1936 to 1938. After 1938, they discarded the illusion that they were something they had long ceased to be; with the anti-Communism of the last years, the Radicals finally began acting like a party of the center.

Conclusion

By the end of 1938 French democracy had ceased to function, though the forms subsisted, shadows and ghosts of the past, for another eighteen months, until those dreadful meetings of the National Assembly on July 9 and 10, 1940, when the representatives of republican France silently accepted their revocation. The Republic perished slandered and unmourned. The shoddy theatricality of those last meetings should not obscure the abdication of the preceding, peacetime years. The Third Republic was not overthrown by the German invasion; it went under because of peacetime crisis, a crisis materially not so severe as the First World War, yet spiritually as devastating. The tried political processes had suited the contented society of the Third Republic; in the halcyon days the Radicals had administered power and distributed benefits, but had grown unaccustomed to govern; they were unable to cope with the unexpected, awful challenges of the 1930's. The party and all of parliament abdicated to Daladier, who was, in this respect, the precursor of Marshal Pétain.

During the 1930's, the Radical party sustained two long-range changes: the directing circles of the party were aging and becoming more moderate, and the Radical voters were shifting to the right; thus, after 1936, the party found its support well in the center. Its political posture, however, did not faithfully reflect this shift. From 1920 to 1936, with brief stays in 1926 and 1934, the party's program and outlook drifted decisively leftward. In 1920, more than half the deputies had accepted at least part of the program of the conservative Union des Intérêts Economiques; in 1936, the party advocated the reform of the Bank of France, the nationalization of the arms industry, and the creation of the Wheat Board. Then, after 1936, the program and attitudes became more moderate. This shift in direction parallels that of the Catholics, as analyzed by René Rémond: both groups were driven to the left by the Depression and the fear of fascism, and to the right thereafter by the fear of Communism.*

It is tempting to regard the end of the Radical Republic as an inevitable outcome of such a profound sociological shift; the very underpinnings of Radicalism were disintegrating. Undoubtedly this is true in the long run; one cannot imagine a revived Radical party under present French social conditions. Yet the decline and fall of the Radicals was not simply, or even primarily, the result of gradual sociological attrition. The failure of the 1930's was essentially a political failure of individual politicians; the change of opinion in the electorate was secondary. The Radical Republic was a distinctly political affair, and the political performance of the Radicals is the key to their downfall.

When a party plays a role as important as that of the Radical party, it is worth asking whether any general conclusion can be drawn from its experience. Can anything be learned from the Radicals' sorry performance? In his book on political parties, Maurice Duverger used the French Radicals, who pre-eminently exhibited the natural characteristics of a middle-class party, as the model for the caucus or cadre party. In their spasmodic activity, their loose party ties, their feeble control over their own parliamentarians, and their sloppy ideology, the Radicals strongly resembled, for example, the British Conservatives; and they provide a model for the pragmatic, "brokerage" parties that are becoming standard in the West.

In one important respect, however, they differed from most pragmatic parties of the postwar era: the latter are highly disciplined, whereas the Radicals had no discipline worthy of the name.† Party discipline has become crucial for the form of modern democracy; a

---

* See Rémond, *Les Catholiques,* p. 11. It may be objected that the comparison does not hold because the Catholics in France were not a party, and had no way of adopting a unified policy; rather, the center of gravity of Catholic opinion shifted first to the left and then to the right, but with some Catholics remaining on the left and some on the right at all times. Still, they are not unlike the Radicals, for the unity of the party was, as we have seen, of little importance, and it, too, changed in response to shifts in general opinion. Left-wing Radicals, like left-wing Catholics, remained so until the end; nonetheless, both became anti-Communist. Radicalism was, in its broader aspects, a "political culture," within which its socially heterogeneous membership shared a common world view, and in this, at least, it was comparable to Catholicism. That two such different groups followed a broadly parallel development leads one to suspect that such was the movement of the general political climate.

† That some parties, like the Radicals, operate within a multi-party system, while others operate within a two-party system, does not seem to make much difference with respect to their internal organization, their relations with their electors, or the type of politician that emerges.

disciplined party concentrates and mobilizes the diffuse power of its voters, but an undisciplined party disperses it even further.[1] A disciplined-party system leads to a quasi-plebiscitary form of democracy, but an undisciplined-party system remains a purely representative democracy.[2] That the Radicals were undisciplined has therefore been very important for the form of French democracy. But since there are few undisciplined caucus parties outside France, and since the most important of them, those in the United States, have developed in a peculiar way, comparative analysis of the Radical party in its totality is liable to yield meager results.

Still, a party may be compared with other parties on particular points, and the Radicals' experience may be applied in other situations. One of the essential functions of the modern party is to act as a broker between conflicting interests, and in this the Radicals were adept. When brokerage is the key political function, then the type of politician produced will tend toward the slick operator of the Chautemps breed. The type of politician produced by Radicalism seems fairly characteristic of modern parties. Also, in modern democracy, it is becoming increasingly necessary for all parties to participate in government,[3] and it will be remembered that the Radicals prided themselves on being above all "a party of government." One effect of governing is that doctrine and conviction give way to administration and manipulation, the edge of principle being blunted by constant decision making. That the governing experience had precisely this effect on the Radicals is clear. By the 1930's the slick broker and the urbane administrator had become as typical of the Radicals as they are of today's dominant parties.

It is to be hoped that the situation facing the Radicals in the 1930's was in some ways unique; it seems unlikely that an economic crisis comparable to the Great Depression will occur or that there will be another Hitler. Still, the Great Depression was not all that great in France, and her politicians were spared from making the drastic readjustments that the more serious crisis caused in the United States, Germany, and, to a lesser extent, England. The French were faced with a stagnating economic situation more closely parallel perhaps to the sluggishness of the British and American economies in the late 1950's—a situation ultimately dangerous, but at no specific moment critical. France was the one major European country that had the opportunity to make its economic readjustments from calculation rather than crisis—she could study foreign devaluations, deflationary experiments, attempts at Keynesian policies, systematically planned economies, and so forth; she was the one major country whose hand was not forced—at least domestically—by events.

The Radical party was not hindered by doctrinal commitment in confronting the country's situation, and the party leadership consisted of men of a caliber as high as one could reasonably expect. The Radicals were conscious of being on trial, of being called to make decisions of historical import. If it is possible to generalize beyond one party's reaction to a specific situation, it would appear that the Radical party's responses in these conditions are highly instructive, since the challenges, though heightened, were not essentially extraordinary, and since the party, though unique, was not remarkably dissimilar to other middle-of-the-road, reformist parties.

The party's response to the crisis of the 1930's was, of course, disheartening. No important problem was faced. When difficulties arose, the characteristic action of the leaders was to resign—as Chautemps did three times, and Daladier did after February Sixth—or to do nothing, as Albert Sarraut did during the Rhineland crisis. Instead of investigating the new economic conditions conscientiously, the party almost automatically formulated slogans that they and their electors could understand, and then fought for these slogans as for revealed truth until overwhelmed by the facts. Problems were debated only from symbolic and easily attained positions, so that the whole political struggle took place in a fantasy world. The very single-mindedness of the debates attracted attention, but the struggle was so out of touch with reality that it generated nothing but ephemeral passion. Thus the economic problems of the depression focused on the salaries of the hapless fonctionnaires; the balance of payments problem was turned into a crusade against devaluation; the threat of Hitler was to be parried by a hysterical anti-Communism and the quixotic proclamation of an imperial destiny. Panic over the Leagues drove the party into the Popular Front, just as panic over Communism drove it out.

The party's structural organs were unadapted to their role. The Group was able to overcome the tyranny of the leadership only once, to defeat Georges Bonnet; otherwise the deputies' wishes were ignored. The only time that the entire party machine was mobilized against a government—Laval's—the operation took some months and achieved a success so tardy as to be irrelevant. The Congress was unable to impose any coherent policy upon the leaders. When, after a lifetime of July Fourteenth oratory, the Radicals were faced with really defending the Republic in the summer of 1940, they did nothing. The leaders themselves were unprepared for what faced them in the 1930's, or rather, their preparation positively prevented successful action.

The Radicals looked on themselves as men of the left, yet their material interests were on the center or the right—the classic French conflict between the heart and the pocketbook. In a tranquil era this tension was not serious; in a period of crisis it became disastrous. The *mystique des gauches,* in its various guises of republican defense, anticlericalism, the Popular Front, and nostalgia for the Great Revolution, enthralled even so moderate a man as Herriot, whose hostility to "reaction" crippled his political maneuverability.

During the years 1932 to 1934, the narrow interests of the party and its clientele all argued for allying with the center against the Socialists, and the center was justifiably puzzled by the Radicals' refusal to understand where their real interests lay. In 1932 the Radicals' attachment to the left was so strong that a break with the Socialists was unthinkable. During the first two years of the legislature, the Radicals made no attempt to resolve the contradiction between interest and outlook. The mystique of the left proved no guide to the economic problems that overwhelmed the successive governments, so they borrowed the congenial deflationist theories of the center and right.

Thus commenced a pattern of immobility followed by crisis; there was no movement from 1932 to 1934 despite an intolerable situation; then, through crisis, came the total renunciation of the dogmatically left-wing political position held a moment earlier—a political capitulation before an economic imperative. This capitulation took place without political preparation, so it was misunderstood and resented. The resentment grew as the new right-wing alliance proved as bankrupt as the old left-wing one, for the tension between political attitude and economic policy remained unresolved. Then the party made a sudden lurch back to a policy dominated by purely political considerations, when it committed itself to the Popular Front. When this in turn failed, the party reversed itself once more.

With each reversal, the Radicals' faith in the rejected alternative was diminished. The experience of 1932–34 made the Radicals reconsider their political attitudes and economic doctrine, but no resolution of the conflict between them emerged. The entry into the Popular Front implied a repudiation of the economic policy that had dominated the deflationary years, but no new economic policy was elaborated. The rupture of the Popular Front brought an apparently decisive rejection of the earlier naïve leftist attitude, but all that replaced it was the potent but sterile ideal of anti-Communism. The period ended, then, with the economic doctrine and the mystique having eliminated each other; only habit remained to bind the people to the Radical party.

Just as serious as the inability to deal with new problems as they arose, was the ease with which the most hallowed traditions of political behavior were sloughed off when the situation really became critical. Many Radicals tacitly abandoned the rights of man; many abused parliament; many deserted the Republic. At a certain point the intensity of the Hitler menace became so great that it swept away all convictions; the party hysterically descended to unbridled anti-Communism, which, in this instance at least, was but a scapegoat for their own considerable failings, and an outlet for their impotent anguish. The ease with which anti-Communism engulfed the Radicals is doubly disturbing—not only because it was irrelevant and indeed diverted attention from the most urgent tasks, but also because it went against their traditional political comportment.

It was only the severity of the final crisis that forced the inadequacies of this traditional balancing party into brutal relief, proving that such a party, while the most apt to govern in normal times, was the least apt to meet extreme situations. One might very well offer as the epitaph of the whole party the disillusioned judgment that Pertinax delivered upon Daladier: "His success as a politician, his failure as a statesman, the misfortune of France: all effects of a single cause."[4]

Notes

Complete authors' names, titles, and publication data are given in the Bibliography, pp. 301–14. The full names and departments of all Radical deputies will be found in the Index, identified by an asterisk.

INTRODUCTION

1. Until recently this remarkable phenomenon, the Radical party, had scarcely been studied. The best prewar monograph was by a German, Rudolf Semler; the French have generally produced either empty eulogies by Radicals (Gaston Maurice, Albert Milhaud) or partisan denunciations (Raymond Cartier). In the past three years, however, three excellent monographs have appeared: Daniel Bardonnet has examined the party structure in its formal and actual relations; Francis de Tarr has given a fine account of the party history following World War II; and Gil Alroy, in his unpublished dissertation (perhaps the most exciting work of the three), has considered the party's thought and style in their functional relationship to the social structure of twentieth-century France. Other studies are also listed in the Bibliography.

2. This attitude on the part of the right has been pointed out by Alroy, Chap. 2, pp. 28–29. (Each chapter in this dissertation is numbered from p. 1.)

3. Hoffmann, "Paradoxes," p. 15.   4. Elgé, pp. 219–20.

5. *Tableau des partis,* pp. 158–59.   6. *La Politique,* p. 50.

7. From Berl's article reprinted in *La Tribune républicaine* (Meuse), May 15, 1936. See also Alroy, Chap. 2, pp. 2–4, for a similar set of statements.

8. Bendix and Lipset, p. 4. See also Lipset, *Political Man,* p. 113, for a similar statement.

9. Mounier, p. 907.

10. Daniel Halévy, quoted in Fourcade, p. 42. See also Halévy, "Le Parti radical-socialiste," p. 425, and Maxence, pp. 235–36.

11. *L'Homme libre,* Aug. 27, 1937. See also "B. S." (François Goguel), "Le Parti radical-socialiste," p. 187.

12. *Le Temps,* Oct. 25, 1937, speech.

13. See, for example, Campinchi's speech at Soustons, Landes, *Le Temps,* July 17, 1936; Bauzin's speech at Mayenne, *ibid.,* Oct. 6, 1936; the Radical manifesto, *ibid.,* Oct. 18, 1936; Kayser speech, in Parti Républicain Radical et Radical-Socialiste, *33ᵉ Congrès . . . tenu à Biarritz les 22, 23, 24 et 25 octobre 1936,* Oct. 24, p. 369. (Henceforth the proceedings of all party Congresses will be referred to simply as *Congress,* with the date.)

14. Cartier, p. 105.

15. Both Siegfried's statement (from *Tableau des partis,* p. 159) and Williams's own are from Williams, *Politics in Post-War France,* p. 104.

16. See Truman, p. 282.   17. Leites, pp. 113, 131.

18. Bonnet, *Défense de la paix,* I, 43.   19. *Aux écoutes,* Sept. 19, 1936.

20. Trotsky, *Ecrits, 1928–1940,* II, 9.   21. See *Le Temps,* March 12, 1937.

22. The American sociologist Seymour Martin Lipset has shown how liberalism and fascism tend to be the moderate and extremist ideological expressions of the center, i.e. of the lower middle classes and peasants, and how voters who had once voted as democrats were the prime subjects of fascist conversion (*Political Man*, pp. 131–40).

23. The memoirs of Herriot and Lucien Lamoureux are clearly based on the notes they took at the time, but even these are partial and summary. For Herriot, see *Jadis*, Vol. II. Lamoureux published 52 installments of his memoirs, dealing with the period 1932–37, in *Le Bourbonnais républicain* intermittently from Dec. 17, 1950, to March 22, 1953, and from March 13, 1955, to Aug. 26, 1956; these cover up to p. 1765 of his typed memoirs with what appears to be considerable thoroughness. Citations to the earlier period will be given to *Le Bourbonnais républicain*, to the later period by page number of the manuscript. Other memoirs include Paul-Boncour, *Entre deux guerres*, Vols. II and III; Bonnet, *Défense de la paix*; and Zay, *Souvenirs et solitude*.

24. I have seen the file done by Lucien Bauzin when he was *chef de cabinet* for Raymond Patenôtre.

25. *Le Petit Journal*, *L'Oeuvre*, *Le Petit Parisien*, and *L'Ere nouvelle* reproduced it with alterations; *La Dépêche de Toulouse* copied the first two paragraphs. Only *La République* had a different version. All appeared on Nov. 8, 1933.

26. *L'Information sociale*, Nov. 16 and Nov. 23, 1933.

27. *Le Temps*, Feb. 12, 13, 14, 1937.

CHAPTER I

1. Dupeux, p. 124; Chevallier, *Histoire des institutions politiques de la France moderne*, p. 549.

2. François Albert, cited by Louis Vincelles, *L'Homme libre*, Dec. 20, 1932.

3. See *Le Temps*, Jan. 6, 1937; Campinchi's speech at Royan, *Royan*, June 6, 1937; Lamoureux's memoirs, *Le Bourbonnais républicain*, April 1, 8, 15, 22, 1956.

4. See Lhomme, pp. 273–95, and Bleton, *Les Hommes des temps qui viennent*.

5. Cot, "Le Rajeunissement des partis," p. 165.

6. See the Maurice Thorez speech, Jan. 22, 1936, in *Oeuvres*, Vol. II, fasc. 8, p. 13; Marécot, pp. 1457–58; Bonte, p. 812. To Trotsky and his followers, the Radicals were not representative: "If the party of Herriot and Daladier has its roots in the masses of the petty bourgeoisie and in a certain sense even among the workers, it is solely for the purpose of duping them in the interests of the capitalist regime" (*Ecrits, 1928–1940*, II, 16). The Chichery speech, made before the Federation of the Seine, March 30, 1939, may be found (in typed form) in the Lucien Bauzin papers.

7. Alroy calls this policy *morcellisme*, a conscious attempt to protect and expand small holdings (Chap. 3, pp. 36–51).

8. Gourdon, pp. 227–29. He used as his basic sources the 1952 survey of the Institut Français d'Opinion Publique, *Etudes des opinions et professions de l'électorat R.G.R.*, and the *Statistique professionelle des maires radicaux*, furnished by the Ministry of the Interior.

9. Chevalier, pp. 31–33.

10. The only possible sources of such information are the membership lists of individual committees, but in the few of these that I have seen, the occupation of the party worker is generally omitted. This omission is characteristic both of the party's indifference to systematic organization, and of its essentially liberal ideology in which class differences had little importance.

11. See McKenzie, p. 246, for this relationship in both the Conservative and Labour parties. See also Dogan's table in *L'Origine sociale,* p. 328, which shows that the higher the political position, the less likely it is to have a working-class occupant.

12. See Bardonnet, *Evolution,* pp. 49–51. Milhaud, *Congress,* Oct. 5, 1933, p. 7, claimed 120,000. Information is very sparse after 1933; two estimates in *Esprit,* May 1, 1939, were 80,000 (by Goguel, p. 176), and 200,000 (by Raymond Millet, p. 209). A note in *Le Temps,* May 6, 1936, citing "a former secretary-general" (Milhaud?), claimed that membership was 108,000 or 109,000, instead of the official 116,000. An article in *Les Nouvelles de l'Ouest,* June 16, 1939, says it was 125,000, although in 1936 it had fallen to 70,000.

13. *La République,* Oct. 23, 1932.

14. McKenzie, p. 244. Admittedly, the French figure applies to the mid-1930's and the British one to the early 1950's, but the contrast is still valid.

15. Rimbert, "L'Avenir du parti socialiste," p. 125.

16. Borkenau, p. 101, claims 15,000 in 1933; the commentator in *Esprit,* May 1, 1939, p. 157, says 25,000; the official historian, Jacques Chambaz, reports 30,000 in 1934, p. 138n. Duverger's figure of 45,000 in 1933, drawn from Thorez, therefore seems too large (*Political Parties,* p. 88).

17. McKenzie, p. 245.

18. Chambéry, Feb. 16, 1936, 842; Thonon, Feb. 8, 1936, 700; Lons-le-Saunier, Jan. 26, 1936, 600; Privas, August 13, 1938, 300; Gourdon, April 4, 1932, 800; Dôle, Sept. 23, 1934, 200, etc.

19. St.-Jean-d'Angély, June 7, 1936, 800; Dax, July 14, 1936, 600, Nov. 11, 1936, 2,000; Melle, Nov. 20, 1932, 550; Royan, Oct. 19, 1932, 400; Angers, March 15, 1934, 4,000. Since electoral campaigns were relatively undeveloped, it is unlikely that as many as 300 worked actively in the district.

20. Duverger, *Political Parties,* p. 64.

21. *L'Oeuvre,* Sept. 25, 1938, and *Le Citoyen* (Finistère), Sept. 21, Dec. 3, 1933.

22. Based on lists given to me by Michel Geistdoerfer, former deputy.

23. Duverger, *Political Parties,* p. 42. Local radicalism has been exhaustively treated by Bardonnet, *Evolution,* pp. 31–70.

24. Bardonnet, "L'Organization locale du parti radical," pp. 73, 81–85, 98–110.

25. Interview with Ducos, June 1, 1960.

26. See Frédérix, pp. 121–22.

27. See Bardonnet, *Evolution,* pp. 74–77, 93–101, for the best discussion of these two unique institutions.

28. Typed minutes of the meeting of the Federation of the Seine, Feb. 2, 1935, pp. 9–10, from the papers of Lucien Bauzin.

29. Duverger, *Political Parties,* pp. 183–84.

30. *Congress,* Oct. 6, 1933, p. 234.

31. *Congress,* Oct. 25, 1934, p. 54; also Oct. 26, pp. 153–64.

32. McKenzie, pp. 188–99.

33. See *L'Information sociale,* July 26, 1934, p. 12, for an excellent account of the battle between the party worker and the parliamentarian.

34. On the Bureau, see particularly Bardonnet, *Evolution,* pp. 110–18; *Esprit,* May 1, 1939, p. 176.

35. *Congress of Lille,* 1906, pp. 85–88, quoted in Bardonnet, *Evolution,* p. 112.

36. Kayser, Roche, Robert Lange, Alfred Dominique, Pfeiffer, Ripault, Gaboriaud, Milhaud, Robert Louis, Sableau, Manescau, Fabius de Champville, Anxionnaz.

37. Piot, Chauvin, Deyris, Guernut, Martinaud-Déplat, Riou, Tony Révillon, Grisoni.

38. Parliamentarians: Julien, Archimbaud, Liautey, Ducos, Delthil, Lorgeré, Zay,

Courson, Férin, Monnerville. Non-parliamentarians: Louis Ripault, Kayser (three terms), Alfred Dominique, Mmes. Kraemer-Bach and Eliane Brault, Marcel Sableau, Sanguinetti, Bauzin, Lange, Herbert Couquet, Emile Laurens. Piot and Martinaud-Déplat each served one term as a parliamentarian and one term as a non-parliamentarian.

39. William Bertrand, *Le Journal de Marennes,* June 11, 1933.

40. Kayser, "Le Parti radical-socialiste," p. 272.

41. Interviews with Jacques Kayser, March 8, 1961; Léon Martinaud-Déplat, Nov. 7, 1960; Paul Anxionnaz, March 15, 1961.

42. *Jadis,* II, 545 (May 29, 1935).

43. It printed a series of 21 "Documents radicaux" such as Jammy Schmidt's *Le Parti radical devant la situation financière,* Ducos's *Le Parti radical et les anciens combattants,* and reprints of speeches by Herriot, Daladier, and Delbos.

44. *Congress,* Oct. 25, 1936, p. 423.

45. André Liautey, *ibid.,* Oct. 27, 1937, p. 18.

46. Speech at the regional Federation of the Southwest, reported in *Le Journal de Marennes,* June 19, 1938.

47. For the role of the parliamentarians, see Bardonnet, *Evolution,* pp. 135–73; Duverger, *Political Parties,* pp. 183–86.

48. Lavau, p. 1891.

49. *Le Journal de Seine-et-Marne,* Sept. 28, 1935.

50. For the senatorial renaissance, see Soulier, pp. 176–93, 499. Jules Jeanneney, the president of the Senate, is often said to have been a Radical, but he was not.

51. Goguel, *Le Rôle financier,* pp. 256–60.

52. Chambre des députés, *Notices et portraits, 15ᵉ législature, 1932,* and *16ᵉ législature, 1936.*

53. The social categories are slightly altered from those used by Dogan in his study of parliamentarians in the 1956 Chamber, "Les Candidats et les élus," Table XI, p. 456.

54. Duverger, *Political Parties,* p. 184.

55. De Tarr, p. 156.

56. *La Défense républicaine* (Charente-Inférieure), April 29, 1933. Ellipses in original.

57. *L'Action républicaine* (Tulle), May 9, 1936.

58. Almond, pp. 406–7.

59. *L'Homme libre,* Oct. 24, 1936; it is revealing that such electoral determinism should be uttered by Frossard, who himself drifted with impunity from Socialism to Communism to dissident Socialism, to simple opportunism, and finally to Vichy.

60. Jean Luchaire in *Notre Temps,* cited in *L'Ere nouvelle,* Nov. 20, 1932; also see Lamoureux, *Le Bourbonnais républicain,* Sept. 4, 1936. The very competent political analyst of *Le Bulletin quotidien* labeled the Radical deputies pro- and anti-Popular Front solely on the basis of their electoral alliances, and predicted their legislative behavior accordingly. (May 20, 1936, p. A-6 *bis.*)

61. *Congress,* Nov. 4, 1932, p. 139.

62. Interview with Robert Fong, journalist and former party worker, at Rochefort, Aug. 20, 1959; and *Le Journal de Marennes,* March 5, 1939.

63. See Duverger, *Political Parties,* p. 149; Bardonnet, *Evolution,* pp. 228–42; Headings, pp. 70–75, 112, 264–66; Frédérix, pp. 123–28; Hayward, pp. 2–5.

64. See Pataut, I, 93; Barral (book), pp. 277–87.

65. From a table published in *Marianne,* July 19, 1933: Communists 38.3; Republican Socialists 50.1; SFIO 50.4; Radicals 51; Popular Democrats 51.5; Independents 51.7; Républicains de Gauche 52; Centre Républicain 52.9; Gauche Radicale 53.8; Fédération Républicaine 57.

66. *Social Movements*, pp. 123-24. See also Lipset, pp. 264-70; Duverger, "Generations in Conflict"; Hyman, pp. 73-74, 92, 123-54; Neumann, "The Conflict of Generations," pp. 623-28, and "Toward a Comparative Study," p. 410.

67. Interview, Nov. 10, 1960.

68. *Le Procès de la République*, I, 49. Other deputies, of course, joined the party simply because it was the easiest road to power (interviews with André Cornu, Oct. 25, 1960, and Guy La Chambre, Nov. 30, 1960), or as a way to work up a business clientele (*Esprit*, May 1, 1939, p. 172).

69. On the Young Turks, see Nicolet, *Le Radicalisme*, p. 84; Alroy, Chap. 8, pp. 26-29; Millet and Arbellot, *Ligues et groupements*, pp. 58-60; Debû-Bridel, "La Crise des partis," p. 272; Werth, *Lost Statesman*, p. 8, and "Le Mouvement 'Jeunes Turcs,'" pp. 100-105; Kayser, "Jeunes turcs ou jeunes radicaux," *Le Citoyen* (Quimper), Dec. 15, 1932; *La République*, Jan. 31, 1934; *L'Information sociale*, June 21, 1934, p. 11; Bardonnet, *Evolution*, pp. 177-79; Duverger, *Political Parties*, pp. 152-53, 166.

70. The following is a rough list of the left-wingers: *deputies*—Zay, Monnerville, Mendès-France, Corsin, Ravel, Gaston Martin, Le Bail, Fouilland, Cot, de Tessan (slightly older but generally classed as a Young Turk), Ferru, Bergery; *party workers*—Kayser, Lange, Sauger, Huss.

71. *La République de l'Oise*, May 13, 1934.

72. At the Congress of Nantes, for example, Jammy Schmidt ran into a great deal of heckling from the Young Turks in presenting a stodgy and unimaginative defense of the actions of the Radical Group (*Congress*, Oct. 25, 1934, pp. 70-107).

73. Interview with Pierre Barral, June 19, 1960.

74. Mistler, "Du nouveau en politique?" p. 176.

75. Neumann, "Toward a Comparative Study," p. 410.

76. May 22, 1936; reported in *Bulletin du parti radical et radical-socialiste*, June 2, 1936.

77. Nov. 22, 1933.

78. The Herriot army bill, July 12, 1932, 115 for, 33 abstentions, 11 against; war debt repayment, Dec. 13, 1932, 134 for, 11 abstentions, ten against; Paul-Boncour bill, Jan. 27, 1933, 131 for, nine abstentions, 14 against; Sarraut government formation, Nov. 3, 1933, 150 for, 11 abstentions.

79. Thirty-seven in the vote of Dec. 28, 1935.

80. *L'Oeuvre*, Jan. 16, 1936. Aubaud, the secretary-general, had read numerous communications from the federations demanding discipline.

81. *Le Temps*, Jan. 25, 1936.

82. *Le Petit Journal*, Nov. 7, 1934.

83. Zay, *Souvenirs*, p. 60.

84. Sauvy, *L'Opinion publique*, p. 45.

85. Nov. 6, 1934.

86. Herriot spoke 26 times, Delbos 24 times, Malvy 24 times. Among those who spoke less than their share were Campinchi, president of the Group in 1936, and Cot. Queuille, although eleven times minister in eight years, spoke only once, as did Paganon; among those who were totally silent were Aubaud—secretary-general from 1934 to 1936—and Jules Julien, six times minister. The few fourth-line deputies who spoke were Mortier (six times), Mahagne (three times), Sénac (three times), Ledoux and Mège (twice), Fernand Augé, Ferdinand Augé, Lacourt, Perrot, Picard, Pouchus, and Raude (once).

87. On political financing in France, see Pollock, pp. 284-97, 305-19; Lewinsohn, pp. 225-34; Bardonnet, *Evolution*, pp. 251-62; Fusilier, pp. 146-60, 258-76; Sérampuy [Goguel], "Le Comportement," pp. 657-67; Meynaud, pp. 148-49; Bourgin and Carrère, pp. 216-17.

88. Lewinsohn (p. 228), 40,000–50,000; Pollock (p. 284), 40,000–60,000. Gaston Martin (*Congress,* Oct. 25, 1934, p. 57) claimed that each election cost between 25,000 and 30,000 francs.

89. Halévy (*La République des comités,* pp. 191–92) gives a harsh analysis of Radical financing. Coste, a party worker, said at the Federation of the Seine that the party paid no money to candidates (Bauzin papers, typed minutes, Feb. 2, 1935, p. 15).

90. See Kahn's report, *Congress,* Oct. 25, 1936, p. 423; he also complains that the loss of 50 seats hurt resources. Coste claimed that the abolition of ex officio members would cost 110,000 francs (Bauzin papers, typed minutes, Feb. 2, 1935, p. 15).

91. Parti socialiste, *XXXV*^e *Congrès national, 4, 5, 6, et 7 juin, 1938, Royan. Rapports,* pp. 184–86.

92. Bauzin papers, typed minutes, Feb. 2, 1935, p. 15.

93. Lewinsohn, p. 228.

94. Pollock, pp. 285–95.

95. *Ibid.,* p. 296.

96. Caillaux, Malvy, Paganon, Landry, Bénazet, Dumont, Régnier, Valadier, Elbel, and Lamoureux.

97. Meynaud, *Les Groupes de pression,* p. 149.

98. Fusilier, pp. 265–67, 270.

99. Pollock, pp. 315–16.

100. *Aux écoutes,* April 9, 1932; the paper adds that the secretary-general, when asked about this figure, said it was only a million.

101. Those who accepted all or part of its frankly conservative program. (Bourgin and Carrère, pp. 216–17.)

102. *Le Temps,* Nov. 25, 1932; Robert Lacoste, *La Tribune des fonctionnaires,* Nov. 26, 1932; also "Observateur," *Candide,* May 5, 1932.

103. Goguel, "Le Comportement," p. 658.

104. The paper of François Albert, leader of the left-wing Radicals, claimed that these were Blum's motives in 1932, *L'Oeil de Paris,* June 4, 1932, p. 6.

105. Lamoureux, *Le Bourbonnais républicain,* Oct. 18, 1936, Aug. 22, 1937; Charles Laurent, *La Tribune des fonctionnaires,* Oct. 7, 1933.

106. *Congress,* Oct. 30, 1937, p. 522.

107. *La République de Chinon,* Oct. 19, 1933.

108. Dominique Carravaggio, *Le Journal,* Dec. 19, 1935.

109. *La France radicale,* Dec. 1932.

110. Coulondre, p. 17.

111. "Rayon X," *L'Oeil de Paris,* May 28, 1932.

112. *Le Temps,* June 6, 1935. See Herriot's account in *Jadis,* II, 549.

113. Beau de Loménie, p. 63.

114. Lévy, *The Truth About France,* p. 141.

115. This weakness had been clear to the initiated earlier: "M. Daladier's reputation for bravery is one of the most agreeable jokes of the day" (*Le Canard enchaîné,* Feb. 1, 1933).

116. De Monzie, Lamoureux, and Paul-Boncour all became permanently alienated from Daladier for this reason during his first ministry. See de Monzie, *Ci-devant,* pp. 99–100; Lamoureux's memoirs, *Le Bourbonnais républicain,* Jan. 4, 1953; Paul-Boncour, II, 101. See also Bonnet's testimony, March 22, 1951, in *Commission de 1933 à 1945,* IX, 2684, on Daladier's run-ins with Paul-Boncour.

117. *Le Procès de la République,* I, 170.

118. De Monzie, *Ci-devant,* p. 15.

119. *L'Ordre,* April 27, 1932.

120. Zay, *Souvenirs*, p. 323.

121. *Ibid.*, p. 321.

122. Bardonnet, *Evolution*, p. 124.

123. Semler, p. 81.

124. This is completely contrary to the observation of German politics made by Max Weber: "But that party leaders should emerge from the ranks of the press has been an absolute exception." ("Politics as Vocation," pp. 97–98.)

125. Chaintron, p. 1540.

126. Hamon, II, 138–39; Champeaux, II, 204.

127. Interview with Rolland, Jan. 23, 1961.

128. *Esprit*, May 1, 1939, p. 185.

129. E.g. Marcus, p. 163, in which *La République* is called "the Radical party's newspaper," and Dupeux, *Le Front Populaire*, pp. 87–95, in which *La République* is used as the exclusive source for Radical attitudes toward the Front, thus weighting attitudes in a conservative direction. Bodin and Touchard, on the other hand, use *L'Oeuvre*. Of the 19 clearly Radical statements they insert, 15 come from *L'Oeuvre*. Two others, written by Bayet, who also wrote in *L'Oeuvre*, are from *La Lumière*, and there is also one statement by Zay in the Chamber as well as an electoral declaration by Rucart. Of those cited, only Herriot, Daladier, and Israël are not clearly far to the left.

130. See note, p. 46.

131. *La Tribune de l'Aisne* printed 3,000 copies in 1934; *La Tribune républicaine* (Verdun) printed 5,000 in 1935, as did *L'Avenir de Pithiviers* in 1936; *La République tourangelle* printed only 2,000 in 1933, and *Le Journal de Seine-et-Marne* only 1,500 in 1931. Lamoureux claims 7,000–8,000 for *Le Bourbonnais républicain* in the 1936 campaign (*Le Bourbonnais républicain*, Feb. 26, 1956). Chichery (in *La Voix du Centre*, Jan. 1, 1938) claimed that that paper had a circulation of 3,000.

132. Emile Roche's figures (interview, Jan. 16, 1961).

133. In *La République de l'Ain*, from the elections of 1932 until the end of the year, of 41 outside articles, 13 were by Bayet and seven by Milhaud. Sometimes a Parisian would regularly write the editorial, as in *Le Réveil de la Creuse*, in which Milhaud was to be found no fewer than 40 times in 1936.

134. An analysis of the editorials in *La République des travailleurs* (Gers) in 1932 gives the following results: *left-wing writers*—François Albert, three; Bayet, 17; Kayser, one; Mendès-France, one; Jammy Schmidt, one; Bertrand de Jouvenel, one; *moderate-left writers*—Andre Sauger, one; Henri Clerc, one; *moderate writers*—Herriot, one; *conservative writers*—Milhaud, four; Lamoureux, two; Caillaux, two; Pierre Dominique, one; Gardey, one; Pfeiffer, one; Proust, one.

135. *Ouest-Océan* during 1933 printed Kayser and Bayet principally, but sometimes also Milhaud and Roche; after 1934, when the paper turned to the left, Kayser dominated, with Roche entirely absent; in 1936, when it turned to the right, Kayser and Bayet were banished. In 1933 *La République de Chinon* was dominated editorially by Bayet, but he was dropped after February and replaced by Mistler, Milhaud, and Borel, all on the right.

136. The source of my titles is basically *L'Annuaire de la presse* for a single year, 1933. I included only those papers whose political identity was listed in the *Annuaire*, with the exception of the Socialist papers, which were clearly under-represented, and for which I used a list supplied by my colleague, Donald Baker. Four categories have been used, "Radical," "republican," "moderate-conservative," and "Socialist." The political affiliation in the *Annuaire* is often distressingly vague. Depending on the area, "republican" may mean either left, right, or center. The papers classed as right-wing, on the other hand, are unmistakable—"union nationale," "conservateur," "libérale,"

etc. Of 606 papers used, 132 are Radical, 232 moderate and right, 179 republican, and 63 Socialist.

137. Forty-eight per cent of the titles are ostensibly non-political—"journal," "nouvelles," "gazette." Thirty-nine per cent are overtly political, in that they propound some ideal—"républicain," "progrès," "combat." Twelve per cent are ostensibly non-political but have covert political overtones—"avenir," "action," "éclaireur," "impartial."

138. Furthermore, of the eight Radical papers, six were dailies, which were less doctrinaire than the weeklies and appealed to a different public. Thus "petit" had very limited appeal as a symbol.

139. Ten republicans and three right-wingers used "républicain." "Tribune" was acceptable to the moderates (six), but not the republicans (o). The Socialists had one "républicain," but no "démocrate."

CHAPTER 2

1. Particularly Alain's *Eléments d'une doctrine radicale.*

2. E.g., Goguel, "The Historical Background," p. 31.

3. Kayser, "Le Radicalisme des radicaux," p. 70.

4. If the village of Roussillon in the Vaucluse is at all representative, such an attitude was the dominant fact of provincial politics. See Wylie, pp. 206–39.

5. See de Tarr, pp. 2–5, Alroy, Chap. 2, pp. 2–7, and Kayser, "Le Radicalisme des radicaux," pp. 72–73, for some pleasant examples of this way of thinking.

6. Article in *Paris-Soir,* reprinted in *La République de l'Indre,* March 19, 1939; the same citation is to be found in Jammy Schmidt, *Idées et images radicales,* p. 5. Italics in original.

7. *La France radicale,* editorial, May 1, 1932.

8. Bayet, *Le Radicalisme,* p. 11. Alroy has an interesting section on what he calls the "rationalist jargon," chap. 3, pp. 16–23.

9. Sarraut, p. 245.

10. Appeal of Senators Henri Roy, Marcel Donon, and Fernand Rabier in *L'Avenir républicain* (Loiret), Oct. 8, 1932.

11. Jammy Schmidt, *Les Grandes Thèses radicales,* 217–25.

12. *L'Abeille des Vosges,* Nov. 11, 1933.

13. *Journal officiel de la République française, annales de la Chambre des députés: débats parlementaires* (henceforth *J.O.Ch.*), Jan. 16, 1936, p. 31.

14. See Alroy, Chap. 2, pp. 7–9.

15. Cabanis (left-winger), *L'Avenir de Pithiviers,* March 12, 1938.

16. Delbos (moderate), *Congress,* Nov. 3, 1932, p. 25.

17. Sarraut, p. 247.

18. Herriot, *Pourquoi je suis radical-socialiste,* pp. 54–56.

19. Campinchi, *Congress,* Nov. 10, 1936, p. 335.

20. Cited in Bourgin and Carrère, p. 120.

21. De Jouvenel, *Après la défaite,* p. 61.

22. See Section 20 of the Program of Nancy in Nicolet, *Le Radicalisme,* pp. 48–53.

23. *Congress,* Oct. 30, 1936, p. 525.

24. Declaration of the party, *Congress,* 1935, p. 481. My italics.

25. On the question of the *salariat,* see the excellent analysis in Alroy, Chap. 5, particularly pp. 29–41; also Chap. 4, pp. 23–34, and Chap. 6, pp. 13–26.

26. *Le Jacobin,* Nov., 1936.

27. Archimbaud, *L'Avenir du radicalisme*, pp. 14, 17. See also Cazalis, *Le Démocrate* (Dax), Nov. 3, 1935, and Pierre Cot, *Le Démocrate savoyard*, March 17, 24, 1934.

28. Semler, p. 39.

29. Bayet, pp. 45–87.

30. *Congress*, Oct. 24, 1936, p. 339.

31. Bertrand de Jouvenel had already examined this doctrine and showed its complete failure in *L'Economie dirigée*, pp. 41–42.

32. *Congress*, 1931, pp. 460–61.

33. Printed in Nicolet, *Le Radicalisme*, pp. 48–53.

34. Cf. Avril, pp. 77–78, and Declaration, *Congress*, 1931, p. 458.

35. (1) Immediate reduction of defense expenditure; (2) a national system of unemployment insurance, workers' compensation, and agricultural insurance; (3) nationalization of the insurance companies and the railroads; *Le Temps*, April 12, 1932.

36. *Congress*, Oct. 24, 1936, p. 332.

37. *La Tribune républicaine de la Haute-Garonne*, Jan. 7, 1934.

38. Declaration of the party, read by Paul Bastid, moderate, *Congress*, 1931, p. 454; speech of President Daladier, moderate left, *Congress*, Oct. 29, 1936, p. 414; speech of the Minister of Commerce, Fernand Gentin, moderate, *Congress*, Oct. 26, 1938, p. 172.

39. I have managed to find only one printed "program," extremely abbreviated, in a party worker's handbook for 1937, a $1\frac{1}{2}$" by 3", 14-page work entitled *Calendrier du militant*; this was at the time of the declining Popular Front, and the contents were considerably more moderate than earlier versions.

40. Ginet, *Barodet*, 1936.

41. Herriot speech at La Tour du Pin, reported in *Le Temps*, April 19, 1932.

42. Hoffmann, "Paradoxes," p. 15.

43. *Congress*, May 11, 1934, pp. 47–61.

44. Maurice Allehaut, *ibid.*, p. 64.

45. *Congress*, Oct. 28, 1937, pp. 199–217.

46. Simmel, "The Sociology of Sociability," p. 259.

47. *Congress*, Oct. 28, 1937, p. 219.

48. De Jouvenel, *L'Economie dirigée*, p. 29.

49. Regarding this new enthusiasm for the Radicals, Daniel Halévy says: "In the interior of this party which was absurdly led but at the same time was close to power, they thought something might be done" (*La République des comités*, p. 171).

50. Charles Dulot, *L'Information sociale*, May 17, 1934.

51. Cot, *Le Procès de la République*, I, 49.

52. *Congress*, Oct. 5, 1933, p. 26.

53. *Congress*, Nov. 3, 1932, p. 14.

54. *La République*, March 16, 1933, in reply to Bergery's defense of his resignation from the party.

55. *Mantes-républicain*, March 8, 1933.

56. *Ibid.*, March 15, 1933. Herriot, as president, characteristically distorted this thought: "We understand your reasons, since you write me that, in your opinion, only revolutions have given history access to the plain" (*ibid.*, March 22, 1933).

57. Kayser, "Le Radicalisme des radicaux," pp. 71–72. This idea is challenged by Leites, pp. 17–18.

58. Kayser states that only Caillaux was competent. "The radicalism of the Radicals was neither economic nor financial. The history that inspired and impregnated it was not yet, at this period, open to economic facts and sociology" ("Le Radicalisme des radicaux," p. 82).

59. Bergery interview, Oct. 18, 1961; Durand interview, Nov. 5, 1960.

60. Maurice Rolland interview, Jan. 23, 1961.

61. *J.O.Ch.*, Jan. 27, 1933, p. 354. In 1926 Herriot had formed a one-day government which was overwhelmed by a financial panic. See Bonnefous, IV, 159–64.

62. Speech reported in *Le Temps,* April 12, 1936, p. 6.

63. *Congress,* Oct. 27, 1934, p. 255.

64. *Ibid.,* pp. 269–73.

65. Declaration of the party, *Congress,* 1931, p. 458. Charles Dulot claimed that Daladier's very serious attempt to put economic questions into their proper perspective was utterly distorted by malicious emphasis on Woergl, which was meant only as an example (*L'Information sociale,* Nov. 8, 1934). The distortion, however, was effective.

66. Reported in *Le Bourbonnais républicain,* Sept. 2, 1934.

67. Durand, Chap. 14, pp. 2–3.

68. Gaston Martin, *Le Démocrate de Lot-et-Garonne,* Nov. 6, 1932.

69. In addition, Caillaux was Minister in the abortive Bouisson cabinet. The four non-Radicals were: Germain-Martin in the Herriot cabinet; Henri Chéron in the Paul-Boncour cabinet; François Piétri in the second Daladier cabinet, until he resigned over the Chiappe affair; and Reynaud in the third Daladier cabinet, after November 1938.

70. In the 1932–36 legislature, the following Radicals sat in the Finance Committee: Bernier, Durand, Jacquier, Lamoureux, Malvy, Marchandeau, lawyers; Nogaro, Palmade, professors of law; Dezarnaulds, Marcombes, doctors; Jammy Schmidt, Archimbaud, journalists, the latter with theological training; Jaubert, agronomist; Catalan, Deyris, tax auditors; Bonnet, inspector of finances; Lassalle, department head, Ministry of Finance. Of these, only Bonnet, Lamoureux, Malvy, and Marchandeau were notably important; some of the others had transient ministries—Durand, Jacquier, Jaubert, Lassalle, Marcombes, Palmade. Those who tended to dominate the debates of the committee were Lamoureux and Malvy, *rapporteur-général* and president, on the right; and Lassalle, Deyris, and Dezarnaulds, on the left. This should be compared with the Socialist representation in 1932: Auriol, Bedouce, Blum, Lafont, Marquet, Moch, Monnet, Renaudel, Spinasse, and Valière, all leaders in the party. It is noteworthy that three of the Radicals of minor importance, Deyris, Catalan, and Lassalle, because of their training as *fonctionnaires* in the financial administration, were regarded as experts, although checking tax returns is scarcely adequate training for making economic policy.

71. *L'Echo de la Nièvre,* Nov. 27, 1937.

72. *Congress,* Oct. 6, 1933, pp. 281–82.

73. Gardey, Malvy, Lamoureux, Bonnet, Régnier, Palmade, Nogaro. When it was felt that the Popular Front Chamber of 1936 should have a left-wing deputy as *rapporteur-général* of the Finance Committee, the best that could be dug up was Jammy Schmidt, who had many admirable qualities, among which was not, unfortunately, financial competence.

74. "The capitalist regime, rotten, war-mongering, incapable of establishing peace, creator of unemployment, of agricultural crises, of misery, impotent to bring prosperity and justice to the world, is slowly dying" (*L'Avenir républicain,* Feb. 3, 1934).

75. *Ibid.,* Dec. 3, 1932.

76. *La France du Centre,* Aug. 27, 1933.

77. *Le Journal de Die et de la Drôme,* Sept. 30, 1933.

78. *Le Démocrate de Lot-et-Garonne,* Sept. 17, 1933.

79. *La Tribune des fonctionnaires,* Oct. 7, 1933.

80. Rémond, *La Droite en France,* p. 198.

81. André Liautey, *L'Union démocratique de la Haute-Saône,* April 29, 1932.

82. Arnoud Denjoy, *La République des travailleurs,* Sept. 19, 1937.

83. The Radicals claimed to have authorized 15 billion francs in budget cuts and new revenue to balance the budget, of which 11 to 12 billion were actually received by the Treasury (Bonnet, *Le Redressement financier*, pp. 13–15).

84. Nathan and Delouvrier, p. 86; Oualid and Rivet, p. 465, estimated that in 1936 the real budget was 77 billion francs instead of the official 46.5 billion, which, of course, compounded the problem. Marion, p. 12, estimated the real budget at 80 billion francs.

85. Dessirier, *Paris-Midi économique et financière*, quoted in *La Tribune des fonctionnaires*, June 18, 1932.

86. Motion of the Radical Assembly of Dax, Sept. 24, 1933 (*Le Démocrate* (Dax), Oct. 15, 1933).

87. *L'Echo des Alpes*, Nov. 4, 1933. Italics in original.

88. Albert Chichery, *La Voix du Centre*, Jan. 28, 1933. See also the doubts about the virtues of deflation expressed by the moderate William Bertrand: cutting salaries means lowering purchasing power (*Le Journal de Marennes*, July 3, 1932). Some other Radicals were also skeptical: the proposals are undemocratic and outdated (*L'Aube républicaine*, Nov. 11, 1933); a balanced budget is not the national necessity claimed by the press (*Le Démocrate savoyard*, Feb. 2, 1933). Paul Elbel (*La Gazette vosgienne*, Nov. 8, 1933) was upset by the simple-minded solutions produced.

89. *Barodet*, 1936, pp. 1478–79.

90. See Sauvy, *L'Evolution économique*, pp. 229, 247–54; *L'Opinion publique*, pp. 73–78; and *La Nature sociale*, pp. 272–73. Also Goguel, *La Politique des partis*, pp. 334–41, Nathan and Delouvrier give the most complete description, pp. 77–94.

91. Notably developed in the Chamber, June 28, 1934; see Bonnefous, V, 263–65.

92. Zay, *La France du Centre*, July 1, 1934.

93. Aubaud's paper, *La République de l'Oise*, Dec. 10, 11, 1934.

94. Thiébaut, *La Tribune républicaine*, Feb. 1, 1935; Thiébaut was, of course, not a left-winger. Cot was also opposed (*L'Oeuvre*, Nov. 30, 1934).

95. *Congress*, Oct. 27, 1934, p. 268.

96. Sauvy, *L'Evolution économique*, p. 229. Italics in original.

97. *Congress*, Oct. 29, 1937, pp. 345–47.

CHAPTER 3

1. Côtes-du-Nord was one of the six poorest departments of France. See Hoffmann, *Le Mouvement Poujade*, pp. 205–8.

2. Although no major electoral study has been made of the Côtes-du-Nord, two minor ones, by Roger Huon and A. de Vulpian, have been used here.

3. *Dinan-républicain*, Oct. 28, 1937.

4. *Le Républicain des Côtes-du-Nord*, June 4, 1959.

5. Aug. 31, 1933; May 24, 31, Aug. 30, Oct. 25, 1934; Jan. 24, Aug. 1, 8, 1935; Nov. 12, Oct. 8, 1936; April 4, Oct. 21, 28, Dec. 6, 9, 23, 1937; April 7, Aug. 25, Sept. 1, 15, 1938; July 13, 27, Aug. 3, 1939.

6. Interview, June 27, 1959.

7. Letter dated May 21, 1936, Geistdoerfer papers.

8. Letter dated Aug. 29, 1930, Geistdoerfer papers.

9. *Dinan-républicain*, March 23, 1933; *Loudéac-républicain*, April 7, 1933; *La Démocratie bretonne*, March 18, 1933.

10. Letter to Gaston Lefèvre, secretary-general of the federation, April 14, 1934, copy

in Geistdoerfer papers. See also *Dinan-républicain*, Jan. 4, 1934, Aug. 10, 1933, May 10, 1934, Feb. 20, 1936, April 29, 1937; *La Démocratie bretonne*, Feb. 15, 1936.

11. Lemonnier and Bethuel. Lorgeré interview and memoirs, pp. 274, 277. Lorgeré at that time was intriguing with the councillors-general of Caulnes and Evran against Geistdoerfer.

12. Siegfried noted as early as 1913 that Dinan was without contact with St.-Brieuc, *Tableau politique*, p. 121.

13. *Ibid.*, p. 120.

14. Letter of the secretary-general, Lefèvre, dated Oct. 19, 20, 1932, Geistdoerfer papers.

15. *La Démocratie bretonne*, Sept. 2, 1933. See also *La Nouvelliste*, Aug. 30.

16. *Dinan-républicain*, Oct. 6, Nov. 24, Dec. 1, 1932, but particularly Aug. 10, 1933.

17. *Les Cahiers de Job Coz*, Sept. 15, 1933.

18. *Dinan-républicain*, Sept. 7, 1933.

19. *La Gauche*, Sept. 24, Nov. 12, 1933; *Dinan-républicain*, Aug. 31, Sept. 7, 14, 21, 28; Oct. 19, 26, Nov. 11, 1933; Jan. 4, 1934.

20. *La Démocratie bretonne*, Sept. 2, 9, 16, 23, 30, Oct. 14, Nov. 11, 1933; *L'Eveil breton*, Oct. 1; *La Charrue rouge* (Lannion), Sept. 10; *L'Union malouine et dinannaise*, Sept. 1, 15; *L'Eclaireur du Finistère*, Sept. 9; *La Nouvelliste*, Aug. 30; *Les Cahiers de Job Coz*, Sept. 15.

21. *La Démocratie bretonne*, Oct. 21, 1933; *L'Eveil breton*, Oct. 10, 1933.

22. *Les Cahiers de Job Coz*, Nov. 15, 1933.

23. Geistdoerfer letter to Gaston Lefèvre, April 14, 1934.

24. Nomination for 1932, *Dinan-républicain*, April 28, 1932; annual meeting, *ibid.*, Nov. 9, 1933; before partial cantonal election, *ibid.*, April 19, 1934; before regular cantonal election, *ibid.*, Sept. 20, 1934; banquet, *ibid.*, May 30, 1935; committee for 1936 elections, *ibid.*, April 2, 1936.

25. It seems to have played no part in the nomination of the other councillors-general.

26. *Dinan-républicain*, April 30, 1936, May 5, 1932.

27. *Ibid.*, Jan. 21, 1937.

28. *Ibid.*, March 11, May 20, Sept. 16, 1937.

29. *Ibid.*, Oct. 19, 1933; Feb. 1, 8, May 3 ("le parti socialiste Ponce Pilate!"), Oct. 18, Dec. 20, 1934; Feb. 21, March 4, 1935; Jan. 7, 1937, and throughout 1937.

30. *Ibid.*, April 28, 1932.

31. *Ibid.*, Dec. 20, 1934; April 28, 1932; May 5, 1932.

32. *Ibid.*, April 26, 1934; also Dec. 20, 1934.

33. *Ibid.*, March 23, 1933, Nov. 14, 1935, Feb. 20, April 23, May 21, Aug. 6, 1936, Jan. 20, March 17, July 7, 1938.

34. *Dinan-républicain*, March 1, 1934, Dec. 19, 1935, Feb. 6, 27, April 16, Oct. 8, 1936.

35. *Ibid.*, April 28, 1932.

36. *Ibid.*, March 23, 30, April 6, 20, July 27, 1933; March 1, 1934; Feb. 26, July 4, 1935; May 12, June 25, Sept. 10, 1936; Jan. 21, June 3, Sept. 2, Nov. 18, Dec. 23, 1937; Feb. 24, March 4, Dec. 22, 1938; May 4, 1939.

37. *Ibid.*, April 4, 1940.

38. De Vulpian, pp. 111–12.

39. *Dinan-républicain*, June 22, Sept. 21, 1933, Aug. 13, 1936.

40. *Ibid.*, Jan. 26, 1933.

41. *Ibid.*, Jan. 10, 1935.

42. *Ibid.*, April 28, 1932.

43. *Ibid.*, Oct. 6, Nov. 24, 1932.

44. *Ibid.*, Dec. 22, 1932.

45. *Ibid.*, Feb. 2, Nov. 2, Dec. 7, 14, 1933.

46. *Ibid.*, March 23, May 11, 1933.

47. *Ibid.*, Feb. 15, 1934.

48. *Ibid.*, Feb. 22, 1934.

49. *Ibid.*, March 8, 15, 22, 29.

50. *Ibid.*, March 21, April 4.

51. *Ibid.*, Feb. 14, July 11, Aug. 22, Nov. 14, 1935.

52. *Ibid.*, Nov. 21.

53. *Ibid.*, Sept. 12, 19, Oct. 10, 17, 24, 1935.

54. "Je n'aime pas, pour ma part, l'expression, 'l'Italie a attaqué l'Ethiopie,' c'est trop abstrait pour moi. Je dis: des italiens et des éthiopiens se tuent. Des hommes se battent. Cela me suffit" (*ibid.*, Oct 10, 1935).

55. *Ibid.*, Oct. 8, 1936.

56. "Syndicalism, which has been infiltrated in a regrettable way by political elements that should not be present . . . is playing a role that is not its own and is at the root of the disturbances and uncertainty of the present" (*ibid.*, April 29, 1937).

57. *Ibid.*, April 29, 1937.

58. *Ibid.*, Jan. 27, 1938.

59. *Ibid.*, March 31, 1938.

60. *Ibid.*, May 26, June 2, 9, 16, 23, 30, July 7, 19, 21, 1938.

61. *Ibid.*, Sept. 29, Oct. 6, 20, Nov. 17, 1938.

62. *Ibid.*, Dec. 1, 15, 1938.

63. *Ibid.*, Dec. 1, 1938.

64. *Ibid.*, May 18, 1939.

65. *Royan*, June 26, 1932. The deputies Bertrand, Hesse, Longuet, and Sclafer were members. See Pitois, p. 173.

66. The sources used here are the following local papers: *Ouest-Océan* (La Rochelle), *La Défense républicaine* (La Rochelle), *Royan*, *Le Journal de Marennes*, *L'Indépendant* (Saintes), *Le Démocrate* (Jonzac), *L'Echo saintongeais* (St.-Jean-d'Angély), and *La Voix socialiste* (Charente-Inférieure), and interviews with Robert Fong, party worker and former journalist with *La France de Bordeaux* and *Royan*, Aug. 17, 20, 1959.

67. *Le Démocrate*, Jan. 18, 1936.

68. *La Lumière*, June 30, 1939.

69. *La Voix socialiste*, April 26, 1932.

70. *Ouest-Océan*, Feb. 14, 21, 27, 1934; also *La Voix socialiste*, Feb. 17, March 10, 1934.

71. See *Ouest-Océan*, March 7, 14, 21, 24, April 11, 14, May 19, 24, Sept. 8, 1934.

72. *Ibid.*, Feb. 14, 1934.

73. *Ibid.*, Sept. 8, 1934.

74. *La Défense républicaine*, Jan. 16, Feb. 6, March 6, 13, 20, 1935; *Ouest-Océan*, Dec. 15, 1934; Feb. 9, 12, 23, 1935.

75. *Ouest-Océan*, Oct. 10, 1935, motion of the Committee demanding collaboration with the parties of the left.

76. *Le Démocrate* (Jonzac), Feb. 17, 1934.

77. *Le Journal de Marennes*, Feb. 11, 1934.

78. For the elections, *Le Démocrate* (Jonzac), April 11, 25, 1936; *Le Journal de Marennes*, April 5, 19, May 10; *Ouest-Océan*, April 4, 11, 18; *La Défense républicaine*, April 1, 22, May 2; *Royan*, April 29, May 5.

79. *La Défense républicaine*, June 6, 17, 1936; *Ouest-Océan*, July 4.

80. *Ibid.*, Feb. 13, 1937.

81. *Royan*, Feb. 14, April 11, 18, 25, May 2, 16, 30, June 6, 1937.

82. See *Ouest-Océan,* Oct. 2, 1937.
83. *L'Indépendant* (Saintes), May 28, 1938.
84. See above, pp. 35–36.
85. Printed in *La Voix socialiste,* March 18, 1939.

CHAPTER 4

1. Marcus, pp. 52–53, p. 83n.; Goguel, *La Politique des partis,* pp. 487–88.
2. Rémond, "Explications du 6 février," p. 224.
3. *Aux écoutes,* June 25, 1932, p. 16; my italics, ellipses in original.
4. For example, the editorial in *La Lumière,* May 21, 1932, declared that it was clear there would have to be collaboration in government after the country had spoken so plainly. This judgment was general, but not universal. C. J. Gignoux wrote very accurately: "The country expressed no positive wish, only disapproval" (*Le Bulletin quotidien,* May 25, 1932, citing *La Journée industrielle,* May 18–24, 1932). See also the brilliant analysis of the 1932 elections by Charles Seignobos in *L'Année politique,* Nov. 1932.
5. Blum at Narbonne, *Le Temps,* April 12, 1932. Tardieu at the Salle Bullier, *Le Temps,* April 8, 1932: "In the face of the essential problems [there is] a real community of republican groups that have been divided since the end of 1928. Foreign policy, national defense, finance, social and economic policy, all these issues together unite [the republicans] and oppose them to the Socialists." See Chevallier, *Histoire des institutions politiques de la France moderne,* pp. 570–71, for an outstanding analysis of Tardieu's tactics; also Bonnefous, V, 117–19, for the campaign; and Herriot, *Jadis,* II, 282–85.
6. *Le Temps,* April 19, 1932.
7. Speech at the Salle Rameau, Lyons, *Le Temps,* May 6, 1932.
8. See comments by Bergery, *Mantes-républicain,* May 18, 1932; Goguel, *La Politique des partis,* p. 259; Pierre de Pressac wrote in *Revue politique et parlementaire,* June 10, 1932, p. 517: "It is not too much to say that the Radicals are embarrassed by the extent of their victory"; *La Lumière,* May 17, 1932: "A victory beyond their wildest hopes." Milhaud, who directed whatever national campaign existed, wrote later that on the very eve of the election a contagious enthusiasm took hold of the local campaigns, new candidates appeared, and the party, which had been discouraged by constant defeats in by-elections, suddenly came to life (*Le Démocrate du Rhône,* April 29, 1936).
9. The figure of 130–40 was advanced by him in an interview with *La Volonté,* April 24, 1932; "Observateur," in *Candide,* May 12, 1932, claims that Herriot expected he would be faced with only 95 Socialists.
10. Interview in *Le Temps,* April 30, 1932; see also his speech at Lyons, Salle Rameau, *ibid.,* May 1, 1932; also the statement he made in an interview quoted by Tardieu in his speech at Belfort, *ibid.,* April 30, 1932: "When a statesman has benefited once in his life from Socialist support, he can never solicit it again." Herriot's anti-Socialist tone in the campaign was adopted, according to Jacques Kayser, who was a member of the Bureau at this time, entirely on his own and presented to the Bureau as a fait accompli (Kayser interview, March 8, 1961).
11. Conservatives, 27; moderates, 29; moderate-left, 35; left, 18.
12. The 90 pro-deflation statements were made by 25 out of 37 conservatives, 22 out of 44 moderates, 32 out of 54 moderate-lefts, 11 out of 28 left-wingers.

13. Divided as follows: 13, 13, 12, and 6.

14. *La Tribune des fonctionnaires,* June 18, 1932.

15. *La Tribune ariégoise,* April 30, 1932; *L'Avenir du Cher,* April 30; also Mège, *Le Nontronnais,* April 17; Courson, *Le Républicain de Chinon,* May 5; Chichery, *La Voix du Centre,* April 6, May 7; Berthod, *Le Démocrate du Jura,* May 7; Chautemps, *Le Républicain de Loir-et-Cher,* April 10. Emile Kahn analyzed the operation of discipline in the 360 second ballots among the parties of the left and found only three instances where it had failed, two involving Radicals—Potut in Nevers and Couillerot in Louhans (*La Lumière,* May 7 and May 14, 1932).

16. See Blum's speech to the Socialist Congress, May 30, 1932, *Le Temps,* June 1; also Louis Lévy's careful analysis of the elections in *Révolte,* Oct. 1932, pp. 15–21. For an example of local complaints see *La Voix socialiste* (Charente-Inférieure), May 7.

17. Borkenau, pp. 107–10; Willard, p. 196; Bécarud, "Esquisse"; Goguel, *La Politique des partis,* p. 258; Walter, pp. 216–30.

18. Werth, *Lost Statesman,* p. 11. Also Marcus, p. 7: "[Herriot] invited the Socialists to participate, but after an exchange of views in which they demanded economic and social reforms that Herriot felt powerless to grant, the offer of participation was turned down"; Debû-Bridel, *L'Agonie,* p. 160; Bonnefous, V, 123–24, is more restrained and not inaccurate, but misses the point; Goguel, *La Politique des partis,* p. 261; Soulié, p. 354, gives the most accurate account; Chevallier, *Histoire des institutions politiques de la France moderne,* pp. 576–77, is also good.

19. See Piétri's contribution in Aubert, pp. 100–101.

20. *Le Matin,* May 10, 1932.

21. *Le Bulletin quotidien,* May 4, 1932. See also Lautier, *L'Ordre,* May 4, 1932; Senatus in *L'Avenir,* May 4, May 10; de Kerillis, *L'Echo de Paris,* May 10; also *L'Oeil de Paris,* May 14, p. 4, for an analysis of the centrist tactics by the leader of the left-wing Radicals, François Albert. *L'Information sociale,* May 15, 1932, has a good press analysis, pp. 13–14.

22. Piétri, of the Flandin wing, describes these divisions very frankly in Aubert, pp. 100–101.

23. *La République,* quoted in *L'Information sociale,* May 19, 1932.

24. May 3, 1932. Also *La Volonté*: "Electoral Cartel, then Concentration," May 4, 1932.

25. Kayser interview, March 23, 1961.

26. *Mantes-républicain,* May 18, 1932; see also his speech at the Executive Committee reprinted in *ibid.,* June 8; and the article by Kayser in *La République de l'Oise,* June 4, 1932.

27. *Jadis,* II, 292. For this crucial meeting, which is generally ignored, see *Le Bulletin quotidien,* May 21, 1932; *La République de l'Oise,* May 22; *Le Petit Journal,* May 21; and *L'Echo de Paris,* May 21.

28. *Le Figaro,* May 29, 1932.

29. Two Socialist pamphlets illustrate the Socialist point of view in this affair, *Radicaux et socialistes (1932–1936),* and Blum, *Les Radicaux et nous (1932–1934).* Herriot's version can be found in *Jadis,* II, 297–305; in *Congress of Clermont-Ferrand,* May 12, 1934, pp. 185–92; and in an interview in *Le Temps,* April 18, 1936. Mead gives a long account in which he blames the Socialists (pp. 149–57).

30. Cf. Raoul Aubaud, then secretary-general of the party: "It is possible that the Radicals did not bring the necessary enthusiasm for a governmental collaboration with the Socialists" (*La République de l'Oise,* Oct. 19, 1935); Kayser: "I am one of those who asked at the end of the month of May that the leaders of our party offer the Socialist party the chance of collaborating in achieving a bold program. This offer was

not made" (article reprinted in *L'Echo des Alpes*, Jan. 7, 1933); also Henri Guernut, *La Tribune de l'Aisne*, June 21, 1934.

31. *Le Journal de Marennes*, June 12, 1932. My italics.

32. *L'Information sociale*, June 30, p. 8.

33. *Le Temps*, May 30, 1932.

34. Herriot's cabinet had 21 Radical ministers out of 29; Paul-Boncour's, 18 out of 29; Daladier's first, 15 out of 23; Sarraut's first, 16 out of 25; Chautemps' second, 17 out of 26; Daladier's second, 16 out of 26.

35. Speech at La Tour du Pin, *Le Temps*, April 19, 1932; also speech at Lyons, *ibid.*, April 13.

36. *La Dépêche de Toulouse*, which, because of the Sarrauts, was well informed on Radical politics, published a list of the probable ministers on May 27, three days before the negotiations, that included no Socialists.

37. Five conservatives, 11 moderates, three moderate-left, no left-wingers.

38. The official biography states this bluntly. See Antériou and Baron, p. 135.

39. Herriot, mod. (pres.); Dalimier, mod., Berthod, mod., Hesse, mod. (vice-presidents); Marcombes, mod., Jouffrault, mod., Ferrand, cons. (secretaries); Jammy Schmidt, left (secretary-general).

40. The others were Cot, Bergery, and Jammy Schmidt; in addition there were two not very pro-Herriot moderates, Bonnet and Hesse. See *Le Temps*, June 8, 1932; *La Dépêche de Rouen*, June 8; *Aux écoutes*, June 11; *Candide*, June 9.

41. See particularly Blum's speech, *J.O.Ch.*, June 7, 1932, p. 2246; also Lamoureux, *Le Bourbonnais républicain*, June 12, Pierre Laine, *Le Populaire*, June 8, and *Aux écoutes*, June 11, for analyses of the parliamentary maneuvering.

42. *La Tribune des fonctionnaires*, June 11, 1932; *Le Journal de Rouen*, June 11; *Candide*, June 16; *L'Oeil de Paris*, June 18; *Aux écoutes*, June 18, p. 14; Pierre du Clain [François Albert], *La Lumière*, June 18; *L'Information sociale*, June 20; Soulié, p. 373; Herriot, *Jadis*, II, 314–15. *La Volonté*, June 11, claimed that the crisis never occurred.

43. *Aux écoutes*, July 2; see also *L'Oeil de Paris*, July 9; *Le Temps*, June 30; *Le Populaire*, June 29; *L'Ordre*, June 29; *L'Humanité*, June 28; *La Volonté*, June 29; *Le Quotidien*, June 29; *La Dépêche de Rouen*, June 29; *Candide*, June 30; R. Pinon, *Revue des deux mondes*, July 15. And from the principal actors in this minor drama: François Albert in *La République de l'Oise*, July 1; Bergery in *Mantes-républicain*, July 13; Lamoureux in *Le Bourbonnais républicain*, July 3; Herriot, *Jadis*, II, 346.

44. For the whole problem, see Paul-Boncour's testimony, March 9, 1948, *Commission de 1933 à 1945*, II, 787; Weygand, p. 386. See also Bayet, *La Lumière*, July 9; Pierre du Clain, *ibid.*, July 16; *La République*, July 10; *Candide*, July 14; *Aux écoutes*, July 16, p. 12; Pierre Cot, *Le Démocrate savoyard*, July 23; Gaston Martin, *Le Démocrate de Lot-et-Garonne*, July 21.

45. William Bertrand, *Le Journal de Marennes*, July 17.

46. *Le Démocrate savoyard*, July 23.   47. *Le Journal de Marennes*, July 17.

48. *L'Avenir du Cher*, Aug. 7.   49. *La Lumière*, July 16, 1932.

50. Notably in Henri Roy's speech in the Senate, *Journal officiel de la République française, annales du Sénat: débats parlementaires* (henceforth *J.O.S.*), July 15, 1932, pp. 1104–07.

51. For the Congress, the stenographic report is essential; also, *L'Echo de Paris*, Nov. 4–6; *Le Populaire*, Nov. 3–5; *Le Figaro*, Nov. 3–5; *Le Temps*, Nov. 4–6; *L'Ere nouvelle*, Nov. 3–5; *La Volonté*, Nov. 3–5; P. de Pressac in *Revue politique et parlementaire*, Dec. 10, pp. 554–62; *L'Information sociale*, Nov. 10, pp. 1, 7; *Marianne*, Nov. 9, p. 3; *La Lumière*, Nov. 12; *Aux écoutes*, Nov. 12, pp. 20–23; *La République*, Nov. 3–5, also article by Roche, "Après Toulouse," Nov. 10; *Mantes-républicain*, Nov. 16, 4

pages on Bergery; *L'Avenir*, Nov. 15, article by L. Philouze on Roche article; Eugène Lautier in *L'Homme libre*, Nov. 21; *La Volonté*, Nov. 15; Herriot, *Jadis*, II, 351–54. Soulié, pp. 398–401, gives a more sympathetic view than my own.

52. Editorial, Nov. 10.

53. *Congress*, Nov. 5, pp. 370–412.

54. *Ibid.*, Nov. 4, pp. 147–230.

55. *Ibid.*, pp. 136–46.

56. *Ibid.*, Nov. 3, pp. 45–57 for Kayser, 61–80 for Bergery.

57. Herriot, *Jadis*, II, 351.

58. *Congress*, Nov. 3, 1932, pp. 90–114.

59. P. de Pressac, *Revue politique et parlementaire*, Dec. 12, 1932, p. 557.

60. *Ouest-Océan* (Charente-Inférieure), Nov. 16, 1932. The extraordinary ascendancy of Herriot was commented on frequently: Gaston Martin, *Le Démocrate de Lot-et-Garonne*, Nov. 13, 1932; Emile Roche, *La République*, Nov. 10; Albert Milhaud, *L'Ere nouvelle*, Nov. 16; *Aux écoutes*, Nov. 12, 20; *L'Information sociale*, Nov. 10; *Le Temps*, Nov. 5, article by Raymond Millet and editorial.

61. *Le Démocrate savoyard*, Nov. 12.

62. *La République*, Nov. 19.

63. *Le Temps*, Nov. 10–11; *La Lumière*, Dec. 17, and Pierre du Clain, Nov. 21; also Lamoureux's memoirs, *Le Bourbonnais républicain*, Nov. 2, 1952. Soulié, p. 402: "Malvy and Lamoureux . . . take the lead of the opposition of the 'orthodox' financiers. . . . At the end of the month of October, at Landernau, in a carefully prepared speech, Lamoureux publicly stated his position; he refused to consider borrowing and demanded massive budget cuts and increased taxation."

64. See *La Lumière*, Dec. 17, for an account of a protest meeting by the Senate Radicals because of the inadequacy of the budgetary compressions; also *Aux écoutes*, Nov. 19, p. 6.

65. See particularly *La Tribune des fonctionnaires*, Oct. 15, 22, 29, Nov. 5 (account of a meeting and protest parade), Nov. 19, Dec. 3.

66. *Ibid.*, Dec. 17, 1932.

67. On Herriot's fall, see Goguel, *La Politique des partis*, p. 294; Soulié has a long and sympathetic treatment, pp. 407–17; Bonnefous, V, 132, and Paul-Boncour, p. 273, are also useful.

68. Mège, *Le Nontronnais*, Dec. 18; Perrein and Hérard, *Le Réveil démocratique de Maine-et-Loire*, Dec. 17; Girard, *L'Action jurassienne*, Dec. 17; Liautey, *L'Union démocratique de la Haute-Saône*, Dec. 20; Tony Révillon, *La République de l'Ain*, Jan. 1, 1933; Marc Rucart, *La République des Vosges*, Dec. 17, 1932. Kayser himself, before Herriot had made his stand public, came out strongly against payment, *La République de l'Oise*, Dec. 5, 6; see also *Le Temps*, Dec. 13, for a report of the Radical meeting. Only after the defeat did he become a staunch defender of Herriot's views, *ibid.*, Dec. 21. Of 28 statements on the debts, only eight favored Herriot's stand, and five of these not for the policy itself, but for the spiritual nobility Herriot had shown; only three seemed convinced that repayment was a good thing.

69. *Le Temps*, Jan. 13, 1933; meeting on the morning of Jan. 12.

70. The meeting of Jan. 17 received full reports in only a few papers: *Le Temps*, Jan. 19; *La France de Bordeaux*, Jan. 18; *Le Journal*, Jan. 18. The Radical papers (*L'Oeuvre*, *L'Ere nouvelle*, *La République*, *La Dépêche de Toulouse*) suppressed any mention of it; nor was anything to be learned from the other major papers.

71. Jean Piot (*L'Oeuvre*, Jan. 23), Kayser (*La République*, Jan. 21), and Nogaro (*L'Ere nouvelle*, Jan. 24) all seem to be referring, albeit obliquely, to the passions aroused at this meeting.

72. See *Le Temps,* Jan. 19, for the full text.

73. Palmade, Jacquier, Nogaro, at the Jan. 19 meeting.

74. Blum, p. 11: the offer "was long and carefully prepared." Blum also stated at the Congress of Avignon that Daladier had approached each Socialist individually (*Le Populaire,* April 18, 1933). *Aux écoutes,* Feb. 4, 1933, p. 7, claimed that Daladier had been negotiating with the Socialists for three weeks.

75. *Mantes-républicain,* Feb. 8, 1933. Blum wrote later: "There had been a growing hope in the Socialist group that Daladier's arrival in power was at last going to permit the initiative we awaited . . . since the beginning of the legislature: a determined and daring attempt to leave the beaten path . . . [and to] reanimate and renew the national life" (*Les Radicaux et nous,* p. 11).

76. My sources for this crisis, with the exception of Lamoureux's memoirs and Blum's pamphlets, are almost exclusively journalistic. Most of the newspapers carried substantially similar accounts—*Le Temps, L'Oeuvre, Le Petit Journal, La France de Bordeaux, Le Petit Parisien.* Quite different reports are to be found in *L'Ere nouvelle,* whose editor, Gaboriaud, was active in the party at this time, in *Le Progrès de Lyon,* which suddenly had exhaustive reports (inspired by Herriot?), and in *La Dépêche de Toulouse,* which gives the best account of Jan. 30, its owner, Maurice Sarraut, being intimately involved in the negotiations. See also Louis Joubert, "Chronique politique," *Le Correspondant,* Feb. 10, 1933, 470–77; Louis Joxe, "Le Ministère Daladier," *Europe nouvelle,* Feb. 4, 1933, 100–101; P. de Pressac, *Revue politique et parlementaire,* Feb. 10, 1933, 358–63.

77. *Mantes-républicain,* Feb. 8, 1933.

78. *Le Journal de Rouen,* Jan. 31; *La France de Bordeaux,* Jan. 31; *Aux écoutes,* Feb. 4; *La Lumière,* Feb. 4.

79. *Radicaux et socialistes,* p. 9.

80. Particularly "Observateur," *Candide,* Jan. 26, 1933; also *La Volonté* cited in *Le Bulletin quotidien,* Jan. 30; and P. du Clain, *La Lumière,* Jan. 28.

81. *Le Bourbonnais républicain,* Nov. 30, 1952; see also Bonnet's statement to the press at 4:15 P.M., when he said that he would probably be Minister of Finance. *L'Oeuvre,* Jan. 31, 1933.

82. Feb. 1, 1933.

83. *Radicaux et socialistes,* p. 9, cited by Lapaquellerie, pp. 134–35. In interviews, Martinaud-Déplat and Georges Bonnet both claimed that the offer to the Socialists had been only for the record, and that financial worries dominated all.

84. *Le Progrès de Lyon,* Feb. 1.

85. *Mantes-républicain,* Feb. 6.

86. See *La République,* Jan. 31; *L'Ere nouvelle,* Jan. 31.

87. Bertrand in *Le Journal de Marennes:* on Feb. 5 he was desolate, Feb. 12 pleased, March 12 delighted.

88. Feb. 2, 1933.

89. For example, in February a measure against the fonctionnaires was squeezed through, which pleased the conservatives, but had the merit, in the eyes of the fonctionnaires, of asking for only 20 francs per head; *La Tribune des fonctionnaires* of Feb. 25 conceded a loss in principle, but claimed a victory in fact.

90. Marcus, pp. 5–30; Bonnefous, V, 160–66; Ligou, pp. 391–95; Louis, pp. 387–89; Lamoureux, in his memoirs, acknowledges that the Socialists' divisions helped him considerably with his financial bills (*Le Bourbonnais républicain,* Dec. 28, 1952).

91. Bergery resigned in March. See his extraordinary letter of resignation in *Mantes-républicain,* March 15, 1933, cited above, p. 69.

92. In 1925, Herriot had overthrown the Briand government in which Caillaux, as Finance Minister, had demanded full powers (Bonnefous, IV, 156–58). In 1935, he was

involved in bringing down the Bouisson government, in which Caillaux was once again Finance Minister. Caillaux, on the other hand, had engineered Herriot's resignation from the Poincaré government at the Congress of Angers in 1928 (*ibid.*, pp. 288–89; Soulié, pp. 307–11).

93. A deflationary "douzième provisoire" in February, and the budget in May.

94. In April, Blum had already denounced Radical attempts to split the Socialists and achieve Concentration (*Le Populaire*, report of Congress, April 18, 1933). See rumors about these maneuvers in de Pressac, *Revue politique et parlementaire*, May 10, 1933, pp. 585–90, July 10, p. 167, Nov. 10, pp. 332–35; *Aux écoutes*, July 15, p. 5; Sept. 23, p. 10; and Joubert, *Le Correspondant*, Aug. 10, p. 474. Bayet and Milhaud both denied the existence of such a policy (*La République de l'Ain*, June 11, and *L'Europe nouvelle*, March 11); but a number of left-wing Radicals denounced any attempt to split the Socialists, which they realized would be disastrous for them (Kayser, *La République de l'Oise*, July 26; Jammy Schmidt, *ibid.*, July 27; Archimbaud, *Le Journal de Die et de la Drôme*, Sept. 30; and Zay, *La France du Centre*, Sept. 24). Reibel, a member of the center, testified later to the February Sixth Commission that Daladier's subsequent proposals for Concentration were "nothing new for us because you [Daladier] certainly remember a conversation that I had with you last September" (*Commission d'enquête chargée de rechercher les causes et les origines des événements du 6 février 1934 et jours suivants* (henceforth *Commission du 6 février*), Annexe No. 3385, p. 599).

95. On the vote defeating the government, 28 broke with the party.

96. See Lamoureux's memoirs for an exhaustive account in two installments, *Le Bourbonnais républicain*, Jan. 4, Jan. 11, 1953; also *La Lumière*, Sept. 2, 1933.

97. *Le Bourbonnais républicain*, Feb. 15, 1953.

98. *Congress*, Oct. 6, pp. 223–34, 272–77, 277–86.

99. *Ibid.*, pp. 235–72; deputies: Mendès-France, Clerc, Mahagne, Deyris; party workers: Laffery (Seine), Bertrand de Jouvenel (Seine-Inférieure), Weyman (Algiers), Parouteau (Seine-et-Marne), Sennac (Seine-et-Oise), Luciani (Algiers), Cristin (Seine), Galimand (Seine-Inférieure), Willard (Alpes-Maritimes)—the only conservative. Note the dominance of the Paris region and the Seine-Inférieure.

100. *Congress*, Oct. 10, pp. 311–51.

101. *Ibid.*, pp. 312–14.

102. *Ibid.*, p. 311.

103. See copy in *Le Réveil démocratique de Maine-et-Loire*, Sept. 23.

104. See the left-wingers Archimbaud, Zay, and Gaston Martin's statements in favor of the Socialists and rigorous deflation: *Le Journal de Die et de la Drôme*, Sept. 30, 1933; *La France du Centre*, Aug. 27; *Le Démocrate de Lot-et-Garonne*, Sept. 17; also a fortiori the conservatives, e.g., Charles Bedu, *L'Avenir du Cher*, Sept. 9, 1933.

105. Henri Clerc, *L'Echo des Alpes*, Nov. 4, 1933.

106. *La France du Centre*, Oct. 26; other left-wingers who gave unstinting praise to Daladier: Dupuis, *Le Patriote de Châteaudun*, Dec. 12; de Tessan, *Le Journal de Seine-et-Marne*, Oct. 28,

107. *L'Echo de Paris*, Oct. 24, 1933.

108. Oct. 26 at 10 A.M.

109. Nogaro, quoted in *Le Journal des débats*, Oct. 27.

110. At the Congress of the Alliance Démocratique, St.-Etienne, *Le Temps*, Oct. 30.

111. See his demand for immediate and complete equilibrium in *La République des travailleurs* (Gers), Oct. 15.

112. *J.O.Ch.*, Nov. 3, p. 3985.

113. *Le Temps*, Nov. 5, 1933; a number of deputies changed their votes so the official figure reported was 320 in favor; but it was the original vote that counted. *J.O.Ch.*,

Nov. 3, 1933, p. 3986. See de Pressac, *Revue politique et parlementaire,* Nov. 11, 337–38; Pinon, "Le Ministère Sarraut," *Revue des deux mondes,* Nov. 15, 471–75; *Aux écoutes,* Oct. 28; Hutin, *L'Echo de Paris,* Oct. 25; Gaston Martin, *Le Démocrate de Lot-et-Garonne,* Nov. 12; L. Le Page, *L'Eclaireur du Finistère,* Nov. 11.

114. The meeting was Nov. 6. *Le Petit Journal* claims only 15 present, *La Dépêche de Toulouse,* only 20; it was in their interest to minimize the meeting's importance. But however few attended, they were enough to overturn the government. See also *Le Temps,* Nov. 8; *Le Populaire,* Nov. 7; *Aux écoutes,* Nov. 11; Louis Proust, *La République tourangelle,* Nov. 18; Zay, *Souvenirs,* p. 196.

115. Le Page, *L'Eclaireur du Finistère,* Nov. 11. See p. 11 of this issue for a discussion of the reporting of this meeting.

116. *L'Oeuvre,* Nov. 22, report of a speech before the Radical Group.

117. *J.O.Ch.,* Nov. 23, pp. 4284–85. See Soulier, pp. 158–60, for an excellent description of this sitting, one of the few in which the events of the sitting itself overturned a government. Also Suarez, *Les Heures héroiques,* p. 142; Lamoureux, *Le Bourbonnais républicain,* Feb. 15, 1953; *Le Canard enchaîné,* Nov. 29, 1933; Bonnefous, V, 181–82.

118. L.-O. Frossard, now the leading right-wing Socialist, was a Freemason; he had led the attack on Sarraut within the Socialist party and then led the defense of Chautemps in the same place, on essentially the same program. See *Aux écoutes,* Dec. 9, p. 17; Dec. 23, p. 13; Bonnefous, V, 180, 182–84.

119. *Le Temps,* Dec. 4. The measure was to have provided six billion francs and the Chamber succeeded in voting 4.7 billion; see Jenny, *Revue politique et parlementaire,* Jan. 10, 1934, p. 153.

120. *J.O.Ch.,* Dec. 8, 1933, p. 4494. Auriol: "For us the choice is painful, humiliating, intolerable; . . . we will not accept this choice. We will not be dupes, nor accomplices."

121. For example, when Daladier kept the Socialists out of the government in 1933, his reward was an advance made by the Bank of France to the Treasury; see the statement by Moret in *Dalloz,* 1936, IV, 175ff., cited in Lair, p. 47. Also *Revue d'économie politique,* 1937, p. 617: "The diminution of the national gold reserve in 1933 was the result of the flight of capital at this time, which coincided with the first serious political crisis; on the other hand, gold flowed in during 1934." Kirchheimer points out that the extravagant political powers of the Bank of France far surpassed those of other national banks. The government was reduced "to a state of perpetual dependency upon the bankers. . . . Scarcely has the government begun to develop a timid program of social reform when the *crise de confiance* . . . gets into full swing. . . . With a little help from the governor and regents of the bank . . . the untrustworthy government disappears." ("Changes in the Structure," pp. 268–70.)

122. Lair, pp. 9–10.

123. Charles Morice, *Le Petit Parisien,* Nov. 27, 1933. See also Bonnet's speech to the Group, where he said that no bonds had been sold since the fall of the Daladier government, and that if the financial bill were not voted, the situation would become intolerable (*Le Temps,* Nov. 18).

124. See Perrot, p. 207, for a pleasant account of the moral approach to the Gold Standard and other doctrines sacred to the majority of Frenchmen.

125. *J.O.S.,* July 15, 1932, pp. 1104–7; Jan. 17, 1933, pp. 24–25.

126. See *Aux écoutes,* Dec. 16, 1933; *Les Cahiers de Job Coz,* Dec., 1933, pp. 8–9.

127. *J.O.Ch.,* Nov. 3, 1933, p. 3973; for Caillaux's tutelary role, see Goguel, *Le Rôle financier,* p. 254.

128. It was estimated the conversion would save 1,332 million francs, plus an addi-

tional 500 million for 1933. See "Chronique financière," *Revue politique et parlementaire,* Oct. 10, 1932, p. 159.

129. Only the Paul-Boncour bill was opposed by a significant number of Radicals: nine opposed, 13 abstained, six absent. On the other bills: July 12, 1932: 156 for, one abstained, two opposed, one absent; vote on Article 83, Feb. 28, 1933: 155 for, one abstained, one opposed; vote on Lassalle amendment, Oct. 23, 1933: 157 for, four abstained, one opposed; vote on Gounin amendment, Nov. 23, 1933: 158 for, three abstained, none opposed. Cf. Goguel, *La Politique des partis,* p. 293: "The Radicals were . . . opposed to the reduction of state expenses, if not in principle, at least in fact, as soon as it became a question of a precise measure affecting some interest."

CHAPTER 5

1. For the Stavisky scandal, see Werth, *France in Ferment,* pp. 79–99; Bonnefous, V, 192–96; Goguel, *La Politique des partis,* pp. 482–84; Suarez, *Les Heures héroiques;* Soulier, p. 220; Brogan, pp. 652–58; *Dans les coulisses,* pp. 15, 30–36; Tardieu, p. 332; and Lauréat Odilon Joseph Bernard, pp. 63–135.

2. Raynaldy in the Sacazan affair.

3. See Soulier, pp. 220, 315, 348–49, 376–77; Brogan, p. 656; Bonnefous, V, 197; *Dans les coulisses,* pp. 40–42; Goguel, *La Politique des partis,* p. 484.

4. Printed in *La Tribune picarde,* Feb. 3, 1934.

5. *Aux écoutes,* Feb. 3, p. 6. Blum, in *Le Populaire,* Jan. 31, claimed he did resign; *L'Oeuvre,* Feb. 1, echoes this rumor.

6. According to Herriot's statement in the Cadillac Committee, printed in *Le Petit Parisien,* Jan. 29, 1934.

7. See the reserve of *La Dépêche de Toulouse,* Jan. 29, 30; *L'Ere nouvelle,* Feb. 5. In the local press, I have found only expressions of reserve or hostility with regard to the formation of the Daladier government. For example, Clerc, *L'Echo des Alpes,* Feb. 3; Aubaud, *La République de l'Oise,* Feb. 2; Zay, *La France du Centre,* Feb. 4 (all left-wingers); Noël (Sireyjol), *Le Nontronnais,* Feb. 3; Charles Bedu, *L'Avenir du Cher,* Feb. 3; Raoul Girard, *L'Action jurassienne,* Feb. 3 (right-wingers).

8. The political crisis surrounding the riots of February Sixth has been well analyzed by Eugen Weber in *Action Française,* pp. 327–32. My analysis was written before I had seen Weber's, and since it agrees in all essentials, it has been left unchanged. The best contemporary description of the formation of the Daladier government is Suarez, *La Grande Peur,* pp. 11–45. See also Suarez, *Les Heures héroiques,* pp. 170–80; Bonnefous, V, 198–99; Werth, *France in Ferment,* pp. 118–24; and Goguel, *La Politique des Partis,* p. 484.

9. Daladier's undersecretary at the Presidency of the Council, Martinaud-Déplat, canvassed the leaders of the center following Fabry's expulsion and concluded that Daladier would not get sufficient support from them. Testimony of Foures, Laniel, and Martinaud-Déplat in *Commission du 6 février,* no. 3385, pp. 598–600.

10. See *Le Populaire,* Jan. 31: "M. Edouard Daladier has formed a ministry that probably will not survive its presentation to the Chamber."

11. The best analysis of February Sixth I have found is Rémond, "Explications du 6 février"; other recent studies are Beloff, pp. 9–35; and Warner, pp. 377–85. Werth, *France in Ferment,* remains the most colorful, complete, and accurate account. The best guide to the debates of the February Sixth commission is the reports of the *Commission du 6 février, Annexes,* particularly documents 3383, 3384, 3385, 3388, and 3391.

Also of interest are the testimonies in the *Commission de 1933 à 1945,* particularly Lebrun, May 27, 1948, IV, 951; Paul-Boncour, March 16, 1948, II, 812; and Blum, June 18, 1946, I, 124. Other useful studies are Marcus, pp. 48–56; Goguel, *La Politique des partis,* pp. 481–90; Bonnefous, V, 198–214; Chevallier, *Histoire des institutions politiques en France de 1789,* III, 318–19; *Dans les coulisses,* pp. 63–73; Duverger, *Cours de vie politique,* p. 96; Genin, "Le 6 février"; Lamoureux's memoirs, *Le Bourbonnais républicain,* May 3, 10, 1953; Bankwitz, pp. 558–59; Bonnevay, *Les Journées sanglantes;* and Paz, "Le 6 février."

12. See *Le Populaire,* Feb. 4, 1934. Some left-wing Radicals shared the Socialists' feelings: see meeting of the Group, Jan. 11, 1934, Raoul Aubaud, *La République de l'Oise,* Feb. 4.

13. Fabry, p. 38; Suarez, *La Grande Peur,* pp. 32–35, 39, and 47. See also *Commission du 6 février,* No. 3385, pp. 601–2; Victor Basch, *Les Cahiers des droits de l'homme,* Feb. 20–March 10, 1934, p. 100, says this is the only rational explanation; also Werth, *France in Ferment,* pp. 130–41.

14. Blum, *Le Populaire,* Aug. 28, 1934; also in *Les Radicaux et nous,* p. 6. Blum gave the full details of this offer for the first time after the war in *Commission de 1933 à 1945,* I, 123–24, June 18, 1947; Daladier confirms this (*ibid.,* p. 12). Marcus (pp. 66–70) makes a great deal of this sudden Socialist conversion.

15. Paul-Boncour testimony, *Commission de 1933 à 1945,* March 16, 1948, II, 812. Marc Rucart, *La République des Vosges,* Feb. 24, 1934, reports that he was at a banquet with several members of the cabinet when they learned by telephone of their resignation; Lorgeré says the same thing in his unpublished memoirs.

16. See his testimony before the *Commission du 6 février* that the chief reason for resignation was the fear of having the blood of hundreds upon his hands, Document no. 3391, pp. 699–700.

17. Cot, *Le Procès de la République,* I, 70–71; Goguel, *La Politique des partis,* p. 489; Genin, p. 81; Duverger, *Cours de vie politique,* p. 96.

18. *Commission du 6 février,* no. 3391, p. 698; speech at Orange, *Le Temps,* April 9, 1934. See also Roche's polemic with Cot, *La République,* Sept. 18, 1934; Roche throws Cot's capitulation back in his face.

19. See *Crapouillot,* "Le Six février," Jan. 1935, pp. 24–25; Paz. p. 639.

20. Beloff, pp. 31–35. Beloff's suggestion gets the support of only unreliable sources like André Simon, p. 67. The ministers, Martinaud-Déplat, Lorgeré, and La Chambre, in interviews, were all quite categoric in rejecting such a hypothesis. Bankwitz, II, 558, says that Weygand would do nothing against the government, although his sympathies were with the demonstrators.

21. *Commission de 1933 à 1945,* March 16, 1948, II, 812.

22. Trotsky, pp. 10–11.

23. Interview with André Cornu, Oct. 25, 1960. Lebrun's testimony, June 8, 1948, *Commission de 1933 à 1945,* IV, 984. See also *La Dépêche de Toulouse,* Jan. 29, 1934; and Fischer, pp. 32–38.

24. De Jouvenel, *Après la défaite,* p. 63.

25. Deyris, *Le Démocrate* (Dax), March 18, 1934; the motion of the Committee of Auch (Gers), Feb. 23, 1934, printed in *La République des travailleurs,* March 1, 1934.

26. Aubaud, *La République de l'Oise,* Feb. 12, 13, 1934; Zay, *La France du Centre,* Feb. 11.

27. For example, Cot, *Le Démocrate savoyard,* April 21. Though his opposition was very weak, he officially absented himself from the vote; and a short time later (*ibid.,* May 19) he was again advocating that the experiment continue; see also Marc Rucart,

La République des Vosges, Feb. 24; and Henri Guernut, *La Tribune de l'Aisne,* Feb. 15.

28. Deyris, *Le Démocrate* (Dax), March 18; Leculier, *Le Jura démocratique,* Feb. 6.

29. For example, the left-wing de Tessan, *Le Journal de Seine-et-Marne,* Feb. 14, 17, supported Doumergue unreservedly.

30. *La Concorde,* Feb. 22, 1934; the same idea was expressed in *Le Démocrate* (Jonzac), Feb. 17. According to *Le Temps,* Feb. 11, in the meeting that marked participation in the Doumergue government, many of the Radicals accepted a temporary Union, but not one that would break them from the left. But what was the Union if not a break from the left?

31. The only report of the Feb. 7 meeting is by a deputy, Charles Bedu, *L'Avenir du Cher,* Feb. 24, since February Sixth crowded all other events out of the papers. The meetings of Feb. 8 and 9 are fairly well documented in the press, particularly *Le Petit Journal, Le Petit Parisien, La Dépêche de Toulouse, Le Journal, L'Oeuvre.*

32. *L'Oeuvre* says that Mendès-France, Cudenet, Zay, Bouëssé, and Rucart abstained; Bedu (*L'Avenir du Cher*) also notes the beginnings of opposition. Herriot, on the contrary, maintained that the party supported his entry into the government unanimously. See *Jadis,* II, 378–79.

33. Siegfried, *De la IIIe à la IVe République,* pp. 57–58.

34. Quoted in Werth, *Lost Statesman,* p. 9.

35. Quoted by Albert Milhaud (secretary-general), *L'Ere nouvelle,* March 3, 1934.

36. The best reports of the meeting are by Milhaud, *L'Ere nouvelle,* Feb. 14, 17, March 3, April 7. Much of the Paris press ignored the meeting; the rest reported it strangely, most of the articles being two days late, which indicates a certain amount of secrecy. The best Paris report is in *Le Petit Journal,* Feb. 17, to be supplemented by *Le Petit Parisien,* Feb. 17. *La Dépêche de Toulouse* gave two reports, Feb. 16 and Feb. 18, which seemed to be about two different meetings, although they were not. According to *Le Petit Journal,* the Congress was demanded by the federations of the Nord, Seine, Seine-et-Oise, Rhône, etc. The inclusion of Rhône, which was Herriot's creature, is highly suspect. Milhaud himself says that the Seine-Inférieure and Seine-et-Oise took the initiative. *L'Oeuvre,* Feb. 15, mentions that Loiret, Zay's federation, was extremely active.

37. *L'Ere nouvelle,* April 28, 1934.

38. *Le Petit Journal, Le Petit Parisien, L'Ere nouvelle,* March 6; *Le Temps, La Dépêche de Toulouse,* Milhaud in *L'Ere nouvelle,* March 7.

39. Martinaud-Déplat in the Executive Committee, reported in *Le Petit Parisien,* Jan. 1, 1934.

40. The 14 he accused were Chautemps, Hesse, Renoult, Durand, Dalimier, François Albert, Bonnet, Hulin, Bonnaure, Garat, Proust, Puis, Cot, and Gardey. See Tardieu, p. 332.

41. See Headings, p. 264.

42. *La Concorde,* April 4, 1934.

43. Herriot, *Jadis,* II, 392–93.

44. See *Le Démocrate savoyard,* March 10, April 21, 1934.

45. *Le Bourbonnais républicain,* Feb. 11.

46. *La République de Chinon,* Feb. 15. Italics in the original.

47. At the federation, March 18, 1934; reported in *La Réveil démocratique,* March 24.

48. *La République des Vosges,* Oct. 20, 1934.

49. *La Démocratie bretonne,* Feb. 29, 1936; *L'Union démocratique de la Haute-*

Saône, March 30, 1934; *Le Jura démocratique,* Jan. 19, 1934, citing *L'Abeille jurassienne* and *La Vie dôloise.*

50. *Le Citoyen,* Dec. 3, 1933, March 1, 1936.

51. *La République de l'Oise,* April 18, 1934.

52. Marcel Déat, *Le Républicain de Chinon,* March 22, 1934.

53. Goguel, *La Politique des partis,* p. 491; Bonnefous, V, 219–22.

54. *L'Action jurassienne,* March 28, 1934.

55. *Le Démocrate savoyard,* Feb. 17, 24, 1934.

56. *La République des travailleurs,* Feb. 11, April 22, 1934.

57. Barral (thesis), p. 729; *Le Démocrate* (Dax), Feb. 11, 18, March 18; *Ouest-Océan,* Feb. 10, 14, May 7.

58. See *L'Avenir républicain,* Feb. 18; *La France du Centre,* Feb. 11.

59. *L'Ere nouvelle,* April 7.

60. Brachard, Hulin, René Richard, Deyris, and Lassalle.

61. Cot, Catalan, Crutel, Dupuis, Le Bail, Longuet, Lorgeré, and de Tessan; some even voted for him on all three occasions—Geistdoerfer and Gout.

62. Augé, Cornu, Ducos, Ferrand, Girard, Martinaud-Déplat, Maupoil, and Eugène Roy.

63. Wassy (Haute-Marne), March 11, 1934, legislative, and St.-Dizier, cantonal, March 4. Both were to replace the deputy Rollin, who had been killed at the train crash in Lagny.

64. Melle, April 11, 1934.

65. Cantonal elections at Châtellerault, April 11.

66. The best discussion of the election is in *L'Information sociale,* May 10, pp. 10–12. For Milhaud's side, see *L'Ere nouvelle,* April 21, May 5, June 16.

67. Of these, four (Dalimier, Renoult, Hesse, and Proust) were eventually reintegrated when the heat was off.

68. *L'Echo des Alpes,* April 21, 1934.

69. "Bulletin d'action radicale," *L'Information sociale,* June 21, p. 11.

70. *La Dépêche normande,* May 25.

CHAPTER 6

1. See Binion, pp. 320–22; Bonnefous, V, 271–77; Zay, p. 210; Lamoureux, *Le Bourbonnais républicain,* Aug. 31, 1952; Soulié, pp. 448–50; Herriot, *Jadis,* II, 445–49.

2. *Le Populaire,* July 26, 1934.

3. Speech at the Federation of the Rhône, July 29, 1934, reprinted in *Le Démocrate* (Rhône), Aug. 4.

4. See Milhaud, *L'Ere nouvelle,* Aug. 8, 1934.

5. "Interim," July 17, 1934, *La République*; Mistler, Aug. 13, 20; Roche, July 26, 27, 30, Aug. 1, 7, 28, Sept. 5, 6, 7, 9, 12, 13, 19, 20; Riou, Aug. 30, Oct. 2, all in *La République*; Cot, *L'Oeuvre,* Sept. 7; Kayser, *La République,* Aug. 6, *L'Oeuvre,* Oct. 7; Hoog, *L'Aube,* Aug. 28; Blum, *Le Populaire,* Aug. 20, 19, etc.

6. Georges Dupeux's discussion, pp. 89–91, is complete and seems essentially accurate.

7. Kayser, *L'Oeuvre,* Oct. 7, 1934. Mounier, p. 888.

8. *Congress,* Oct. 27, 1934, p. 278.

9. Sept. 24 and Oct. 4.

10. Cornu unconvincingly attempted to demonstrate that Marchandeau's project was

different from Doumergue's and channeled the discussion into such pleasant fantasies —for the time—as referendums (*Congress*, Oct. 25, 1934, pp. 28–29).

11. Federation of Loiret, *L'Avenir républicain,* Oct. 13, 1934; Federation, *L'Union démocratique de la Haute-Saône,* Oct. 23; Federation of Finistère, *L'Eclaireur du Finistère,* Oct. 27; Federation of Lot-et-Garonne, *Le Démocrate,* Sept. 30; Federation of Savoy, *Le Démocrate,* Oct. 27.

12. Noël, *Le Nontronnais,* Nov. 11; Potut, *L'Echo de la Nièvre,* Nov. 17; *Le Démocrate* (Jonzac), Nov. 10; Bedu, *L'Avenir du Cher,* Nov. 17.

13. *Congress,* Oct. 26, 1934, pp. 153–67; also P. Simon, *Revue bleue,* Nov. 11, 1934, p. 825; Charles Dulot, *L'Information sociale,* Nov. 8.

14. Printed in *Le Républicain de Chinon,* Nov. 8, 1934.

15. See particularly his speech, *Congress,* Oct. 27, 1934, p. 286.

16. Declaration of the party, *ibid.,* p. 381.

17. See Dupeux, p. 90; Kayser said it was a very useful Congress with solid unanimity and no equivocation [!], *L'Oeuvre,* Oct. 30, 1934.

18. *Le Populaire,* Oct. 30, 1934.

19. Déat, p. 13.

20. Nov. 4, 1934, text in *L'Alliance démocratique,* Nov. 14; also the reports of conversations between the Radicals and the Alliance Démocratique in *Le Petit Journal, Le Petit Parisien,* and *L'Oeuvre,* Oct. 12, 1934, and the advances made to the Radicals in *L'Alliance démocratique,* Aug. 15, Oct. 10, 1934.

21. Lamoureux's memoirs, cited in Bonnefous, V, 299; complete text in *Le Bourbonnais républicain,* Oct. 5, 1952. See also Marchandeau's speech to the Group, Nov. 8, *Le Temps,* Nov. 10.

22. Bonnefous's account of the fall of the Doumergue government and the formation of the Flandin cabinet, V, 300–301, seems to be more balanced than Soulié's, pp. 452–54; Herriot, *Jadis,* II, 462–80, gives a wonderful story of the events; also Goguel, *La Politique des partis,* pp. 497–500.

23. *La France du Centre,* Nov. 11, 18, 1934; also *Le Courrier de la Creuse,* Nov. 11.

24. Herriot at Château-Thierry, *Le Temps,* Nov. 26, 1934; Herriot and Caillaux in the Executive Committee, Jan. 25, 1935, *Le Temps;* Roche, p. 104; Deyris (moderate left), *Le Démocrate* (Dax), Dec. 16, 1934; Jammy Schmidt and Aubaud (left), *La République de l'Oise,* Nov. 16, 1934, Feb. 16, 1935; Raoul Girard (conservative), *L'Action jurassienne,* Dec. 22, 1934; Thiébaut (moderate), *La Tribune républicaine,* Nov. 23, 1934; Elbel (moderate left), *La Gazette vosgienne,* Nov. 17, 1934; Delbos (moderate), *La Dépêche de Toulouse,* Jan. 23, 1935.

25. There were very shocked comments by Bedu (conservative) and Zay (left) in *L'Avenir du Cher,* Feb. 16, *La France du Centre,* Feb. 10, 1935.

26. Sauvy, *L'Evolution économique,* p. 263.

27. *L'Oeuvre,* Dec. 11, 1934.

28. *L'Avenir du Cher,* Dec. 15, 1934, Jan. 19, 1935; *La République de l'Oise,* Dec. 30, 1934, Jan. 13, 1935.

29. Fernand Augé (moderate left), *Le Démocrate de Seine-et-Marne,* Jan. 26, 1935; also Potut (conservative), *L'Echo de la Nièvre,* Dec. 22, 29, 1934; *Le Journal de Seine-et-Marne,* Feb. 2, 1935, reports the federation congratulating de Tessan (left), for opposing the bill; Mortier (conservative), *Le Démocrate de Seine-et-Marne,* Feb. 2, 1935; Gers, motion applauding Catalan (left), *La République des travailleurs,* Dec. 31, 1934; Thiébaut (moderate), *La Tribune républicaine,* Dec. 21, 1934, apologizing for voting the bill; Guernut (moderate left), apologizing, *La Tribune de l'Aisne,* Jan. 24, 1935.

30. See report in *L'Oeuvre,* Jan. 18, 1935.

31. *La République de l'Oise,* April 8, 1934, Aug. 3, 1934.

32. *La Tribune de l'Aisne,* Oct. 18, 1934.

33. *Ouest-Océan,* Sept. 5, 1934.

34. Loiret: *L'Avenir républicain,* Sept. 8, 1934; Loire, *Le Montbrisonnais,* July 28, 1934.

35. See Kayser, Oct. 7, and Cot, Oct. 9, both in *L'Oeuvre.*

36. On the Common Front, see Joll, pp. 36–52; Albertini, pp. 133–34; Borkenau, pp. 120–27; Chambaz, pp. 63–70; Marcus, pp. 56–79; and Allen, pp. 365–70.

37. Oct. 10; Chambaz, p. 76; also Borkenau, p. 129; and Dupeux, p. 82.

38. Herriot's comment cited in *Le Petit Parisien,* Sept. 13, 1934. On negotiations with the Common Front, see Herriot, *Jadis,* II, 456.

39. Herriot, *Jadis,* II, 460.

40. *Le Démocrate savoyard,* Oct. 20, 1934; also left-wing complaints in *Le Démocrate de Seine-et-Marne,* Oct. 10; *La Gazette des Vosges,* Oct. 13; *La République des Vosges,* Oct. 20; *La République des travailleurs* (Gers), Oct. 7, 11, 14.

41. *Le Journal de Die et de la Drôme,* Oct. 6, 1934.

42. Chambaz, pp. 75–76; Joll, p. 49.

43. Victor Basch and P. Bouillon, Dec. 15; Kayser, Dec. 18, 1934.

44. See *La France du Centre,* Feb. 17, 1935, *L'Avenir républicain* (Gien), Feb. 2, March 2, 31, 1935.

45. *Le Temps,* Feb. 4, 1935.

46. *L'Oeuvre,* Jan. 11, 1935, report by Perney on his talks.

47. Bonnefous, V, 325–28; Goguel, *La Politique des partis,* pp. 501–2.

48. Reported in *La France de Bordeaux,* May 8, 1935.

49. The Alliance Démocratique stated that Concentrationist lists had been established in 59 towns having more than 5,000 inhabitants (*Le Temps,* May 9, 1935).

50. For Grenoble, Barral (book), p. 478; for Rouen, Eude, p. 95; also Crutel, *L'Eveil,* May 12, 1935. In the Seine-et-Marne, de Tessan made a joint list with the centrists on condition that their leader not run in the legislative elections of 1936 (*Le Journal de Seine-et-Marne,* Feb. 22, 1936). For the last three towns, *La République des travailleurs,* April 14, 1935; *La Gazette vosgienne,* April 1935; *Le Démocrate de Lot-et-Garonne,* May 5, 12, 17, 1935.

51. *Le Temps,* May 14, 1935.

52. See Aubaud's complaints to this effect, *La République de l'Oise,* April 4, 1935; also editorial in *Le Temps,* May 12.

53. Examples of Radicals on two competing lists: La Rochelle, *Ouest-Océan,* May 4; Niort, *L'Echo de l'Ouest,* May 19; Dôle, *L'Action jurassienne,* May 18; Brive, *La Corrèze républicaine,* April 23; Tours, *La République tourangelle,* May 11. Examples of isolated Radical lists: Morlaix, *L'Eclaireur du Finistère,* May 11; *Le Journal de Marennes,* May 12; Amiens, *La Défense républicaine,* March 9, April 27; Gien, *L'Avenir républicain,* May 18. Examples of Radical and Socialist lists: Château-Thierry, *La Tribune de l'Aisne,* May 9; St.-Jean-d'Angély, *L'Echo saintongeais,* May 5; Vesoul, *L'Union démocratique de la Haute-Saône,* May 8; *L'Avenir de Pithiviers,* April 27, May 4, for Pithiviers; Chambéry, *Le Démocrate savoyard,* May 18.

54. "J.T.," *L'Indépendant* (Saintes), April 27, 1935.

55. *L'Alliance démocratique,* May 17, 1935; editorials in *Le Temps,* May 14, 15; Lamoureux, *Le Bourbonnais républicain,* May 26.

56. Goguel, *La Politique des partis,* pp. 501–2. Yet the 1938 elections took place within a few days of Munich, when the Radicals were at the height of their anti-Popular Front reaction, and so a municipal councillor who was right-wing in 1938 may not have been in 1935.

57. *L'Oeuvre,* April 26, 1935.

58. *La France de Bordeaux,* May 25, 26, 1935. Also reports of the May 29 meeting of the Group, particularly the accounts in *Le Petit Journal,* May 29, *Le Temps,* May 30, and *Le Canard enchaîné,* May 29.

59. Forty-five voted for, 86 against, 16 abstained, and nine were absent. Practically the only reason given for overthrowing Flandin by all groups was his demand for full powers after having done nothing for seven months: Picard (mod. left), *L'Abeille des Vosges,* June 15, 1935; Aubaud (left), *La République de l'Oise,* June 1; Berthod (mod.), *Le Démocrate du Jura,* June 22; Liautey (mod. left), *L'Union démocratique de la Haute-Saône,* June 11; Thiébaut (cons.), *La Tribune républicaine,* June 14.

60. *J.O.Ch.,* May 30, 1935, p. 1741.

61. Report of the Delegation of the Left, *Le Temps,* May 31.

62. *Le Populaire,* June 2.

63. *Le Démocrate du Jura,* June 22.

64. Bouisson speech, *J.O.Ch.,* June 4, 1935, p. 1778; Potut, *L'Echo de la Nièvre,* June 8; Thiébaut, *La Tribune républicaine,* June 14; Liautey, *L'Union démocratique de la Haute-Saône,* June 11.

65. *J.O.Ch.,* June 4, 1935, pp. 1777–79. Goguel: "But Bouisson, a cynical, uncultured politician known for his business connections, aroused the disgust of the Chamber by the brutal and down-to-earth way he presented his program, for which he, in turn, asked for full powers. The cabinet was overthrown the very day of the ministerial declaration" (*La Politique des partis,* p. 503). Also Soulier, p. 165, and Bonnefous, V, 337–39.

66. Leites, p. 128.

67. Text in *Le Temps,* June 7, 1935.

68. Blum, *Le Populaire,* June 9, 1935.

69. Radical Group, *Le Temps,* June 7. Daladier's statement reported in *Le Petit Journal,* June 29.

70. *Le Temps,* June 8, 1935. Herriot, *Jadis,* II, 551.

71. *La République de l'Oise,* June 8; Laval's giving pensions to Henri Maupoil cited by Picard, *L'Abeille des Vosges,* June 15; Liautey, *L'Union démocratique de la Haute-Saône,* June 11; Ferrand, *Le Courrier de la Creuse,* June 9; that deflation would be limited, Ferrand, *ibid.,* Guernut, *La Tribune de l'Aisne,* June 13, Thiébaut, *La Tribune républicaine,* June 14; Liautey's statement in *L'Union démocratique de la Haute-Saône,* June 11.

72. Cf. Dupeux: "It was then that the tension within the Radical-Socialist party reached its greatest intensity" (p. 92).

73. Kayser, "Le Parti radical-socialiste," p. 273.

74. *L'Echo de Paris,* Nov. 6, 7, 8, 16, 1935.

75. Duclos, p. 1303; telegram from the Communist party read by Roche, *Congress,* Oct. 28, 1937, p. 241.

76. Raymond Rethoré, *Le Jacobin,* June, 1937.

77. Borkenau, pp. 116–17: "The whole policy of the Popular Front . . . was directed against an imaginary danger," p. 206: "To pretend to see in the leagues a French fascism is to take a bogey seriously." Also Girardet.

78. *Le Montbrisonnais,* May 2, 1936; Métayer (very pro-Popular Front), *Barodet;* Perrot, *ibid.*

79. *La Démocratie bretonne,* Feb. 2, 1933; Crutel, p. 47; letter from Taittinger, head of the Jeunesses Patriotes, reprinted in *L'Avenir républicain,* June 9, 1934.

80. The responsibility for these last two attacks was not unquestionably attributable to any of the right-wing groups, but the Radicals took them as political plots. See Herriot, *Jadis,* II, 518; *L'Abeille des Vosges,* March 23; *Le Démocrate savoyard,* June 1.

81. *Le Petit Journal,* June 26, 1935.
82. *La République de l'Oise,* Oct. 20, 1935.
83. *Le Jura démocratique,* Oct. 31, 1936.
84. The figures are: less than 5 per cent, 119 constituencies; 5–10 per cent, 37 constituencies; 10 per cent or more, 26 constituencies.
85. Mitton, *Le Patriote de Châteaudun,* June 30, 1935.
86. Menon, *Ouest-Océan,* March 30, 1935. Italics in original.
87. Jean Vincent, *Le Bourbonnais républicain,* April 21, July 28, 1935.
88. *La Nouvelle Chalosse* (Landes), March 29, 1936.
89. Chautemps, cited by Raymond Millet, *Le Temps,* Oct. 19, 1935.
90. *Congress,* 1935, Oct. 26, p. 376.
91. *La Défense républicaine* (Somme), June 22, 1935.
92. *Le Démocrate du Jura,* June 22.

CHAPTER 7

1. *Le Bourbonnais républicain,* July 7, 21, 28, Aug. 11, 1935.
2. H. Bonnet, secretary-general of the Federation of Eure-et-Loir, *Le Patriote de Châteaudun,* Nov. 12, 1936.
3. *Le Démocrate du Jura,* Feb. 1, April 25, July 5, 7, 1936. This is also an interesting illustration of how the party workers might be considerably more extreme than the voters.
4. Interview by Raymond Millet, *Le Temps,* March 26, 1932.
5. Mitterand interview, Feb. 24, 1961; Le Brun expressed the same idea, Nov. 10, 1960.
6. Mirkine-Guetzévitch, p. 20.
7. *Le Populaire,* Oct. 3, 1934.
8. Speech reported in *L'Oeuvre,* Oct. 6, 1934.
9. François Albert, writing as Pierre du Clain, *La Lumière,* Sept. 17, 1932.
10. "LD.," *Le Démocrate* (Jonzac), Oct. 28, 1933. André Lorgeré denounced the Breton Socialists to me as opportunists, clerical or anti-clerical as the circumstances warranted, whereas the Radicals were rigid, doctrinaire, and really on the left.
11. Béluel, president of the Federation of the Haute-Garonne, *La Tribune républicaine de la Haute-Garonne,* Jan. 7, 1934.
12. Bastid interview, Feb. 12, 1961.
13. "Un Rochelais," *La Défense républicaine,* March 8, 1933.
14. Blum in *Le Populaire,* June 10, 1935.
15. Kayser, "Le Parti radical-socialiste," p. 277; also Borkenau, p. 140.
16. *Le Temps,* Oct. 17, 1937.
17. This apprehension is reported in Kayser, "Le Parti radical-socialiste," pp. 277–78; Charles Dulot, *L'Information sociale,* Oct. 31, 1935; an excellent series of articles in *Le Temps* by Raymond Millet, Oct. 19, 24, 25; and Marécot, pp. 1456–61.
18. See Gaston Martin, *Le Démocrate de Lot-et-Garonne,* Nov. 17, 1935; Marécot (p. 1461) says it is quite extraordinary that the party maintained its unity in unequivocally adhering to the Popular Front.
19. *Congress,* pp. 422–45.
20. Report in *Le Temps,* Oct. 26; also *Jadis,* II, 602.
21. *Congress,* Oct. 26, 1935, p. 427.
22. *Ibid.,* pp. 376, 412.

23. *Ibid.*, p. 481.

24. *Le Bourbonnais républicain*, Nov. 3, 1935.

25. Crutel, *L'Eveil*, Nov. 3.

26. Lamoureux in *Le Bourbonnais républicain*, Aug. 11, Sept. 15, 1935; his speech at Vichy, *Le Temps*, Sept. 2; Blum in *Le Populaire*, Sept. 5, 10.

27. Zay, *La France du Centre*, Sept. 15, 1935.

28. Interview with Raymond Millet, *Le Temps*, Oct. 24, 1935.

29. See Bonnefous, V, 354–55, for a good outline of his tactics.

30. Blum, *Le Populaire*, Nov. 15, 1935.

31. *Jadis*, II, 567, 607, 610.

32. *Le Petit Provençal*, Nov. 10, 1935; also, Blum apparently made this condition clear at a meeting of the Delegation of the Left, Nov. 27, reported by de Kerillis, *L'Echo de Paris*, Nov. 28.

33. *Le Petit Provençal*, Nov. 10.

34. *La France du Centre*, Nov. 17; *La République tourangelle*, Nov. 16, expressed identical sentiments.

35. Mitton, *Le Patriote de Châteaudun*, Aug. 18, 1935. Also attacking the decree laws were Delabie, *La Défense républicaine* (Somme), Nov. 16, who wondered who would ratify them; Deyris, a member of the general assembly in the Landes, who characterized them as "disastrous" in *Le Démocrate* (Dax), Oct. 13; the Federation of the Seine-Inférieure, reported unanimously opposed in *L'Eveil*, Sept. 29; and the Bloc Républicain in Montbrison, whose opposition is reported in *Le Montbrisonnais*, Dec. 14.

36. Bedu, *L'Avenir du Cher*, Aug. 24, Dec. 21; *L'Action républicaine* (Tulle), Sept. 28; *La Tribune républicaine de la Haute-Garonne*, Aug. 11, 17, 25; Thiébaut, *La Tribune républicaine*, Jan. 24, 1936; Sclafer, *Le Démocrate* (Jonzac), Jan. 18; Courson, *La République de Chinon*, Jan. 9; and Lamoureux, *Le Bourbonnais républicain*, Nov. 17, 1935. Even the moderate-left Henri Guernut enthused, in *La Tribune de l'Aisne*, Oct. 17, 1935.

37. *Le Temps*, Nov. 14. See also Blum, *Le Populaire*, Nov. 14; *L'Oeuvre*, Nov. 13; *Candide*, Nov. 14; and Herriot, *Jadis*, II, 609–10. *L'Oeuvre* says it was unanimity less two, which alters the situation only slightly.

38. Communiqué in *Le Temps*, Nov. 16.

39. Blum, *Le Populaire*, Nov. 17.

40. *Jadis*, II, 615, Nov. 28, 1935; Bonnefous, V, 358–60.

41. *Le Démocrate de Lot-et-Garonne*, Dec. 8, 1935.

42. For example, Liautey's paper, *L'Union démocratique de la Haute-Saône*, mentioned Ethiopia only once in 1935, on Dec. 17, although all autumn the paper was filled with continual attacks on the Leagues. *La République de Loir-et-Cher*, on the other hand, carried a long series of articles about it: Aug. 28, Sept. 1, 8, 15, 22, and 29, 1935.

43. Potut, *L'Echo de la Nièvre*, Oct. 19; *L'Action républicaine* (Tulle), Sept. 14. Of 42 papers examined, ten were indifferent, four pro-Mussolini, 11 strongly pro-League of Nations, seven mildly pro-League, and ten reluctantly felt they had to support the British.

44. Such sentiments can be found in *Le Journal de Marennes*, Sept. 15; *Ouest-Océan*, Sept. 21; Mortier, *Le Démocrate de Seine-et-Marne*, Oct. 5 (speech to General Assembly); Raoul Aubaud, *La République de l'Oise*, Sept. 26; and Henri Guernut, *La Tribune de l'Aisne*, Aug. 29—the author a former secretary-general of the Ligue des Droits de l'Homme!

45. Lamoureux, *Le Bourbonnais républicain*, Sept. 22; Cot, *Le Démocrate savoyard*, March 21, 1936.

46. See Soulié, pp. 464–69.

47. *La République de l'Oise,* Sept. 26, and Dec. 16, 17, and 19.

48. Lair, p. 52.

49. Oct. 31, Nov. 14, Nov. 21; see *Jadis,* II, 607–11.

50. *Ibid.,* p. 611.

51. *Ibid.,* pp. 607–11. Even Henri de Kerillis agreed that these statements had saved the cabinet. *L'Echo de Paris,* Dec. 16. 1935.

52. *Ibid.,* Nov. 8.

53. Herriot, *Jadis,* II, 635. Note also the great stress he placed on the insults in the meeting of the Executive Committee on Jan. 19, as reported in *Le Temps,* Jan. 21, 1936.

54. Rolland interview, Jan. 24, 1961. Also Marc Rucart, *La République des Vosges,* Jan. 25, 1936.

55. Sénac, *La République des travailleurs,* Jan. 13, 1936; Ferrand, *Le Courrier de la Creuse,* Jan. 19. See also Thiébaut, *La Tribune républicaine,* Jan. 3: he voted for the policy, which was that of the left, not for the man. Lamoureux, *Le Bourbonnais républicain,* Jan. 12: he voted against the foreign policy, but for the budget. *Le Journal de Marennes,* Jan. 5, published the communiqué of the Radicals who voted for the government; they decided to do it after Laval's speech; also, because they did not want to endanger the budget or the law on the Leagues.

56. *Candide,* Dec. 19, 1935.

57. Knapp, p. 68; Bardonnet (*Evolution,* p. 108), gives a more detailed account of this point of view.

58. Bonnefous, V, 370–71; it should be noted that 93 Radicals had already voted against Laval on Dec. 28 without provoking his resignation.

59. *Ibid.,* p. 371.

60. Goguel, *La Politique des partis,* pp. 506–7.

61. *L'Avenir du Cher,* Jan. 25; see also Georges Potut for identical sentiments, *L'Echo de la Nièvre,* Jan. 25.

62. Liautey, for example, said, "I acknowledge a mastery of maneuver that no one would dream of contesting" (*J.O.Ch.,* Jan. 16, 1936, p. 32).

63. De Tessan, *Le Temps,* Jan. 16. Also *La Dépêche de Toulouse, L'Ere nouvelle, La France de Bordeaux, Le Petit Journal, Le Petit Parisien, L'Oeuvre,* Jan. 15–18.

64. See above, p. 42.

65. *L'Oeuvre,* Jan. 17; *Le Temps,* Jan. 18.

66. Cited in Bonnefous, V, 371.

67. *Jadis,* II, 635; the other statements and rumors are from *L'Oeuvre,* Jan. 18, 19. Bertrand's speech in the Charente-Inférieure, "It was actually with relief that I decided, without awaiting the decision of the Executive Committee, to follow President Herriot into retirement" (*Le Temps,* Feb. 5, 1936).

68. See, for example, *La Dépêche de Toulouse,* Jan. 18.

69. At the majority Group meeting, *Le Temps,* Jan. 19.

70. Jan. 18: *La Dépêche de Toulouse,* Jan. 19; Jan. 21: *Le Temps,* Jan. 22.

71. Besides Soulié's account of Herriot during this period, see the admirable and sympathetic article by Marc Rucart in *La République des Vosges,* Jan. 25, 1936.

72. *Le Temps,* Dec. 20, 1935.

73. Dominique Caravaggio, *Le Journal,* Dec. 19, 1935, cited by Herriot, *Jadis,* II, 626, as a faithful account of the incident; the incident is also reported by Archimbaud (who was sitting with Herriot on the platform), *Le Journal de Die et de la Drôme,* Dec. 28; Lamoureux's memoirs, *Le Bourbonnais républicain,* Feb. 26, 1956; and Milhaud, *La France de Bordeaux,* Jan. 19, 1936, and *La Tribune républicaine de la Haute-Garonne,* Dec. 29, 1935.

74. Interview with Addé-Vidal, Feb. 18, 1961.

75. Kayser, "Le Parti radical-socialiste," p. 289.

76. The Senate Radicals passed a motion trying to persuade Herriot to change his mind on Jan. 17 (*La Dépêche de Toulouse,* Jan. 18). Chautemps is promoted in *Le Journal de Marennes* of Dec. 29, 1935. I have seen a letter dated Jan. 10, 1936, from Chautemps to Roland Manescau, the extreme-right-wing secretary-general of the Jeunesses Radicales, in which Chautemps said that he (Manescau) would understand why he did not want to take part in any fight between friends.

77. *J.O.Ch.,* Jan. 16, 1936, pp. 30–31.

78. *L'Oeuvre,* Jan. 16. Archimbaud is said to have agreed and, according to *Le Petit Parisien* of the same date, Zay did also.

79. Jan. 25, 1936. See also on this crisis, Pierre du Clain, *La Lumière,* Feb. 1; Bonnefous, V, 373–75; Goguel, *La Politique des partis,* pp. 507–8; Marcus, p. 163; Herriot, *Jadis,* II, 638; Soulié, pp. 476–77. Zay, pp. 196–97, gives an excellent description of the formation of the government. Gaston Martin wrote that the attitude of the right had brought about Concentration on the left (*Le Démocrate de Lot-et-Garonne,* Feb. 2).

CHAPTER 8

1. Feb. 3; reported in *Le Temps,* Feb. 5, 1936.

2. Lamoureux's memoirs, *Le Bourbonnais républicain,* Feb. 26, 1956.

3. Both Auriol's and the Communists' statements reported in *Le Temps,* March 19, citing *L'Ere nouvelle.*

4. Executive Committee, March 18, *Le Temps,* March 20; Kayser, "Le Parti radical-socialiste," p. 280; *La Lumière,* March 15. The conservative Radicals sent a letter, a copy of which is in Geistdoerfer's papers, to all the deputies, denouncing the Auriol proposal and denying that the Radicals accepted the program.

5. Laurens, *La République de Loir-et-Cher,* April 29; *La République de la Corrèze,* May 10, regrets that Jaubert is now tied by an imperative mandate; Bastid is reported as signing, *Le Temps,* April 30; Lallemant signed, *La Défense républicaine,* May 2; Girard signed, but still the Socialists attacked him, *L'Action jurassienne,* April 18; Cabanis signed, *L'Avenir de Pithiviers,* May 2; Sénac refused to sign and was defeated, *La République des travailleurs,* April 9; both Cornu and Durand were asked to sign and refused, and the Socialists fought them.

6. Zay, *Souvenirs,* p. 199.

7. *Ibid.,* p. 65.

8. Chautemps maintained later that he had not said a word in the cabinet meeting; but most of the decisions were taken outside the formal meeting (letter addressed to Pertinax, July 1943, in the Bibliothèque de Documentation Internationale Contemporaine).

9. *Le Temps,* March 8.   10. *Ibid.,* March 11.

11. *La République de Loir-et-Cher,* April 26.   12. *Le Démocrate* (Dax), May 3.

13. *La Tribune républicaine de la Haute-Garonne,* May 3.

14. *Le Républicain de Chinon,* Jan. 30, 1936.

15. Nicolas le Rouge, *Le Citoyen* (Quimper), Jan. 16 (a left-wing constituency).

16. Cabanis, *L'Avenir de Pithiviers,* May 2, his italics; Cot also had to come out in favor of private property, *Le Petit Savoyard,* May 2.

17. Chambonnet: *Le Réveil de la Creuse,* April 17; Malvy, *La Gauche quercynoise,* April 18, his italics; Sclafer, *Le Démocrate* (Jonzac), April 25; Queuille, *La Montagne corrézienne,* April 5.

18. *La Tribune picarde* (Somme), May 2. Italics in the original.

19. Raymond Millet, *Le Temps,* Oct. 19, 1935; Pfeiffer in *Le Capital,* reprinted in *Le Réveil de la Creuse,* April 10, 1936.

20. Bonnefous, V, 420; Dupeux, p. 131. The published returns of 115 deputies were considerably exaggerated; not until very late did the Radicals manage to have more than 108 or 109, not counting those who were "apparenté."

21. Percentage of strength in 1936 Chamber compared to strength in 1932 Chamber: left, 86 per cent; moderate left, 70 per cent; moderate, 58 per cent; conservative, 75 per cent.

22. Manent, *Congress,* Oct. 24, 1936, p. 275.

23. Ribera, p. 27.

24. Goguel, *La Politique des partis,* p. 514; in 1937 he says, "many of them encouraged the opposition of their friends in the Senate" (p. 515).

25. *Le Bulletin quotidien,* May 20, 1936, p. 115 A-6 *bis,* claimed that 27 were opposed. *Le Temps,* May 6, quotes a former secretary-general (Milhaud?) as predicting an opposition of 26.

26. Leites, p. 87.

27. From *La Dépêche de Toulouse,* cited in *Le Temps* editorial, Aug. 14, 1936. Georges Potut (*L'Echo de la Nièvre,* June 13, 1936) used the same argument. Paul Marchandeau (*L'Eclaireur de l'Est,* May 9, 1937) also said he was loyally supporting the government.

28. Lamoureux's memoirs, *Le Bourbonnais républicain,* April 29, 1956.

29. See Goguel, *La Politique des partis,* pp. 513-15.

30. Zay, *Souvenirs,* pp. 428-29; Bastid interview, Feb. 12, 1961.

31. Audry (pp. 119, 124) claims a majority of Radicals was opposed to intervention; this is accepted by Albertini (p. 155) and Van den Esch (p. 54). Toynbee (pp. 139-40) blames the Radicals. On the Spanish question, see also Thomas, pp. 213-14, 218-19, 223-25, 234-35; Broué and Témime, pp. 299-302; Feiling, p. 299; Zay, *Souvenirs,* pp. 114-15; Cot, *Le Procès,* I, 22, 138. The controversy between Blum and Jean Piot is in *L'Oeuvre,* March 6, 8, 10, 1939, and *Le Populaire,* March 7, 9. Blum, *Commission de 1933 à 1945,* I, 219, July 22, 1947; Lamoureux, *Le Bourbonnais républicain,* June 3, 1956, and unpublished memoirs, pp. 1824-25.

32. *Commission de 1933 à 1945,* pp. 216-17.

33. See Laurens addressing Chautemps at a Radical meeting at Herbault, Jan. 31, 1937: "Thanks to you we have nonintervention in Spain and have avoided war in Europe" (*La République de Loir-et-Cher,* Feb. 7, 1937).

34. See the Los Rios letter in Brasillach, pp. 216-18; also Toynbee, pp. 140-41; Van den Esch, pp. 52-54; Audry, p. 119.

35. Wilson to Secretary of State, Aug. 10, 1936, in *Foreign Relations of the United States, 1936,* p. 477; also Straus to Secretary of State, July 27, 1936, p. 448, *ibid.*

36. Pp. 114-15. Zay, according to Blum, had one of the three sets of minutes taken at the cabinet meeting on Aug. 8 (*Commission de 1933 à 1945,* I, 217). Cot also said Daladier favored the Republicans (interview, Dec. 21, 1960). The rumors of the time agreed with this (*Aux écoutes,* Sept. 26, 1936, pp. 22-23); and Piot was sure enough to write in 1939 that Daladier's sympathy was public knowledge. Blum's denial of this statement at that time (*Le Populaire,* March 9, 1939) concerns only the cabinet meeting of Aug. 8, when the decisions had already been made, and when, according to Dezarnaulds, "Blum obliged us all to decide unanimously in favor of nonintervention" (letter to the author, Sept. 5, 1962).

37. Bastid interview, Feb. 12, 1961.

38. Cot interview, Dec. 21, 1960.

39. *L'Oeuvre,* Feb. 17, 1939.

40. André Liautey has written me: "I can only confirm your impressions regarding my Radical colleagues in the cabinet," in a letter dated Nov. 9, 1962.

41. Thomson, pp. 199–200.

42. Sauvy, *L'Opinion publique,* pp. 72–73; italics in original.

43. Duverger, *Cours de vie politique,* p. 97. Albertini (p. 159) also stresses the social reforms.

44. Dupeux prints the program on pp. 179–83.

45. Both at the Executive Committee, *Le Temps,* Jan. 21, 1936.

46. *Congress,* Oct. 24, 1936—Chautemps, p. 332, Marchandeau, p. 374, Dominique, p. 391.

47. *Ibid.,* p. 415. Also speech at Apt, *Le Temps,* March 21, 1937.

48. Reported in *L'Oeuvre,* Nov. 11, 1938.

49. *La République des travailleurs,* July 11, 1937; also Gaston Riou, a very conservative deputy, praised the government's "generous workers' policy" (*La République des Cévennes,* June 26, 1937).

50. *Congress,* Oct. 23, 1936, pp. 112–44.

51. *J.O.Ch.,* Feb. 26, 1937, p. 796.

52. *Congress,* Oct. 27, 1938, p. 384.

53. Reprinted in *Le Réveil de la Creuse,* Oct. 2, 1936.

54. *La République des Cévennes,* Oct. 10.

55. *Le Journal de Marennes,* Oct. 3.

56. Particularly during Mendès-France's economic debate with Potut; in which the latter claimed that "devaluation is contrary to Radical doctrine" (*Congress,* Oct. 23, 1936, pp. 181–214).

57. *Congress,* Oct. 24, 1936, pp. 344–61.

58. Arnaud Denjoy, Councillor-General of the Gers, *La République des travailleurs,* Aug. 1, 1937.

59. Latty and Royer, "Les Radicaux," p. 106.

60. *L'Union démocratique de la Haute-Saône,* May 19, 1936. Also letter to the author, Oct. 31, 1960.

61. *L'Avenir de Pithiviers,* July 9, 1938. See also Arnaud Denjoy, *La République des travailleurs,* Aug. 1, 1937; Mitton, in *Le Patriote de Châteaudun,* Aug. 30, 1936, said he was happier with the Wheat Board than with all the other reforms put together; he repeated this on Feb. 2, 1937; Delattre, *Sedan-républicain,* Aug. 8, 1936; Bernier, *Le Progrès de Loches,* July 2, 9, 16, 1936; on July 27, 1939, he wrote that he had always been in favor of the Wheat Board and now everyone was in favor.

62. *Congress,* Oct. 26, 1938, p. 323. Alroy has shown how the Radicals managed to use the Wheat Board to strengthen the economic position of the peasants who most strongly supported them (Chap. 6, pp. 41–43).

63. *J.O.Ch.,* Feb. 26, 1937, pp. 795–96.

64. Kayser, "Le Parti radical-socialiste," p. 290.

65. De Jouvenel, *Après la défaite,* p. 120.

66. *J.O.Ch.,* June 6, 1936, p. 1343.

67. *Le Temps,* May 23, July 3.

68. *La Tribune républicaine,* May 8, June 12, 1936.

69. *Le Temps,* June 13, 1936, report of the meeting of June 11.

70. Blois, June 28, reported in *Le Temps,* June 29.

71. *La République des Cévennes,* Dec. 5, 1936; also Oct. 10, 17. Also Lamoureux, *Le Bourbonnais républicain,* Sept. 27; Georges Potut, *L'Echo de la Nièvre,* Aug. 22; *La Tribune républicaine de la Haute-Garonne,* autumn, 1936.

72. Archimbaud, *Le Journal de Die et de la Drôme,* May 21, 1938; Crutel, *L'Eveil,* Aug. 29, 1936; Perrier, Barral (thesis), p. 684; Albert and Georges Le Bail, *Le Citoyen* (Quimper), Aug. 27, Sept. 8, and Oct. 10, 1936; H. Bonnet and Mitton, *Le Patriote de Châteaudun,* Aug. 23, 1936, April 24, 1938.

73. William Bertrand, *Le Journal de Marennes,* Aug. 30, 1936; *Le Républicain de Loir-et-Cher,* Aug. 16; Bernier, *Le Progrès de Loches,* Jan. 14, 1937, March 2, 1939; V. Rotinat, *La République de l'Indre,* Jan. 22, 1939.

74. For example, Gaston Thiébaut, *La Tribune républicaine,* Sept. 4, 18, 1936, April 8, 1938.

75. *La République de l'Oise,* Oct. 25, 1936.

76. *L'Avenir républicain,* April 4, 18, 1938; *Sedan-républicain,* Aug. 15, 1936, Dec. 12, 1936.

77. *Le Démocrate du Jura,* June 6, Oct. 31, 1936.

78. Reported in *Le Temps,* Sept. 16.   79. *Congress,* Oct. 22, 1936, p. 27.

80. Oct. 25.   81. *Congress,* Oct. 22, p. 23.

82. *L'Oeuvre,* Oct. 24.   83. *Congress,* Oct. 24, p. 354.

84. Kayser, "Le Parti radical-socialiste," p. 281.

85. *Congress,* Oct. 24, 1936, p. 373.

86. *Marianne,* Oct. 28; *Vendredi,* Oct. 30.

87. *La Lumière,* Oct. 30.

88. H. Bonnet, *Le Patriote de Châteaudun,* Nov. 1, 1936. See also Kayser, "Le Parti radical-socialiste," p. 281.

89. Armand Dupuis, speech at the Executive Committee, May 22, 1936, in *Bulletin du parti républicain-radical et radical-socialiste,* June 2; Lamoureux, *Le Bourbonnais républicain,* May 3; Crutel, *L'Eveil,* May 9; Rucart, *La République des Vosges,* May 23; Kayser, *La République de l'Oise,* July 11.

90. *Congress,* Oct. 26, 1936, p. 25.

91. *Dinan-républicain,* Oct. 22, 1936.

92. *Congress,* Oct. 29, 1938, p. 665.

93. *L'Oeuvre,* Nov. 11, 1938.

94. *Ibid.* For Paul Bastid, anti-Communism was a "negative mystique," which diverted attention from the massive problems facing the country (*ibid.,* Nov. 20, 1938).

95. Maizy, p. 152.   96. *La Lumière,* June 11, 1937.

97. Oct. 16, 1937.   98. *Le Temps,* Oct. 17, 1937.

99. *Esprit,* May 1939, p. 206.   100. Oct. 17, 1935.

101. *La République des Cévennes,* Oct. 31, 1936.

102. *Ibid.,* Dec. 5, 1936.

103. *Le Temps,* Dec. 18, 1936.

104. Note on the decline of the Popular Front prepared by Ducos for the author.

105. Bardonnet, *Evolution,* pp. 186–96.

106. The principal sources for this discussion are the collections of the two principal newspapers, *La Relève* of the dominant faction, edited by Roland Manescau, and *Le Jacobin* of the dissident left-wing minority, edited by Jacques Mitterand; complete collections of both, unavailable at the Bibliothèque Nationale, were loaned to me by Manescau and Mitterand. In addition I used copies of *La Jeune Gauche,* paper of one of the left-wing splinter movements, personal papers and clippings assembled by Manescau, the general Paris press, and interviews with Manescau, Mitterand, Ribera, Laforêt —all former Jeunesses Radicales—and additional information from interviews with Kayser, Anxionnaz, Roche, and Bauzin. Bauzin's papers, especially a mimeographed circular by Sableau complaining about the Federation of the Seine's support of the dissident left, dated May 19, 1937, were also illuminating.

107. See *La Jeune Gauche,* Nov. 15, 1934, Dec. 15, 1934, special issue, Jan. 20, 1935; mimeographed circular no. 2, 1935, Fédération des Jeunesses Radicales de France, Jan. 28, 1935, minutes of the Executive Committee, Jan. 12 and 24, 1935.

108. Eight hundred members in 1933, 2,000 in 1934, as many as 8,000 at the beginning of 1935 (Millet interview with Sableau, *Le Temps,* Feb. 18, 1935; Bardonnet, *Evolution,* p. 190).

109. *Ouest-Eclair,* Oct. 27, 1934; also see praise from *La Croix* [!] and *L'Aube* of the same date, and of the very conservative Radical René Besnard in *La République tourangelle,* Oct. 28, 1933.

110. *Le Temps* report by Raymond Millet, Feb. 17 and 18. Sableau (*La France radicale. Bulletin official des jeunesses,* March 1935) comments on its effects. The report is reprinted in Millet and Arbellot, pp. 56–62.

111. In an interview in *Le Courrier royal,* May 5, 1937, Sableau said 28,000; the Federation of the Aude alone claimed 2,700 members (*Le Bourbonnais républicain,* Sept. 19, 1937). These figures are probably exaggerated; Bardonnet thinks it was probably closer to 15,000 real adherents (*Evolution,* p. 190). This is quite a few for France. The Jeunesses Socialistes in 1935 had only 16,328, although this rapidly increased to a high of 54,000 in 1937 (Parti socialiste, *XXXVIe Congrès,* p. 191).

112. The Federations of the Oise and the Aube also withdrew; those who did not attend the Congress of Carcassonne were the Seine, sections of the Seine-et-Oise, the Jacobin section of Seine-Inférieure, the Oise, Pas-de-Calais, Meurthe-et-Moselle, Aube, and Vosges (*Le Jacobin,* May 1937). See also *La Lumière,* Nov. 5, 1937.

113. *La Jeune Gauche,* special issue, Jan. 20, 1935.

114. "Pour un radicalisme de combat," *La Relève,* Feb. 20, 1937.

115. Sableau, interview in *La Petite Gironde,* cited in *Le Temps,* editorial, April 12, 1937; Manescau, *La France radicale,* March 1933.

116. Speech, Carcassonne, *Le Temps,* April 19, 1937.

117. Sableau to Millet, *Le Temps,* Feb. 18, 1935; statement quoted by Eudlitz in a specially printed number of *La Jeune Gauche* for members of the Jeunesses Radicales only, Jan. 20, 1935.

118. At Carcassonne, *Le Temps,* April 19, 1937.

119. *La Relève,* Oct. 1, 1938.

120. Manescau, *ibid.,* Nov. 20, 1938.

121. Henry Ivan, "Où va le parti radical?" *Le Pays réel,* Feb. 1938, pp. 29–47, 36–38. See also Sableau, "La France aux français," *La Relève,* Jan. 15, 1938.

122. *Ibid.,* May 5, 1938.

123. "B.S.," *Esprit,* May 1939, p. 173; see also Bardonnet, *Evolution,* pp. 194–95.

124. See Ramonet's report on violence to the dissident Paris federation of the J.R.'s on Nov. 13, 1936 (*Le Jacobin,* Nov. 1936). See also *La République,* Oct. 23, 1936. Crutel recounts an attack at the Brasserie de Strasbourg (*L'Eveil,* Nov. 1, 1937).

125. *Le Temps,* Oct. 24, 1937, p. 8.

126. *La Lumière,* Nov. 5, 1937.

127. *Aux écoutes* (Feb. 13, 1937, p. 6) reports a meeting of the Bureau of the party where the complaint was made that the Jeunesses was losing its troops to fascism.

128. *Le Républicain de Chinon,* June 10, 1937, letter from Sableau.

129. Manescau interview, March 11, 1961; he and Kayser said Roche was not deeply involved. Anxionnaz, who was assistant secretary-general of the party at the time, said that Bonnet and Roche were involved, but that Milhaud was too much a republican to get his hands dirty with such people (interview, March 15, 1961).

130. Present at Carcassonne: Mistler, Riou, Paul Richard, Lamoureux, Castel, Ducos, Meyer, Daille, Compayré, Pecherot, Delcos, Baron, Badie, Malric, Bousgarbiès, Alber-

tini, deputies; Delthil, Guilhem, Raynaud, Garrigou, Lavergen, Rambaud, Loubet, Loubat, Presseq, Maulion, senators (*La Relève,* May 1937).

131. According to *Le Temps,* April 19, 1937; 10,000, if one believes *La Relève,* May 1937.

132. Note prepared by Ducos for the author.

133. *Royan,* Nov. 8, 1936.

134. *Ibid.,* April 11, 18, 25, May 2, 16, June 20, and July 11, 1937.

135. *Le Démocrate,* Jonzac, May 1; Royan, May 2.

136. *Royan,* April 25.

137. Speech at Blois, *L'Oeuvre,* March 21, 1938.

138. Werth, *Lost Statesman,* p. 9.

CHAPTER 9

1. "First of all," said Zyromski, "it is incontestable that the government of M. Chautemps is not a real government of Popular Front because of its very composition" (Socialist Congress, July 12, 1937, reported in *Le Populaire,* July 13). Vallat's and Marin's speeches, *J.O.Ch.,* June 29, 1937, pp. 2060–61, 2056.

2. *Ibid.,* p. 2054.

3. *La République de Loir-et-Cher,* June 20, 27, 1937.

4. Millet remarked in 1935 that some Radicals were willing to have an electoral coalition with the left, although they would prefer that the words "Front Populaire" be changed into something less aggressive (*Le Temps,* Oct. 19, 1935).

5. *Ibid.*

6. Herriot's speech at Salle Rameau, Lyons, *ibid.,* April 14, 1932.

7. Paul Richard, *Barodet,* 1936, p. 1200.

8. *J.O.Ch.,* June 29, 1937, p. 2061.

9. See Chautemps's statements before the Group, *Le Temps,* June 23, and *J.O.Ch.,* June 29, pp. 2069–72; and Bonnet's speech, *Congress,* Oct. 29, 1937, pp. 340–52.

10. *La Lumière,* July 2, 1937. *Aux écoutes* reports crises on the following issues: the replacement of Labeyrie as Governor of the Bank of France by Beaudoin (July 10, 24, 1937); the railways and wheat prices (Aug. 28); the declaration of Rambuteau (Sept. 18, Oct. 2). *La Lumière* reports a crisis over the run on gold (Oct. 8). By November even *Le Temps* was talking about the Socialists' dissatisfaction (editorial, Nov. 10).

11. Roche speech in the Nord, *Le Temps,* Sept. 28.

12. *Congress,* Oct. 29, pp. 322–52.

13. *Ibid.,* p. 353.

14. *Ibid.,* p. 355.

15. Reported in *Candide,* Nov. 4.

16. Roche interview, Jan. 16, 1961.

17. *Congress,* Oct. 29, pp. 379–80.

18. *Ibid.,* Oct. 30, pp. 544–49.

19. *Candide,* Nov. 4, 1937.

20. Kayser, "Le Parti radical-socialiste," pp. 282–83.

21. See *Revue de Paris,* Oct. 1, 1937, for a good and extensive analysis, pp. 712–17.

22. Lamoureux, *Le Bourbonnais républicain,* Oct. 17, 1937.

23. Goguel, *La Politique des partis,* p. 522.

24. Lamoureux's memoirs, p. 1786; Daladier, *Congress,* Oct. 28, 1937, p. 189; Ripault, reporter on general policy (*ibid.,* Oct. 30, p. 503), claimed a gain of 200,000 votes over the elections of 1936; also the motion read by Mazé (*ibid.,* p. 544). A close analysis made by the Alliance Démocratique claimed the Popular Front had lost 400,000 votes, that there were only 639 Popular Front councillors-general as against 858 anti-Popular Front (*Elections cantonales,* p. x).

25. Editorial and report of meeting, *Le Temps*, Oct. 15, 1937; *Le Populaire*, Oct. 14–17, 24, 26, 29.

26. *Congress*, Oct. 28, 1937, p. 190. See also Raymond Millet's "enquête" (*Le Temps*, Oct. 17), which pointed out that the Socialists were far worse in this matter than the Communists. See also p. 182n., above.

27. *Le Journal de Marennes*, Oct. 17; *Le Temps*, Oct. 16.

28. *Le Temps*, Oct. 17.

29. See the joint letter of Liautey and Maugière, deputies, and André Maroselli and Moïse Lévy, senators, in *L'Union démocratique de la Haute-Saône*, April 5, 1938; and report of the meeting of the federation, Oct. 16, 1938, Oct. 18, 1938, *ibid*.

30. *J.O.Ch.*, Jan. 13, 1938, p. 24.

31. *J.O.Ch.*, Jan. 13, pp. 28–29.

32. Bonnet, *Défense*, p. 60.

33. Report of Cadillac meeting, Jan. 15, 1938. *L'Epoque*, Jan. 16. Paul Bernier (*Le Progrès de Loches*, Jan. 20) said that he talked with Chautemps many times during the evening and did not think that at any time he desired to resign; but he gradually became irritated at the pettiness of the debate, and toward two in the morning (therefore *before* the Ramette speech, but after successfully getting the support of the Socialists!) he let Bernier understand that he was considering leaving. *La Lumière* (Jan. 21) said that Chautemps did not yield to a fit of bad humor, but that the resignation was a plot.

34. Halévy, *1938*, pp. 7–18.

35. *Le Populaire*, Jan. 15, 1937.

36. See the report in *L'Epoque*, Jan. 16, 1938, which claims that he purposely exaggerated Blum's reply at the meeting of the Group.

37. *L'Epoque*, Jan. 17. Most papers give these figures. *L'Epoque* gives 32–24 with 40 abstentions; *Le Populaire* increased the number to 80 abstentions, but was alone in this contention. *L'Humanité* of Jan. 17 says he got 31 out of 107 votes.

38. Jan. 21, 1938.

39. *Candide*, Jan. 20. Potut, one of Bonnet's supporters, wrote, "It is useless to speculate now on whether he could have done better in managing his tactics better" (*L'Echo de la Nièvre*, Jan. 22, 1938).

40. In addition to the standard Paris newspapers the account of Bonnet's attempt has been constructed from the following sources: *La République de l'Oise*, Jan. 16, 20; *Sedan-républicain*, Jan. 22; G. Riou, *La République des Cévennes*, Jan. 22 (who claims very interestingly that the Communists went into opposition over Delbos's foreign policy); Rotinat, *La République de l'Indre*, Jan. 22; Bernier, *Le Progrès de Loches*, Jan. 20; *L'Eveil* (Rouen), Jan. 25; *La Frontière* (Belfort), Jan. 18; and Lamoureux's memoirs, p. 1765.

41. Bullitt dispatch, Feb. 21, reporting a conversation with Chautemps, *U.S. Foreign Relations, 1938*, pp. 24–25.

42. Bonnet interview, Dec. 4, 1960.

43. Sinsout, *La Dordogne républicaine*, Oct. 1, 1960.

44. E.g., Crutel, *L'Eveil*, Jan. 25, 1938.

45. *Sedan-républicain*, Jan. 21, 1938.

46. *J.O.Ch.*, Jan. 21, 1938, pp. 43–44.

47. *U.S. Foreign Relations, 1938*, two dispatches of Feb. 21, pp. 24–27, 28–29.

48. *J.O.Ch.*, Jan. 13, 1938, p. 23.

49. Speech at Soings-en-Sologne, *La République de Loir-et-Cher*, March 26, 1938. The party's explanation followed this line, as in Chichery's speech, Federation of the Seine, March 30, 1939 (Bauzin papers).

50. *Commission de 1933 à 1945*, III, Feb. 10, 1948, p. 661. Also Paul-Boncour's testimony, *ibid.*, IV, March 9, 1948, p. 801; and his *Entre deux guerres*, III, 81.

51. *Le Démocrate* (Dax), April 3, 1938.

52. *Commission de 1933 à 1945*, Marin's testimony, Feb. 10, 1948, III, 661.

53. *L'Oeuvre*, March 10, 1938.

54. *Le Petit Troyen*, April 10, 1938; also Albert Le Bail, *Le Citoyen* (Finistère), March 19.

55. *L'Oeuvre*, March 12.

56. André Guerin, *L'Oeuvre*, March 12.

57. *L'Oeuvre*, March 14.

58. Statement in the Group, April 4, 1938 (*La République*, April 5). He demanded Union Nationale in the Bureau, March 17; the Group was reported to be very unhappy, March 22 (*Le Petit Parisien*, April 5; *Le Progrès de Lyon* and *La Dépêche de Toulouse*, March 18, 23).

59. *La Dépêche de Toulouse*, April 1, 4, 1938.

60. *Sedan-républicain*, April 9.

61. *Le Petit Parisien*, April 4.

62. *L'Oeuvre*, April 3. Ellipses in original.

63. *La Lumière*, Nov. 18, 1938. Lamoureux writes that when he succeeded Reynaud as Finance Minister he treated the grateful senators with the respect Reynaud had refused them (Memoirs, p. 1880).

64. See Sauvy, *L'Opinion publique*, p. 45.

65. *L'Oeuvre*, April 1, 4, and 6, 1939.

66. *Aux écoutes*, Dec. 17, 1938; *La Lumière*, Sept. 2, 1938; Jan. 1, Nov. 3, 1939; *L'Oeuvre*, April 1, 20, 1939.

67. See *Aux écoutes*, Feb. 12, 1938, p. 23.

68. See below, pp. 246–47.

69. Frossard, pp. 174–75.

70. Lamoureux's memoirs, p. 1859. The quaestor was the Assembly's watchdog over its own funds, supplies, and internal management.

71. Paul-Boncour reports that Perfetti called Daladier during the formation of the Daladier government and implies that the Perfetti group helped prevent his being foreign minister in the Daladier government, III, 100; also Liautey interview on the Perfetti group.

72. Halévy, *1938*, p. 50.

73. See Faure's telegram to Bonnet, *La Dordogne républicaine*, Oct. 1, 1960.

74. Oct. 28, 1938.

75. *Commission de 1933 à 1945*, Blum testimony, July 30, 1947, I, 255; *U.S. Foreign Relations, 1938*, p. 712, Bullitt to Secretary of State, Oct. 3, 1938.

76. De Monzie, *Ci-devant*, pp. 6–41; Roche, p. 280; Fabre-Luce, *Histoire secrète*, pp. 56–80; Zay, *Carnets secrets*, pp. 3–19; Lamoureux's memoirs, pp. 1784–87; Champeaux, II, 144–47, 149, 159–61; Lombard, pp. 225–28; *Commission de 1933 à 1945*, Sarraut testimony, Feb. 10, 1948, III, 662–64.

77. *L'Oeuvre*, Sept. 24; Zay, *Carnets secrets*, p. 9; Champeaux, II, 159–61.

78. Lamoureux's memoirs, pp. 1786–87.

79. Fabre-Luce, *Histoire secrète*, pp. 79–81.

80. Vincent Rotinat, *La République de l'Indre*, Oct. 1.

81. *La République de l'Indre*, Oct. 16; *La Voix du Centre*, Oct. 15.

82. Raymond Millet, *Le Temps*, Oct. 19; Zay, *Carnets secrets*, p. 28.

83. *Dinan-républicain*, May 4, 1939.

84. *Le Démocrate savoyard*, Oct. 8.

85. *La Frontière,* Dec. 12, 1938.

86. *Le Réveil de la Creuse,* March 3, 1939.

87. *L'Echo de la Nièvre,* Feb. 25, 1939.

88. *Congress,* Bayet, Oct. 29, 1938, pp. 641–49; Daladier, Oct. 27, pp. 368–89.

89. *Ibid.,* Oct. 26, pp. 155–77.

90. See *La Lumière,* Nov. 5, 18; *Aux écoutes,* Nov. 19, p. 24

91. *Congress,* Oct. 28, pp. 528–30.

92. *L'Oeuvre,* Jan. 16, 1939; *Le Temps,* Jan. 17.

93. Potut (conservative) said in *L'Echo de la Nièvre* on Nov. 26, 1938, that it was technically good, but brutal, and compared it unfavorably with Blum's policy the preceding spring!

94. *Le Temps,* Jan. 17; Potut, *L'Echo de la Nièvre,* Jan. 21.

95. *L'Agence radicale,* Jan. 26, 1939, No. 6 (mimeographed). *Le Jacobin,* Jan. 27, said Martinaud-Déplat was in charge of the operation.

96. There was one delegate for every 25 cards or fraction thereof held; in 1939 there were 254 elected delegates and 168 ex officio members (Bauzin papers).

97. Bauzin interview, July 3, 1959; on the election, see *La France radicale,* Jan., 1939; *L'Echo républicain de Neuilly,* Feb. 12; *L'Oeuvre,* Jan. 12, 14; and a typed speech by Bauzin at the General Assembly, Feb. 27, in the Bauzin papers.

98. *L'Oeuvre,* March 10.

99. *Le Temps,* Jan. 17.

100. *L'Oeuvre,* March 26.

101. *J.O.Ch.,* March 19, 1940, p. 576.

102. Voting figures from *Le Temps,* March 21, 1940.

103. *La Dépêche de Toulouse,* March 22, 1940; Milhaud, *L'Ere nouvelle,* March 23; Bayet, *L'Oeuvre,* March 25; Delattre, *Sedan-républicain,* April 14; Thiébaut, *La Tribune républicaine,* March 30; Bernier, *Le Progrès de Loches,* March 28; Riou, *La République des Cévennes,* March 30; and Archimbaud, *Le Journal de Die et de la Drôme,* April 13, 1940.

104. Galimand said of Reynaud: "He has proved by the rapidity with which he brought his cabinet together that his foresight did not fail him." *J.O.Ch.,* March 22, 1940, p. 596. Also Vincent Badie's hostile speech, pp. 598–99, and Blum's reply, pp. 604–5.

105. *L'Epoque,* March 23, 1940.

106. Bonnet confirmed the reports in the press that he was trying to defeat the government (interview, Dec. 4, 1960).

107. Nicolet, *Le Radicalisme,* p. 100; 11 on Tony Révillon's list, p. 66.

108. According to Badie's list, the 14 included himself, Manent, Emmanuel Roy, Mendiondou, Gout, Hay, Isoré, Delaunay, Thiébaut, Crutel, Pascaud, Pecherot, Albert Le Bail, André Albert. *Commission de 1933 à 1945,* VIII, March 30, 1950, p. 2271.

109. Soulié, pp. 499–500.

110. Aron, p. 152; for the whole July session see *ibid.,* pp. 127–55; Odin, pp. 31–33, 35–36; Barthe, pp. 70, 93; Paul-Boncour, III, p. 274; Manent, *Commission de 1933 à 1945,* IV, letter, pp. 509–10; Maurice Netter told me that Herriot persuaded the deputy Lucien Bossoutrot—who was from the same arrondissement as Netter—to vote for Laval's project, much to his later regret (interview, March 6, 1961).

111. Nicolet, *Le Radicalisme,* p. 100.

112. Romains, *Bataille,* Nov. 8, 1945.

113. From a list supplied by M. André Schmidt of the Place de Valois; it was published more or less correctly in *Le Monde,* Dec. 23, 1944.

114. Micaud, "French Political Parties, p. 116.

115. Chevallier, *Histoire de la France moderne,* p. 604, n. 1: "To talk of this as Union Nationale in the sense of Poincaré in 1926 . . . or of Doumergue in 1934 . . . seems to go too far."

116. *L'Oeuvre,* Jan. 9, 15, 26, 1939.

117. Goguel, *La Politique des partis,* p. 234.

118. Jan. 3, May 2, 1937; May 22, 29, 1938.

119. Three-way fights: Nice (1st), March 26, 1939; Marseilles (1st), April 2, 1939; Aubusson, March 26, 1939; Marennes, April 2, 1939. Withdrawal for right: Riom (2d), Sept. 6, 1936; Céret, April 10, 1938—some Radical voters going to the PSF, the rest staying away. Against Socialists: Lapalisse, Jan. 3, 1937; La Tour du Pin (2d), Aug. 6, 1939; Charolles (2d), Nov. 1, 1938. Against Communists: Montluçon, April 30, 1939. Recommending abstention: Mulhouse (1st), April 30, 1939. The Socialists withdrew three times in favor of Radicals during the legislature: Falaise, May 30, 1937; St.-Brieuc (1st), April 2, 1939; Loudun, June 18, 1939. (Numbers in parentheses indicate the constituency.)

120. Bécarud, pp. 51–52.

121. Chichery speech at the Federation of the Seine, March 3, 1939, typed manuscript from Bauzin's papers.

122. *Le Temps,* March 28, 1939; letter by Marcel Gitton in *L'Humanité,* April 7; letters by Rivière, of the Socialist federation and Citerne, Communist, and article, in *Le Courrier du Centre,* March 29; and Guernut in *La France de Bordeaux,* March 30.

123. *Le Démocrate* (Dax), Jan. 15, 1939.

124. *L'Oeuvre,* Jan. 5, 1940.

CONCLUSION

1. See Ehrmann, p. 886.

2. See Leibholz, pp. 96–100.

3. See Kirchheimer, "Waning of Opposition," p. 152.

4. Pertinax, p. 199.

Bibliography

The Bibliography is divided into three parts. The first is an alphabetical list of the books, articles, memoirs, and theses consulted in the preparation of this study. The second is a list of the Radical newspapers published throughout France during the 1930's. (The provincial newspapers are divided into four categories, according to their relationship to the local parliamentarian.) The third is a list of interviews with former Radical politicians.

WORKS CONSULTED

Alain. Eléments d'une doctrine radicale. Paris: Gallimard, 1925.

Albertini, Rudolf von. "Zur Beurteilung der Volksfront in Frankreich (1934–1938)," *Vierteljahreshefte für Zeitgeschichte,* April 1959, 130–62.

Allen, Luther. "The French Left and Soviet Russia to 1936: Interaction between French Party Alliances and Franco-Soviet Diplomacy." Unpublished doctoral dissertation, University of Chicago, 1955.

Almond, Gabriel A. "Comparative Political Systems," *Journal of Politics,* XVIII (1956), 391–409.

Alroy, Gil Carl. "Radicalism and Modernization: The French Problem." Unpublished doctoral dissertation, Princeton University, 1962.

Anglès, Raoul. Le Parti radical et la question d'Espagne. Paris: Editions Etoile, 1939.

Antériou, J. L., and J.-J. Baron. Edouard Herriot au service de la République. Paris: Editions du Dauphin, 1957.

Archimbaud, Léon. L'Avenir du radicalisme. Paris: Fasquelle, 1937.

———. L'heure des jacobins. Paris: Imprimerie de l'Oeuvre, [1937].

Aron, Robert. L'Histoire de Vichy. Paris: Fayard, 1954.

Aubaud, Raoul. "Le Parti radical en France," *L'Entente,* July–Sept. 1935.

Aubert, Louis, *et al.* André Tardieu. Paris: Plon, 1957.

Audry, Colette. Léon Blum, ou la politique du juste. Paris: Juillard, 1955.

Avril, P. "Les Origines du radicalisme: II, Les Crises du XXe siècle," *Cahiers de la République,* No. 3 (1956), pp. 72–79.

———. "Radicalisme et socialisme," *Cahiers de la République,* No. 4 (1956), pp. 8–16 and No. 7 (1957), pp. 109–19.

Bankwitz, Philip C. F. "Weygand: A Biographical Study," Unpublished doctoral dissertation, Harvard, 1952.

Bardèche, Jean. "Le Radicalisme d'Alain." Unpublished thesis, Institut d'Etudes Politiques, Paris, 1955.

Bardonnet, Daniel. Evolution de la structure du parti radical. Paris: Montchrestien, 1960.

————. "L'Organization locale du parti radical." Unpublished memoir for the Diplôme d'Etudes Supérieures, Institut d'Etudes Politiques, Paris, 1957.

Barodet. See France, Chambre des Députés.

Barral, Pierre. Le Département de l'Isère sous la Troisième République, 1870–1940. Paris: Colin, 1962. Cahiers de la Fondation Nationale des Sciences Politiques, No. 115.

————. "Le Département de l'Isère sous la IIIème République (1870–1940): Histoire sociale et histoire politique." Thesis for the *doctorat ès lettres,* University of Paris, 1959. More complete on the political history than the published work.

Barthe, Edouard. La Ténébreuse Affaire du Massilia: Une Page d'histoire (18 juin 1940–octobre 1940). Paris: Imprimerie Dupont, 1945.

Bauzin, Lucien. Unpublished papers.

Bayet, Albert. Le Radicalisme. Paris: Valois, [1932].

Beau de Loménie, Emmanuel. La Mort de la IIIe République. Paris: Editions du Conquistador, 1951.

Bécarud, J. "Esquisse d'une géographie électorale du parti communiste français entre les deux guerres (1920–1939)." Unpublished thesis for the *doctorat de l'université,* University of Paris, 1952.

Beloff, Max. "The Sixth of February," in James Joll, ed., The Decline of the Third Republic. London: Chatto and Windus, 1959. St. Anthony's Papers, No. 5.

Bendix, Reinhard, and Seymour Martin Lipset. "On the Social Structure of Western Societies: Some Reflections on Comparative Analysis," *Berkeley Journal of Sociology,* (1959), 1–15.

Benoist, Charles. "Le Programme radical-socialiste," *Revue universelle,* Oct. 1, 1934.

————. "Radical, radicaux, radicalisme," *Revue universelle,* Aug. 15, 1934, pp. 507–10.

Berl, Emmanuel. La Politique et les partis. Paris: Rieder, 1932.

Bernard, Lauréat Odilon Joseph. "Democratic Crisis of 1934 in France." Unpublished doctoral dissertation, Boston University Graduate School, 1957.

Bernard, Philippe. Economie et sociologie de la Seine-et-Marne (1850–1950). Paris: Colin, 1953. Cahiers de la Fondation Nationale des Sciences Politiques, No. 43.

Berteloot, Joseph. "La Crise du radicalisme," *Travaux de l'action populaire,* Nov. 1946, pp. 53–66.

————. "Le Radicalisme à la croisée des chemins," *La Vie intellectuelle,* Oct. 10, 1937, pp. 70–80.

———. "Vieux Radicalisme et jeune radicalisme," *Etudes,* LXXIV (Oct. 5, 1937), 97–105.

Binion, Rudolph. Defeated Leaders: The Political Fate of Caillaux, Jouvenel, and Tardieu. New York: Columbia University Press, 1960.

Bleton, Pierre. Les Hommes des temps qui viennent: Essai sur les classes moyennes. Paris: Editions Ouvrières, 1956.

Blum, Léon. Les Radicaux et nous (1932–1934). Paris: Librairie Populaire, 1936.

Bodin, Louis, and Jean Touchard. 1936: Le Front populaire. Paris: Colin, 1961. Collection Kiosque.

Bois, Elie J. Le Malheur de la France. London: Hachette. n.d.

Bois, Paul. Paysans de l'Ouest: Du Structure économique et sociale aux options politiques depuis l'époque révolutionnaire dans la Sarthe. Collection: Société et idéologies. The Hague: Mouton, 1961.

Bonnefous, Edouard. Histoire politique de la Troisième République, Vol. IV, Cartel des Gauches et Union Nationale (1924–1929); Vol. V, La République en danger: Des ligues au Front populaire (1930–1936); Paris: Presses Universitaires de France, 1960–62.

Bonnet, Georges E. Défense de la paix. Vol. I, De Washington au Quai d'Orsay. Geneva: Constant Bourquin, 1946.

———. Le Redressement financier réalisé par les gouvernements radicaux-socialistes, juin 1932–février 1934. Paris: Comité Exécutif, [1934].

Bonnevay, Laurent. Les Journées sanglantes de février 1934: Pages d'histoire. Paris: Flammarion, 1935.

Bonte, Florimond. "Le Front populaire et le parti radical," *Cahiers du bolchevisme,* July 15, 1935.

Borkenau, Franz. European Communism. New York: Harper, 1953.

Bourgin, Georges, and Jean Carrère. Manuel des partis politiques en France. Paris: Rieder, 1924.

Bracher, Karl Dietrich. "Problems of Parliamentary Democracy in Europe," *Daedalus,* Winter 1964, pp. 179–98.

Brasillach, Robert, and Maurice Bardèche. Histoire de la guerre d'Espagne. Paris: Plon, 1939.

Brogan, Denis W. The Development of Modern France (1870–1939). London: Hamish Hamilton, 1940.

Broué, Pierre, and Emile Témime. La Révolution et la guerre d'Espagne. Paris: Editions de Minuit, 1961.

Cameron, Elizabeth R. Prologue to Appeasement. Washington, D.C.: American Council on Public Affairs, 1942.

Cartier, Raymond. Histoire du radicalisme. Paris: Centre de Propagande des Républicains Nationaux, 1939.

Chaintron, Jean. "Le Parti radical et radical-socialiste," *Cahiers du communisme,* XXXI (Dec. 1955), 1536–48.

Chambaz, Jacques. Le Front populaire pour le pain, la liberté et la paix. Paris: Editions Sociales, 1961.

Champeaux, Georges. La Croisades des démocraties. Vol. I, Formation de la côterie de la guerre; Vol. II, De l'affaire tchèque au revirement de la cité. Paris: Editions du Centre d'Etudes de l'Agence Inter-France, 1942–43.

Chastenet, Jacques. Histoire de la Troisième République. Vol. VI, Déclin de la Troisième: 1931–1938; Vol. VII, Le Drame final: 1938–1940. Paris: Hachette, 1962–63.

Chautemps, Camille. Letter addressed to Pertinax, July 1943. Bibliothèque de Documentation Internationale Contemporaine, Paris.

Chevalier, Louis. Les Paysans: Etude d'histoire et d'économie rurales. Paris: Denoël, 1947.

Chevallier, Jean-Jacques. Histoire des institutions politiques de la France moderne (1789–1945). Paris: Dalloz, 1958. Etudes politiques, économiques et sociales, Vol. Vi.

———. Histoire des institutions politiques en France de 1789 à nos jours. Paris: Cours de Droit, 1949.

Chichery, Albert. Le Problème agricole et le parti radical. Paris: Comité Exécutif. n.d. Documents radicaux, No. 4.

Chopine, Paul. Six Ans chez les Croix de Feu. Paris: Gallimard, 1935.

Commission de 1933 à 1945. See France, Assemblée Nationale.

Commission du 6 février. See France, Chambre des Députés.

Cot, Pierre. Le Procès de la République. 2 vols. New York: Maison Française, 1944.

———. "Le Rajeunissement des partis," in Henry de Jouvenel, ed., Le Rajeunissement de la politique. Paris: Editions Corrêa, 1932. Pp. 155–73.

Coulondre, Robert. De Staline à Hitler: Souvenirs de deux ambassades, 1936–1939. Paris: Hachette, 1950.

Crutel, Octave. France, réveille-toi. Paris: Editions de la Pensée Nouvelle, 1949.

Cuzacq, René. Les Elections législatives à Bayonne et au pays basque de 1919 à 1939: L'Entre deux guerres. Mont-de-Marsan: Jean Lacoste, 1956.

Danos, Jacques. "Le Front populaire: Comment on mène la gauche à la défaite," *Les Temps modernes* (special issue, *La Gauche*), X (May–July 1955), 1803–26.

———, and Marcel Gibelin. Juin 36. Paris: Editions Ouvrières, 1952.

Dans les coulisses des ministères et de l'etat-major (1932–1940). Paris: Documents Contemporaines, n.d.

Déat, Marcel. Flandin, suprême espoir. Paris: Grandes Conférences des Ambassadeurs, 1934.

Debû-Bridel, Jacques. L'Agonie de la IIIe République, 1929–1939. Paris: Editions du Bâteau Ivre, 1949.

———. "La Crise des partis: I, Le Parti radical, ou le cobra à la dent pourrie," *Revue hebdomadaire,* Dec. 17, 1932, pp. 268–76.

Delmas, André. A gauche de la barricade. Paris: Editions de l'Hexagone, 1950.

Demaison, André. "Les Voix de la France," *La Revue des deux mondes,* Feb. 1, March 15, June 15, Oct. 15, Nov. 15, 1929.

Derisbourg, Jean Pierre. "Evolution politique du département du Pas-de-Calais depuis la fin de la première guerre mondiale jusqu'à nos jours." Unpublished thesis, Ecole de Droit, Paris, 1958.

Derruau-Boniol, S. "Le Département de la Creuse: Structure sociale et évolution politique," *Revue française de science politique,* VII (Jan.–March 1957), 38–66.

Dogan, Mattei. "Les Candidats et les élus," in Maurice Duverger, François Goguel, and Jean Touchard, eds., Les Elections du 2 janvier 1956. Paris: Colin, 1957. Pp. 425–66. Cahiers de la Fondation Nationale des Sciences Politiques, Partis et élections, No. 82.

———. "L'Origine sociale du personnel parlementaire français élu en 1951," in Maurice Duverger, ed., Partis politiques et classes sociales en France. Paris: Colin, 1955. Pp. 291–328. Cahiers de la Fondation Nationale des Sciences Politiques, Partis et élections, No. 74.

Duclos, Jacques. "Les Enseignements du congrès radical-socialiste," *Cahiers du bolchevisme,* Nov. 1, 1935, pp. 1299–1304.

Ducos, Hippolyte. Unpublished notes, prepared for the author.

Duhamel, Georges. "La Politique intérieure," L'Age d'or; Vol. II, Etudes: Panorama de la France entre les deux guerres (1919–1939), pp. 21–27. Paris: Calmann-Lévy, 1946.

Dupeux, Georges. Le Front populaire et les élections de 1936. Paris: Colin, 1959. Cahiers de la Fondation Nationale des Sciences Politiques, No. 99.

Durand, Julien. Unpublished memoirs.

Duverger, Maurice. Cours de vie politique en France et à l'étranger. Paris: Cours de Droit, 1957.

———. "Generations in Conflict," *Yale French Studies,* XV (Winter 1954–55), 12–16.

———. Political Parties: Their Organization and Activity in the Modern State. Trans. by B. and R. North. London: Methuen, 1954.

Ehrmann, Henry W. "Direct Democracy in France," *American Political Science Review,* LVII (Dec. 1963), 883–901.

Elections cantonales: Conseils généraux et conseils d'arrondissement par départements et circonscriptions, scrutins des 10 et 17 octobre 1937. Paris: Editions de l'Alliance Démocratique, [1938].

Elgé, L. "Le Facteur des tempéraments dans la vie des partis," *Esprit,* May 1, 1939, pp. 213–21.

Esch, P. A. M. van den. Prelude to War: The International Repercussions of the Spanish Civil War (1936–1939). The Hague: Martinus Nijhoff, 1951.

Eude, Robert. Les Maires de Rouen, 1800–1950: Etude historique et biographique. Dieppe: Imprimerie Dieppoise, 1950.

Fabre-Luce, Alfred. Histoire secrète de la conciliation de Munich. Paris: Grasset, 1938.

———. Journal de la France, mars 1939–juillet 1940. Paris: Imprimerie J. E. P., 1940.

Fabry, Jean Joseph. De la Place de la Concorde au Cours de l'Intendance. Paris: Editions de France, 1942.

Feiling, Keith G. The Life of Neville Chamberlain. London: Macmillan, 1946.

Fischer, Jacques. Doumergue et les politiciens. Paris: Editions "Le Jour," 1935.

Fourcade, Jacques. La République de la province. Paris: Grasset, 1936.

Fournier, M. "Le Parti radical de 1906–1914." Unpublished thesis, Institut d'Etudes Politiques, Paris, 1949.

France. Assemblée Nationale. Rapport fait au nom de la commission d'enquête sur les événements survenus en France de 1933 à 1945. Par M. Charles Serre. 9 vols. Paris: Presses Universitaires de France, 1951. (*Commission de 1933 à 1945.*)

France. Chambre des Députés. Journal officiel de la République française, annales de la Chambre des Députés: Débats parlementaires. 1932–40. (*J.O.Ch.*)

———. (*J.O.Ch.*) Documents parlementaires.

———. Notices et portraits. 15e législature, 1932; 16e législature, 1936. Paris: Imprimerie de la Chambre des Députés, 1932, 1936.

[*Barodet*]. ———. Rapport fait au nom de la commission chargée de réunir et de publier les programmes et engagements électoraux des candidats aux élections législatives des 1er et 8 mai 1932. No. 2145. Par M. Théodore Valensi, député.

[*Barodet*] ———. Rapport fait au nom de la commission chargée de réunir et de publier les programmes et engagements électoraux des candidats aux élections législatives des 26 avril et 3 mai 1936.

———. Rapport général fait au nom de la commission d'enquête chargée de rechercher les causes et les origines des événements du 6 février 1934 et jours suivants, ainsi que toutes les responsabilités encourues. Par M. Marc Rucart. Paris: Chambre des Députés, 1934. (*Commission du 6 février.*)

———. Commission d'enquête chargée de rechercher toutes les responsabilités politiques et administratives encourues depuis l'origine des affaires Stavisky. Paris: Imprimerie de la Chambre des Députés, 1935. 7 vols.

France. Sénat. Journal officiel de la République française, annales du Sénat: Débats parlementaires. 1932–40.

Frédérix, Pierre. L'Etat des forces en France. Paris: Gallimard, 1935.

Frossard, L.-O. De Jaurès à Léon Blum: Souvenirs d'un militant. Paris: Flammarion, 1943.

Fusilier, R. "Les Finances des partis politiques," *Revue politique et parlementaire,* CCXI (Oct., Nov. 1953), 146–61, 258–76.

Geistdoerfer, Michel. Unpublished papers.

Genin, Lucien. "Le 6 février 1934." Unpublished thesis, Institut d'Etudes Politiques, Paris, 1952.

Girardet, Raoul. "Note sur l'esprit d'un fascisme française, 1934–1939," *Revue française de science politique,* V (July–Sept. 1955), 529–46.

Goguel, François. Géographie des élections françaises de 1870 à 1951. Paris: Colin, 1951. Cahiers de la Fondation Nationale des Sciences Politiques, No. 27.

———. "The Historical Background of Contemporary French Politics," *Yale French Studies,* XV (Winter 1954–55), 30–37.

———. La Politique des partis sous la IIIe République. 3d ed. Paris: Editions du Seuil, 1958.

———. Le Rôle financier du Sénat français. Paris: Bibliothèque d'Histoire Politique et Constitutionnelle, 1937.

———. La Vie politique et les partis en France. Paris: Cours de l'Institut d'Etudes Politiques, 1950–51.

———— (*pseud.* Bernard Sérampuy). "Le Comportement du patronat français," *Esprit*, Feb. 1, 1938, pp. 657–67.

———— (*pseud.* B. S.). "Le Parti radical-socialiste," *Esprit*, May 1, 1939, pp. 171–87.

Gourdon, Alain. "Le Parti radical," in Maurice Duverger, ed., Partis politiques et classes sociales en France. Paris: Colin, 1955. Pp. 219–39. Cahiers de la Fondation Nationale des Sciences Politiques, Partis et élections, No. 74.

Graham, James Q., Jr. "The French Radical and Radical-Socialist Party, 1906–1914." Unpublished doctoral dissertation, Ohio State University, 1962.

Grosser, Alfred. "The Evolution of European Parliaments," *Daedalus,* Winter 1964, pp. 153–78.

Guérin, A. "Le Congrès de Vichy et les directives radicales," *Europe nouvelle,* XVI (Oct. 14, 1933), 975–76.

Halévy, Daniel. 1938: Une Année d'histoire. Paris: Grasset, 1938.

————. "Le Parti radical-socialiste," *Revue universelle,* May 15, 1934, pp. 425–39.

————. La République des comités: Essai d'histoire contemporaine (1895–1934). Paris: Grasset, 1934.

Hamon, Augustin, and X. Y. Z. Les Mâitres de la France. Vol. I. La Féodalité financière dans les banques; Vol. II, La Féodalité financière dans les assurances, la presse, l'administration et le parlement; Vol. III, La Féodalité financière dans les transports ferroviaires, routiers, aériens, maritimes, dans les ports, canaux, entreprises coloniales. Paris: Editions Sociales Internationales, 1936–38.

Hayward, J. E. S. "Educational Pressure Groups and the Indoctrination of the Radical Ideology of Solidarity, 1895–1914," *International Review of Social History*, VIII (1963), 1–17.

Headings, Mildred J. French Freemasonry under the Third Republic. Baltimore: Johns Hopkins Press, 1949. Johns Hopkins University Studies in Historical and Political Science, Ser. 66, No. 1.

Heberle, Rudolf. Social Movements: An Introduction to Political Sociology. New York: Appleton-Century-Crofts, 1951.

Herriot, Edouard. Jadis. Vol. II, D'une guerre à l'autre, 1914–1936. Paris: Flammarion, 1952.

————. Pourquoi je suis radical-socialiste. Paris: Editions de France, 1928.

Hoffmann, Stanley. Le Mouvement Poujade. Paris: Colin, 1956. Cahiers de la Fondation Nationale des Sciences Politiques, No. 81.

————. "Paradoxes of the French Political Community," in Hoffmann *et al., In Search of France.* Cambridge: Harvard University Press, 1963. Pp. 1–117.

Huon, Roger. "Etude régionale: Les Côtes-du-Nord," *Cahiers des groupes reconstruction,* Jan. 1955, pp. 17–26.

Hyman, Herbert H. Political Socialization. Glencoe: Free Press, 1959.

Imann, Georges. La Journée du 6 février. Paris: Grasset, 1934.

Ivan, Henry. "Où va le parti radical?" *Le Pays réel,* Feb. 1938, pp. 29–47.

Jammy Schmidt. *See* Schmidt, Jammy.

Jaray, Gabriel-Louis. "Les Responsabilités de la défaite," *Cahiers de politique étrangère du journal des nations américaines,* n.s. VII–VIII (1951), 51–63.

Joll, James B. "The Making of the Popular Front," in James Joll, ed., The Decline of the Third Republic. London: Chatto and Windus, 1959. St. Anthony's Papers, No. 5.

J.O.Ch. See France, Chambre des Députés, Journal officiel.

Jouvenel, Bertrand de. Après la défaite. Paris: Plon, 1941.

———. L'Economie dirigée. Paris: Valois, 1928.

Kayser, Jacques. "Le Parti radical-socialiste et le Rassemblement populaire (1935–1938)," in Société d'Histoire de la IIIe République, *Bulletin,* April–July, 1955, pp. 271–84.

———. "Le Presse de province sous la IIIe République," *Revue française de science politique,* V (July–Sept. 1955), 547–71.

———. "Le Radicalisme des radicaux," Tendances politiques dans la vie française depuis 1789. Paris: Hachette, 1960. Pp. 65–88. Colloques: Cahiers de civilization.

———. "Souvenirs d'un militant (1934–1939)," *Cahiers de la République,* No. 12 (March–April 1958), pp. 69–82.

Keyserling, Hermann. Europe. Trans. by Maurice Samuel. New York: Harcourt, Brace, 1928.

Kirchheimer, Otto. "The Waning of Opposition in Parliamentary Regimes," *Social Research* XXIV (Summer 1957), 127–56.

———. "Changes in the Structure of Political Compromise," *Studies in Philosophy and Social Science,* IX (1941), 264–89.

Knapp, W. F. "The Rhineland Crisis of March 1936," in James B. Joll, ed., The Decline of the Third Republic. London: Chatto and Windus, 1959. St. Anthony's Papers, No. 5.

Kriwkowski, Serge, and Raoul Reynier. Les Radicaux de gauche au service de la République. Marseilles. No publisher, n.d.

Labourie, Raymond. "Eléments pour une étude sociale et politique régionale: La Seine-Inférieure," *Cahiers des groupes reconstruction,* June 1954, pp. 3–10.

Lachapelle, Georges. Elections législatives, 22–29 avril 1928: Résultats officiels. Paris: Librairie Roustan, 1928.

———. Elections législatives, 1er et 8 mai 1932: Résultats officiels. Paris: *Le Temps,* 1932.

———. Elections législatives, 26 avril et 3 mai 1936: Résultats officiels. Paris: *Le Temps,* 1936.

Lair, Marcel. "La Banque de France de 1928 à 1939." Unpublished thesis, Ecole Libre des Sciences Politiques, Paris, 1942.

Lamoureux, Lucien. Unpublished memoirs.

Landry, M. Pour l'avenir du radicalisme. Paris: Comité Exécutif, 1938. Documents radicaux, No. 4.

Lapaquellerie, Yvon. Edouard Daladier. Paris: Flammarion, 1940.

Latty, Lionel, and Jean-Michel Royer. "Les Radicaux," in Jacques Fauvet and Henri Mendras, eds., Les Paysans et la politique dans la France contemporaine. Paris: Colin, 1958. Pp. 101–18. Cahiers de la Fondation Nationale des Sciences Politiques, No. 94.

Laval, Pierre. Laval parle. Paris: La Diffusion du Livre et Librairie Ch. Béranger, 1948.

Lavau, Georges. "Destin des radicaux," *Les Temps modernes* (special issue, *La Gauche*), X (May–July 1955), 1886–1906.

Lazareff, Pierre. De Munich à Vichy. New York: Brentano's 1944.

———. Dernière Edition. Montreal: Valiquette, 1942.

Léger, Bernard. Les Opinions politiques des provinces françaises (1928–1932). Paris: Librairie Universitaire, 1934.

Leibholz, Gerhard. "The Nature and Various Forms of Democracy," *Social Research* V (Feb. 1938), 84–100.

Leites, Nathan. On the Game of Politics in France. Stanford: Stanford University Press, 1959.

Letellier, Gabrielle, Jean Perret, H. E. Zuber, and A. Dauphin-Meunier. Enquête sur le chomage. Vol. I, Le Chomage en France de 1930 à 1936. Paris: Sirey, 1938.

Leuwen, François. "Le Congrès de Biarritz," *Revue de Paris*, Nov. 11, 1936, pp. 424–32.

———. "Le Congrès de Nantes," *Revue de Paris*, Nov. 15, 1934, pp. 427–34.

Lévy, Louis. "Après les élections législatives: Essai sommaire sur le radicalisme français," *Révolte*, Oct. 1932, pp. 15–21.

———. The Truth about France. Trans. by W. Pickles. Harmondsworth, Middlesex: Penguin, 1941.

Lewinsohn, Richard. L'Argent dans la politique. Trans. from the German by Georges Blumberg. Paris: Gallimard, 1931.

Lhomme, Jean. Le Problème des classes. Doctrines et faits. Paris: Sirey, 1938.

Lichtheim, George. The New Europe: Today—and Tomorrow. New York: Praeger, 1963.

Ligou, Daniel. L'Histoire du socialisme en France (1871–1961). Paris: Presses Universitaires de France, 1962.

Lipset, Seymour Martin. "The Changing Class Structure and Contemporary European Politics," *Daedalus*, Winter 1964, pp. 271–303.

———. Political Man: The Social Bases of Politics. New York: Doubleday, 1960.

Lombard, Paul. Le Chemin de Munich. Paris: Editions de France, 1938.

Long, Raymond. Les Elections législatives en Côte-d'Or depuis 1870. Paris: Colin, 1958. Cahiers de la Fondation Nationale des Sciences Politiques, No. 96.

Lorgeré, André. Unpublished memoirs.

Louis, Paul. Histoire du socialisme en France. 5th ed. Paris: Rivière, 1950.

Loyer, Pierre. Les Dessous maçonniques du radicalisme. Paris: Affinités Françaises, 1936.

McDonald, Neil A. The Study of Political Parties. New York: Doubleday, 1955. Short Studies in Political Science.

McKenzie, Robert T. British Political Parties. London: Heinemann, 1955.

Maizy, H. "Les Groupes antiparlementaires de droite en France de 1933 à 1939." Unpublished thesis, Institut d'Etudes Politiques, Paris, 1951.

Manescau, Raymond. Unpublished papers.

Manévy, Raymond. La Presse de la IIIe République. Paris: Forêt, 1955.

Mansire, P. "L'Evolution politique de la Seine-Inférieure sous la IIIe République," *Annales de Normandie*, Oct.–Dec. 1956, pp. 309–19.

———. "La Presse en Seine-Inférieure sous la Troisième République (1871–1939," *Etudes de presse,* n.s. VII (1955), 12–15.

Marcus, John T. French Socialism in the Crisis Years, 1933–1936. New York: Praeger, 1958.

Marécot, D. "Le Congrès radical et le Front populaire," *Cahiers du bolchevisme,* Dec. 1, 1935, pp. 1450–64.

Marion, Marcel. Petite Histoire du second cartel, 1932–193?. Paris: Domat-Montchrestien, 1935.

Maurice, Gaston. Le Parti radical. Paris: Rivière, 1929.

Maxence, Jean-Pierre. Histoire de dix ans, 1927–1937. Paris: Gallimard, 1939.

Mazé, Pierre. Le Parti radical-socialiste dans la guerre et dans la résistance. Paris: Comité Exécutif, 1944.

Mazedier, René. Histoire de la presse parisienne de Théophraste Renaudot à la IVe République, 1631–1945. Paris: Editions du Pavois, 1945.

Mead, Robert O. "The Struggle for Power: Reformism in the French Socialist Party (SFIO), 1919–1939." Unpublished doctoral dissertation, Columbia University, 1952.

Mendras, Henri. "Les Organisations agricoles," in Jacques Fauvet and Henri Mendras, eds., Les Paysans et la politique dans la France contemporaine. Paris: Colin, 1958. Pp. 231–51. Cahiers de la Fondation Nationale des Sciences Politiques, No. 94.

Meynaud, Jean. Les Groupes de pression en France. Paris: Colin, 1958. Cahiers de la Fondation Nationale des Sciences Politiques, No. 95.

Micaud, Charles A. "French Political Parties: Ideological Myths and Social Realities," in Sigmund Neumann, ed., Modern Political Parties. Chicago: University of Chicago Press, 1956. Pp. 106–54.

———. The French Right and Nazi Germany, 1933–39: A Study of Public Opinion. New York: Duke University Press, 1943.

Michon, Georges. Les Puissances d'argent et l'émeute du 6 février. Paris: Imprimerie Centrale de la Bourse, [?1934].

Milhaud, Albert. L'Histoire du radicalisme. Paris: Société d'Editions Françaises et Internationales, 1951.

Millet, Raymond, and Simon Arbellot. Ligues et groupements: De l'extrême droite à l'extrême gauche. Paris: Editions du Temps, [?1935].

———. "Notes sur les partis modérés," *Esprit,* May 1, 1939, pp. 205–12.

Mirkine-Guetzévitch, Boris. "Le Gouvernement et la vie politique sous la IIIe République," in Benoit-Levy, ed., L'Oeuvre de la IIIe République. Montreal: Editions de l'Arbre, 1945.

Mistler, Jean. "Du nouveau en politique?" in Henry de Jouvenel, ed., Le Rajeunissement de la politique. Paris: Editions Corrêa, 1932. Pp. 175–89.

Montigny, Jean. Toute la Vérité sur un mois dramatique: De l'armistice à l'Assemblée nationale, 15 juin–15 juillet 1940. Clermont-Ferrand: Editions Mont-Louis, 1940.

Monzie, Anatole de. Ci-devant. Paris: Flammarion, 1941.

———. La Saison des juges. Paris: Flammarion, 1943.

Mounier, Emmanuel. "Bilan spirituel: Court Traité de la mythique de gauche," *Esprit,* March 1, 1938, pp. 873–97.

Nathan, Roger, and Paul Delouvrier. Politique économique de la France. Paris: Cours de Droit, 1950.

Neumann, Sigmund. "The Conflict of Generations in Contemporary Europe," *Vital Speeches,* V (1939), 623–28.

———. "Toward a Comparative Study of Political Parties," in Sigmund Neumann, ed., Modern Political Parties. Chicago: University of Chicago Press, 1956. Pp. 395–421.

Nicolet, Claude. "Bibliographie du radicalisme," *Cahiers de la République,* No. 2 (1956), pp. 106–12.

———. Pierre Mendès-France, ou le métier de Cassandre. Paris: Juillard, 1959.

———. Le Radicalisme. Paris: Presses Universitaires de France, 1957. Collection "Que sais-je?" No. 761.

Odin, Jean. Les Quatre-Vingts. Paris: Tallandier, 1946.

Oualid, William, and R. Rivet. "Structure budgétaire," *Revue d'économie politique,* LIII (Jan.–Feb. 1939), 456–86.

Parker, R. A. C. "The First Capitulation: France and the Rhineland Crisis of 1936," *World Politics,* VIII (April 1956), 355–73.

Parti républicain-radical et radical-socialiste. 29e Congrès du parti républicain-radical et radical-socialiste tenu à Toulouse les 3, 4, 5, et 6 novembre 1932. Paris: Comité Exécutif, 1932. The following *Congrès* reports are published in Paris by the Comité Exécutif in the same year the Congress is held.

———. 30e Congrès . . . tenu à Vichy les 5, 6, 7, et 8 octobre 1933.

———. Congrès extraordinaire . . . tenu à Clermont-Ferrand les 11, 12, et 13 mai 1934.

———. 31e Congrès . . . tenu à Nantes les 25, 26, 27, et 28 octobre 1934.

———. Congrès extraordinaire . . . tenu à Lyon les 28, 29, 30, et 31 mars 1935.

———. 32e Congrès . . . tenu à Paris les 24, 25, 26, et 27 octobre 1935.

———. 33e Congrès . . . tenu à Biarritz les 22, 23, 24, et 25 octobre 1936.

———. 34e Congrès . . . tenu à Lille les 27, 28, 29, 30, et 31 octobre 1937.

———. 35e Congrès . . . tenu à Marseille les 26, 27, 28, et 29 octobre 1938.

———. Statuts et règlements du parti: Congrès de Biarritz, 1936. Paris: Comité Exécutif, 1936.

Parti Socialiste. XXXVe Congrès national, 4, 5, 6, et 7 juin 1938, Royan: Rapports. Paris: Libraire Populaire, 1938.

———. XXXVIe Congrès national, 27, 28, 29, et 30 mai 1939, Nantes: Rapports. Paris: Librairie Populaire, 1939.

Pataut, Jean. Sociologie électorale de la Nièvre au XXe siècle, 1902–1951. Paris: Editions Cujas, 1956. 2 vols.

Paul-Boncour, Joseph. Entre deux guerres: Souvenirs sur la IIIème République. Vol. II, Les Lendemains de la victoire, 1919–1934; Vol. III, Sur les chemins de la défaite, 1935–1940. Paris: Plon, 1945–46.

Paz, Maurice. "Le 6 février: Rapport général," *Cahiers des droits de l'homme,* Sept. 20–Oct. 10, 1934.

Peltier, Philippe. "Politique et psychologie rurales dans les Hautes-Pyrénées depuis 1871." Unpublished thesis, Institut d'Etudes Politiques, Paris, 1957. 2 vols.

Perrot, Marguerite. La Monnaie et l'opinion publique en France et en Angleterre de 1924 à 1936. Paris: Colin, 1955. Cahiers de la Fondation Nationale des Sciences Politiques, No. 65.

Pertinax. Les Fossoyeurs: Défaite militaire de la France, armistice, contre-révolution. Vol. I, Les Derniers Chefs de la IIIe République, Gamelin, Daladier, Reynaud. New York: Editions de la Maison Française, 1943.

Pitois, Pierre. Les Buts politiques de la Ligue des Droits de l'Homme. Paris: Centre de Propagande des Républicains Nationaux [1935].

Pollock, James Kerr. Money and Politics Abroad. New York: Knopf, 1932.

Prade, Y. Georges. "Après le congrès radical," Revue bleue, Nov. 2, 1935, pp. 725–28.

Quéval, Jean. Première Page, cinquième colonne. Paris: Fayard, 1945.

Radicaux et socialistes (1932–1936). Paris: Librairie Populaire, 1936.

Rémond, René. La Droite en France de 1815 à nos jours. Paris: Aubier, 1954.

——. "Explications du 6 février," Politique, n.s. Nos. 7–8 (July–Dec. 1959), pp. 218–30.

——, and Aline Coutrot. Les Catholiques, le communisme, et les crises, 1929–1939. Paris: Colin, 1960. Collection Kiosque.

Révillon, Marie Michel Tony. Mes Carnets (juin–octobre 1940). Paris: Odette Lieutier, 1945.

Ribera, Marcel. Parti radical et France nouvelle. 1944. No publisher, n.p.

Rimbert, Pierre. "L'Avenir du Parti socialiste," Revue socialiste, LIV (Feb. 1952), 123–32.

Roche, Emile. Caillaux que j'ai connu. Paris: Plon, 1949.

Romains, Jules. "L'Impardonnable Péché des radicaux: La Chute d'un grand parti," Bataille, Nov. 8, 1945.

Rupied, Jean. Elysée, 1928–34: Anecdotes et souvenirs. Paris: Peyronnet, 1952.

Sarraut, Maurice. "Collectivisme et radicalisme," Revue d'histoire politique et constitutionnelle, III (April–June 1937), 245–57.

Sauvy, Alfred. L'Evolution économique: Supplément au cours enseigné en 1950–51. Paris: Cours de Droit, 1951–53. Pp. 614–27.

——. La Nature sociale. Paris: Colin, 1957.

——. L'Opinion publique. Paris: Presses Universitaires de France, 1956.

Schmidt, Jammy. Les Grandes Thèses radicales. Paris: Editions des Portiques, [?1932].

——. Idées et images radicales. Paris: Excelsior, 1934.

Schram, Stuart. Une Etude de sociologie électorale: Traditions religieuses et réalités politiques dans le département du Gard. Alençon: Imprimerie de Corbière et Jugain, 1953.

Semler, Rudolf. Frankreichs Radikalsozialisten und ihre Presse. Würsburg-Aemühle: Triltsch Verlag, 1940.

Sérampuy, Bernard. See Goguel, François.

Sieburg, Friedrich. Who are these French? Trans. by Alan Harris. New York: Macmillan, 1932.

Siegfried, André. De la IIIe à la IVe République. Paris: Grasset, 1956.

——. Géographie électorale de l'Ardèche sous la IIIe République. Paris: Colin, 1949. Cahiers de la Fondation Nationale des Sciences Politiques, No. 9.

——. Tableau des partis en France. Paris: Grasset, 1930.

———. Tableau politique de la France de l'Ouest sous la Troisième République. Paris: Colin, 1913.

Simmel, Georg. "The Sociology of Sociability," trans. by Everett C. Hughes, *American Journal of Sociology,* LV (Nov. 1949), 254–61.

Simon, André. J'accuse! New York: Dial Press, 1940.

Simon, Philippe. "Le Congrès radical de Clermont-Ferrand," *Revue bleue,* LXXII (June 2, 1934), 405–8.

———. "Le Congrès radical de Nantes," *Revue bleue,* LXXII (Nov. 3, 1934), 823–28.

———. Essai d'une doctrine radicale. Paris: Cahiers de la Quinzaine, n.d., [?1934].

———. "Le Parti radical en quête d'une mystique," *Revue bleue,* LXXII (Dec. 1, 1934), 897–900.

Sorre, Maurice. "Eglise, école, politique: Résultats d'enquête sur la sociologie électorale du département de la Haute-Garonne," *Cahiers internationaux de sociologie,* VIII (1950), 134–46.

———. "Les Pères du radicalisme," *Revue française de science politique,* I (Oct.– Dec. 1951), 481–97.

Soulié, Michel. La Vie politique d'Edouard Herriot. Paris: Colin, 1962.

Soulier, Auguste. L'Instabilité ministérielle sous la troisième République (1871– 1938). Paris: Sirey, 1939. Bibliothèque d'Histoire Politique et Constitutionnelle, Vol. IV.

Suarez, Georges. La Grande Peur du 6 février au Palais-Bourbon. Paris: Grasset, 1934.

———. Les Heures héroiques du cartel. Paris: Grasset, 1934.

Tannenbaum, Edward R. The Action Française: Die-hard Reactionaries in Twentieth-Century France. New York: Wiley, 1962.

Tardieu, André. La Profession parlementaire. Paris: Flammarion, 1937.

Tarr, Francis de. The French Radical Party from Herriot to Mendès-France. London: Oxford University Press, 1961.

Taylor, Edmond. "Democracy Demoralized: The French Collapse," *Public Opinion Quarterly,* IV (Dec. 1940), 630–50.

Thibaudet, Albert. Les Idées politiques de la France. Paris: Stock, 1932.

———. La République des professeurs. Paris: Grasset, 1927.

Thomas, Hugh. The Spanish Civil War. New York: Harper, 1961.

Thomson, David. Democracy in France: The Third and Fourth Republics. London: Oxford University Press, 1952.

Thoré, Jacques. "Les Radicaux à Clermont," *Revue de Paris,* June 1, 1934, pp. 665–74.

Thorez, Maurice. Oeuvres. Vol. II, fasc. 8. Paris: Editions Sociales, 1952.

Tony Révillon. *See* Révillon, Marie Michel Tony.

Toynbee, Arnold J. Survey of International Affairs, 1937. Vol. II, The International Repercussions of the War in Spain (1936–37). London: Oxford University Press for Royal Institute of International Affairs, 1938.

Trotsky, Leon. Ecrits, 1928–1940. Vol. II, Où va la France? Paris: Quatrième Internationale, 1958.

Truman, David B. The Governmental Process. New York: Knopf, 1951.

United States. Foreign Relations of the United States, 1936. Vol. II, Europe. Washington, D.C.: Government Printing Office, 1954.

———. Foreign Relations of the United States, 1938. Vol. I, General. Washington, D.C.: Government Printing Office, 1955.

Vinatrel, Guy. Les Falsificateurs de l'histoire et la défense des libertés républicaines en février 1934. Paris: Imprimerie Petites-Affiches, 1954.

Vulpian, A. de. "Physionomie agraire et orientation politique dans le département des Côtes-du-Nord, 1928–1945," Revue française de science politique, I (May 1951), 110–32.

Walter, Gérard. Histoire du Parti communiste français. Paris: Aimery Somogy, 1948.

Warner, Geoffrey. "The Stavisky Affair and the Riots of February 6th, 1934," History Today, June 1958, pp. 377–85.

Weber, Eugen. Action Française: Royalism and Reaction in Twentieth-Century France. Stanford: Stanford University Press, 1962.

Weber, Max. "Politics as Vocation," From Max Weber: Essays in Sociology. Translated and edited by H. H. Gerth and C. Wright Mills. New York: Oxford University Press, 1958.

Werth, Alexander. France in Ferment. New York: Harper, 1935.

———. Lost Statesman: The Strange Story of Pierre Mendès-France. New York: Abelard-Schuman, 1958.

———. "Le Mouvement 'Jeunes Turcs': Phénomène radical d'entre les deux guerres," Cahiers de la République, No. 2 (1956), pp. 100–105.

Weygand, Maxime. Mémoires. Vol. II, Mirages et réalités (1918–1939). Paris: Flammarion, 1957.

Willard, Claude. Quelques Aspects du fascisme en France avant le 6 février 1934. Paris: Editions Sociales, 1961.

Williams, Philip. Politics in Post-War France. London: Longmans, Green, 1954.

Wright, Gordon. Rural Revolution in France: The Peasantry in the Twentieth Century. Stanford: Stanford University Press, 1964.

Wylie, Laurance. Village in the Vaucluse. Cambridge, Mass.: Harvard University Press, 1957.

Ybarnégaray, Jean. Le Grand Soir des honnêtes gens, le 6 février 1934. Paris: Grandes Conférences des Ambassadeurs, 1934.

Zay, Jean. Carnets secrets. Ed. by Philippe Henriot. Paris: Editions de France, 1942.

———. Souvenirs et solitude. Paris: Juillard, 1946.

RADICAL NEWSPAPERS

There were five Paris dailies linked to the Radical party: La République, L'Ere nouvelle, L'Oeuvre, La Volonté, and Le Quotidien. The four Radical Paris weeklies were: La France radicale, Le Jacobin, La Jeune Gauche, and La Rélève; the Bulletin du parti républican-radical et radical-socialiste appeared irregularly. The following is a list of provincial Radical weeklies and dailies. The names in parentheses are those of the parliamentarians involved, and, where necessary, of the department in which the paper was issued.

1. Newspapers in which the political director was openly Radical or in which the owner or inspirer was a Radical, or in which a weekly column was written by a Radical: *L'Avenir républicain* (Loiret; Dezarnaulds); *L'Avenir du Cher* (Bedu); *L'Action jurassienne* (Pieyre, senator, Girard, deputy); *Le Bourbonnais républicain* (Lamoureux); *Le Citoyen* (Finistère; Georges Le Bail, senator, Albert Le Bail, deputy); *Le Démocrate de Lot-et-Garonne et du Sud-Ouest* (Gaston Martin); *Le Démocrate savoyard* (Cot); *La Dépêche dauphinoise* (daily; Paganon); *La Dépêche de Toulouse* (daily; Albert and Maurice Sarraut, Delbos); *Dinan-républicain* (Geistdoerfer); *L'Echo des Alpes* (Clerc); *L'Echo de la Nièvre, du Cher et de l'Allier* (Potut); *L'Echo républicain de l'arrondissement de Dieppe* (Galimand); *L'Eclaireur de l'Est* (daily; Marchandeau); *L'Eveil* (Rouen; Crutel); *La France du Centre* (daily; owned by the father of Jean Zay); *La Frontière* (Belfort; Miellet); *La Gauche quercynoise* (Malvy); *L'Indicateur* (Isère; Ginet); *Le Journal de Marennes* (Bertrand); *Le Journal de Seine-et-Marne* (de Tessan); *Mantes-républicain* (Bergery); *Le Nontronnais* (Sireyjol); *Le Patriote de Châteaudun* (director Valadier, senator; weekly column Mitton, deputy); *La Petite Charente* (Rethoré); *Le Petit Comtois* (daily; Durand); *Le Petit Haut-Marnais* (daily; Lévy-Alphandéry, deputy, Cassez, senator); *Le Petit Savoyard* (Borrel, senator); *Le Petit Troyen* (daily; Brachard); *Le Républicain de Chinon* (Courson); *La République des Cévennes et du Rhône* (Riou); *Le Progrès de l'Allier* (daily; Régnier); *Le Progrès de Loches* (Bernier); *La République des Vosges* (Rucart); *Le Radical de l'Hérault* (1932–34; Vincent Badie); *La République de l'Oise* (daily; Aubaud, Jammy Schmidt); *Sedan-républicain* (Delattre); *Le Sud-Ouest* (daily; Garat); *La Tribune de l'Aisne* (Guernut); *La Tribune républicaine* (Verdun; Thiébaut); *La Voix du Centre* (Chichery).

2. Newspapers with which the deputy or senator was not openly affiliated, but for which he frequently wrote special articles. *Le Démocrate* (Rhône; Herriot); *Le Démocrate du Jura* (Berthod, Dumont); *Le Courrier de la Creuse* (Ferrand); *La République de l'Indre* (Rotinat); *La République des travailleurs* (Gers; Gardey, Philip, senators); *Le Réveil de la Creuse* (Ferrand, senator); *Le Réveil démocratique de Maine-et-Loire* (Hérard, Perrein); *La Tribune du Libournais* (Roy); *L'Union démocratique de la Haute-Saône* (Liautey).

3. Newspapers that printed speeches and articles written for other papers by the local deputy and an occasional article especially for the local paper: *L'Abeille des Vosges* (Picard); *L'Action républicaine de la Corrèze* (de Chammard); *L'Avenir de Pithiviers* (Chevrier, Cabanis); *Le Bonhomme Sarthois* (Caillaux); *Le Courrier de Céret* (Delcos); *Le Démocrate* (Dax; Deyris, Lassalle); *Le Démocrate* (Jonzac; Sclafer); *Le Démocrate de Seine-et-Marne* (Mortier); *Le Jura démocratique* (Leculier); *La Dépêche normande* (Briquet, Chauvin, Mendès-France); *L'Echo saintongeais* (Longuet); *L'Echo du Léman* (Jacquier); *L'Echo de l'Ouest* (Deux Sèvres; Richard); *L'Echo de Bretagne* (Cadoret 1932–34); *L'Eclaireur du Finistère* (Mazé); *La Gazette vosgienne* (Elbel); *L'Indépendant* (La Réole; Thorp); *L'Indépendant de Saône-et-Loire* (Couillerot); *Le Journal de Die et de la Drôme* (Archimbaud); *La Montagne corrézienne* (Queuille); *La Parole républicaine* (Vendée; Daroux); *Le Patriote morézien* (Jura; Durand, Dumont, Berthod); *Le Républicain de Loir-et-Cher* (Chautemps, Lau-

rens); *Le Républicain* (daily; Vitry; Férin); *Le Républicain du Gard* (daily; Bosc, Bazile, senators); *La Loire républicaine* (daily; Corsin); *Le Républicain de Lavaur* (Compayré); *La République de l'Ain* (Fribourg); *La République tourangelle* (Besnard, senator); *La République de Loir-et-Cher* (Laurens); *La Tribune républicaine de la Haute-Garonne* (Ducos); *La Tribune ariégoise* (Cazals); *L'Union républicaine* (daily; Margaine); *Le Montbrisonnais* (Loire; Corsin and Ravel); *Le Lovérien* (Eure; Mendès-France); *Le Gâtinais* (Loiret; Chevrier); *L'Ouest* (daily; Hérard).

4. Weeklies that supported the Radical deputy but never printed anything by him: *La Corrèze républicaine et socialiste; Le Cri de Bigorre; La Défense républicaine* (Amiens); *La Démocratie bretonne; La Démocratie* (Aude; organe de la Fédération radical-socialiste); *La Démocratie havraise; La Dépêche de Louviers; L'Echo de l'Aude* (Limoux); *L'Indépendant de Gray et de la Haute-Saône; Le Journal de Montreuil; Loudéac-républicain; Le Morvan républicain; La Nouvelle Chalosse* (Landes); *Ouest-Océan* (La Rochelle); *Royan; La Tribune picarde* (Somme); *Valence-républicain; L'Indépendant* (Saintes); *La Défense républicaine* (La Rochelle); *Les Cahiers de Job Coz* (Lannion, monthly).

INTERVIEWS

Charles Addé-Vidal, Feb. 18, 1961; Paul Anxionnaz, March 15, 1961; Pierre Barral, June 19, 1960; Barsalou, Jan. 6, 1960; Paul Bastid, Feb. 12, 1961; Lucien Bauzin, June 10, July 3, 1959; Gaston Bergery, Oct. 18, 1961; Georges Bonnet, Dec. 4, 1960; Henri Caillevet, Nov. 25, 1959; André Cornu, Oct. 25, 1960; Pierre Cot, Dec. 21, 1960; Pierre Dominique, March 7, 1961; Pierre Dezarnaulds, Jan. 24, 1961; Hippolyte Ducos, June 1, 1960; Julien Durand, Nov. 5, 1960; Robert Fong, Aug. 17, 20, 1959; Michel Geistdoerfer, June 10, Aug. 12, 1959; Raymond Gruny, July 4, 1959; Jules Julien, June 20, 1960; Jacques Kayser, May 14, Oct. 28, 1959, March 8, 1961; Guy La Chambre, Nov. 30, 1960; Henri Laforest, March 17, 1961; Lucien Lamoureux, May 11, Sept. 5, 1960; Charles Laurent, Oct. 25, 1960; Pierre Le Brun, Nov. 10, 1960; André Liautey, Oct. 29, 1960; André Lorgeré, Dec. 19, 1959; Roland Manescau, March 11, 1961; Léon Martinaud-Déplat, Nov. 7, 1960; Marcel Massot, Dec. 15, 1959; Jacques Mitterand, Feb. 24, March 1, 8, 1961; Maurice Netter, March 6, 1961; Marcel Ribera, March 14, 1961; Emile Roche, Jan. 16, 1961; Maurice Rolland, Jan. 24, 1961; Albert Sarraut, Jan. 29, 1961; René-William Thorp, July 21, 1959.

Index

Index

This index includes the names of all Radical deputies, whether mentioned in the text or not. They are identified by asterisks, with their departments indicated in parentheses. Superscript numbers refer to their constituencies.